Urbanizing Frontiers

Urbanizing Frontiers:
Indigenous Peoples and Settlers in
19th-Century Pacific Rim Cities

Penelope Edmonds

UBCPress · Vancouver · Toronto

20 19 18 17 16 15 14 13 12 11 10   5 4 3 2 1

Printed in Canada on ancient-forest-free paper (100% post-consumer recycled) that is processed chlorine- and acid-free.

Library and Archives Canada Cataloguing in Publication

Edmonds, Penelope
  Urbanizing frontiers: indigenous peoples and settlers in 19th-century Pacific rim cities / Penelope Edmonds.

Includes bibliographical references and index.
ISBN 978-0-7748-1621-2 (bound); ISBN 978-0-7748-1622-9 (pbk.);
ISBN 978-0-7748-1623-6 (e-book)

  1. Indigenous peoples – Urban residence – Great Britain – Colonies. 2. Urbanization – Great Britain – Colonies. 3. Colonial cities – History – Case studies. 4. Indigenous peoples – Great Britain – Colonies. 5. Great Britain – Colonies – Race relations. 6. Indians of North America – Urban residence – British Columbia – Victoria – History – 19th century. 7. Aboriginal Australians – Urban residence – Australia – Melbourne (Vic.) – History – 19th century. 8. Victoria (B.C.) – History – 19th century. 9. Melbourne (Vic.) – History – 19th century. I. Title.

JV305.E36 2009   323.1109171'24109034   C2009-906603-3

UBC Press gratefully acknowledges the financial contribution of the International Council for Canadian Studies, through its Publishing Fund. Publication of this work was assisted by a publication grant from the University of Melbourne.

UBC Press
The University of British Columbia
2029 West Mall
Vancouver, BC V6T 1Z2
www.ubcpress.ca

Contents

Illustrations

Acknowledgments

THIS BOOK REPRESENTS a political, intellectual, and personal journey, and I have been fortunate to share it with many generous and talented people. I especially thank Patricia Grimshaw, Department of History, University of Melbourne, for her encouragement, insights, and friendship. Andrew May reminded me to pay close heed to the archives and was excited by my new approaches to the urban. Thanks also to David Goodman for our discussions regarding comparative history and theory.

I am also indebted to the generosity of many on the other side of the Pacific Ocean. Foremost, I thank Robert McDonald, Department of History, University of British Columbia, for his support and incisive commentaries. Jean Barman literally walked me through the University of British Columbia's library stacks and pointed the way in a new place. Thanks to Chris and Karla for their friendship and for taking me kayaking on Vancouver's English Bay when I needed it most.

Special thanks to Patrick Wolfe, for conversations over many years and for graciously reading an early version of this manuscript. Tracey Banivanua Mar, Jane Carey, and Julie Evans also read chapters of this book and mixed honesty with enthusiasm and supportive engagement. I am also grateful to Adele Perry, University of Manitoba, and Lynette Russell, Monash University, Melbourne, for their insightful comments. I was extremely fortunate to have careful and attentive readers in Scott Sheffield, Department of History, University of the Fraser Valley, and Lisa-Ann Chilton, Department of History, University of Prince Edward Island, who gave valuable feedback on the penultimate manuscript. Special thanks also to Michelle Berry, who listened with enthusiasm to long readings at Clydesdale, Christine Edmonds, and Kat Ellinghaus.

I thank the Department of History, University of Melbourne, for an Australian Postgraduate Award and for two research grants supporting research and travel in the development of this study. Publication support grants from the University of Melbourne and the International Institute of Canadian Studies helped to make this book a reality. I wish to thank Joy Murphy Wandin, senior Wurundjeri elder, for graciously acknowledging this work when I wrote to her in 2004. I thank Paul De Leur for loving support, the creation of maps, and assistance with image production. Finally, thanks to lovely Lily, who shared her precious time in the earliest months of her life, allowing me to finalize this book.

Urbanizing Frontiers

Introduction

In 1886 the American ethnologist Franz Boas visited Victoria, the provincial capital of British Columbia, on the Northwest Coast of Canada. Founded in 1843 on the territory of Lekwammen peoples as a fort for the Hudson's Bay Company, by the late nineteenth century Victoria was heralded as one of the future lights of the British Empire on the Pacific Rim. Boas described the street-scape as follows: "The stranger coming for the first time to Victoria is startled by the great number of Indians living in this town ... we met them everywhere. They dress mostly in European fashion. The men are dock workers, craftsmen or fish vendors; the women are washerwomen or working women ... certain Indian tribes have become indispensable to the labour market and without them the province would suffer great economic damage."[1] Across the Pacific Ocean sat another edge of empire, Port Phillip, later called the Colony of Victoria, in the southeastern region of Australia. Its premier city, Melbourne, was founded in 1837 and built on the lands of the Wurundjeri peoples. For several decades Wurundjeri peoples and other groups of the Kulin Nation were present in the streets of early Melbourne, as many had been pushed off their traditional lands.[2] Later, however, town officials repeatedly attempted to segregate Aboriginal people from the developing town space. Town Council minutes note on several occasions the "inconvenience and immorality of the Blacks being in the town."[3] By 1850 immigrants such as Johann and Carl Graf would write home to Germany with descriptions of Aboriginal people in Melbourne such as the following: "Certainly one sees very few in the district of 15 to 20 miles around the town and those who occasionally come into the town, come only to beg some food and they are more polite in this than many civilised persons."[4] By 1888, only two years after Boas remarked on the many First Nations people in the streetscape of Victoria, British Columbia, there were apparently so few Aboriginal people in Melbourne that the director of the Melbourne Zoological Gardens placed Aboriginal people from distant Coranderrk Station on display in an ethnographic village as part of the Centennial Exhibition. Thomas Avoca, his wife Rose, and two children not related to them were chosen for a staged demonstration of the habits of the passing Aboriginal race, "whose mode of life are being forgotten" reported *The Age* (see Figure 1). On display as a living diorama, with their weapons carefully arranged around them, Thomas and

Figure 1 "Native Camp at Melbourne Zoo," 1888 Centennial Exhibition, Melbourne.
Museum Victoria.

Rose were to be viewed by local and international tourists to "marvellous Melbourne." *The Age* continued, this "party of blacks," selected from Coranderrk Station, was to "throw the boomerang in the presence of strangers" and would be "especially interesting to people from the old world."[5]

By the late nineteenth century in the rapidly growing and increasingly industrialized cities of Europe and the colonies alike, residents craved the spectacle of touring troupes of "primitive" peoples and displays of "savagery" in museums, zoos, circuses, and Wild West shows. Urbanizing modernity hungered for the telling of its own past. As Tony Bennett has observed, ethnographic villages were "sacrificial offerings to the processes of colonization and modernization which, it was envisaged, would eventually remove them entirely from view."[6] It was presumed that the exhibition of colonized Indigenous peoples was the final rite that would signal their removal from the stage of world history. The spectacle of an ethnographic village – a display of supposedly pre-contact Indigenous authenticity in Melbourne, an increasingly industrialized city of empire that was described at the time as "London reproduced" – was therefore compelling.[7] This was especially so when contrasted with the mixed city space of Victoria, British Columbia, which was filled with seemingly assimilated First Nations in European dress whose clear value as labourers fascinated Boas. By 1911, however, after increases in white settlement, many decades of land dispossessions, and multiple strategies for their removal by Victoria city officials, the Lekwammen were paid to leave their city reserve.

Despite different historical circumstances, the overriding commonality for Indigenous peoples in both of these Pacific settler cities was, ultimately, dispossession and displacement. How should we understand the story of urban dispossession in these settler colonies, which were marked by differing but related sequences of change? And how should we understand the shifting constructions of race and segregation in these two urbanizing port cities at the far reaches of Britain's empire?

Colonial frontiers did not exist only in the bush, backwoods, or borderlands; they clearly sat at the heart of early town and city building, a process crucial to the settler-colonial project. Building on this central proposition, *Urbanizing Frontiers* takes a close look at race, segregation, and Indigenous and non-Indigenous lives in these two Pacific Rim cities, which were fashioned by British settler colonialism between the years 1835 and 1871, a period that began with the first European settlement at Port Phillip and ended with British Columbia becoming a province of the Dominion of Canada. Bringing a postcolonial perspective to urbanizing colonial environments, this book explores the racialized politics of these two settler-colonial landscapes at the spatial, imaginative, social, and legal levels and in a comparative context. More importantly, it examines the racialized transformations of these developing cities and proposes that these urbanizing colonial precincts can be viewed as formative sites on the Pacific Rim, where bodies and spaces were rapidly transformed and mutually imbricated in sometimes violent ways, reflecting the making of plural settler-colonial modernities. In the chapters that follow, I explore the powerful narratives of British imperial city building, the willful shaping of white settler-colonial polities, and the unmooring of these narratives at the unruly edges of empire.

Reimagining the Colonial Frontier

Settler colonialism's nineteenth-century frontier has been routinely conceptualized as a distinctly non-urban geographical space that sits somewhere out in the country or borderlands. The frontier is frequently portrayed as a liminal zone without rules, a zone that was characterized by violence, forced removal, and dispossession for Indigenous peoples. The frontier has also been inaccurately conceptualized by some historians as a linear phenomenon that marked civilization from savagery, as a site where they can record "official," martial-style engagements between males as a reflection of colonial relations. Instead, I wondered about early cities and towns as developing frontiers, as equally charged and often-violent sites of racialized spatial contestations. These frontiers were mosaic-like – mercurial, transactional, and, importantly, intimate and gendered.[8] For too long historians of Canada and Australia have imagined the colonial frontier as a problem of the backwoods, prairie, or bush, and ignored the early development of towns and cities as vital sites of contestation. The frontier must be reimagined. This book, therefore, considers another terrain: settler colonialism's urbanizing frontier from the mid- to the late nineteenth century and the lives of Indigenous and non-Indigenous people in these settler-colonial cities of the Pacific Rim.

The presence of Indigenous peoples in settler-colonial cities at the edges of Britain's empire has often been erased from historical consciousness. Today, tourist brochures continue to tout Victoria, British Columbia, as more English than the English. This belies the great number of First Nations who lived (and still live) and worked in the city and the city's history of racialized, often violent spatial contestations. Many previous studies, especially in Australia, have ignored the dynamic interactive contact histories of the colonial cityscape, as if Indigeneity stopped at the urban. Alternatively, as in the case of Victoria, when the presence of First Nations was recorded in nineteenth-century records, the language often evoked savagery, violence, and fear.

Astoundingly, in her study *Urban Aborigines,* which was published in 1972, Faye Gale describes Aboriginal people in the Australian cityscape as virtual newcomers, as urban immigrants.[9] Although it is true that many Aboriginal people in southeastern Australia were partitioned in remote mission stations from the mid-nineteenth century and began to re-enter cities only with the project of assimilation in the interwar period, many studies have overlooked a long and complex history of Indigenous people in early Australian towns and cities that stretches back into the nineteenth and late eighteenth centuries. There has been a pervasive amnesia in Australia regarding the contested and racialized nature of cities and towns that persists well into the present. Yet Aboriginal people have not forgotten. As historian Gary Foley recalled of the 1950s and 1960s, "There was segregation in my town ... the theatre was segregated, the bars were segregated ... it was done through convention."[10]

Much scholarship in Canada on the historical development of towns and cities has also failed to include First Nations. As Jordan Stanger-Ross notes, Canadian historians have been slow to examine the significance of the urban Aboriginal experience.[11] Evelyn J. Peters observes that many researchers have explored the ways in which the Western city is seen as a gendered, racialized, and heterosexual space, yet little work has examined how the city in postcolonial settler societies excludes Indigenous peoples and cultures. Peters comments on the lack of geographic research on Canadian Aboriginal people and their relative absence from the discipline of historical geography itself. For decades in Canada, writes Peters, "policies responding to Aboriginal urbanization have been informed by a discourse that defines Aboriginal and urban cultural life as incompatible."[12]

Indigenous peoples may have been dispossessed, but they have not been entirely displaced from cities.[13] Today, large proportions of Aboriginal people live in urban centres. In Canada, according to the 2001 census, almost half of the people who identify themselves as Aboriginal (Indian, Métis, or Inuit) reside in urban areas. Projections show that this proportion will increase. In British Columbia around 4.4 percent of the population identifies as Aboriginal, and in Victoria, the provincial capital, around 3 percent identifies as Aboriginal. In Australia, many Aboriginal people live in major metropolitan areas. In the state of New South Wales, almost half of the Indigenous population lives in the greater Sydney region. In Melbourne, which represents the majority of people in the state of Victoria, 0.4 percent of the population identifies as Indigenous, compared to 0.6 percent of people in the state as a whole.[14]

Commenting on the lack of scholarly attention to Indigenous people in early colonial cities, Nicholas Blomley observes suggestively of Vancouver that "the issue of native title was easy to imagine as something outside the city," but the "visible presence of many native people in the city seemed to complicate things in important ways."[15] Although many Aboriginal people live in our postcolonial cities, they remain places of the most thoroughgoing extinguishment of Native title.[16] It is little wonder that there has been a striking absence of historical work on Indigenous people in developing settler-colonial cities; to put it plainly, issues of sovereignty are at stake here, and recognition of Indigenous people's historical presence would be an admission that Indigenous peoples are not newly arrived immigrants to cities – they owned and occupied the land well before settler cities were established and were implicitly part of their physical and imaginative creation.

Much of the international literature on colonial cities has regularly privileged franchise-colonial over settler-colonial formations. Metropolitan perspectives are usually placed in the foreground, largely omitting the lived realities and gendered and racialized contours of settler cities, as well as the dynamic histories of intimate and mixed relations between Indigenous peoples and newcomers at the local level. Yet early towns and cities were often the greatest sites of contestation, as many newspapers and settler reports of the time attested. The nineteenth century's urbanizing frontier is now a hidden history. This is strange, because the presence of Aboriginal people in and around colonial towns and cities created much anxiety, as evinced in colonial reportage, artwork, and cartoons, where fear of mimicry, mendicancy, and cross-contamination of cultures prevailed. Despite a lack of critical scholarship on nineteenth-century towns and cities as crucial frontier sites, sources relating to Melbourne and Victoria between 1835 and 1871 reveal a rich and diverse body of material in letters, diaries, newspapers, Aboriginal Protectorate records, municipal and legal records, colonial dispatches, and town council minutes, to name only a few sources, that attests to the racialized socio-spatial politics of these cities. Indigenous-European interactions in urbanizing Canadian and Australian colonial landscapes have not been studied sufficiently, and this book seeks some redress to what is more than mere oversight – it is a form of collective amnesia that has had, and continues to have, political effects.

Scholars have routinely conceptualized the frontier as the remote bush, back-woods, or borderlands and ignored towns and city spaces as vital contact zones, as if urbanizing zones were not also part of the settler-colonial project. Further-more, the field of urban space has been dominated either by traditional geog-raphy or an (at times) apolitical cultural geography, approaches that have been somewhat deficient. As one scholar observed, the urban planning and environ-ment field is a mainstream discourse that is often pre-theoretical and landscape-focused and tends to repeat familiar topics such as land-use zoning, development control, garden suburbs, and new towns. The reviewer argued that works in this traditional vein have offered only "glimpses of the Indigenous peoples whose lives were unalterably changed, cultural practices ... compromised and destroyed, and land rights extinguished for the good of the British empire."[17] In accounts of urban settlement in both North America and Australia, Indigen-ous dispossession is routinely written out of the story. And much traditional and historical geography has largely failed to examine settler cities through the interpretive lens of settler colonialism.

This pervasive trend of privileging city planning and infrastructure over culture and identities, of focusing on colonial cities without attention to the dispossessed and displaced Indigenous peoples on whose land these cities were built, as well as the wider issues of settler colonialism and race, represents a methodological schism between the disciplines of history and urban studies. This is at first glance characterized by a failure to synthesize urban and municipal records with Indigenous archives and is more broadly indicative of an incom-plete encounter between urban studies and postcolonial approaches. Upon deeper inspection, however, as I trace in Chapter 2, this schism is also a glaringly ideological and, thus, historiographical problem that reflects settler-colonial hegemonies themselves – that is, the promotion of "New World" cities as being built upon tabula rasa and the representation of Indigenous peoples as being either absent or anomalous to urbanizing colonial environments. *Urbanizing Frontiers* seeks to redress this scholarly gap by conceptualizing the nascent urban towns and cities of the Pacific Rim as dynamic settler-colonial frontier zones. The book seeks to indigenize, or indeed, re-indigenize historical understandings of the settler-colonial city by focusing on human stories and individual lives transformed in the context of British colonizing structures and urbanization in the Pacific Rim. Some may find my use of the term *indigenize* problematic. I use this term in a dual sense. First, as a non-Indigenous writer, it is not possible for me to proffer an Indigenous perspective. I do use *indigenize*, however, to capture a sense of historical reclamation as I attend to the everyday lives of Indigenous peoples in the city as they are suggested by the historical sources. Second, I use *indigenize* to suggest the presence and agency of Indigenous peoples and their cultures within the history of settler-colonial urbanism in these two sites. The term acknowledges the transactional, mixed nature of these early settlements at the edge of the Pacific, places that were double sites of negotiation. Just as Indigenous peoples were colonized, so too were newcomers and new spaces indigenized, albeit in highly uneven ways and within asymmetrical relations of power.[18]

There has been a general reluctance to see city space as postcolonial space. During the last two decades, however, a growing body of research has begun to examine the racialized politics of Australia's and Canada's postcolonial cities, that is, the cities of the twentieth and twenty-first centuries.[19] The postcolonial city has been conceptualized as a place in which identity is constituted through race, space, and the law. Yet postcolonial cities frequently hide their histories and the conditions of their own production. Scholars have often privileged the postcolonial city without looking at the antecedent structures and processes upon which it was formed. It is my contention that postcolonial cities have syncretic pasts with extended genealogies of segregation and partition. I eschew any suggestion of a break between the present and the past, which is suggested by the term *postcolonial,* and instead read the city as a continuing and vital structure of settler colonialism. Today's cities may, therefore, be understood through a close examination of the socio-spatial histories of race found in the nineteenth century's developing urban landscape.

Colonial Cities, Postcolonial Cities: The Production of Space and Race

As recent historical scholarship attests, there has been intense concern in the last few decades with the spatiality of empire and with articulating the diverse relations of place, race, and empire. More than ever, historians are looking to other disciplines and incorporating the spatial models of cultural and critical geographies, postcolonialism, and law to analyze power, place, and formations of race in colonial settings.[20]

Race and urban space have one overwhelming and pervasive commonality: they have each been conceived as natural, given, and elemental. Space has been viewed conveniently as empty, geometric, passive, and elemental, while race is (still) conceived as being ostensibly anchored deeply in human biology.[21] In the last few decades, however, new and vital fields of inquiry – including post-colonial and critical race theory, historical geography, and critical legal and urban histories – have emanated from the imperial and spatial turns. Cultural theorists and others have rejected the notion that urban "spaces, and the arrangement of bodies in them, emerge naturally over time," and on this premise they have attempted to strip away the apparently naturalized evolution of change in cities to show that the development of social space is a process of uneven power inscription that reproduces itself and creates oppressive spatial categories.[22] Although it is often unacknowledged, the formative historical materialist work of Henri Lefebvre, who in *The Production of Space* (1974) proposed the idea of social space as a process, has informed much of this thinking.[23] Lefebvre asked, "Is the city a work or a product?" and "what or whom does it signify?" Crucially, Lefebvre asserted that space, so often deemed passive and natural, is never void of political meaning. As he argued, space is a process – that is, each present space is "the outcome of a process with many aspects and many contributing currents."[24]

Lefebvre's proposition, that space itself is a dynamic social product, was radical. Significantly, Lefebvre highlighted the ways in which the unequal distribution of power in social space becomes naturalized and its operations forgotten. That is, spaces obscure the conditions of their own production.[25] The classed, gendered, and racialized relations of city space became naturalized, or conventional, and it is difficult to understand how they came to be that way. Thus, settler-colonial cities themselves became somehow natural and inevitable, and we do not see the constitutive relationships of Indigenous dispossession and displacement that inhere in their present space. There is something distinctive about settler-colonial cities. As Jane Jacobs notes, they possess a "very specific local politics deeply marked by the historical legacy of the colonial dispossession of Indigenous peoples."[26] Accordingly, unless the broader processes of settler colonialism are revealed, we will not see what is particular about the operations of urban settler-colonial space and how subjects and spaces are produced with all their local and historical specificities. Few scholars have adequately charted the deep symbolic and economic genealogies of how settler cities and their inhabitants came to be weighted with particular meanings.

In this book urbanizing frontiers are defined as contested and highly transactional spaces in which rapidly developing settler-colonial settlements and towns were formed on expropriated Indigenous land. I use the term *urbanizing* to indicate an active spatial and cultural process, as well as to signal a nascent stage of town and city development in these nineteenth-century settler colonies. Although the early existence and structure of these cities differed from more modern twentieth-century urban spaces, in the chapters that follow I show that these places were in fact formative sites of an embryonic urban settler-colonial modernity, which would later become fully realized and in which the governance of spaces would become more formalized and bureaucratized.

Just as the city and notions of social space have been reconfigured, so too has the notion of race been radically rethought in the last three decades. Accordingly, growth in theorizations on the construction of race and moves to de-centre race in concert with ideas about the racialization of social relations have led scholars to pay more attention to the city and the processes that reproduce racial divisions in time and space.[27] Scholars working in this broad field of concern seek to expose hierarchies that emerge from and in turn produce oppressive spatial categories.[28] Yet historians still grapple with identifying the specific processes through which race is materialized and mediated through space and place. Lefebvre, however, proposed a solution to overcome the masking effect of the operations of power. He suggested that one must track generative processes. The way to understand the nature of space, Lefebvre asserted, is to "reconstitute the process of its genesis and the development of its meaning."[29] I take Lefebvre's injunction to mean an examination of the specific historical conditions and transformations that produced settler-colonial spaces. Without attending to the broader processes of settler colonialism and its multivalent strategies, the distinctive spatial commerce of settler cities and how the lives and subjectivities of its inhabitants were shaped cannot be made apparent. Historical inquiry can bring the local and particularized nature of a syncretic space such as the city and its relations into focus.

What is the political and spatial character of the settler-colonial city? Settler cities are crucial aspects of the settler-colonial process, and many urbanists and historians of colonialism have failed to fully identify that they have spatial and political features that make them distinctive from other colonial formations. The towns and cities of Britain's imperial Pacific Rim were, symbolically and economically, vital sites of colonial endeavour. The formation of the settler-colonial city marked an unprecedented space in the New World and signified a key moment in both empire and colonial modernity. Settler-colonial cities were crucial transitional sites in which Indigenous lands were rapidly converted to property. When outlying areas were seen to be unruly and outside the reach of the law, the colonial order was often first established at the municipal level. Around the Pacific Rim, these towns and cities became nodes in active transimperial networks through which bodies, ideas, and capital increasingly flowed in the circuits of empire. The settler-colonial city has been represented in much triumphalist European literary and visual culture of the nineteenth century as the most potent symbol of progress, as the highest stage of commerce and civilization, and as the consummation of empire.[30]

The physical features of settler-colonial cities in the New World were (and remain) distinctive. They were often gridded, expansive entities that rolled out over apparently empty lands. With their outer limits frequently existing only in the imaginary realm of maps, they pointed to a future of settler progress and prosperity. The rapid increase of immigrant populations to these colonial towns and the growth of industrialization over the latter part of the nineteenth century drove a continually developing set of regulations to govern how Indigenous and non-Indigenous peoples could inhabit city spaces. As Elizabeth Grosz notes, bodies and cities are mutually defining entities whose relations are regulated and mediated by the state.[31] Crucial to these transformations were the eventual regulation, partition, and sequestration of Aboriginal peoples and attempts to control so-called mixed-race relationships. The anxious development of these cities reflected the uneasiness of the colonial polity itself; who would and would not be considered full members of this ideally white polity was mirrored in exclusions in the streetscape. Bodies and spaces were rapidly reconfigured, and racial partitions were only amplified in the colonial townscape. The settler-colonial city was a site in which the appropriation of Indigenous land was coupled with aggressive allotment and property speculation, a site in which property relations were constructed quickly through rhetorical celebrations of making a white, civilized British space.[32]

Despite differing local histories, some colonial features repeat themselves with an uncanny persistence in these two cities on the Pacific Rim. As I show in later chapters, close attention to the micro-geographies of the streetscape reveals that Indigenous peoples were often depicted as inconvenient wanderers – as nuisance, vagrant, or prostitute – constructed identities that tell us much about the deeper structures of settler colonialism and its manifestations in urban environments, both in the past and the present. In the nineteenth century, these cities became charged sites in which issues of civilization and savagery; race, gender, and miscegenation; and law and sovereignty were played out, and these contests indeed had global ramifications as colonial outposts emerged uneasily as settler states connected through powerful British transimperial networks.

Urbanizing Frontiers reflects on how these urbanizing histories as antecedent forces have shaped the postcolonial present in terms of land rights, treaties, and ongoing Native title negotiations in British Columbia and southeastern Australia. The outcomes for each site have been similar in their trajectory of Indigenous dispossession, but they have also differed. In Victoria, British Columbia, one former city-based land treaty has been honoured, and reparations have been paid to local Indigenous peoples. In Melbourne, the lack of treaty, land rights, and reparation was controversially highlighted at a sit-in held by the Black GST group (stop genocide, recognize sovereignty, and make treaty) at the Kings Domain during the 2006 Commonwealth Games. Early city histories therefore have vital implications for cities that are nominally postcolonial, cities in which Indigenous peoples continue to assert their sovereign rights in urban environments.

Comparative and Transnational Approaches to Pacific Rim Cities

The study of nineteenth-century cities such as Melbourne and Victoria is necessarily a study of British colonialism and the particular economic and discursive features of the colonies that built them. To understand the broader imperial processes that shaped these places and the cultural and legal frameworks that came to bear particularly on Indigenous peoples and the construction of white and non-white identities in the cityscape, this study also looks, at times, to their metropolitan counterpart, London, since ideas concerning Melbourne and Victoria were frequently formed in relation to the Empire's centre. Patricia Nelson Limerick has observed that the potential of comparative history is its promise to help us avoid provinciality and stay unsettled. We may begin studying what seems to be a local colonial frontier and soon find ourselves considering global processes.[33] We gain new insight into the making of Indigenous, white, and other identities in local cityscapes when they are placed in tension with the often broader and countervailing global and imperial metanarratives of race and Britishness. It is important to mark out the complex interplay between localized, on-the-ground cultures and transimperial narratives of British colonial expansion and city building that prevailed throughout the nineteenth century.

Over the last decade there have been calls for more comparative and transnational studies of British settler societies and a greater integration of the parallel scholarship on Australia, Canada, and Aotearoa New Zealand and their respective settler-Indigenous relations. As Chapter 1 outlines, Victoria, British Columbia, and Melbourne, Australia, are ideally suited for comparative study. Melbourne and Victoria were each planted on Aboriginal lands, amidst groups of peoples whose cultures were rich and diverse. Europeans imagined both places at the periphery of Britain's empire as Edens. They were understood as gifts of Divine Providence for the Anglo-Saxon races and were thus drawn into racialized, transimperial narratives of settlement. Europeans utilized Indigenous knowledge and labour, whether through surveying and fencing the landscape or building towns and cities, to establish themselves, map the territory, claim it epistemologically, and fashion it into a European cognate space. Each colony was directed largely from the Colonial Office in London, however partial and attenuated this direction was at times. By the 1850s these cities and their colonies were each transformed by the Pacific gold rushes and the rapid influx of immigrants and wealth associated with them – developments that, in turn, marked a further loss of land and control for Indigenous groups.

A comparative study promises to reveal the particularity of the colonial urban encounter, while throwing the specificity of each site into relief and tracing key aspects of the global system of British colonialism in the emerging nineteenth-century city. Although there are many similarities between these two British settler-colonial cities, crucial departures lie in disparities between the economic and discursive formations that came to structure the respective colonies: the fur trade versus pastoralism and differing formations of industrial economy, treaty making or its absence, varying degrees of immigration, and attitudes to intermarriage and mixed-race relationships. Thus, by answering the call of scholars such as Frederick Cooper and Ann Stoler to look not only at metropole-periphery relations but also at hierarchies between related colonies, this book examines the development of settler-colonial British spaces of settlement and traces structures with "distinct but related sequences of change."[34] Despite diverse histories and circumstances, the overriding commonality for Indigenous peoples in both sites of the Pacific was dispossession, eventual segregation, and displacement.

Urbanizing Frontiers locates these settler colonies within the rich cultural and political sphere of the Pacific Rim, which I view as a trans-Pacific world, a vital site of inquiry. This wider focus offers an innovative perspective to understand the vast interconnected world of Pacific settler societies and their contact histories.[35] There are several caveats, however. Comparative history is challenging, and in an effort to contextualize and explain what historian Marc Bloch once described as local pseudo-causes, care must be taken not to use hindsight to promote an easy positivism, as if all colonial formations were magically related. Likewise, Indigenous peoples in each site were highly diverse and had distinct and unique cultures; therefore, any notion of a monolithic Indigeneity is avoided. More importantly, these colonies were shaped as much by their relations with local places and peoples as they were by British interests and policies.[36] Consequently, I trace the experiences of the diverse Indigenous groups whose lands were settled to reveal the unique ways they refashioned or refuted the social categories of colonizers and confronted colonization in the streetscape.

The Imagined City and Its Dislocations: Transactional Spaces and the Intimate, Urbanizing Frontier

Mary Louise Pratt's idea of the contact zone augments the notion of the settler-colonial city as an urbanizing frontier.[37] This concept and associated ideas of mutual cultural transformations and mixed, shared spaces and identities have become highly resonant in colonial studies. Furthermore, several decades of scholarship in the field of urban history have promulgated the notion that instead of the "hard" city of planning, built form, infrastructure, and external economistic processes, a "softer" city may be tracked to reveal the flow of information, relationships, and identities and give insight into the lived experiences of city dwellers themselves. Consequently, the streetscape can be considered as both a contact zone and a fundamental dimension of social power.[38] I look closely at the daily lives of Indigenous peoples and newcomers in the developing streetscapes, where racialized subjectivities and racialized spaces were co-fashioned.

In line with postcolonial scholarship, this book traces disjunctures and fissures in the colonial city-building project. This study charts both shared and indigenized spaces and moments when imaginings of segregations, partitions, and a white, imperial spatial hegemony were resisted and subverted by Indigenous peoples. In Melbourne, Aboriginal peoples resisted official efforts to move their camps from the town perimeter. They jumped fences and burned them down; they engaged in acts of resistance against the imposed cadastre of newly enclosed Indigenous lands. In the First Nations reserve in Victoria on Vancouver Island, residents threw rocks at police who intruded into their space and fought well into the early twentieth century to keep their city reserve lands. Locating these acts of agency and spatial alterity in the colonial streetscape illuminates a history of dynamic exchange between Indigenous peoples and newcomers that is often absent in traditional colonial histories. It is also important to mark out stark ruptures between the Anglo-Saxon expectations, morals, and aspirations of bourgeois metropolitans and local settlers who defied partitions by brokering diverse relations with Indigenous peoples. This approach counters scholarship that posits colonialism as a unilinear projection from the metropole by denying the interactivity and subversions of the urbanizing frontier. This book seeks new visions of Indigenous and non-Indigenous city dwellers who lived at the edge of empire, often a far cry from the mores and ideas of British metro-politan elites and city builders who occupied the civilized spaces of a fictive racial purity.

In response to Cooper and Stoler's call for an examination of the "stretch between the public institutions of the colonial state and the intimate reaches of people's lives," the chapters explore intimate encounters between Indigenous and non-Indigenous peoples in the city.[39] The urbanizing frontier was an intim-ate frontier, a place of shared domestic and collaborative moments as well as sexual violence between Indigenous women and non-Indigenous men. If there is a striking absence of historiography on Indigenous peoples in the colonial cityscape, then studies of Indigenous women and the many instances of mixed-race relations in colonial towns and cities are even more scant, especially in Australia. Yet, as scholars such as Adele Perry have shown, these new settler-colonial polities were made through the bodies of Aboriginal and white women. Contact zones are typically conceived of as spatial sites, but women's raced and classed bodies were also vital contact zones.[40] Yet in many urban histories, women are given small walk-on parts – if they have any role at all. Significantly, Chapters 3 through 8 of this book also examine the lives of Indigenous women and issues of gender and mixed-race relationships in colonial towns and cities, subjects that have been doubly neglected by scholars but were of intense concern for many nineteenth-century writers and city dwellers. Several decades of fem-inist and postcolonial scholarship have shown the constitutive nature of gender in imperial relations, and this is particularly true in the city, where social rela-tions were writ large.[41] Building on Judith Butler's and feminist geographers' premise that the fashioning of bodies and spaces are interrelated, it is clear that bodies and spaces in the colonial cityscape were mutually imbricated and co-produced.[42] Paying attention to Indigenous women's bodies as particular sites of anxiety in the streetscape can tell us much about imagined colonial orders that were both imposed and defied. As Tony Ballantyne and Antoinette Burton maintain, the body can be read like a transcript that reveals the gender assump-tions that underpin empires in all their complexity.[43] I have attempted to in-corporate – or to write in, as it was so often written out – an examination of Indigenous women and the implications of gender in the settler-colonial city-scape. There is nothing soft, however, about the gendered dynamics of these urban settler cities: they were frequently characterized by the hard exigencies of sexual abuse and the potency of mixed and at times affectionate relations. The study of sex, race, and fears of miscegenation provides an essential contour, and at times a violent fault line, of the urbanizing settler project that cannot be overlooked. Indeed, these relations, as Stoler reminds us, were formative in the "making of racial categories and in the management of imperial rule."[44] As I became interested in the gendered contours of the developing streetscape and the lives of Indigenous and white women, these settler-colonial cities revealed much about the racial imperatives of empire.

The (Dis)locations of Empire: Where Was Empire? Whose City Was White?

Indigenous people in many historical studies have been typically isolated as the raced subject. This study, in line with critical race theory and whiteness studies, maintains that the category of whiteness is also a racialized condition and that city spaces were imagined and constructed legally and socially as white or, initially, Anglo-Saxon spaces. Whiteness has been the subject of intense international scholarly concern over the past decade and has been conceptualized as a marker of identity – indeed, not as a colour but rather as a strategy of power or a set of political relations.[45] Whiteness, too, can be authorized though space and environments. Just as Indigenous identity was constructed and litigated in the cityscape, so too were the often frustratingly fugitive parameters of whiteness and its entitlements. As much as whiteness was concerned with bodies, sex, and fictive ideas of racial purity, the notion of whiteness as property, which in turn directed the segregation of bodies, was also paramount in rapidly urbanizing settler landscapes.[46] This book therefore attends to the racialized exigencies of both bodies and spaces in the colonial cityscape. In Chapters 3 to 8, I examine the making and unmaking of these racialized bodies and spaces.

Victoria and Melbourne were imagined as white cities of empire. British Columbia was to be the England of the Pacific and a white man's province, and according to one writer, the Colony of Victoria, southeastern Australia, was another England.[47] Yet where was empire, and whose city was white? These colonial cities were not as white as many wished and imagined. They were instead new transcultural sites in which Britain's narrative identity was confounded and subverted. In line with renewed concerns regarding the spatiality of empire, this book interrogates the British imperial vision of a contiguous cartographic, legal, and white urban space, offset and at times destabilized by the particular unruly refractions and subversions of colonialism at the local level. It is a story of British settler-colonial cities built on Indigenous land and their co-production with local Indigenous people and their cultures.

In seeking to bring colonized and colonizer into one analytic frame, I have employed archival collections that are often treated disparately, such as legal archives and criminal records; municipal, legislative, and urban-planning archives; and Indigenous and missionary archives. Archive collections, of course, differed for each city, and they must be considered within their own context.

Although early missionary archives for Melbourne were important to this study, a similar body of material was not available for Victoria, British Columbia. Likewise, crime records for Victoria were more complete than for Melbourne; consequently, newspaper reports of crime in Melbourne had to be relied upon. I have accounted for the varying biases in each set of records.

In writing about Victoria and Melbourne, I faced a methodological challenge that all historians encounter when writing about colonialism. If all of the written sources have been created by colonizers, the available information on Indigenous peoples will always be partial and biased. This asymmetry inevitably constructs Europeans as initiators and Indigenous peoples as mere reactors. Charting Indigenous people's presence and agency in the nineteenth-century settler-colonial city is a challenging task. When European accounts of Aboriginal people appear in letters, diaries, and newspapers, they are often stereotypical and derogatory, and this necessitates continuous counter-readings. Finding accounts that moved beyond tired constructions was challenging. I sought them out and located moments that are illuminating, notwithstanding the important caveats in postcolonial debates on the authenticity of the Indigenous voice as constructed in imperial records.[48] It is not possible for me to know or to be able to thoroughly interpret Indigenous people's experiences in nineteenth-century Melbourne and Victoria. Instead, as a way forward, and in line with Lefebvre, I chart the generative historical and social processes through which social spaces and geographies of exclusion were created. Through this process of reclamation, I seek to re-Indigenize historical understandings of the settler-colonial city. Nihal Perera has suggested that such acts of political indigenization can be viewed as resistance to colonialism.[49] Such efforts are especially important since settler colonies such as Canada and Australia have not decolonized: settlers and descendants did not return to their place of origin, and the colonies over the generations have become "home."

Through critical counter-colonial readings of traditional archives, however, and by incorporating neglected Indigenous archives and listening to Indigenous voices, we may reclaim the histories of settler cities and, thus, reimagine the frontier. This historical endeavor has crucial political implications for the assertion of Indigenous rights and sovereignties in urban and rural landscapes today and may go some way towards an intervention in settler colonialism's ongoing project of re-territorialization and the formation of modern settler-colonial states. To reflect on the postcolonial city we must understand its syncretic past. An exploration of the antecedent relations of race and public space in these colonial cities, and the shifting sites of Indigenous oppression and ongoing acts of cultural assertion, helps us to understand uneven relations of power in the frontiers of our postcolonial cities today.

A Note on Terminology

Nomenclature, like racialization, is a shifting and complex practice. When addressing Australian material, I use the term *Aboriginal* to refer in general to Aboriginal people of the Port Phillip region, and I use *Kulin Nation* when speaking of the confederation of five cultural-linguistic groups in the Port Phillip region. When historical detail permits, I identify specific groups such as Wurundjeri and Boonwurrung, and I use the terms *Native* or *black* as they are used in the historical material. In the chapters on British Columbia, to avert any suggestion of cultural equivalence or any suggestion of a monolithic Indigeneity between two very distinct and diverse populations on opposite sides of the Pacific Ocean, I use the term *First Nations*. I use the terms *Indian* or *Native* when this appears appropriate within the context of the British Columbian historical or archival material addressed. More generally, I use the commonly accepted term *Indigenous* for both the British Columbian and southeastern Australian contexts.

The term *mixed-race,* as used in the nineteenth century and today, has connotations of a fictive biological and racial purity. The term is always inadequate, yet I like many authors have not found a more adequate term. I use the terms *mixed-race* and *miscegenation* in their nineteenth-century historical contexts. The term *white* is often used as shorthand for a diverse range of ethnicities that originated in western Europe and Britain. *White* like the term *black* is often read as a monolithic category and is weighted with an array of connotations. In both case studies, I use the term *white* in cases where it is found in the historical material and particularly when I want to emphasize the theme of whiteness and the idea of a white race. In general, however, I use the terms *European* or *newcomer* to denote recently arrived Europeans, mostly Anglo-Saxons, who sought to create new British imperial spaces at the edges of empire.

Finally, nineteenth-century images of Indigenous peoples must be approached with sensitivity, and I have sought permission to use them from institutions and descendents where possible.

1

Extremities of Empire: Two Settler-Colonial Cities in Comparative Perspective

THE SETTLEMENTS OF MELBOURNE and Victoria were planted on land amid the diverse cultures of Indigenous peoples. Melbourne began in 1835 as a small settlement built on the banks of the Yarra River in the region of Port Phillip by overstraiters from Van Diemen's Land who sought to open up new country for pastoralism. Victoria, Vancouver Island, formerly Fort Victoria, was selected as a key fur-trading fort by the Hudson's Bay Company in 1843 (see Figure 2). Both cities have temporal parity: they were each transformed radically when gold was discovered in southeastern Australia in 1851 and on the Fraser River in British Columbia in 1858. Following in the footsteps of San Francisco and the 1849 gold rush, these two British imperial cities were imagined as hubs of empire, as lights of civilization and Britishness on the Pacific Ocean.[1] This type of racialized anticipatory geography grew with the gold rushes and only increased with the rise of the British Empire and the upturn in wealth that accompanied industrialization in these colonies in the late nineteenth century.[2]

Port Phillip (which became the Colony of Victoria in 1851) and its premier port city, Melbourne, and British Columbia (which was formed from the amalgamation of the colonies of Vancouver Island and British Columbia in 1866) and its port city, Victoria, soon took their place in the aspirations of colony builders as new fields of colonization and industry for the Anglo-Saxon races. By the 1860s each city and its territory was configured in transcontinental terms as part of the grand narrative of British empire and race. In 1848 the *Illustrated London News* had no doubt about the expansive powers of empire when it lauded the transformative and spatial vigour of the Anglo-Saxon race in an opinion piece titled "Emigration and Colonisation":

> With a rapidly increasing population, and with the prospect before us that other civilised nations, who cannot now compete with us in commerce or manufacture, will, at no distant period be able to do so, the question of the subsistence of our people becomes the utmost urgency. As a people it may truly be said that we are pre-eminent amongst the nations of the earth. Our spirit rules the world. Our wisdom enters into the composition of the everyday life of half of the globe. Our physical as well as our intellectual presence is manifest in every climate under the sun. Our sailing ships and steam vessels cover the seas and rivers. Wherever we

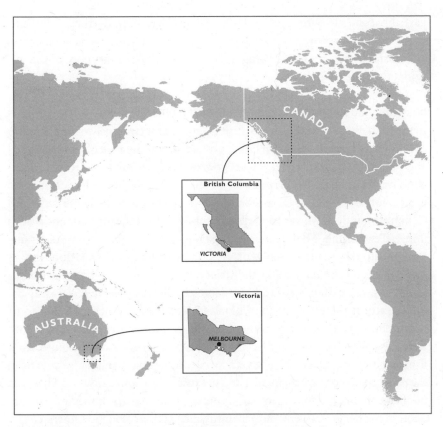

Figure 2 Melbourne (Victoria) and Victoria (Vancouver Island).
Cartography by Paul de Leur.

conquer, we civilise and refine ... No place is too remote for our enterprise or our curiosity ... We have spread ourselves over all regions. We have peopled North America, civilised India, taken possession of Australia, and scattered the Anglo-Saxon name and fame in language, literature, religion and laws, ideas and habits, over the fairest portion of the globe.[3]

Nineteenth-century Anglo-Saxon claims – which mobilized the appropriation of new territories for gold seeking, settlement, and industry and stamped them with the imprimatur of Divine Providence – clearly transcended individual colonies and were far greater than, and indeed prefigured, any discrete or local-ized ideas of nation. Britain's territorial claims in these distant edges of empire must, therefore, be viewed properly in global, transnational terms and in the context of late nineteenth-century imperial narratives of race and empire. How-ever, Anglo-Saxon expansionist aspirations were often overstated, and their partiality comes to light when we look at these colonial sites as they really were. In the middle years of the nineteenth century, British control was often partial and unstable, and notions of Anglo-Saxon unity resided far more in the imagination than in reality.

Imagining the Antipodes and the West beyond the West

In the mid-nineteenth century, British Columbia sat tenuously on the margins of European colonial control; it hung "precariously at the edge of Britain's literal and symbolic empire," writes Adele Perry. In its transformation from a culturally diverse Indigenous territory to a conjunction of two colonies built on protocolonial mercantile expansion underwritten by the British Empire, British Columbia was the "awkward and disappointing child of the fur trade and British imperial expansion."[4] Before the heady gold rush days of the 1850s would transform it into the wealthy Colony of Victoria, with "marvellous Melbourne" as its premier city, the early colonial district of Port Phillip sat rather uncertainly at the edge of Britain's control and largesse. Melbourne's low status as the southernmost periphery of the Colony of New South Wales extended to its earliest European residents, many of whom would become pastoralists. They were described by the *Sydney Gazette* in 1837 as persons of ill-repute, as "a drunken and worthless set." The *Gazette* noted that many residents came from the penal colony of Van Diemen's Land because of "various causes which would not make them desirable in any community." Edward Curr opined in 1839 that many of the labourers were "old gaol birds and expiree convicts." Others, clearly of the lower orders, had come over on an adventure and would "take advantage of the absence of power to behave in a lawless and intimidatory manner."[5] Often lacking funds and in fear of becoming another of Britain's antipodean convict repositories, Port Phillip would appeal to Britain to send immigrant labour to help it to become a free settler society.

Studying these sites comparatively not only offers avenues to trace the commonalities and dissonances of two settler-colonial locales, it also illuminates these edges of empire in new and compelling ways. For an analysis of the global system of British colonialism not only necessitates an examination of the co-production of the edges of empire and the metropole but also requires an exploration of the hierarchy of colonial spaces throughout the British Empire.

Longstanding European economic and cultural discourses on the two regions shaped the way these imperial spaces were imagined before Europeans ever set foot on their shores. Although Europeans had partial knowledge of the Australian continent's coastline by the 1780s, and even though various explorations had refuted the idea of a great southern supercontinent, the myth of *terra australis incognita* persisted in the popular imagination. Deep European cultural lineages had represented Australia, the great southern land, as a world turned upside down, as an empty, inverted, and perversely antipodal continent.[6] The area that would come to be known as British Columbia was the enigmatic West beyond the West. Until the introduction of rail in 1885, which traversed the Rocky Mountains, an overland journey to British Columbia was an arduous haul and the stuff of heroic travelogue for non-Aboriginal writers.[7]

The particular European imaginings of these two distinct regions, separated by the Pacific Ocean, would collude in the formative and specific ways that Indigenous peoples would be represented, in the way that European appropriation of Indigenous lands would be rationalized, and in the way that these new settler-colonial spaces would be called into being. Exploration and the exercise of mapping – the semiotic practice of inscribing British imperial destiny onto Aboriginal space, with all of its connotations of colonial possession and erasure of Indigenous presence – meant that imperial spatial constructs of these new edges of empire often preceded actual physical invasion. The physical appropriation of Indigenous land and the imposition of European settler-colonial spatial disciplines followed, with the eventual surveying, division, and commodification of land. As will be shown, at the edges of the Pacific Ocean, a new imperial geography created distinct and, indeed, unprecedented settler-colonial spaces at the great expense of the traditional Indigenous owners.

European Expansionism, Geopolitical Tensions, and the Imperial Contest

Over three decades ago, the historian K.M. Dallas emphasized the formative transimperial and organizing role of mercantilist, sea-based trade and observed that the actions of settling and persisting in extended settlement should be understood in relation to geopolitical circumstances and events in Europe, America, Southeast Asia, and other lands in the Pacific Ocean.[8] Accordingly, and as many scholars now argue, British colonialism must be understood as part of a great contest among the European empires. New World spaces were ultimately reorganized not only through European imaginings but also through European transimperial networks of trade and commerce and the resultant movement of ideas, capital, and bodies reconfigured with local Indigenous cultures.

James Cook's three voyages between 1768 and 1779 unlocked the Pacific for Europeans. On his first voyage, made between 1768 and 1771, Cook and his crew circumnavigated New Zealand, charted over eight thousand kilometres of the Australian coastline, made contact with Aboriginal peoples on its eastern shores, and, without their agreement, claimed the eastern seaboard for Britain. During Cook's third voyage, made between 1776 and 1780, he revisited Hawaii and mapped the Pacific Northwest Coast, sojourned at what would come to be known as Nootka Sound on the west coast of Vancouver Island to trade with First Nations people, and then journeyed further north to Alaska. Cook's expeditions ushered in a period of extensive and enduring contact between Europeans and the peoples of the Pacific and opened the area for exploitation. Within several decades European expeditions to this region were commonplace.[9] The European search for goods and trade with Pacific peoples only intensified, and it was Cook who first recognized the commercial viability of tapping into existing fur trade networks.

By the late eighteenth century, the increasing profitability of furs in the Orient caused the Pacific Northwest Coast to become a site of intense geopolitical interest and tension. Nootka Sound became an international hotspot. Amidst the presence of ships from many European nations, Spain, having built a fort on the site, formally took possession of Nootka Sound on 24 June 1789.[10] This seemingly audacious act of imperial assertion spurred the British to claim the area for the King of England and led to confrontation. In July the Spanish navy seized several English trading ships by claiming that the English had contravened Spanish sovereignty, and it forcibly dispersed First Nations with whom the British were trading.[11] Diplomatic claims and counter-claims over this distant bay ensued between the European powers, and political tensions increased for Britain. The British demanded restitution and Spain's renunciation of its traditional claims to sovereignty in the unoccupied territories of America. However, in that same year, the French Revolution began, and the possibility of Britain engaging in war with France and Spain was great. Not only did the prospect of an Anglo-Spanish war seem imminent, but also the French, weakened by revolution, were threatened by this expansionist act and perceived it an as attempt to break the Franco-Spanish alliance. In defence of Spain, the French debated posting fourteen vessels to Nootka Sound, but in effect the crisis served only to plunge France, in a time of revolution, into lengthy debates about foreign policy, national interests, and the people versus the king.[12]

In the southern Pacific Ocean, the British and French also tested each other. In 1788 the British established a penal colony at Port Jackson (now Sydney) on Australia's southeastern coast. Around the same time, the French naval officer and explorer Jean-François de Galoup, Comte de La Pérouse, who had also mapped the west coast of North America, was sent on a scientific voyage to chart the great southern continent, although it is claimed that he had secret orders to investigate the trade possibilities that Cook had identified. La Pérouse arrived at the settlement of Port Jackson only a few days after it was founded by the British.[13]

Back on the other side of the Pacific, at Nootka Sound, the British, knowing that the revolution had weakened the French, continued to make their claim against Spanish interests.[14] When the possibility of war between Spain and Britain increased, a settlement was made. British ships and prisoners taken by the Spanish were released, and a period of Spanish exploration and mapping followed. In 1792 George Vancouver, on behalf of the British, also made serious explorations of the San Juan archipelago and Puget Sound, during which he named the Gulf of Georgia and Point Grey, the site of present-day Vancouver. British possession of Nootka Sound was confirmed by the Nootka agreement of 1794, a settlement between the British and Spanish governments.[15]

By this time, too, Britain and France were at war; in its midst a dramatic and yet diplomatic meeting between Matthew Flinders and Nicholas Baudin occurred in 1802 on the southern coastline of Australia as the two passed each other during their circumnavigations. Flinders and Baudin met on successive days on *Le Geograph* outside what would become Encounter Bay. Flinders cordially proffered the copy of a map he had made to Baudin. In an act of imperial possession at the edge of the Pacific, Flinders had inscribed hundreds of place names connected with his own life on the map of Australia.[16] Baudin also reconceptualized the land through French eyes by charting the southeastern coast line of Australia and Tasmania, transposing the landscape onto maps, and naming the various straits, channel islands, and promontories after a panoply of royals and figures such as Napoleon and Josephine.

A year later, in 1803, the creation of the first settlement in Port Phillip Bay at Sorrento was prompted by British fears that French vessels would attempt to claim part of the southern shore. Urgent messages had been sent to London to warn that French vessels were probing the coastline. Britain was determined to stop republican France from imperial expansion. It quickly dispatched a small fleet, headed by Lieutenant Colonel David Collins as lieutenant-governor, that carried three hundred convicts and military and civil forces. When the fleet arrived, writes Michael Cannon, officers "mounted their cannon to sweep the bay, drilled their men, flogged their convicts ... and waited for the French invasion which never came."[17] Baudin's ships had been called back to France. The French were so weakened by their military engagements in Europe that they withdrew from the contest for territory in the southern Pacific Ocean.[18]

The French, the Spanish, and the British would imagine new lands on these edges of the Pacific Ocean. Parts of the Pacific Northwest Coast are inscribed with Spanish names, with remnants of a possessive imperial imagining, to this day. Likewise, the French left their mark on Australia's southern shores in acts of anticipatory geography. At both edges of the Pacific, Britain's expansionist ambitions prevailed as Britons sought to inscribe Indigenous lands with their own worldview.

Dallas has likened the Pacific Ocean at this time to a vast new oilfield. In his view Britain's mercantilist maritime and geopolitical interests in forestalling the French far outweigh the conventional historical explanation for the settlement of Australia. Dallas argues persuasively that Australia was more than a mere New World repository for Britain's criminals and that its appropriation was motivated by more than the need to offset the loss of the American colonies after the American Revolution.[19] Without entering into these debates at length, there is clear value in looking synchronically at global trade relations between European powers and at the geopolitical tensions that ensued throughout the trans-Pacific world. From the mid-seventeenth century to the mid-nineteenth century, the British Committee for Trade and Plantations was powerful and highly active. Each edge of empire had its origins in mercantilist economics and European imperial expansion – the organized fur trade on the Pacific Northwest Coast and the sealing and whaling industry (smaller and less organized than the fur trade) in Australia, which circulated across the Tasman Sea to New Zealand. European settlement came slowly to Vancouver Island, and it was directed largely by the interests of the Hudson's Bay Company. In contrast, the coastal mercantilism of the Port Phillip region was short-lived and quickly gave way to a rapacious pastoralism, a very different form of economy that would drastically alter the lives of Aboriginal peoples in southeastern Australia. The Colony of New South Wales' origins as a penal colony ensured that state rather than private interests quickly dominated.

Impact on Indigenous Peoples: Disease and Transformation

The net effect of mercantilist and colonizing endeavours would be devastating for the Kulin Nation and the Coast Salish. As was the case in many regions of the Pacific, the Indigenous peoples of Vancouver Island and the Port Phillip region suffered large population losses because of smallpox epidemics that preceded actual invasion.[20] Before Fort Victoria was built on Lekwammen territory in 1843, the geopolitical manoeuvres of European powers seeking territorial control in the Pacific Northwest – their dispatches, their cartography, and their bickering in parliaments – may have occurred initially and largely outside of the awareness of First Nations. Yet a range of forces had altered social and cultural life for the Lekwammen prior to this event. The physical incursion into Indigenous space was preceded by epidemic disease, which caused great population loss and had a brutal impact on social structures. For at least a century following contact with traders in the 1770s, the Lekwammen suffered the effects of bacterial and viral diseases, including smallpox, malaria, influenza, dysentery, whooping cough, typhoid fever, typhus, tuberculosis, and syphilis.[21] Although it is difficult for historians to accurately determine the size of the population on the Northwest Coast prior to these epidemics, current scholarship estimates that it was between two hundred thousand and four hundred thousand people.[22]

Sea traders brought venereal and respiratory diseases, which no doubt produced misery and population loss, to First Nations communities in the late eighteenth century. However, several more waves of epidemic disease swept the Northwest Coast and devastated populations. The smallpox epidemic of 1775 near present-day Vancouver "probably hit the Songhees before they even met a European," writes John Lutz.[23] Smallpox came to the Lekwammen's territory again in 1801, and the epidemic was followed by measles in 1824.[24] Another smallpox epidemic that broke out at Victoria in the summer of 1862 caused profound disruption to First Nations societies along the Coast. Entire villages were lost, with perhaps only a few survivors. In sum, First Nations settlement patterns were altered because of devastating population losses; remnant groups were forced to unite to form new mixed groups; cultural practices were transformed; and food-gathering and -processing systems, which had formerly relied on large numbers of people, were disrupted.[25] The Hudson's Bay Company employees who arrived on Vancouver Island to trade furs encountered peoples already changed by several disease epidemics. The period from the 1850s to the 1880s was one of rapid population decline for the Lekwammen.

Turning to the southeastern coast of Australia, the weight of evidence shows that smallpox epidemics probably spread southward via river systems from the Sydney area on the east coast to the Port Phillip region. These epidemics possibly explain Australia's relatively small Aboriginal population on contact with Europeans.[26] The smallpox epidemics of 1790 and 1830, which occurred in central New South Wales, may have moved into the Port Phillip region, and many European witnesses certainly noticed the pockmarked faces of some older Aboriginal people during the late 1830s and 1840s. Since similar diseases in North America had killed from 40 to 60 percent of the Indigenous population, some scholars estimate that the pre-smallpox population of Victoria could have been between thirty thousand and fifty thousand; however, fifteen thousand is the figure most often cited.[27]

Coast Salish peoples and the peoples of the Kulin Nation eventually suffered the loss of their land and were pushed into reserves and systems of missionization, where pernicious assimilative trajectories resulted in transformations and the loss of language and culture, the effects of which are still present today.[28] The Kulin Nation and the Coast Salish, highly diverse cultures located on opposing edges of the Pacific Ocean, experienced similar patterns of disease, land expropriation, and missionization through British colonization throughout the

late eighteenth and nineteenth centuries. Apart from implicitly distinct Indigenous cultures, which came to shape colonial patterns, crucial differences
and departures also lay in key economic, legal, and demographic disparities:
the fur trade versus pastoralism; treaties or their absence; differing levels of
industrialization, which demanded different terms of engagement with colonial
labour systems; and variable attitudes towards intermarriage, miscegenation,
and assimilation. Importantly, Indigeneity in both places was made and remade
over time by these European colonial structures. Shifting constructions of race,
or racializations, in these two edges of empire were profoundly more different
than is often acknowledged.

The Fur Trade versus Pastoralism: Economics and Labour

Varying colonial economic and discursive formations came to frame particular
Indigenous subjectivities and their representations in markedly different ways
in Port Phillip and British Columbia. Because British Columbia was dominated
initially by the Hudson's Bay Company – and later by huge fisheries and forestry
industries that required large pools of capital and wage labour – colonial interests
had shaped Indigenous peoples as labourers by the late nineteenth century.
British Columbia, with its long-term mercantile and industrial systems, would
later be dubbed the "company province." First Nations workers were crucial to
the fisheries and forestry industries, and these workers came to form the backbone of the colonial economy by the late nineteenth century.[29]

By contrast, in southeastern Australia the Port Phillip region's early contact
with maritime mercantile systems of sealing and whaling had, by the late 1830s,
given over to a boom in pastoralism and an influx of European settler-colonists.
Pastoralism was yet another form of industrialization in which markets were
also created in the metropole. Yet, unlike the fisheries and forestry industries
of British Columbia, the pastoral industry of Port Phillip did not require many
Aboriginal people as labourers. Despite some southeastern Aboriginal people
being used opportunistically by colonists as an itinerant labour force, mainly
in the growing pastoralist industry and for seasonal harvesting, Aboriginal
people would in general be constructed as a silently vanishing and economically
redundant population.[30] Both industrial systems on each side of the Pacific
Ocean would eventually restructure the environment in such a way as to remove
Indigenous people from their lands. The influx of thousands of immigrants in
search of gold only exacerbated the strain on Aboriginal cultures. Despite varying economic and political formations, the Kulin Nation and the Coast Salish
would both suffer a thoroughgoing dispossession of land by the close of the
nineteenth century, when both regions emerged as full-fledged British settler

colonies with land as their key object. It is also important, however, to acknowledge the diverse cultural formations that were shaped in these two sites, including widely varying racializations and markedly different attitudes towards mixed-race relations and miscegenation. As Victoria Freeman points out in relation to Pacific Rim settler colonies, various attitudes towards sexuality, class, race, and gender and histories of cross-cultural contact influenced policies towards racial mixing, and it is these particular historical circumstances that must be traced.[31]

British Columbia: The Land-Based Fur Trade and the Hudson's Bay Company

The sea- and land-based fur trades, which operated in Canada long before the building of Fort Victoria, shaped the lives of the Lekwammen. The early trade in furs began inland and increased markedly when European craftsmen found that the underfur of the beaver matted to make a high-quality felt suited for hat making. French, English, Scottish, and American traders sought to profit from the inland fur trade, and the Hudson's Bay Company, managed from London, was chartered in 1670 to take advantage of the trade.[32]

The peak years of the maritime fur trade were between 1792 and 1812.[33] On the Northwest Coast, James Cook, during his third voyage, observed that fur-bearing animals such as the sea otter were being traded. By 1785 the first trading vessel, the *Sea Otter,* had arrived in Nootka Sound. The profitability of the trade in sea otter pelts with new trading partners such as China bolstered a long period of mercantile trade between the diverse First Nations of the Northwest Coast and Europeans.[34] After 1785 an extensive mercantilist sea- and land-based fur-trading culture developed and co-joined with pre-existing Indigenous trade. The land-based fur trade had come west from Montreal, with the North West Company controlling the majority of trade. The first forts were built west of the Rocky Mountains in the first decade of the nineteenth century, although various European and American trading vessels continued to visit the Northwest Coast until the 1820s.[35] In 1805 Simon Fraser, a representative of the North West Company, set up the first permanent fur-trading fort at McLeod Lake.[36] In 1821 the Hudson's Bay Company, which had an organized bureaucratic style and a policy to stay close to waterways, amalgamated with the North West Company. Restructuring of the trade led to the formation of a systematic mercantilist operation dedicated to exploiting the resources of the area known as New Caledonia.[37]

Although the sea- and land-based fur trades were both mercantilist systems, the impact of the land-based fur trade on First Nations was greater. As Jean Barman and Cole Harris have observed, with the land-based fur trade came sustained ties that replaced the fleeting contact that characterized relations between ship-based Europeans and Aboriginal peoples.[38] If the locus of trade in the maritime operation was the ship, on land it was the fort – described as a node in a system of trade embedded in Indigenous territory – that ultimately formed a power base for the development of a British presence and British capital.[39]

How did the land-based fur trade affect First Nations? How do the themes of force, coercion, and consent that run through contact histories present themselves in British Columbian colonial history? Some of the chief historiographical debates regarding this period of contact and mercantilism are worth considering. Although many writers have contributed to this debate, the approaches of two key authors, Robin Fisher and Cole Harris, provide a sense of the anatomy of the debates on the fur trade and its consequences for First Nations.

In the late 1970s, Robin Fisher's publication *Contact and Conflict* represented the beginning of a body of new historical work that reconsidered the history of First Nations in British Columbia. Fisher observed that the field was dominated by anthropologists.[40] His central argument was that it was crucial to make a distinction between the mercantilist culture of the maritime and land-based fur trade and the period of settlement and white domination that followed. The settlement period, Fisher argued, could be dated roughly from the beginning of the gold rush in 1858, which led to the demise of the fur trade and the degradation of Indigenous cultures. Crucially, Fisher proposed that rather that being an unmitigated disaster for Indigenous peoples, as some authors had maintained, the fur trade had ushered in a period of reciprocal relationships between First Nations and Europeans, a period during which First Nations culture was simultaneously disrupted and invigorated by contact with Europe. Furthermore, Fisher proposed that Native people played only a small role in the new settler economy and that by the end of the 1880s the "process of establishing white domination was complete."[41]

This cultural enrichment thesis has since been contested vigorously in more recent historical studies.[42] These studies have presented the argument that in attempting to move away from the "fatal impact" theories that prevailed in colonial histories that eradicated First Nations agency, Fisher instead privileged notions of First Nations cultural autonomy and the reciprocity of exchanges between European and First Nations. Furthermore, many now claim that the brutality and violence of the Hudson's Bay Company and traders who kept First Nations in check has been understated. These critics also note that the devastating effects of disease and the impact of environmental change on First Nations has likewise been given scant attention. Since then, as Harris notes, "Native voices have repoliticized issues of land and cultural appropriation."[43] In the last three decades, a new intellectual climate and accompanying scholarship have come to the fore, and the latter crucially considers the nexus of imperial geo-politics, violence, colonial law, and the dominance of commercial capital that altered the lives of First Nations.[44]

Harris, writing within the genre of new scholarship on the fur trade, empha-sizes the strategic nature of the expansion of European power and makes use of themes from Foucauldian-inspired work and the thinking of cultural geog-raphers to argue that the aim of traders was to "reconfigure an alien territory and discipline people so that an ordered, profitable, trade was possible therein."[45] It is important to note that this genre, which emerged in the early 1990s, has a spatial and global emphasis and seeks to locate European-Aboriginal contact within the context of the various imperial and geopolitical contestations of the eighteenth and nineteenth century and the movement of capital that mobilized these processes.

Fisher, by contrast, asserted Indigenous autonomy and argued that Aboriginal peoples "to a large extent controlled both the trade and their culture." He argued that trade had been mutually beneficial and offered the "continuous absence of major interracial conflict" as proof.[46] More recent work, however, has starkly revealed the harsh and retaliatory violence used by maritime and land-based fur traders.[47] On land, fort operations were run in a military fashion, and displays of organized violence were used to intimidate or discipline First Nations. As Harris and others argue, and as the historical record clearly attests, gun boats, muskets, cannons, and floggings were part of the repertoire in the performance of violence used to underscore trader might, at least until a fur trade culture was established and other techniques of coercion and control were developed.[48] Fort Victoria was no exception. The elaborate shows of violence by the Hudson's Bay Company at trader forts was partly a product of the forts' acute vulnerability since they were small fortified enclaves placed amidst large First Nations popu-lations. Harris argues that these displays of violence, which could not be backed up with manpower, provided lessons in might and terror that were often used in concert with other stratagems of control or coercion.[49]

In seeking to depart from totalizing Foucauldian analyses that understate Indigenous agency, several authors, including Fisher and John Lutz, maintain that First Nations allowed forts to exist in their own territory for their own economic benefit.[50] First Nations accepted the forts "out of self interest rather than fear," writes Fisher, and they "can hardly be described as a conquered people."[51] First Nations economies, with their culture of gift-giving and estab-lished trade routes, existed prior to European contact. As Lutz contends, the Lekwammen economy was well suited to join with a European-style economy, with each subsidizing the other for its own gain. Lutz outlines this process well in his account of the Lekwammen's encounter with Europeans. The links between European and First Nations economies that Fisher and Lutz (and indeed Harris) suggest (although neither overtly identifies the theoretical basis of such thinking) have been interpreted by historical materialists as the "articulation of modes of production," a feature that is notable in colonial formations in which the Indigenous economy at times subsidizes the imposed European economic system.[52]

In short, Northwest Coast Aboriginal peoples were very experienced in the business of trade – not only among themselves but also with newcomers. The Hudson's Bay Company operated its coastal enterprise among peoples who had several generations of experience in maritime trade with Europeans. Competition was vigorous up and down the Coast as Aboriginal groups played different European and American traders against one another.[53] The strategy of monopolizing trade extended to the land-based trade, in which First Nations groups would congregate around a particular fort and act as middlemen to prevent other groups from trading directly with the fort. As trading intermediaries, they dealt furs between the Hudson's Bay Company and other Aboriginal groups that hunted and trapped furs in the Interior. It is little wonder then that forts held strong economic value for First Nations groups and were jealously coveted. In the case of Fort Victoria, as we shall see, the Lekwammen moved their villages to the fort's immediate vicinity soon after it was built, and Chief Factor James Douglas wrote that they "considered themselves to be specifically attached to the establishment."[54] Clearly, both First Nations and Hudson's Bay Company fur traders were strategic players in the complex world of trade relations.

Unlike the situation in southeastern Australian, where a short-lived mercantilism based on trans-Tasman sealing and whaling was followed by a swift move to pastoralism (which required not trade with Aboriginal peoples but their removal from the land), the culture of at least fifty years of maritime and land-based fur trade created entirely different social relations in the Pacific Northwest. Whereas maritime traders along the Coast were itinerant, culturally detached, and never really imbricated in local First Nations cultures, Europeans who formed the land-based trade were, like their Indigenous counterparts, changed through ties of marriage and culture. The system of land-based fur trade relied on cross-cultural relations that created a distinctive culture. Traders, who were representatives of the Hudson's Bay Company, married First Nations women or women of mixed decent. Many of the traders themselves were of mixed ancestry and spoke Chinook, a pidgin trader language.

Fisher was correct to assert Indigenous autonomy and to bring into focus the interdependence of the trade relationship, and other scholars have since also correctly detailed violence and coercion in the trade and the strategic nature of the fur traders' intent. For a time, a balance may have existed between First Nations and traders, with each group benefitting in socio-economic terms, and with First Nations being largely in control of their land and resources. Gradually, however, changes in the trade, the accumulated effects of disease, the onset of settlement, and a reduction in available resources tipped the balance in favour of Europeans. The articulation of First Nations and European fur-trading economies became less favourable to First Nations as settlement proceeded. This disadvantage was coupled in the mid- to late nineteenth century with a reserve system that ultimately anchored First Nations to small areas of land and to a legal system that increasingly sought to define and control them.

Fisher's statement that Native people played only a small part in the new settlement economy has also been thoroughly contested by the work of scholars such as Lutz and Rolf Knight, who have shown that First Nations in fact engaged in multiple forms of wage labour throughout the century and, indeed, formed the backbone of the settler economy. In was only in the late nineteenth century that First Nations were pushed out of the labour force by legislation passed to ensure jobs for an increasingly white population.[55]

Although the extent of coercion and consent for First Nations and the changes and dislocations that they incurred in the face of the fur trade may be debated, a defining feature that separated the fur trade from the settlement period was the ownership of land. During the fur trade, there was great violence, but land was largely under the control of First Nations, because mercantilism left Aboriginal peoples on their land. Settler colonialism, by contrast, sought to remove Indigenous peoples from their land and denied or extinguished Native title. In the Australian pastoral frontier, land, not labour, was the primary object. It was an object that was pursued with rapidity and violence.

Harris argues that traders were not interested in altering Native cultures and that they did not want Native land. Beyond their palisaded forts and few farms, traders "did not claim Native space. They were not colonizers."[56] This may be true of the earliest period of the fur trade; however, by the mid-1840s the Hudson's Bay Company's fur-trading culture had clearly laid the groundwork for settlement. By the late 1840s, the building of settlements and towns was an explicitly stated object imposed by the Crown on the company, and the eventual shift from mercantilism to an industrialized settler economy would radically alter the lives of First Nations.

The Select Committee on Aboriginal Tribes and the Port Phillip Protectorate
British colonizing efforts in Australia began when a convict colony was formed in New South Wales in 1788 and followed by European settlement in Van Diemen's

Land, now Tasmania, in 1803. Aboriginal peoples rapidly lost their lands as settlement ensued. The years between 1824 and 1831 are known in the history of Van Diemen's Land as the Black War, a time of violent contestation and Aboriginal resistance to the appropriation of their land by Europeans. By the 1830s the lives of Aboriginal people in the Colony of New South Wales and in Van Diemen's Land had been brutally interrupted by invasion. In 1835 mercantilists and pastoralists, overstraiters from Van Diemen's Land, sought new lands at the opposite coast, the southeastern edge of Australia, for commercial gain.[57] This district, nominally part of the Colony of New South Wales, would come to be known as Port Phillip and was highly sought out for pastoralism and settlement.

At this time, humanitarian interest in the welfare of colonized peoples in the British settlements, particularly Africa's Cape Colony and Australia, became intense. After the abolition of the slave trade in 1833, the Aborigines Protection Society, seeking to capitalize on its humanitarian and political successes, turned its attention to the condition of the colonized peoples in the outlying realms of the British Empire.[58] In 1837 a select committee convened to inquire into the condition of the Indigenous populations of all the British colonies produced a two-volume report titled *Report of the Parliamentary Select Committee on the Aboriginal Tribes (British Settlements)*.[59] The development of the report was driven by Thomas Foxwell Buxton, a well-known abolitionist, and it was written by members of Buxton's evangelical abolitionist circle, including Anna Gurney, the final author of the report.[60] The report detailed in its Preface the corruption of Britain's empire: "In an age distinguished for its liberality, its enlightened sentiment, and its Christian zeal, atrocities, the most daring and dreadful in their character ... have passed unnoticed and unreproved."[61] Seeking to draw attention to the real operations of Britain's expansionist endeavours, the committee noted that "comparatively little of what was passing on our colonies has been published at home."[62] Drawing on transnational evangelical networks to gather its evidence, committee members sought to appeal to the metropolitan religious public, a strategy used by abolitionists, to force social change, for they believed that a "virtuous public would rebel against such atrocities."[63] The report painted the far reaches of Britain's empire not as new lands or Edens but as the dark places of the earth. Eden had turned sour. The report stated: "Through successive generations the work of spoilation and death has been carried on, until the colonial possessions of the most religious nation in the world" had become the "the dark places of the earth, full of the habitations of cruelty."[64]

Those who have summarized the report have noted that it was characterized by noble idealism but a lack of appreciation for the realities of frontier life.[65] It did, however, lead Great Britain's House of Lords to instigate a protectorate system in Port Phillip, which was implemented by Colonial Secretary Lord Glenelg to "protect" Indigenous peoples in southeastern Australia from over-straiters from Van Diemen's Land and others who had created an outlaw settlement outside the limits of location.[66] It was hoped that the Aboriginal Protectorate would avert the violent clashes that had marked the history of the earlier colonies. Although the report was directed primarily at the Cape Colony and Australia, it also addressed Canada, and its conclusion regarding the "Indian" situation in British North America was damning.[67] The report, of course, predated the establishment of the Colony of Vancouver Island. In general, however, the report's recommendations were minimal compared to its scope of investigation, and over the next century of British expansionism its recommendations regarding the recognition of Indigenous peoples' legal rights were largely ignored.[68]

By 1838 George Augustus Robinson, who had the dubious reputation of having "conciliated" the Aborigines in Van Diemen's Land, had been selected, along with four assistants, as the chief protector of Port Phillip. Lord Glenelg stipulated that the protectors were to "promote the well-being of Aborigines and to represent their interests to the colonial executive or the British government." In addition to physically protecting the Aborigines, they were to civilize them, educate them, convert them to Christianity, and instruct them in agriculture and the building of houses.[69]

The Port Phillip Aboriginal Protectorate lasted from 1839 to 1849 and was generally considered a failure. Although various missions to First Nations peoples on the Northwest Coast were founded throughout the nineteenth century, a protectorate system was never declared. Indeed, possibly because of bitter and violent conflicts over the expropriation of Indigenous land in Australia and the perceived failure of the Port Phillip protectorate, the Colonial Office explicitly avoided the creation of such an institution when the new Colony of British Columbia was created after the gold rush of 1858. For example, in 1858 Colonial Secretary Sir Edward Bulwer Lytton clearly stipulated in a colonial dispatch that *"no nominal protector of the aborigines* – no annuity to a petted chief, – no elevation of one chief above another, *will answer the purpose."*[70] This stance, which was a refutation of the select committee's report, reflected a change in the times. By the 1850s humanitarian sentiments had begun to wane, and less radical and more reactionary views that did not privilege Aboriginal peoples over settlers prevailed.

Gold Rushes at the Extremities of Empire

If the fur trade from British Columbia's interior to Europe was the lifeline of empire,[71] the produce transported to the metropole from Australia Felix (bullion and wool, for example) and, in turn, the goods and immigrants it imported from the Empire's centre formed another vital economic and cultural circuit of the imperial economy. Early Melbourne was primarily a port in the service of squatters and those associated with the pastoral industry. Later, although various industries developed, the production and sale of wool was the economic mainstay until the gold rush.[72]

By the 1850s and 1860s, these two extremities of empire were imagined in powerful ways. The town of Victoria was envisaged as an English village and British Columbia as the white man's province, despite that First Nations represented an overwhelming majority. Melbourne, too, imagined itself as an antipodean London, as a city of white, imperial classicism and as a new seat of empire in the far south.

The Colony of Victoria and Vancouver Island gestured towards each other in newspapers with reportage of imperial milestones and the growth of each colony. Boosted by the fervour of the gold rushes, and speaking to the Royal Geographical Society in London on 12 December 1859, W.C. Grant observed that the Colony of Vancouver Island, if properly developed, "might be made extremely profitable ... the fish if caught and cured under European superintendence ... might be exported profitably to Australia, where salmon and herring are both in demand, and the two distant extremities of the British Empire might thus be made to join hands, with mutual benefit to each other."[73] Mutual enthusiasm did not stop at the prospect of trade. Gold rushes in California (1848–49), southeastern Australia (1851), British Columbia (1858), and New Zealand (1861-63) were deemed to be proof of the imperial destiny of the Anglo-Saxon races; they were events that proved "the finger of Providence was manifest."[74] Rhetorical gesturing between the colonies was common throughout the late 1850s and 1860s. At the time of the Fraser River gold rush in British Columbia, its potential size and impact was projected to be as great as those of California and southeastern Australia. Many hoped that like the centres of San Francisco and Melbourne, the settlement of Victoria, a supply centre for the gold rush, would be made prosperous by gold and immigration. But it was not to be. In 1852, 435 Europeans lived in the Colony of Victoria Island. The 1858 gold rush, while drawing many immigrants and miners to Victoria and the Coast, never drew the tens of thousands of immigrants that swelled the population of California and the Colony of Victoria. As Jean Barman notes, around thirty thousand men and women headed for the mainland of British Columbia in 1858, but three times that number had reached California by 1849, the first year of the gold rush, and that number rose to a hundred thousand the following year. At its peak, the number of people drawn by the gold rush to Victoria was about six thousand.[75] By contrast, in 1851 the population of Melbourne was estimated to be between 23,000 and 29,000. By 1861 that number had increased to between 125,000 and 140,000 people.[76]

The gold rushes radically altered the demographic, economic, and political balance of the regions they affected. Although the Fraser River gold rush was relatively small on a world scale, it shifted the focus of early newcomer settlement from a place directed by the Hudson's Bay Company to one with a relatively independent colonial government. As Barman writes, the handover of authority from the Hudson's Bay Company ended a distinct chapter in British Columbia's history.[77] The gold rush in southeastern Australia prompted the separation of Port Phillip from the colony of New South Wales to form the colony of Victoria. The influx of newcomers to British Columbia and southeastern Australia in the 1850s reorganized bodies and spaces, and new racial tensions emerged as immigrant groups such as Chinese made these places their home. Victoria would remain relatively small. By the 1880s it was eclipsed by growth on the mainland of Vancouver, whose population flourished when it became the terminal point of the transcontinental railway. By 1888 Sydney and Melbourne were two of the largest cities in the British Empire. Rivalling Birmingham and Liverpool, they were port cities with firm ties in an imperial network of trade.

Spatial Strategies of Invasion: Treaties Compared

In general Canada has had a long history of brokering treaties with First Nations, whereas Australia has not. Treaty making or its absence in regard to land is a vital point of departure and debate in the development of Port Phillip and Vancouver Island. Land treaties framed understandings of Indigenous and European rights in land for the future. In Canada, treaty making between the Crown and First Nations began in the seventeenth century. The formation of the territory of Nunavut in 1999 was a partial settlement of the Inuit claim against Canada, and the conclusion of the Nisga'a Final Agreement in 2000 in British Columbia shows that, compared to Australia, a different attitude presides in Canada. Canadians have a long-standing commitment to negotiating difference that has much to do with the political and cultural presence of the Québécois.[78] Historically, however, British Columbia's treaty record was much different from the rest of Canada. As Stuart Banner notes, British Columbia was the only part of Canada that the British treated as *terra nullius* (the notion of land belonging to no one). Apart from fourteen instances on Vancouver Island, Europeans did not acquire land from First Nations by treaty.[79]

In his study of the acquisition of Indigenous land by British and American settlers throughout the Pacific, Banner observes that no two places followed the same process of land acquisition. In tracing this Pacific world, it is clear that in some places Indigenous peoples own much more land than in others, and some

Indigenous people possess treaty rights while others do not. The notion of terra nullius was, however, common to British Columbia and most of Australia. Banner describes the process of land expropriation in Australia as "terra nullius by design" and in British Columbia as "terra nullius as kindness." In the case of the latter, rights in land were at first recognized and then taken away for the "good" of First Nations.[80]

The key object of the settler-colonial project, to expropriate land from its Indigenous owners, ensured that Indigenous space would be remade in these two edges of empire. In Port Phillip one treaty was brokered between Aboriginal peoples and the Port Phillip Association. It was quickly declared null and void by Governor Richard Bourke. On Vancouver Island fourteen land-based agreements, known as the Douglas treaties, were made between Governor James Douglas and First Nations. But these treaties were, in general terms, not honoured. Apart from the Douglas treaties, British Columbia stands in stark contrast to the rest of the country. In sum, these two sites had something in common – the fiction of terra nullius and the very material consequences of Indigenous dispossession.

To date, Native title and Aboriginal land justice continues to cause concern in the State of Victoria. The *Yorta Yorta* Native title case was struck down in 1998 after lengthy litigation that involved infamous debates about matters of history and set a new low for Indigenous land rights claims. In his ruling, Federal Court Justice Olney privileged the uncertain written evidence of pastoralist Edward Curr over the oral testimony of Yorta Yorta claimants. Two more recent claims (the Wotjobaluk and the Gunditjmara) have ended in successful determinations of Native title over small areas and ancillary agreements that give the claimants some say in land-management issues. The Native title won by the Gunditjmara is non-exclusive, that is, they enjoy access, camping, and fishing rights, but these do not affect non-Indigenous rights in the same territory.[81]

A closer look at historical treaties that were either rendered void or dishonoured in Port Phillip and Vancouver Island provides insight into Aboriginal entitlements in urbanizing environments. These agreements tended to prescribe approaches towards Indigenous peoples in settler cities and set the legal conditions for land contestation throughout the nineteenth century, and they continue to profoundly shape land rights negotiations today.

Failed Treaty in Port Phillip

The only "treaty" made in Australia is known as Batman's Treaty of 1835. In this dubious agreement, John Batman, on behalf of the Port Phillip Association from Van Diemen's Land, claimed that the Kulin Nation had exchanged two tracts of land around the Port Phillip Bay area that amounted to six hundred thousand acres in return for goods such as blankets, axes, flour, mirrors, scissors, and handkerchiefs and the promise of an annual rent or tribute.[82] The treaty was in fact two land deeds, or deeds of conveyance, that covered most of present-day greater Melbourne and Geelong. The Port Phillip Association's central aim, motivated by entrepreneurial and humanitarian sentiment, was to make a treaty with Indigenous peoples and then present it immediately to the British government. Land in Van Diemen's Land was becoming scarce, and the association planned to quickly move livestock to Port Phillip as the government and the Colonial Office "ruminated on the merits or otherwise of the Association's claims."[83] By 1834 George Arthur, lieutenant-governor of Van Diemen's Land, was well aware of the association's private plans to settle across the Bass Strait. In fact, his nephew Henry Arthur was one of its members. Arthur had made no secret of his interest in the opposite coast and his desire to bring it under his jurisdiction, although this was not to be. In 1832, after violence had peaked in Van Diemen's Land, he lamented that "a treaty was not entered into with the Natives" and stated that the results of such devastation and loss of Aboriginal life "must ever remain a stain upon the colonisation of Van Diemen's Land."[84] Arthur encouraged the association to broker a treaty with the headmen or *ngurungaeta* of the Kulin Nation, partly for humanitarian reasons and partly to avoid the calamity that had occurred in Van Diemen's Land. Later, in 1837, just after the suppression of the rebellion against British rule, Arthur was appointed lieutenant-governor of Upper Canada (present-day Ontario). He sought to make an example of captured rebels: some were sentenced to hang and others were eventually transported to Port Arthur, the notorious penal establishment set up by Arthur when he was governor of Van Diemen's Land. Canadian-Australian connections such as these reveal the circuits of colonial personnel that linked various colonies.[85]

Therefore, in 1835 the Port Phillip Association was careful to locate its treaty claims within a humanitarian framework. Since the abolition of slavery in 1833, attention had shifted to the Colonial Office and its treatment of Aboriginal peoples in Britain's far-flung colonies. The association described its intentions to the government as that of establishing "a free and useful colony, founded on the principle of conciliation, of philanthropy, morality and temperance ... calculated to ensure the comfort and well being of the natives."[86]

Batman's claim of a treaty with the Kulin peoples of the Port Phillip district and the increased movement of private settlers to the area caused serious challenges to the Crown on several fronts. First, private entrepreneurs treating with Indigenous peoples undermined the Crown's central claim that it owned all land, which was later underpinned by the proposition of terra nullius. Second, by treating, however dishonestly, with Kulin peoples, Batman had implicitly acknowledged Aboriginal rights in land, which the Crown sought to disavow. Batman's Treaty, which claimed that he had gained rights to six hundred thousands acres and subsequent settlement in the area, was thus a radical manoeuvre, and officials in Hobart, Sydney, and London were "determined that the basic sovereignty of the Crown should not vanish by default."[87] A small entrepreneurial group treating with Indigenous peoples without the Crown's imprimatur was seen as a dangerous development by London and the colonial governments, for it signified an acknowledgment of Indigenous rights in land. The Port Phillip Association's treaty was a highly calculated and strategic bid for a vast swath of land, and although issues of sovereignty were hotly debated in the 1830s and were by no means settled, the bid in fact served to consolidate the Colony of New South Wales' position on sovereignty and thus shored up the legal fiction of terra nullius.[88] Authorities were also "troubled by the spread of costly settlements beyond their control," and the treaty was quickly voided on the grounds that the Crown alone had an exclusive right of pre-emption.[89] By contrast, in the early expansionist phases of colonialism in North America and New Zealand, small and relatively weak groups operated largely outside the reach of government. In the United States, the entire land-owning system was based on individual title purchases from Native Americans; in New Zealand, British settlers purchased much of the land from Maori.[90] In Australia, state rather than private interests prevailed. Representatives of the Crown arrived on the shores of southeastern Australia in 1788 to set up a penal colony, and the state centrally administered land, labour, and the market. From the very outset, the southeastern coast of Australia was dominated by the Crown and its perceived entitlement to all lands and land negotiations.

Fast on the heels of Batman's treaty claim and the illegal occupation of land around Melbourne and present-day Geelong, Francis Forbes, chief justice of the Colony of New South Wales, wrote to Governor Bourke. He advised the governor to prevent settlers, operating under the erroneous belief that they had legal title to the land, from purchasing land from Aborigines. The chief justice's letter reveals the hardening position of the colonial government on issues of sovereignty. Forbes urged Bourke to issue a proclamation "defining the true limits of the Colony within your Commission as Governor, declaring that all settlements made on any land within such limits, without the permission of the local government, is illegal and cautioning persons against purchasing any portion of such land from the aboriginal inhabitants under an impression that such purchases will be respected as conferring legal title." Forbes concluded his advice by declaring: "I deem such a measure of the more importance, as the example of Messrs Batman & Gellibrand will be surely followed by other persons nearer home and much trouble may be occasioned if the Crown seems tacitly to assent to the right of the Savage to sell, and of His Majesty's subjects to buy the land of the Colony."[91] The chief justice of the colony thus disavowed outright the "right of the Savage to sell." Described as a "pretence," the treaty was declared null and void on 26 August 1835 in a formal proclamation issued by Governor Bourke. The settlement was declared illegal. The proclamation stated that "every such treaty, bargain, and contract with the Aboriginal natives ... for the possession title, or claim to any lands lying and being within the limits of the Governments of the Colony of New South Wales ... is void and shall be of no effect against the rights of the Crown." Any persons "in possession of any such land" were to be deemed "trespassers" and were "liable to be dealt with in like manner as other intruders upon the vacant lands of the Crown."[92] In early September the proclamation was published in the Van Diemen's Land press, no doubt to deter other eager overstraiters from attempting such a journey. There has since been much debate about the authenticity of the treaty documents themselves, particularly the "signatures" or sacred inscriptions of eight Aboriginal *ngurrengaeta* who represented what is now referred to as the Kulin Nation.

Despite this proclamation to deter land grabbing, it was impossible to stem the tide of settlers to these new pastoral lands. Colonists who were deemed trespassers on the Crown's land were also viewed by the colonial government as potentially valuable speculators, as "good" colonists who would cause the expansion of the wool industry. By 13 April 1836, Lord Glenelg approved Bourke's actions to bow to the inevitable and authorized the unleashing of the "spirit of adventure and speculation" while maintaining the Crown's basic authority over the land, the law, and the Native inhabitants. This was the beginning the great expansionist phase of the wool industry, which would shape southeastern Australia well into the future.[93]

Vancouver Island: Fourteen Treaties

In the early 1850s, James Douglas, as the newly appointed governor of the Colony of Vancouver Island, negotiated fourteen land-based treaties, including several treaties that formed Native reserves in and around the town of Victoria. These reserves and the terms of the treaties that created them became the subject of intense, long-standing legal debates that have carried into the present. The Crown had conveyed title of Vancouver Island to the Hudson's Bay Company in 1849 in fee. As historian Hamar Foster has noted, little mention was made of Native peoples, and it appears that the company had been required to extinguish Native title.[94] By establishing the Colony of Vancouver Island, the Colonial Office had largely left the direction of land policy to Douglas. Douglas sought to treat with Native peoples, and he considered the transactions to be genuine and solemn obligations.[95]

To open up land for settlement, in 1850 Douglas made eleven purchases of land from First Nations near Fort Victoria and west along the Strait of Juan de Fuca. The Hudson's Bay Company had provided Douglas with copies of land cessation agreements, described as deeds of conveyance, which included verbatim copies of agreements between Maori and the British Crown in New Zealand.[96] The contracts, in Company Secretary Archibald Barclay's words, were "a copy with hardly any alteration of the Agreement adopted by the New Zealand Company, in their transactions of a similar kind with the natives there."[97] Foster explains that Barclay had access to the report of a House of Commons Select Committee on New Zealand (1844), which had inquired into Native title in that colony. The select committee concurred with the views of the New Zealand Company and, indeed, with the theories of Emer de Vattel, who upheld only Indigenous occupancy rights, not property rights.[98] Barclay therefore modelled his advice to Douglas on the select committee's finding that Indigenous peoples had the right of occupancy but not property, that is, First Nations claims extended only to their cultivated fields and building sites or villages. Regarding this highly delimited versions of Native title, Barclay advised Douglas that "the uncivilized inhabitants of any country ... have a right of occupancy only, and ... until they establish among themselves a settled form of government and subjugate the ground to their own uses by the cultivation of it ... they have not any individual property in it." This "qualified Dominion," as Barclay termed it, encompassed only land that First Nations had "occupied by cultivation, or had houses built on." All other land, he stated, "is to be regarded as waste and applicable to the purpose of colonisation." Barclay did not tell Douglas that the Colonial Office did not approve of the select committee's report.[99]

Two more "arrangements" were made in Fort Rupert to settle the title to coal deposits. Douglas then purchased land near Nanaimo in 1854, which brought the total number of treaties to fourteen. The purchases represented less than 3 percent of the total area of Vancouver Island.[100] It is unlikely that First Nations actually signed anything; rather, as Sydney Harring notes, they placed an *x* on blank pages, which over a year later were written out in boilerplate treaty language.[101] The so-called treaties were loose and full of discrepancies. The definitions were based on occupation not property, and the deeds of conveyance, writes Harris, were vague documents open to many interpretations.[102] There was confusion about the definition and demarcations of villages. As Harris observes, if *village* meant winter lodges, then which sites counted? Thirteen winter villages have since been located around Fort Victoria in Lekwammen territory.[103] In addition, the term *enclosed fields* did not include camus fields that Coast Salish peoples had cultivated for hundreds of years, and the issue of First Nations mariculture was left undecided. There has also been some suggestion that Native people thought they were signing peace treaties, with *x* representing the sign of the cross.[104] The Douglas treaties, which were actually deeds of conveyance, simultaneously extinguished Native title and asserted it in partial and qualified ways.[105] The deeds effectively acted as a kind of statute of limitations. Native peoples were entitled only to small parcels of land, villages, fields, and sustenance rights, while the remainder of was deemed Crown land.

Treating with First Nations was initially viewed as being warranted and convenient; it was, as Harris surmises, a "ritual in which whites secured what they wanted for little cost."[106] Yet after 1854 Douglas stopped making treaties as farmland and coal-mining sites were secured by the government. Douglas' views on Native title had also altered by this time, and the termination of treaty making was a de facto denial of Native title. As Banner argues, a new and convenient humanitarian sentiment had emerged that purchasing land from First Nations actually harmed them, because transactions tended to be misunderstood, unfair, or forced. Douglas, as a witness to First Nations impoverishment and distress, concurred with this sentiment. The development of the US reservation system had amply shown that land purchases from First Nations were counter to humanitarian opinion, and on advice from the Colonial Office, Douglas embraced this stance, ostensibly for the good of First Nations.[107] It is also possible that Native people had become suspicious of the treaty process on Vancouver Island by this time. As Foster notes, they had experienced the unjust outcomes of the treaties and had seen the tide of settlement that had followed.[108]

In summary, while the Colony of Victoria in southeastern Australia ultimately had no treaty, British Columbia formulated fourteen treaties, including two within the precinct of the city of Victoria. In 1835, and for several years afterwards, the Port Phillip Association attempted to have the Batman Treaty legitimated by the Colony of New South Wales and the Colonial Office in London, but the treaty was never ratified. Fourteen years later in British Columbia, James Douglas treated with First Nations by utilizing the deeds of conveyance of the New Zealand Company and its very limited notion of Native title. By the late nineteenth century, many settlers viewed the Batman Treaty as a foolhardy anomaly, while the very existence of the Douglas treaties in British Columbia largely faded from the public mind.

Why did the legal fiction of terra nullius prevail in Australia and British Columbia? This is a complex question. It is not simply that questions of Indigenous and British sovereignty were in flux and the subject of fierce debate during the early nineteenth century or that the British did not respect varying forms of Indigenous political organization or agriculture in both places, although these were certainly contributing factors. As Banner notes, because the British Crown arrived on Australia's shores before settlers, state interests dominated.[109] Likewise, on Vancouver Island, the Hudson's Bay Company, as proxy for the Crown, was the premier authority. Unlike much of North America, Vancouver Island was settled late and very slowly, and there were no treaties or purchases between individuals or groups and Native peoples. When the Colony of Vancouver Island was formed in 1849, Douglas, as governor, brokered land policy. In other words, the state dominated. Douglas' desire to uphold some rights for Native peoples explains the treaties' existence. Although the Douglas treaties were largely dishonoured, the very existence of treaties has meant that later negotiations over land in British Columbia could occur within a discourse of sovereignty, something that has not occurred in that same way in the State of Victoria. These differences and the presence of a First Nations reserve within the limits of Victoria would shape racialized dynamics in the two cities and the spatial commerce of the urbanizing frontier in distinct and important ways throughout the nineteenth century.

Intimate Frontiers: Intermarriage and Miscegenation

Studying racialized space in the colonial city requires paying careful attention to intermarriage, miscegenation, and mixed-race peoples in the cityscape and to the issues of domestic and everyday life, because these urbanizing frontiers were also intimate frontiers, places of shared, collaborative moments between Indigenous and non-Indigenous peoples. Writers such as Ann Stoler and Jorge de Alva have noted a profound shift from a structural focus on economics and politics to the cultural and discursive aspects of power formation in everyday life in analyses of colonialism since the late 1970s. Indeed, economic and political structures are *transformed* in these intimate power relations of everyday life.[110]

Commenting on the increased attention that has been paid to the intimacies of empire, Stoler describes them as vital political sites. The imperial politics of intimacy clearly have global scope. Stoler directs us to the work of feminist scholars who have attempted to trace the intertwined sexual and racial patterns of dominance that move across historical fields and asks us to consider the gendered dimensions of colonial governance.[111] Attention to intimate relations and gender – as Sylvia Van Kirk, Adele Perry, Ann Stoler, and many other scholars have shown – is crucial. Perry writes that, in the settler colony, "Gender is where the abiding bonds between dispossession and colonization become most clear since settler colonies function on a mutual discourse (often studied separately) of colonization and immigration."[112]

Aboriginal people in Australia were presented in nineteenth-century racial-scientific rhetoric as being the lowest order among all of the races of humankind. While gross and systematic sexual abuse on the colonial frontier was often taken for granted, marriage between Aboriginal women and European men, though not illegal, was often deemed unacceptable and was only grudgingly acknow-ledged as an activity of the "lower orders."[113] In Port Phillip, unlike British Columbia, there was no long-standing tradition of publicly accepted unions between Aboriginal women and European men. Unions between First Nations or Métis women of high rank and European fur traders, which were known as country marriages or marrying *à la façon du pays,* set in train very different social dynamics in British Columbia.[114] These unions profoundly affected the socio-spatial politics of the cityscape and the development of social demograph-ics, particularly in the period before the gold rush, and radically threatened and redefined metropolitan ideas of whiteness and white privilege.

Shoring up a white settler population became a priority in both sites, especially after the 1860s. During the mid- to late nineteenth century, each colony encour-aged and engineered immigration schemes to bring white women to their shores to fortify and expand the white settler population. Prevailing ideas of white women as the civilizing sex, class and gender mores, and ideas of family and domesticity ensured that white women were crucially required in British col-onies. As government officials increasingly feared miscegenation and the sup-posedly degenerative effects of mixed populations, mixed unions became increasingly unpopular. As Lisa Chilton points out, government officials pro-moted the civilizing and settling effects of white women's integration into male-dominated, frontier communities. Their domestic labour was also highly valued.[115] By the late nineteenth and early twentieth centuries, an overt and vigorous transnational discourse of whiteness, of "white man's land" and "white labour," had formed throughout the British settler colonies.[116] Immigration policy was crafted to keep out those deemed a threat to the maintenance of white settler society. British Columbia, for instance, borrowed Australia's colonial immigration laws, which were racially encoded to enforce notions of white labour and white man's lands. As we shall see, these tensions of intimacy, race, and idealized polities played out at the level of everyday life in urbanizing col-onial cities.

Settler-Colonial Cities: A Survey of Bodies and Spaces in Transition

IN 1843 WILLIAM ADENEY, a young Londoner in his twenties, arrived in Melbourne. It was his first visit to the colony, and after taking lodgings in Collins Street, he wrote his impressions in his diary, where he described the notorious dust storms in the town and the poverty of the colonials. He recounted the following scene:

> I was sitting writing a letter the other day and rose to peep through between the blind and window frame to see how the day looked out of doors when at the same moment a black horrible looking face suddenly came into very close proximity to mine but on the other side of the glass. It was that of an old native woman who activated by the same curiosity as my own no doubt wished to see through the same aperture what was inside. As it happened I was regularly startled and could not imagine for a moment what it was. The old woman was as much surprised as I was and after gazing with open mouth a few seconds said *boro boro* but what she wanted I could not understand ... These poor creatures wander through accosting passers by with "give me black money" and various other similar expressions begging bread, etc etc. We are not much troubled by them as my host keeps a great black dog which is quite furious.[1]

William Adeney's compelling diary entry, which describes his face-to-face encounter with an Aboriginal woman in early Melbourne, reveals the powerful intersubjective dimension of the colonial encounter in the developing townscape. It is a first-hand rebuttal of the seemingly popular misconception that Aborigines simply exited the scene once European settlers arrived in 1835. Far from being on the margins, Aboriginal people were present in early Melbourne. As European immigrants planted a town in the traditional lands of the Wurundjeri of the Kulin Nation, encounters between Aborigines and Europeans were continuous, complex, and at times violent. The five cultural-linguistic groups of the Kulin Nation met annually for meetings and ceremonies in what is now the city centre of metropolitan Melbourne. Aboriginal people maintained a presence in the early townscape even as land was surveyed for the creation of new streets. As the European grid plan was laid over Indigenous land, cultural practices were adapted; although many Aboriginal people did not seek to reside permanently in this new European space, they did use it for their own ends.

Adeney's retelling of the window scene also reveals the settler-colonial city as a transactional space. The startling meeting through the aperture of a window suggests new worlds, the transformation of indigenous places, and the rapid refashioning of spaces that accompanied colonialism. It reveals one of many transcultural moments and the repositioning of bodies and spaces. It shows, too, that Melbourne was already a place in which the lines of partition and segregation were drawn, with dogs being used to keep Aboriginal people out of town. The forces of settler colonialism had displaced both Adeney and the unnamed Aboriginal woman. But Adeney was a voluntary traveller, an immigrant seeking land. The woman was caught between the pastoral land grab, which pushed Aboriginal groups off traditional lands, and the expanding cadastral grid of the town, which simultaneously sought to keep Aboriginal people out of the new urbanizing space. It is possible that the woman was starving, because Aboriginal food sources diminished as pastoralism took hold of Aboriginal lands and waterways, which were increasingly enclosed by European fences. Bartering and seeking to "boro" (borrow) goods became one way to survive as traditional life was interrupted.

Until the late 1850s, members of the Kulin Nation lived in and around the Melbourne area. Dispossessed of their lands and with their social structures brutally altered, they ventured into the Melbourne townscape to exchange their labour, to sell goods, to barter, and, at times, to buy munitions. Adeney's window scene refutes Melbourne's pictorial tradition, which depicts Aboriginal people always at the edges of the town. In traditional artwork Aborigines inhabit the realm of the mythic; they look on from the margins at European progress and at the unveiling of empire's ultimate destiny – the bustling settler-colonial city. William Knight's *Collins Street, Town of Melbourne, NSW, 1839* (Figure 3), shows Melbourne as a busy, emergent city, as a place of possibility and progress that influential residents and enthusiasts would initially promulgate as a white, commodified space and later as a European-style vision of imperial classicism famous for its grid. Knight depicts Aborigines in white, flowing robes, which activates allusions of Greek and Roman antiquity and Rousseau's noble savage, the antitheses of modernity and the grid plan of the New World city. The Aborigines look from the edge of recently cleared forest onto the vista of colonial settlement, from one stage of development to another. This spatial positioning implies that Aboriginal people are out of time or that their existence is coeval: they reside in another time, which would pass in the wake of the city and its New World progress.[2] John Skinner Prout uses the same artistic device in his

Figure 3 Collins Street, Town of Melbourne, NSW, 1839 (artist, William Knight).
National Library of Australia.

striking wood engraving *Melbourne in 1846: A View from Collingwood.* The
painting is a nostalgic reminiscence, made in 1887, that depicts two Aboriginal
figures in the foreground looking at a panorama of Melbourne (see Figure 4).

Powerful and symbolic representations of the city as the apotheosis of colonial
endeavour continue to render Indigenous people's presence in the nineteenth-
century city marginal or non-existent. Aboriginal people have been viewed as
anomalous to or incompatible with the emerging settler cityscape, and these

Figure 4   Melbourne in 1846: A View from Collingwood, 1887, wood engraving (artist, John Skinner Prout). State Library of Victoria.

notions have enduring significance for issues of Indigenous sovereignty and emplacement. The genesis of these views can be understood within the context of late eighteenth- and early nineteenth-century stadial theory and Enlightenment ideas about progress and improvement in which the settler city was fashioned symbolically as the emblem of Western commercial and civil development, as the triumph of empire.

Seeking the Settler-Colonial City

In 1973 the geographer Anthony D. King wrote that colonial cities were "laid out by the rulers and not the ruled."[3] He observed the uneven distribution of power within colonial urban environments and that these environments possessed a global dimension. Despite his observations, few scholars have charted in sufficient detail what was distinctive about the spatial commerce of settler-colonial cities and what this distinctiveness has meant for broader transimperial processes and for Indigenous peoples who were dispossessed and displaced.

Many scholars in the fields of urban studies, environmental planning, geography, and colonial and postcolonial studies have attempted to define and analyze the colonial city. For example, in a 1985 survey article, King sought to define the multifarious forms and expressions of colonial cities.[4] This was not an easy task and, of course, since then great change has occurred in theoretical approaches to the study of cities and colonialism. King argued, in line with emerging urban theory, that the city is a social product and that the colonial city could not be understood without understanding the colony of which it was a part.[5] King outlined possible characteristics of colonial cities and methods for typologizing them. For example, he suggested that colonial cities could be defined by analyzing factors such as the degree of Indigenous urban settlement, motives for colonization, the effect and degree of coercion over Indigenous subjects, resource exploitation, and physical and spatial form. Certainly, one could test Zanzibar, Winnipeg, Mexico City, or Rabat in all or any of these ways. But only the suggestion of looking at motives for colonization and the degree of coercion over Indigenous subjects hinted at useful ways to determine a colonial formation and, thus, the racialized dynamics of social space in a city.

There are limitations in the way traditional geographers and urban planners define colonialism, colonies, and colonial cities. Characterizations tend to be functionalistic. They speak of goods and products circulating, but they often omit the important human and cultural aspects of empire's urbanizing landscapes: the displacements and transformations of peoples and ideas. Contextualizing the physical and discursive development of early cities within broader circuits of empire, and within the recursive processes of metropole and periphery, is an approach that has only recently been taken up by urban geographers. Furthermore, until recently, Indigenous peoples have been marginalized within the discipline of geography, and only scant attention has been given to the coercion of Indigenous peoples through various modalities of colonial power and the fashioning of Indigenous and immigrant subjectivities within settler-colonial cityscapes. Although many authors have conceded that colonial cities were and are instruments of cultural and racial dominance, they have largely failed to show the historical particularities of these operations or the deeper genealogies that encode *settler* cities with particular European cultural meanings. Ronald Ross and Gerard Telkamp's *Colonial Cities* (1985) falls into this category.[6] It is peculiar that this volume of essays, which covers colonial cities over five centuries in almost every continent, does not address cities in what King dubiously described as "successfully colonized lands," lands where the Indigenous population was "largely eliminated ... marginalised or to varying degrees absorbed into the population of the colonising power." Such cities, King suggested, might be Sydney in Australia, or Halifax in Canada. Clearly, King was referring to the setter-colonial city, although he did not identify it as such. King suggested that analysis of such colonial cities "would be desirable."[7]

Another feature of scholarly work to date is that views from the metropole tend to dominate. *Imperial Cities: Landscape, Display and Identity* (2003), edited by metropolitan geographers, is concerned with cities of empire. Yet this work barely addresses the rich and dynamic histories of colonized Indigenous and mixed-descent peoples in these imperial cities. An earlier work by Robert Home, *Of Planning and Planting: The Making of British Colonial Cities* (1997), is equally problematic. One reviewer observed that the book shares most of the characteristics of the mainstream discourse, that is, the planning and environment field: it is pre-theoretical and landscape focused and, with a central emphasis on British city-shapers, offers only rare "glimpses of the Indigenous peoples whose lives were unalterably changed."[8]

Such apprehensions of colonial cities tend to privilege a top-down view of empire, and of colonial power, rather than the lived realities of these cities, with rarely a mention of the presence and agency of Indigenous peoples whose lives were radically transformed and whose lands were taken. Crucially, these British or metropolitan studies often conflate colonial and settler-colonial formations, although many colonies exhibited features of both. As Lorenzo Veracini and others note, colonial formations could be and were mixed; at other times, they were in tension with one another.[9] However, the ideal forms of colonial versus settler-colonial cities, which resided in the colonial imagination, were quite different. It is necessary to make the distinction between colonial and settler-colonial geographies clear and to delineate how varying aspirations for them manifested in the building of urban spaces and the organization of peoples. It must be acknowledged that in settler colonies the dispossession of Indigenous peoples and immigration were vital twin facets of the settler-colonial urbanizing project and that these features are mirrored in their cities.

David Hamer's *New Towns in the New World: Images and Perceptions of the Nineteenth-Century Urban Frontier* (1990) is one of the few monographs that specifically examine the settler-colonial cities of Australia, New Zealand, and North America.[10] Hamer explores the symbolism, planning, architecture, and representations of settler-colonial cities in the European literary and visual imagination, but he only indirectly addresses the lived experiences of and cross-cultural encounters between immigrants and the Indigenous peoples on whose land these cities were built. As his title tells us, Hamer's study is concerned with images and perceptions of the urban frontier – as seen mainly through the lens of empire's centre. Few authors have conceptualized the settler-colonial city from the edge of empire as a dynamic socio-cultural phenomenon.

In his promising article "Anglo-Saxon Cities on the Pacific Rim" (1993), Lionel Frost explicitly racializes his title.[11] But the article is a comparative account of infrastructural development. The presence of Indigenous peoples and their dispossession from lands upon which these self-consciously styled "Anglo-Saxon" Pacific cities were built are omitted, as are considerations of identity, power, and culture. Frost does not acknowledge that these immigrant cities were built through the process of settler colonialism; by doing so, he could have provided particular insight into the conditions and nature of their production and cultural forms. Works such as Frost's reflect the incomplete encounter between urban studies and postcolonialism and, indeed, between urban studies and countercolonial and Indigenous historical geographies, encounters that have only just begun. Furthermore, these omissions are not merely methodological problems, they are ideological and representative of settler-colonial hegemonies themselves – that is, of the perpetual disavowing of Indigenous sovereignties and the depiction of Indigenous peoples as being absent or incompatible with the history of urbanizing colonial environments. Settler ideology shapes historiography and geography, and such forgetting regarding colonial urban development continues to this day.

The cities of settler colonies, built on the land of Indigenous peoples in Canada and Australia, are clearly in need of politically engaged transnational and historical research and comparative reflection. At least two decades ago, Gilbert A. Stelter observed the lack of comparative studies in Canadian urban history: "We must look in a comparative way beyond Canada to the cities of the US and other countries which were the products of European expansion if we wish to fully understand our own experience."[12] In 1995, in his review of the urban historiography of Australia and New Zealand, Lionel Frost observed that studies of the cities of the early to middle years of the nineteenth century were scant: work tended to focus on the last three decades of the century. Furthermore, Frost noted that the absence of comparative work was regrettable.[13] Although Frost cited a number of works that analyze Australian cities through the lens of class, not one of these works considers the issue of race, the impact of cities on the lives of Indigenous peoples, or the presence of Indigenous peoples. Nor are the gendered dimensions of cities mentioned. Based on the literature surveyed, one would be forgiven for thinking that only white men of various classes populated Australian cities. Aside from what she would find in the work of Kaye Anderson and others on Aboriginality and postcolonial Sydney, an Aboriginal woman would have to look for a very long time indeed to see herself and her history reflected in the literature of urban studies.[14] Australian scholars have in general failed to ask germane questions regarding the production of racialized and gendered bodies and spaces in settler-colonial cities and the ensuing segregation practices that continue to shape peoples lives. On the other side of the Pacific, Anderson's earlier work, *Vancouver's Chinatown*, was path-breaking for its consideration of the racialized exigencies of one of the Northwest Coast's major cities. Since then, authors such as Adele Perry, Jean Barman, and Renisa Mawani have considered nineteenth-century Victoria, Vancouver Island, and the partition of First Nations men and women, and this work suggests useful avenues of inquiry for this book.[15]

Indigenous Urban Frontiers: Conceptually Unclad?

Historians of the colonial frontier have traditionally ignored the settler-colonial city as a crucial locus of unequal power relations between Indigenous and non-Indigenous peoples and relied instead on triumphalist narratives of empire building that ignore the presence of Indigenous peoples in the city. Furthermore, many studies in the fields of history and urban geography continue to privilege franchise-colonial city formations and fail to highlight the settler-colony's fundamental economic imperative for land, its distinct spatial commerce, and its role as a nodal point in the circuits of empire. In addition, although a range of historians and geographers have asserted that colonial cities were instruments of cultural and racial dominance, few have used the interpretive framework of settler colonialism to demonstrate the historical conditions through which this domination occurred, nor have they attended to the transformation and mutual imbrication of bodies, spaces, and subjectivities in urbanizing colonial environments.

Among those studies that do seek new ways to understand the Indigenous urban frontier, the most compelling work is often by Aboriginal scholars who have their own experiences of living in postcolonial cities at the edges of empire. Over two decades ago, Marcia Langton identified a range of ways that sociologists in Australia, seeking to analyze "urbanising Aborigines," had got it wrong. Reviewing the literature of the time, she observed the paucity of ethnographic materials on the subject, refuted European terminology used to adjudicate Aboriginal urban lifestyles, and noted that white researchers were limited by their Eurocentric values.[16] Langton noted that misconceptions about loss of culture tended to dominate studies. Langton also stated that another Eurocentric narrative, the "culture of poverty," pervaded scholarship, which only served to "explain away the tragic living conditions of Aboriginal people which has resulted from dispossession." Drawing attention to the colonial process itself, Langton rightly argued that these models did not represent the actuality of Aboriginal people's lives but instead reflected relationships between Aboriginal and white society.[17] Langton challenged the unilinear and Eurocentric notion that Aborigines were an adapting culture and pointed out how descriptions in the sociological research failed to match how Aboriginal people in towns and cities saw themselves.

According to Langton, social scientists had failed to "understand the inside story" of Aboriginality, but so too had Marxist writers. Langton refuted the Marxist view of colonial struggles, which promulgated the idea that Aboriginal people's and working-class people's experiences were similar in an attempt to force Aboriginal people into white historical frameworks. This, she argued, was not the view of Aboriginal people. Although Langton believed that this perspective was useful to "explain the structural position of Aboriginal societies within the larger Australian sovereign state," she argued that it did not explain the "inside view" of Aboriginal people and their cultures or their development and effect on the larger society.[18]

In line with Langton, Tim Rowse has argued that the category urban is "historically and politically volatile".[19] In his article "Transforming the Notion of the Urban Aborigine," Rowse interrogates the assimilationist narratives and ideas of progress inherent in many early sociological studies of urbanizing Aborigines in the twentieth century. Rowse argues that it is implicit in early studies (such as those by Faye Gale, who positions Aboriginal people as urban immigrants) that the space of the urban is a metaphor for social evolution (which is encoded in Gale's work with phrases such as *their rural past* and observations about Aboriginal people's urban future).[20] Gale's language, argues Rowse, "produces the Aboriginal subject idealised in assimilationist discourse."[21] Rowse contends that this is also apparent in some recent government policies, where the urban is an ideological category that postulates the transition of an adapting culture. Echoing notions of a Western, historicizing narrative, studies such as Gale's configure Aborigines as evolving migrants. Rowse identifies this phenomenon as settler-colonial ethnogenesis – that is, the positive aspect of settler subject production – and argues that it is a process that has historical parallels with the Australian pioneer legend and the fashioning and duplication of myths about the bush and the city.[22]

In Canada, geographer Evelyn J. Peters has likewise stated that colonial narratives that depict First Nations as "incompatible with urban life" continue to have resonance.[23] Peters has been emphatic about the necessity of resolving Aboriginal peoples' place in terms of local and national geographies in Canada. In seeking to chart a new Canadian geography that is inclusive of Aboriginal peoples, Peters proposed that feminist geography could provide a useful framework.[24] Feminist historical geographers had challenged the discipline by asserting that women created new kinds of spaces and had markedly different experiences of emplacement and power than those represented in traditional male-centred urban models. Indeed, feminist geographers argued that traditional frameworks of understanding were deeply inadequate. As Suzanne MacKenna rightly observed, feminist geography left the discipline "conceptually unclad."[25] Likewise, old models – models based on white, metropolitan, and male-centred geographies – provide inadequate frameworks to explain Indigenous people's experiences of emplacement, power, and segregation in the settler-colonial cities of Australia and Canada. The limitations of traditional historical, urban, and environmental models for examining the settler-colonial city as a cultural formation that was deeply racialized means that the Indigenous urban frontier is also conceptually unclad.

Peters also refuted the notion that Aboriginal people were new migrants and pointed out that writers failed to recognize that Aboriginal people had been removed to make space for settler cities. Langton drew attention to the relationship between Aboriginal people and white society in her consideration of the urban, and it is this relationship that needs to examined. In other words, the dilemmas of race, dispossession, and urbanization in colonial cities and the issues of contemporary Indigenous emplacement must be understood primarily in the context of settler-colonial historical processes. Unless it makes crucial linkages between current urban social issues and settler-colonial patterns of expropriation and the re-territorialization of land, historical geography will continue to be conceptually unclad.

In line with Peters' argument that feminist historical geography challenged the discipline by arguing that women created new kinds of spaces and had distinctly different experiences of emplacement and power, Nihal Perera has suggested a similar strategy to indigenize the history of the colonial city. As he notes, broader studies of colonial urbanism in all its forms have led scholars to focus their analysis on imperial power, but new perspectives could show cultural arenas within which new social spaces and landscapes were indigenized. Many traditional urban studies rarely provide agency to Indigenous populations and are largely focused on the uncontested dominance of European colonizers. In the colonial city, as Perera writes suggestively, "Indigenization and colonization are simultaneously complicit and conflictual: these processes are neither separate nor direct opposites – Indigenization does not begin where colonization ends.[26] Thus, the early development of Melbourne and Victoria – the period prior to wholesale dispossession and displacement, when urbanizing spaces were both shared and contested – involved the dynamic interchanges of the transactional contact zone, processes in which Indigenization and colonization were simultaneously complicit and conflictual.

New frameworks also provide fresh ways to see the agency of Indigenous peoples and the broader transactional processes of the city. As Jay T. Johnson and others argue, although the discipline of geography has frequently marginalized Indigenous perspectives, the growth of an international Indigenous peoples' movement and increased attention to Indigenous rights and knowledges within national and international forums has allowed new approaches to come to the fore. Much of this research has an activist orientation, with some researchers seeking to decolonize the geography discipline to create genuinely anticolonial geographies that are concerned with breaking and "writing the silences of the present as well as the past."[27] Indigenous peoples and peoples of mixed descent did have markedly different experiences of emplacement and power in urbanizing colonial landscapes than European men and women, just as newcomers who lived their lives in these colonies had markedly different experiences than Europeans in the metropole. Indeed, through historical inquiry it is possible to detect the formation of new Indigenized social spaces and landscapes in conjunction with the complicit processes of colonization.

Symbolism and Stadial Theory

> *One can understand a city as a metaphor or symbol for the territory and how to govern it.*
> – Michel Foucault [28]

The new perspectives traced above can assist in uncovering the distinctive syntax of the settler-colonial city and the mechanisms by which it dispossessed Indigenous people. In this section I begin by exploring the symbolic and discursive power of the settler-colonial city and its operations within the British imperial imagination in order to appreciate how it mobilized and legitimated renderings of Western history, settler colonialism, and the conquest of Indigenous space.

The Imagined City and the State

In 1850 a treatise on Melbourne titled *Melbourne As It Is and Ought to Be ... with Remarks on Street Architecture Generally* was penned anonymously. The author wrote:

> Instead of inheriting the labour of fifty generations, we have to commence and carry out everything for ourselves. We have dispossessed the natives of their lands, but have taken possession of neither cities, nor vineyards, nor olive yards ... What then are the true principles on which a town should be planned? ... On the square should be ... the post-office, the focus of international and provincial intercourse, the colonial centre of a system extending its ramifications over the globe. Our ideal of a town should have a noble river ... and a public promenade ... adorned with statues and vases ... [and] eventually a viaduct should be formed to Batman's Hill, on the summit of which, conspicuous to the stranger coming up the river, might be erected a hall for the reception of the busts of great men.[29]

The author's imaginative vision charts a future of imperial classicism for Melbourne in which the emergent town is configured *as* empire. The passage points to a clear line of political intent that reflects the key themes of settler-colonial discourse and its manifestation in the city. Invasion, the dispossession of Indigenous peoples, and the figuring of the town as a classicized nodal point in the British Empire's developing network of global capital are explicit themes. The spatial imperatives of empire are clear; imperialism is an expanding system, a network that is progressively encompassing the globe. Most importantly, the author articulates the settler-colonist's central burden of establishing a *settler-*colonial city and its supporting agrarian or commercial structures, as opposed to establishing a franchise-colonial city by using existing Indigenous social and economic resources. The distinction between these two types of cities had and continues to have profound implications for Indigenous peoples and the spatial commerce between colonizer and colonized in Australia and Canada.

The powerful significance of the settler-colonial city in the nineteenth century must be considered within the context of Enlightenment notions of four stages of human progress and development – hunting, pastoralism, agriculture, and commerce.[30] The discursive vigour of four-stages or stadial theory, as it is known generally, which is rooted in a long-standing tradition of European political theory and international law, should not be underestimated today. British colonists who settled Australia in the early nineteenth century brought with them ideas of landscape, nature, and progress that were current in early industrial Britain. The coalescence of these ideas with the idea that one is entitled to land that one has improved, which was expounded by John Locke in *Two Treatises of Government* (1623-1704), and with the ideas of political economy, which were driven by the rapid changes of the Industrial Revolution, was also an important factor in the creation of particular philosophical views among colonists.[31] These developments were intrinsically bound up with Enlightenment discourse on improvement and human progress. Enlightenment ideas, which refashioned European society in the seventeenth and eighteenth centuries, sought to base the social order on reason, natural law, and the idea of a universal humanity capable of infinite perfectibility. Enlightenment ideas became the "ideological mortar of late eighteenth-century British society."[32] A fundamental aspect of Enlightenment thought, especially from 1750 to 1800, was that the key factor in human socio-economic development was the mode of production.[33]

The work of Adam Smith (1723-90), leader of the Scottish historical school, which is commonly referred to as the Scottish Enlightenment, is generally associated with the ideas of competitive capitalism, free trade, and the price mechanism.[34] Smith has been credited (including by Marx himself) with prefiguring key ideas that influenced Marx. Smith provided Marx with the model of a new tripartite class relationship, which was characteristic of capitalist societies at the time, and with the formulation of a "new concept of surplus ... ascribed to the productivity of labour in general." However, it is Smith's theory of the development of society and the nature of socio-historical processes that is of import here.[35] R.L. Meek has charted the various lineages of four-stages theory. Although there were several general streams of thought that may have led to the emergence of the four-stages model, the key point is that the stages were eventually conceptualized as distinct modes of production.[36] Smith, however, is generally credited with developing a model in which, crucially, the four stages are understood as distinct, hierarchical, and successive modes of production and conceptualized in an evolutive, teleological fashion that figures European society as the highest stage of development. Thus, ideas of stadial progress legitimized and naturalized the taking of land. And these ideas are the key to understanding the views of those who came to the Pacific Northwest Coast and the shores of the great southern continent.

In his consideration of the operation of space, time, and empire, Johannes Fabian points out that geopolitics were based on chronopolitics, the idea that human development was spatial and temporal.[37] Indeed, Hegel asserted that global geometries were relative and wrote that "world history travels from east to west ... for Europe is the absolute end of history, just as Asia is the beginning."[38] In addition to shaping the concerns of space, time, and empire, such ideas also conceptualized imperial Britons as progressive in new ways. As Patrick Wolfe observes: "The four stage theory of the Scottish Enlightenment was not new in holding pastoralism superior to nomadism, agricultural settlement superior to both and urban commerce the highest of all. Neither the ancient Greeks nor the biblical Hebrews would have disagreed. The novelty the Scottish Enlightenment unveiled was not this hierarchical ordering but its cumulative temporality – pastoralists were not merely superior to nomads; they were so because they *had once been* nomads but were so no longer."[39] Cumulative temporality is key here. Thus, British subjects of the commercial stage saw in their classicized Aboriginal subjects both the ancient and pastoral states that they had once embodied. Colonized subjects and other marginalized groups such as women and the lower orders were also represented as occupying a space of alterity that was, as Anne McClintock contends, "prehistoric, atavistic, irrational, inherently out of place in the historical time of modernity."[40] As Nicholas Blomley explains, Locke, who was greatly concerned with the colonization of North America, imagined that the relationship that Native North Americans had with the land and their forms of government were at an earlier stage of development than those of their European counterparts. Their relationship to the land was akin to the state of nature and could be viewed as the origin of private property.

According to Locke, the taking of Native lands could, therefore, occur without Native peoples' consent because the lands were unimproved and could be appropriated by those capable of reclaiming "waste."[41] Emer de Vattel was influenced by Locke's thesis on property as he developed his own treatise on the principles of natural law. He, in turn, influenced the secretary of the Hudson's Bay Company, Archibald Barclay, who advised James Douglas on the wording of the fourteen treaties on Vancouver Island, which focused on occupancy rather than property.[42]

Thus, if the city represented the space of modernity (as was the case in William Knight's painting) and was, indeed, progress itself, then Aboriginal peoples were out of time and space in European understandings of history and philosophy. Aboriginal people in the urban landscape of Australia interrupted the powerful syntax established by stadial theory and its driving Western, historicizing narrative. When rendered on the margins, Aboriginal peoples, in the eyes of Europeans, came to stand in for stadial displacement itself. As Rod Macneil has observed, images of Aborigines in the colonized landscape take on a symbolic function that signifies the act of colonial dispossession rather than the re-identification of the landscape. Images of dispossessed Aboriginal people became not a "literal but an emblematic representation of the colonial process."[43]

In Australia notions of other worlds, times, or stages of human development that would give way to the tide of progress were activated repeatedly to justify the entire colonial project. In 1821 James Wallis claimed that the engravings in his *Historical Accounts of New South Wales* would "serve to show and convince ... from what slender beginnings and in how few years, the primeval forests ... may be converted into plains covered with bleating flocks, lowing herds, and waving corn; may become the smiling seats of industry and the social arts, and be changed from desolate wilderness, into the cheerful village, the busy town, and the crowded city."[44] Wallis' description jumps from "primeval forests," to "herds," to "corn," to the "crowded city," reflecting the four-stages model of social development, which had by this time so thoroughly suffused European expansionist discourse. In these historicizing and stadial narratives, the apotheosis of commerce, progress, and civilization is the crowded New World city. Aboriginal peoples are represented as undeserving because they have been positioned as hunters without rights to land. This is markedly apparent in a letter John Cotton sent from Sydney in 1848, when the Colony of New South Wales was celebrating its sixtieth anniversary:

> Sixty years back then, the site on which this city was built was a wild waste, known only to savage blacks; now it is covered with noble houses, shops, warehouses, banks, barracks ... and is occupied by a large industrious population of Europeans

and in the interior numerous tracts of country afford food for thousands of sheep and cattle. The worthless idle Aborigine has then been driven back from the land that he knew not how to make use of, and valued not, to make room for a more noble race of beings who are capable of estimating the value of this fine country. Is it not right that it should be so?[45]

Narratives such as these also served to mythologize the creation of property based on maximizing value and to position Indigenous rights in land in the early hunting and gathering stage, where proprietary right to the soil did not exist.

Stadial ideas mobilized and rationalized the expropriation of Indigenous land and travelled throughout Britain's many colonies, including the Colony of British Columbia. In 1859, at the height of the gold rush, Alexander Morris delivered a lecture to an enthusiastic crowd at the Mercantile Library Association in Victoria: "In the rapid planning of the Anglo-Saxon civilisation, the finger of Providence was manifest ... one cannot pass though this fair valley without feeling that it is *destined* sooner or later to become the happy hope of civilized men, with their bleating flocks and lowing herds – with their schools and churches."[46] Furthermore, entitlement to colonized lands in this instance was heavily racialized. For Alexander Morris it was the Anglo-Saxon race that was uniquely endorsed by Providence to form centres of trade around the Pacific Rim.

The narrative of these writings depicts, as Blomley observes, a transition from "Edenic nature to improved settlement; from common to private entitlement." The powerful syntax of settler colonialism, or as Blomley terms it, the "*telos* of highest and best use" is apparent. In this narrative schema, the settler city has pride of place: it is the space of progress and commerce, predicated on the absence of Indigenous peoples. As several authors have pointed out, the central relation in these expansionist, pioneering narratives is an exclusive one between God, white men, and the land.[47]

The discursive flipside of the triumphal settler-colonial city, in which emerging metropolitan space was configured as progressive and stadial, was, perhaps, the lavish reverence and nostalgia laid on the ghost town, the white towns lost to the brutish and hostile elements of the Australian landscape. These ruined and abandoned cities were graphic symbols of the syntax of settler colonialism interrupted, the driving narrative of which depicted progress from savagery to settlement, from perceptions of lack of property to private property broken and, indeed, reversed. On the Northwest Coast, a favourite theme of artwork in the mid- to late nineteenth century was, likewise, the dilapidated and abandoned Indian village, an image that operated as a powerful metaphor for the "vanishing" Indigenous population.[48] In both sites, imperial nostalgia lamented for a stage passed.

Returning to *Melbourne As It Is and Ought to Be,* the author's grand and clas-sicized imperial vision of noble rivers, viaducts, and busts of great men not only served to bolster and preserve the colonists' essential identity but also asserted the powerful subject-producing qualities of landscape and architecture.[49] For stadial theory is evolutive, naturalized, and teleological, and it self-fashions the imperial, European progressive subject. In narratives like these, we see how geographies of empire fashion their subjects. In Morris' case it was explicitly the Anglo-Saxon race that was the inheritor of new lands. Thus, the city as rational, ordered place became inseparable from justifications for the expropria-tion of Indigenous land. The settler-colonial city became a synecdoche for empire and its ideological paradigm. The precondition for the highest stage of progress and commerce was the absence of Indigenous peoples in the city. They may have been imagined as worthless and idle, as John Cotton wrote, but this was the imaginative geography of settler colonialism operating in its most idealized form. In reality settlers did use far more than Indigenous lands: they harnessed Indigenous knowledge and labour. The labour of First Nations and Métis in the mining, fishing, and forestry industries of the Northwest Coast and the use of Aboriginal people as agricultural labourers, ranch hands, and domestic servants in Australia attests to this phenomenon.

The city and its ideological links to the state were also important. As Michel Foucault observed, by the end of the eighteenth century, architecture had become political. By this time "one sees the development of reflection upon architecture as a function of the aims and techniques of the government of societies." Every treatise on politics as the art of the government of men necessarily included chapters on urbanism, collective facilities, hygiene, and architecture.[50] Cities had once been viewed as islands beyond the common law, but the problems that they raised and the particular forms that they took reflected the governance of the whole territory. Foucault proposed that the state should be conceived like a large city, that the "model of the whole city became the matrix for the regulations of the whole state." As he put it, "one can understand a city as a metaphor or symbol for the territory and how to govern it."[51] By understanding the city, one implicitly understands the subjects the state seeks to create and the polity it seeks to fashion. And these states were formed explicitly to serve the processes of the settler-colonial endeavor.

Thus, when the author of *Melbourne As It Is and Ought to Be* outlined his preference for specific styles of architecture, certain kinds of transport and com-munications, hygiene and the regulation of bodies, and the symbolic representa-tion of the busts of great men, he was not only acting in a manner that was highly political, he was also prescribing the activity of the modern state. Was the author inspired by James Silk Buckingham's important work *National Evils and Practical Remedies, with the Plan of a Model Town,* which had been published only one year earlier in 1849?[52] The widely travelled Buckingham had a keen interest in New World cities and had toured the United States and Canada in the 1840s. His book proposed a range of economic and political reforms, as well as a plan of a model town. It was a vision of a town in which the architecture and facilities were highly structured by class, a vision that sought to provide services and a measure of egalitarianism and improvement to the working classes but placed wealthy capitalists at the centre of privilege. Buckingham's vision was a city of modern, bourgeois conception, and his treatise represents the beginning of a movement that would only grow in the metropole, one that by the late nineteenth century would reveal the state's increasing attempts to impose administrative order on nature and society. As James C. Scott has noted, large-scale authoritarian city plans represented the imperialistic ideologies of high modernism.[53]

The imaginative vision of a city at the periphery of empire represented in *Melbourne As It Is and Ought to Be,* however, was a somewhat different creature. By detailing the form and activities of the city, the author was prescribing the activities of the *settler-colonial* state. In this case, its creation was necessarily enmeshed in other discourses, and its symbolism differed from that of its metropolitan counterparts.

The settler-colonial city had potent discursive and economic purchase. It was discursively naturalized and rendered inevitable through stadial theory and ideas of progress and improvement, and it was depicted as the apotheosis of settler colonialism, the highest stage of commerce, which replaced the stage of hunters and "wild waste." More than just order on chaos, the city was the symbol of a new stadial order, a metonym of empire, state, and the settler-colonial project. The cities invoked by Wallis, Cotton, Morris, and the anonymous author of *Melbourne As It Is and Ought to Be* thus revealed the concerns of an expansionist settler-colonial modernity and a powerful Western, historicizing narrative. Moreover, this expansionist enterprise in the Pacific was explicitly racialized as the exclusive destiny of the Anglo-Saxon races.

Universal History Begins: Civis Britannicus and the Western, Historicizing Narrative

Empire cannot be unconnected from its temporal and spatial inscriptions. The French geographer Élisée Reclus knew this when, two years shy of the close of the nineteenth century, he wrote a multi-volume work, *The Earth and Its Inhabitants,* on peoples, geography, and empire, in which he noted the annexation of:

half of the planet to the other half, of which West Europe occupied the central point. Thus the world, hitherto incomplete, has as it were, been suddenly revealed in its entirety, *and universal history, in the strict sense of the term, henceforth begins for all the races and peoples of the earth.* Nothing is now wanting to the vast stage that now throbs the great heart of humanity, *already awakening to self-consciousness and henceforth united, at least in all its material relations.* This enlargement of the civilised world cannot fail to be attended by consequences of far-reaching importance ... And now the whole world becomes the theatre of busy life for civilised peoples. *Henceforth the earth knows no limits, for its centre is every where or anywhere on the planetary surface, and its circumference nowhere.*[54]

Perhaps the first dissident geographer, Reclus (1830-1905), a positivist and anarchist, understood the globe as a system that was historically and spatially interrelated.[55] Implicit in Reclus' notion that "universal history, in the strict sense of the term, henceforth begins for all the races and peoples of the earth" was the idea of a linear sequence of history – a Western, historicizing narrative or totalizing trajectory that would sweep all peoples and races up in its path. This Western linear narrative was spatialized. If, as Hegel noted, "Europe [was] the absolute end of History," then the colonization of the far reaches of empire and the spatial and temporal collapse that accompanied the remaking of the world in Europe's image indeed created a totalizing history.

Reclus articulated a schema of European political economy that is a perennial subject of analysis in postcolonial and neo-Marxist scholarship. Inherent in such a schema is a vision of the colonized non-European as an inherently transitional subject, one whose journey necessarily follows an evolutionary trajectory from peasant to labourer to modern Western citizen, a path that mirrored linear historical time. This Western, historicizing process has thoroughly shaped the practice of history writing among Western and non-Western historians.[56] To return to the idea of spatial collapse, when Reclus wrote "Henceforth the earth knows no limits, for its centre is everywhere or anywhere on the planetary surface, and its circumference nowhere," he indicated both a spatial and temporal collapse in which the whole planet, its peoples, and cultures conform to a grand civilizing, Westernizing narrative as the world becomes one mode of production, the commerce stage, through industrial capitalism.

Reclus also wrote about the British (male) subject as the universal subject that travelled the globe when he wrote, "The longer maritime route from London, round the cape, to Melbourne and Sydney, has also, for intermediate station, the British south-African colonies. Thus, during his long voyage of nearly 16,000 miles across half the circumference of the globe, the *civis Britannicus* touches

English territory alone; everywhere he sees his social and political institutions firmly established, everywhere he hears the familiar sounds of his mother tongue; he moves from hemisphere to hemisphere, but scarcely feels that he has quitted his native land."[57] The inflection is thus complete. As Wolfe notes about cumulative temporality, "pastoralists were not merely superior to nomads; they were so because they *had once been* nomads but were so no longer."[58] For Reclus, the corollary, which is key here, was that the spatio-temporal collapse caused by colonialism's expansion would ensure that all humankind, in various temporal and historical stages, would in the rapid blink of an evolutive eye wake up with self-consciousness, and each individual would become the civilized subject, the *civis Britannicus*, of universal history. Reclus' description of a centre that is everywhere and a circumference that is nowhere reveals the transformative power of imperialism and global capital and their material inscription in the New World, where the culture and subjectivities of Indigenous peoples were being transformed. Colonialism initiated a temporal and geographical collapse – a transformation to New World capitalist time and space – and produced new spaces and bodies at the local and global levels.

According to Reclus, it was the Anglo-Saxon race that had annexed lands around the Pacific Rim. It was, he wrote, unquestionably the British and American branches of the Anglo-Saxon race that seemed destined to create an oceanic Britain.[59] Reclus' imagined civilized subject, the civis Britannicus, was also a distinctly masculine identity constructed and enabled entirely by the dominance of a British, globalizing modernity. Civis Britannicus was an exceptional subject who had a global purview and spatial entitlements that few other men or women could possess at the time. With his spatial mobility, he could travel "from hemisphere to hemisphere" but "scarcely feel" that he had left his native land.[60] This was the male, imperial subject exemplified. Civis Britannicus was a subject who was unique, yet he was also configured as the potential everyman of empire, as the subject of universal history. Defined by and made through his global entitlements, civis Britannicus could make transglobal journeys between British settler colonies, where he (not Indigenous peoples) would be configured as native. Highlighting the mutual imbrication of colonial bodies and spaces, civis Britannicus was transimperialism in human frame, the imagined personification of the Anglo-Saxon race, which had annexed lands around the Pacific.

The Spatiality of Empire and Cognate Spaces

The city cannot be understood without studying the colony in which it resides. What was the economic and social value of the settler-colonial city to the British Empire, and what was distinctive about its spatial commerce? Settler-colonial cities were not like franchise-colonial cities, such as New Delhi, where the British formed inward-looking, protective cantonments – enclosed, circumscribed towns within ancient and established cities. Settler-colonial cities were not like the sequestered hill stations of India or the French colonial cities of Algiers and Morocco, which had imperial additions to indigenous built forms and *cordonnes sanitaires* (sanitary lines) to enforce separation between colonizers and colonized.[61]

Unlike the franchise-colonial city, settler-colonial cities were ambitious, imaginative exercises. They were often deemed to be too large, and they invited comparisons with *Gulliver's Travels,* one of the eighteenth century's key analogical texts for Europe's encounter with the New World. When Edwin Lloyd first arrived in the colonial frontier town of Adelaide in 1846, he wrote, "Heat was the order of the day." "My first impression ... was of a long straggling street, very red, very sandy, and very hot. The sand, which was of a bright colour seemed to have stained the houses, the bullocks and even the very inhabitants."[62] For Lloyd, the strange landscape was desolate, provincial, and even apocalyptic. The squatters or bushmen were "wild looking figures, bearded, belted, booted, and spurred; sometimes with long leather leggings and broad brimmed straw hats ... their only weapons were enormous whips, with thongs of some twelve or fourteen feet in length, held in a coil in the hand." The bushmen gathered around the main hotel with "a number of half naked dusky savages, clustered around a storekeeper ... and some more lounging down the street with spears and waddies in their hands, filthy ... Vagrant dogs, ad infinitum, swarm the street, straw hats prevail, louses and bulchers flourish; and the few that retain the costume of the old country amuse you by the antiquated cut of their garments."[63]

As Lloyd approached the town from the port, he observed that "the view here is most dismal and disheartening ... the perfection of desolation and ruin." Adelaide was not the triumphal embodiment of empire in the antipodes, it was a place of desolation and ruin. Moreover, to Lloyd, it was the sense of space that was most disconcerting, for the town plan was oversized, magnified, and bizarrely ambitious. He reflected on a map he had seen in England:

> When remembering the magnificent and extensive city on paper, which figured in England as the representation of this colonial capital, I drew a comparison between it and the half ruinous place before me, I was impressed with the Lilliputian grandeur of the whole affair, that seemed to say in the spirit of its projectors, *"Were my means only as gigantic as my desires."* It seemed like something mighty that had begun and left unfinished ... a beginning without an end, an end without a beginning. It is a town large enough for the metropolis of a great nation, with about three good streets properly built upon. It is quite unwieldy; so large, as with its present population, to preclude public improvement.[64]

The settler-colonial city was audaciously expansive. Its grid was pre-emptive, reaching out over Aboriginal land, truly "a beginning without an end." In 1869 John Martineau, like Lloyd, wrote that "the space covered by Melbourne and its suburbs is compared with an English or European town, out of all proportion large for the population."[65] Spatial representations such as maps for New World cities served to possess Indigenous space and, simultaneously, empty it of its Indigenous inhabitants. Not only did Lloyd register the apocalyptic dissonance of frontier Adelaide as it really was, he also noticed Aboriginal peoples and the absurdity of a map that depicted a town with only three good streets as being "large enough for the metropolis of a great nation." As Hamer has observed, maps such as these encouraged a preoccupation with the future and progress, being "future-oriented and making little sense in the present ... [they] forced people to 'see' and indeed to live in the future ... plats were essentially maps of the future."[66] To Lloyd, however, Adelaide seemed more like the end of the world than a beginning.

Just as celebratory ideas of stadial progress and the Western, historicizing narrative created the universal British subject, civis Britannicus, so they also created the idea of cognate urban space. Of course, what made settler-colonial cities distinctive over those in the Old World was a subject of intense debate. Many saw city building at the edges of empire as a naturalized expression of civilisation. Yet the terms upon which these cities were formed were more complicated. Alexis de Tocqueville, who was concerned with new societies, likened cities to so many other aspects of the New World: they were made out of the invisible luggage that immigrants brought with them.[67] The replication of culture and mentality could be seen most conspicuously in the planning and built form of a city, and it was supported by travel writing and the constant comparisons that writers gave their readers. For example, commenting on the Englishness of Melbourne, James Ballantyne wrote: "Many a one on coming to Melbourne has said that he felt as though he had scarcely gone from home: Everything seems to be just what he left behind him when he quitted the streets of Liverpool, Glasgow or London, for this new shore. Melbourne is London reproduced; Victoria is another England."[68] Most Australian writers described Sydney and Melbourne with urban imagery that was derived directly from contemporary discussions of London. The same styles of urban writing were used, and the same moral topographies were detected or imposed. As subjectivities, the spaces of empire were shaped willfully and coterminously; they became intertwined and mutually interpolated one another. British imperial expansion created the nineteenth-century port city of Melbourne, named after Lord Melbourne, Britain's prime minister. By the mid-nineteenth century, its structure of gridded streets, architecture, cultural and legal life, and economic role as a node in Britain's global empire were imagined as social spaces inscribed with the cultural and economic signatures of Britain.

The Economic Value of the Settler-Colonial City

Not only was the settler-colonial city deemed to be the apotheosis of civilization, emblematic of empire's aspirations, but for political economist Edward Gibbon Wakefield it was also a key economic requirement of the settler-colonial project.[69] Wakefield is known for his promulgation of systematic colonization, a system that sought to combine land, labour, and capital in the right proportions and which was based on the views of Adam Smith, Robert Gourley, and others and underwritten by Benthamite utilitarianism. John Stuart Mill summarized Wakefield's thoughts on the importance of towns as follows: "Every colony shall have from the first a town population, bearing due proportion to its agricultural, and that the cultivators of the soil shall not be so widely scattered as to be deprived, by distance, of the benefit of that town population as a market for their produce ... a place for disposing their surplus."[70] Wakefield also wrote about the economic and civic importance of planned towns; he was involved in Colonel Light's plan of Adelaide; and, through his connection with the New Zealand Association, he planned seven towns, including the town of Britannia, or Wellington, in New Zealand. Later in life, Wakefield travelled to Canada and contributed to the Durham Report, dubbed the Magna Carta of the colonies, which sought to establish a policy for the British Empire by proposing central control of lands for the whole empire, a plan that ultimately failed.[71]

Robert Rotenburg has recently used the notion of primacy to explain Wakefield's insistence on the importance of the colonial city. Rotenburg defines the primate city as "a node in a regional market network that can so dominate suppliers and consumers that large sections of the more distant hinterland would be poorly serviced ... Primacy is also a feature of colonial systems."[72] Thus, the settler-colonial city was necessary and legitimated as a primary market for surplus produce and as a controlled labour pool composed of those who could not afford land. But these cities were also portals for mass immigration schemes throughout the nineteenth century. By mid-century the move from mercantilism to industrialization and modernity had drawn towns, which were based on mercantile trade, into the global grid of empire, as they sent products to the metropole and, in return, received immigrant labour. Jane Jacobs, who writes about the importance of colonial cities and their incorporation into the global power grid of empire, has stated: "The city is also an important component in the spatiality of imperialism. It was in outpost cities that the spatial order of imperial imaginings was rapidly ... realised and it was through these cities that resources of colonised lands were harnessed and reconnected to cities in imperial heartlands."[73] Jacobs not only alerts us to the settler-colonial city, she also pulls us back to economics and the material relationships that structure empire and its dominance. In line with this, Rotenburg, writing on the rapid transformation of Europe's metropolitan cities in the nineteenth century, has sought to understand bourgeois metropolitanism transnationally. It was, indeed, transnational colonialism that financed metropolitanism. Although some presume that these transformations emerged from Europe's internal processes, Rotenburg argues, correctly, that metropolitanism was dependent on capital from a colonial economy. Understanding that metropolitan and colonial cities coproduced one another is crucial. As Rotenburg writes, "Transnational colonialism financed metropolitanism. It arose within the propertied classes of European imperialist commercial centres in the mid-nineteenth century; it grew as the power of the bourgeoisie replaced that of the aristocracy in the management of empire. Metropolitanism reshaped the city to fit the imagined possibilities of the bourgeoisie. The only cities that could afford such reshaping were those that benefited from the colonial economy, the metropoles of London, Paris and Vienna." He notes further that other centres – such as Amsterdam, Brussels, St. Petersburg, and Berlin, as well as industrial ports such as New York – would follow as best as they could, but they would always be in the shadow of these three metropoles.[74]

Colonial cities were also viewed as laboratories for testing new societies. As Hamer observes, many travellers were excited by these new cities because they seemed to offer possibilities that were no longer available to the old cities of Europe.[75] As much as they were laboratories for new social systems, such as democracy, the settler colonies and their cities were also viewed as repositories for an overpopulated Europe. As Edwin Lloyd opined in 1846, "colonisation is a necessary consequence – I had almost said evil of an overgrown community." He then went on to give the example of the death of an old man in London: "A short time ago, I saw the body of an old man ... in the charnel house ... his flesh was wasted to his bones ... In a large and populous city, where abundance existed, and where a great proportion were clothed and fed luxuriously ... home he had none! The question naturally arose, was there no land where this poor being could have earned a subsistence? Had he emigrated, he could not have starved; his labour would have been valued; his services sought after."[76]

Settler cities were, thus, vitally important nodes in an imperial network through which capital and peoples moved. As Alan Lester writes, "bourgeois ideas of legitimate behaviour towards others and corresponding notions of Britishness itself moved through, and were contested within, circuits connecting Britain with each of its colonies."[77] Just as transnational colonialism financed metropolitanism, free settlers in these settler colonies constructed and harnessed transimperial discourses that rationalized settlement and framed particular types of Britishness. These discourses of Britishness were imagined abroad in powerful ways and bolstered the identity of settlers and cities, as is evident in *Melbourne As It Is and Ought to Be,* which presents the city as a classicized node within imperial networks.

Settler cities were nodes in an imperial network through which Europeans moved, but these newly developing towns and cities also displaced and attracted Indigenous peoples. Growing settlements disrupted traditional land ownership, pushed Indigenous peoples out of cities, and reconfigured Indigenous spaces. At the same time, Indigenous people ventured into settled areas for food or employment when squatters or homesteaders pushed them off traditional lands in the outlying frontier. These mutual, albeit uneven, interactions, of colonization and Indigenization, were for a short time part of the tenor of the early settler-colonial landscape.

3

"This Grand Object":
Building Towns in Indigenous Space
[Melbourne, Port Phillip]

In March 1835 I made up my mind to venture across the straits and commence the world again.

— JOHN PASCOE FAWKNER, "REMINISCENCES"[1]

IN 1835 TWO GROUPS of Europeans, both overstraiters from Van Diemen's Land, raced each other to claim the Port Phillip region, the site of present-day Melbourne. Each group, one led by John Batman and the other by John Pascoe Fawkner, drew up allotments as it sought to make a European cognate space and to "commence the world again" through mapping, naming, and, for Batman, ostensibly, treaty making and purchase.[2] Yet the land of the Kulin Nation was a world fully formed and complete unto itself.

Aboriginal people had lived in the area for many thousands of years. The water wells that the Europeans used to sustain themselves and the trails that helped them to find their way to new pastoral lands were part of a rich Indigenous heritage staked in the land. Rather than commencing the world again, Fawkner, Batman, and the Europeans that came after them utilized Indigenous knowledge and labour, and appropriated Indigenous land, to realize their entrepreneurial goals.

Greater Port Phillip and the Kulin Nation

The Kulin Nation had lived around the greater Port Phillip Bay region for around forty thousand years and had constantly adapted to its changes.[3] At the time of contact, the population of the region was around fifteen thousand.[4] The greater region, beyond the bay area, now known as the State of Victoria was home to about thirty-three cultural-linguistic groups, of which the Kulin Nation was a part. Each cultural-linguistic group included smaller groups or clans of several hundred people or more.[5] Each clan or land-owning group had great spiritual attachment to the land and looked after it. Boundaries were well known between groups (see Figure 5).

The people that Europeans met in the immediate vicinity of Port Phillip Bay in 1835 moved over their territories, harvesting food according to seasonal availability. These Kulin people belonged to the Crow *(waa)* and Eagle *(bunjil)* moieties, and exogamous marriage between clans was determined by these

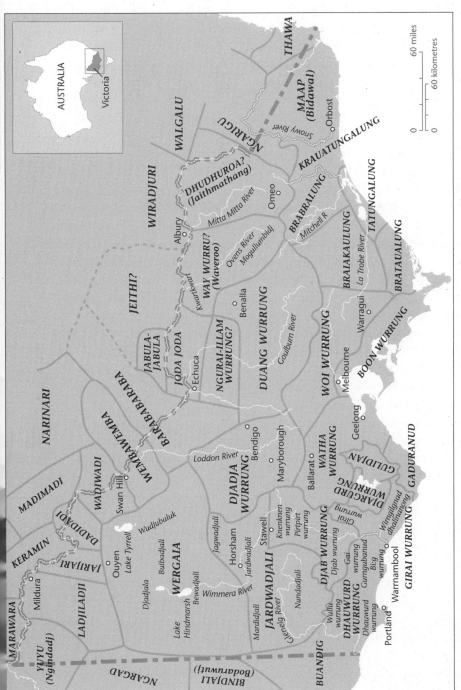

Figure 5 Language map of Victoria at the time of contact. Based on the map by Ian D. Clark, Victorian Aboriginal Corporation for Languages (Melbourne), 1996. Cartography by Eric Leinberger.

patrilineal affiliations. Each clan possessed economic and ceremonial responsibilities for its land, and reciprocity and exchange between groups allowed for mutual access and the management of food and other resources.[6] Small bands composed of several families could travel up to six to ten miles a day over their territory in search of food. The places they visited were also sites of sacred significance, formed by the creator spirits.

When John Pascoe Fawkner arrived on the banks of the river that would become the site of Melbourne in 1835, he was delighted with the terrain but unaware of the extent of Aboriginal peoples' physical and spiritual connection to land. Later, he reminisced about "this noble bay, the fine deep water approach by the lower Yarra." The "beauty of the scenery around Melbourne" was "most exhilarating." He praised the "fine open country to the West" and the wetlands west of the Yarra River.[7] These wetlands were a plentiful source of water birds, fish, and plant foods, particularly in summer months. Aboriginal people, using wooden spears and boomerangs, hunted emus and kangaroos on the surrounding plains and grasslands. Women collected and hunted most of the staples of subsistence. They caught small animals and harvested a wide variety of plants – including the *myrnong*, a tuber-like root – using digging sticks and baskets.[8]

Many European writers presumed that Aboriginal peoples possessed no housing and no agriculture; however, this is simply not the case: the colonial archive is replete with descriptions of Aboriginal shelters and systems of land management. Moving through the landscape required semi-permanent dwellings. Bark huts or *mia mias* were put up with speed. William Thomas, the assistant protector of Aborigines in the Melbourne region, observed that "I have seen in half an hour a village comfortably housed, from the bounty of Providence in the forest around. A few sheets of bark and a sapling, and two forked sticks make at once an habitation."[9] Mia mias were left behind, knocked down, or burned when the group departed the camp.

In places such as the Western District, where food resources were more abundant, Aboriginal people such as the Gunditjmara lived semi-sedentary lives and built more permanent dwellings. The chief Aboriginal protector, George Augustus Robinson, in 1841 saw "permanent villages of a dozen huts near Lake Colac and other similar settlements north of Warnambool and Portland."[10] These dwellings were beehive shaped, with stone walls and thatched roofs. Others were fashioned with sticks covered over with turf. The remains of stone dwellings, along with weirs for fish farming made of woven sticks, exist in the Western District. It was partly on this evidence of permanent habitation that the Gunditjmara Native title claim was recognized. In the Mount William area, extensive canals that extended over six hectares and individual trenches that were fifteen hundred metres long were dug and used to harvest eels. They can still be seen today.[11] The invasion of European pastoralists and town builders would upset the balance between Aboriginal people and their environment and delicate agreements between clan boundaries.

Over the last 160 years, Wurundjeri people, who live on lands in what is now the sprawling site of metropolitan Melbourne, have faced the colonial expropriation of their lands and the envelopment of their lands by concrete and asphalt.[12] Since the late 1830s, as its cadastral spread has moved outward, Melbourne has engulfed many hundreds of meeting places, fishing sites, shell middens, campsites, scarred and carved trees, pathways and water wells, and ceremonial and sacred sites, all of which are evidence of a world fully formed.[13] These sites, some of which have been preserved, are now actively protected through legislation. As Lynette Russell and Ian McNiven note, these sites provide Wurundjeri people with a "tangible link with ancestors and an acknowledgment of their past, present and future ties to the land."[14]

For thousands of years, the site that would become Melbourne, situated on the slopes above the Yarra River falls, had been a meeting place for Aboriginal groups in the bay area. In 1840 William Thomas noted in his journal the significance of the site for Aboriginal groups. Kulin peoples would meet there to have meetings and contests, or "judicial proceedings, which once a year or oftener they met to settle at Melbourne, a spot always resorted to for its central position."[15] For the Wurundjeri, the creator spirit, Bunjil, in the form of an eagle, presided over the land. The river, meandering through the landscape on its way down from the Dandenong ranges, was called Bay-ray-rung by these traditional inhabitants, but Europeans, acting on a mistaken belief about its correct Aboriginal name, named the river Yarra Yarra. This was the place that in 1835 became the small settlement of Bearbrass (a version of an Aboriginal name), which was later dubbed Melbourne.[16]

By the late summer of 1836, Thomas Mitchell, the surveyor general of New South Wales, had looked down upon the greater Port Phillip region and described it in lavish terms: "This highly interesting region lay before me with all its features new and untouched as they fell from the hand of the Creator! Of this Eden it seemed I was the only Adam; and it was indeed a sort of Paradise [and I was] ... permitted thus to explore its mountains and streams." It was a "country ready for the immediate reception of civilised man and destined perhaps to become eventually a portion of a great empire." On an earlier trip, Mitchell had dubbed the southwest country "Australia Felix."[17]

Edward Said, who has highlighted the series of intrinsically spatial strategies of dispossession that the West visited upon colonized societies, stated that it is challenging to think about colonialism without acknowledging the vital imaginative and geographical processes at work in the "production as well as the acquisition, subordination, and settlement of space."[18] As Paul Carter has observed, spatial history begins not in time or place but, culturally, in the act of naming. Through this process "space is transformed symbolically into a place, that is a space with a history."[19] Naming brought Australia into being and contextualized it culturally and philosophically. Steeped in biblical and historical references, appellations such as "Eden," "the Plains of Promise," and the "Great River of the Desired Blessing," names that were inscribed into many early maps of the continent, remind us of the spatial and imaginative qualities of imperial endeavour and that these metaphorical destinations were charged with a divine destiny. The country appeared to British eyes as a "gentlemen's park," seemingly prepared by Providence for the taking.[20] Utopian descriptions litter late eighteenth- and early nineteenth-century travel writing and imperial maps. Announcing imperial desires, they conjure an imaginary or anticipatory geography of a new land for the taking underwritten by Providence. Men of empire sought to possess the new landscape by, first, imaginatively producing a space that could be appropriated and, second, by reaping material rewards from the opening of "new" lands through surveying, mapping, and speculation. The overcoding of Indigenous space with European cultural fantasies prepared the way for and was vital to colonization.

"The Natives on shore": Approaching Melbourne and Foundation Myths

News of Thomas Mitchell's Australia Felix rekindled interest in the new lands across Bass Strait among the pastoralists and merchants of Van Diemen's Land. As early as 1827, petitions had been sent to the Executive Council of New South Wales to allow settlement in this region, but a series of injunctions were put in place to prevent trespass on a terrain that was deemed Crown land. The south-eastern extremity of the continent was well outside Governor Ralph Darling's 1827 limits of location statue.

In Launceston a group of mercantilists formed the Port Phillip Association, and on behalf of this entrepreneurial group John Batman crossed the straits to the new pastoral lands. John Batman and his party entered Port Phillip Bay on the schooner *Rebecca* in late May 1835.[21] With him were "five or six Sydney Aborigines," who he hoped would help him to communicate his intentions to the local Aboriginal people. On 6 June, Batman's party drew up a dubious treaty with eight chiefs or *ngurungaeta* of the Kulin Nation. He then directed his attention to the western side of the bay, where he landed a small party at Indented Head, which was on the land of the Wathawurrung.[22] Later, on 8 June 1835, after travelling upriver on the eastern side of the bay, on the lands of the Boonwurrung peoples, Batman apparently saw the site that would one day become the city of Melbourne. It is commonly believed that he announced, "This will be the place for a village."

Batman's pronouncement has been treated with mythic reverence by historians and eager city builders for well over 150 years. This act of grand colonial imagining by Melbourne's "founder" has long been celebrated in popular visual and literary culture. "This will be the place for a village" was indeed a compelling historical prophecy, for it invoked the symbol of the highest stage of settler colonialism or the consummation of empire: the village or town. One of the primary characteristics of English society was the village. Patricia Seed notes that within English law at the time, to erect a house – to settle – created an almost unassailable right to own a place. To build a village in the New World was within English tradition an "unmistakable sign of intent to remain – perhaps for millennium."[23] Yet, when Batman recorded his journey up the river that he thought was the Yarra, his actual words were "This will be the place for a village – the Natives on shore." He acknowledged Aboriginal people's presence in the land that would become Melbourne, and he had many dealings with them.[24] He returned quickly to Hobart to make his claim to Governor Arthur.[25]

The news of the treaty, which in effect circumvented the 1831 regulations that all land in the colony was to be sold by the Crown, was sensational.[26] Soon after, John Pascoe Fawkner's party (which had gone ahead from Van Diemen's Land to Port Phillip without Fawkner), guided by information from Batman's reports, reached the Yarra River on the schooner *Enterprize* in late August 1835. Fawkner had availed himself of Aboriginal labour. Even as he had loaded the schooner *Enterprize* on the Tamar River in Tasmania in early 1835, preparing to join his party at Port Phillip, one of those he took with him was a "native youth as a ploughman." Stocking the enterprise in order to "commence cultivating the promised land," Fawkner put on board provisions, including "goods of all sorts for the use of the settlement and of myself. Grains of all sorts – ploughs, harrow, garden plants and seeds, 2500 choice young fruit trees and three horses."[27]

There was much mythic self-imagining on the part of Batman and Fawkner. Reminiscing in 1862 on his role in the foundation of Melbourne, Fawkner wrote of his voyage across Bass Strait as if he were the godlike, predestined hero of an epic voyage: "In March 1835 I made up my mind to venture across the straits and commence the world again." Later, some historians would argue that members of Fawkner's party, not Batman's, were the first village makers, with Fawkner being the first "Cain or the first tiller of the soil in this province."[28] Batman also seemed to be skilled at the art of self-memorialization. The nineteenth-century journalist Edmund Finn, known as Garryowen, recalled that "Batman seems to have had a weakness for perpetuating himself in nomenclature, for some of the most prominent localities were very soon branded with his cognomen. The beautiful tree-covered hill ... was called Batman's hill, the Yarra was Batman's river, and the marsh was Batman's swamp, the town was to be called Batmania."[29] The vigorous rivalry between Batman and Fawkner, the "founding fathers," has overshadowed much of the written history of early Melbourne. Rather than replicating this tradition, I look instead at their arrival and the formation of the settlement and pay particular attention to the presence of and first encounters with Indigenous people.

It is hard to discern to what extent Aboriginal people anticipated the arrival of newcomers. Certainly, the escaped convict William Buckley recounted many stories of Europeans to the Wathawurrung peoples with whom he lived for over thirty-two years.[30] The Henty family, from Van Diemen's Land, had been squatting in the Warrnambool area on Portland Bay since 1834. Indeed, they had requested permission to buy twenty-five hundred acres of land adjacent to this southern coast from the imperial government. The request, however, had been denied.[31] The comings and going of the various members of the Batman and Fawkner parties during the winter and spring of 1835 would have raised much curiosity and, probably, concern among Aboriginal people. Information about invaders would have spread fast.[32]

Overstraiters from Van Diemen's Land, who were in search of pastoral lands, may have expected confrontation from Aboriginal peoples. Throughout much of the 1820s and into the early 1830s, Aboriginal people had carried out effective guerrilla warfare in Van Diemen's Land, fighting off invasion and the rapacious violence of European immigrants. Indeed, most of the members of the Port Phillip Association had been on the Black Line, an aggressive, government-sanctioned attempt to capture or force Aboriginal people into the Forestier Peninsula of Van Diemen's Land.[33] These hopeful entrepreneurs, with their wives and displaced Aborigines from the Sydney region, carried these experiences with them. Aboriginal people watched the newcomers closely as they approached up the Yarra River. Fawkner wrote that "the borders of the stream were literally lined with Aborigines."[34] White people quickly began ploughing and fencing land that was a traditional gathering place for the various members of the Port Phillip clans. As noted, planting gardens and erecting houses to mark out the possession of new lands was a distinctive feature of British imperialism; indeed, such acts were key ceremonies of possession in North America and the Pacific.[35] We know little about what these white women thought about their journey and the Aboriginal people they encountered at Port Phillip Bay, because we do not have their writings. Yet Fawkner recalled their foreboding on arriving at the small settlement, where there were numerous Aborigines. He wrote, "Mrs F and her friend Mrs Lancey were much alarmed at first for they had been told by many persons in Launceston that the whole of us would be killed and eaten by these sable gents."[36]

In late 1835 John Helder Wedge, surveyor general and representative of Batman's Port Phillip Association, approached Wathawurrung country from the western side of the bay. His intentions were to survey the land, test the facility of the bay for "transporting the future produce of the country to foreign markets," and observe the "habits and characters of the natives of the country with a view to satisfy my own mind and that of my friends as to the security of residing amongst them." Wedge wrote that he wished to ascertain the "probability or chance of leading the aborigines by degrees to embrace the advantages of ... civilisation."[37] Fortunately for Wedge, he was accompanied and aided by William Buckley, who translated for him, and several Aboriginal people.

Wedge had landed on 7 August 1835 at Indented Head, a peninsula west of the gap on the western side of Port Phillip Bay, where he found the encampment of three men that had been left behind by John Batman's party. "At the encampment," noted Wedge, were seven Wathawurrung "families ... amounting altogether to forty in number, and a person of the name of Buckley who had been residing with them for about thirty years." He found them to be very friendly, and one Aboriginal man, Nullaborin, with whom Buckley lived had never seen a white man before. Wedge sat up at night around the fire with several Aboriginal families, and they later "kept up a conversation a great part of the night amongst themselves with Buckley – they were anxious to know where I had been and were curious to know why I was walking about the country." Wedge continued, "through [Buckley] and from a few days of observation I became quite satisfied, provided the proper steps were taken that the friendly intercourse which had happily been effected by Mr. Batman (and for which every praise is due to him) might be made permanent."[38] Regarding the Aborigines on the western side of the bay, Wedge wrote about their eagerness for European objects and food and had clear opinions about which group could lay claim to barbarity in the colonial encounter:

> Like those of every other country in a state of nature, these people were anxious to be possessed of everything they took a fancy to, tomahawks, knives, blankets, and more especially bread were what they never ceased to importune you for and if they could get it unperceived they did not hesitate to take it. And it is quite incredible the quantity of bread, potatoes, and fresh meat they would devour at one meal. Possessing these propensities I was forcibly struck with the necessity of using great forbearance with these commonly called "savages." But I much doubt, judging from the atrocious acts of barbarity that has marked the career of Europeans amongst them, whether the white man is not more deserving the

epithet than the man of colour and I fear the stains [are] indelibly on the English, if not more so than any other country.[39]

Wedge warned that the "most difficult matter," however, was "inducing ... the servants of the establishment to take the same view respecting [Aborigines], and to act on the same principle towards them." The servants, also from Van Diemen's Land, were no doubt primed with a mixture of fear and aggression, having been steeped in a culture of violence towards Aboriginal peoples. Wedge, fearing a repeat of violent relations in this new place, concluded that "everything depends on the proper person being appointed to superintend them."[40]

Wedge's humanitarian sentiment regarding the peoples of the Kulin Nation was at times genuine, but it was also politically strategic. The Port Phillip Association used the humanitarian guise of "civilizing" the Aborigines of the bay area, in conjunction with an ostensible treaty, in an attempt to justify its illegal appropriation of Aboriginal land to the Crown. Only two months later, after the alleged signing of the Batman treaty, Wedge admitted to his business partners that the Aboriginal "chiefs" who signed the vellum documents had had little authority to sell the land: "There is no such thing as a chieftainship ... but this is a secret that must be kept to ourselves, or it may affect the deed of conveyance." He also suggested that the rations given to the Aborigines should be the poorest grains possible – such as damaged oatmeal, barley, or rice – "anything that could be got at the cheapest." Later, Wedge would quarrel with Batman on several issues, one being the possible use of force on Aboriginal peoples and another the distribution of food to Aboriginal people.[41]

Arriving on 2 September 1835 at the site that would become Melbourne, Wedge was surprised to find members of Fawkner's party already occupying the land. After spending the night with the party and receiving some provisions, he left them, ironically, with a letter declaring that they were trespassing on land that the Port Phillip Association had purchased from a group of Aboriginal chiefs. He told the party that "they were within the limits of the land purchased by Mr. Batman from the natives, in reply to which they stated their determination to hold possession." Much put out, Wedge "pointed out the impropriety of any interference with our land and the unpleasant consequences that would result by their persisting in doing so."[42]

In January 1836 Joseph Tice Gellibrand, another member of the Port Phillip Association, and his party approached the settlement from the direction of Arthur's Seat through Boonwurrung territory on the eastern side of the bay. He could see the many huts and fires of the Boonwurrung people in the distance, and at times his group followed their tracks to find its way. The party landed its boat for the night about three quarters of a mile from Sandy Point and noticed the "many tracks of the natives upon the beach."[43] Later, walking north-west, the group came across "about one hundred native huts and near the huts discovered water," which attested to the large number of Aboriginal people in the area.[44]

An Outlaw Settlement in the Middle of Indigenous Land

Melbourne was an illegal, outlaw settlement. In the minds of political economists and moralists in Britain, it embodied the worst characteristics of the unruly convict colonies. Yet Robyn Annear has quipped that, unlike the penal badlands of Sydney and Hobart, Melbourne had "no British government whipcracker at its helm." It was instead "instigated by small town colonial businessmen for motives of profit and glory."[45] The Port Phillip Association, a small mercantile outfit, sought to gain legitimacy to its claim to land by treating with Indigenous peoples, and it sought fast acknowledgement from the Crown for the claim. Governor Richard Bourke declared the treaty null and void in the proclamation of 26 August 1835, and the settlement was declared illegal. These entrepreneurial "trespassers," the proclamation declared, were "liable to be dealt with in like manner as other intruders upon the vacant lands of the Crown."[46]

Lawless Port Phillip stood in stark contrast to two other new settlements in the Southwest Pacific – South Australia and New Zealand, formed by the South Australian Association and the New Zealand Company, respectively. These were formed deliberately along the lines of political economist Edward Gibbon Wakefield's systematic colonization. By 1840 these British settlements were, in Jan Kociumbus' words, ideally formed around "an expertly calculated ratio of land, labour, and capital designed to maximise profits."[47] They also, theoretically, sought to convert British paupers, seen as an excess and undesirable part of the British population, and Indigenous peoples into "contented, compliant colonial labourers."[48] Port Phillip, however, was based on the squatting system and its ruthless land taking. For these reasons Port Phillip was very attractive to entrepreneurs, and halting the tide of settlement to this outlaw pastoral land was almost an impossibility.

"We destroyed all their bark canoes": Building a Town and a Deportation

Recalling the new settlement of Port Phillip, Fawkner wrote that "King Batman required a muster of his sable subjects ... [there were] upwards of 300 of these children of the wilds, brought in from the Goulburn River on one side, Western Port on the other and from Geelong the Barabool Hill Tribe."[49] By the time that both entrepreneurial parties established themselves uneasily together in the new settlement, it seems that Aboriginal peoples had already begun to view them as a threat. The short-lived, but violent, sealing and whaling industry along the shores of southeastern Australia may have provided some with an early warning, although many had not actually seen Europeans.[50] Unlike the Lekwammen of Vancouver Island, who developed a culture of productive trade with various European groups over many generations, Indigenous peoples of the Kulin Nation quite possibly had few, if any, positive expectations for European newcomers.

As his party erected the first weatherboarded huts, Fawkner was fearful, for he believed that the "Goulburn, the Westernport, and the Barabool Hill tribes planned to murder us all by tomahawking us on the head with their stone axes ... We fed them well with biscuits, potatoes, and many little presents of clothing that I purchased and brought over to give them."[51] Fawkner's tale of settlement presents Fawkner and his colleagues as beneficent invaders, and Fawkner reassures his readers that members of his party left their arms on the boat. While the Europeans were busy carrying materials and putting up shelters, they allowed "these sable gents" to "pass in, amongst, and about us, some occasionally aiding to carry or lift pieces for us." The Aboriginal groups, however, were arranging an attack on the newcomers. Their plan, Fawkner suspected, was to get "one or two of their warriors to attach themselves to keep close to each of us ... I do not believe one of us would have escaped."[52]

This story about how the Melbourne party of Aborigines warned the settlers about the attack is one that has resonated in settler folklore. According to Fawkner, Derrimut, or Derah Mat, referred to by some as a chief, formed a friendship with the boy William Watkins and warned him of the impending attack. The Aboriginal people "were all armed with their stone tomahawks hidden under the skin rugs that they wore as elaborate cloaks, and each one we found had a spear with him, some had the spear hidden in the long grass near the hut, and were dragging it along with their toes." Seeking to warn the Aborigines, Fawkner loaded one of his muskets and fired a shot above their heads. Soon, the Aborigines, under armed threat, were partitioned to the other side of the river. Fawkner recalled that "Buckley was sent to tell these murderous blacks that they must quit our huts and cross the Yarra ... they consented to do so, and Batman found one man and I found another to work my two boats, and we thus transported nearly the whole of these savages across the Yarra. Myself and the others stood armed as did Batman's Europeans, whilst this deportation took place."[53] "We destroyed all their bark canoes that we could find," wrote Fawkner, "and out of gratitude to Derrimut, gave him clothes and food." Derrimut was encouraged to take Fawkner's boat out on the bay to shoot swans, geese, and ducks for the Europeans and to work with the crew, Aboriginal men named Baitbainger, Negrinoule, and Benbow.[54] The destruction of canoes, which were valuable possessions for Aboriginal people, and the removal of Aboriginal people to the other side of the river were proclamations of European possession that deliberately marked a new settler space.

"Faces crowded to the windows": White Settlement in Aboriginal Space

By 1837 the ragged settlement of turf huts, wattle and daub houses, and several dozen canvas tents, some of which were mere tarpaulins propped up with forked sticks, had expanded greatly. In February, the Governor of the Colony of New South Wales, Richard Bourke, anxious to view the progress of the new settlement, arrived in Port Phillip.[55] The governor would inspect the country and proclaim the foundation of a city.

On the first Sunday after the governor's arrival, a service was held in the new church and schoolhouse. Wurundjeri people peered through the windows at the strangers inside. "The scene was certainly interesting," observed the keen-eyed Rev. George Langhorne, an experienced missionary from the Cape of Good Hope, who led the devotions:

> There was a motley congregation, the Governor and his suite, the police magistrate, his superintendent, the survey officers of the MS Rattlesnake, the soldiers and convict labourers, and around the building with their faces crowded to the windows were groups of about 100 blacks and last not least in the midst stood [William] Buckley, his tall figure erect among the congregation ... and often as I glanced at his desponding countenance contrasted with the excitement and glee manifested in the faces of his former sable companions at the windows, I would have given something to have read his thoughts and theirs.[56]

William Buckley had been made interpreter to the new administration. This strange, lone figure, who had lived for over three decades with local Aboriginal people, suspected that the future for Aboriginal people would be bleak.[57] The outlaw settlement was beset with tensions. "Future strife was already brewing," wrote Langhorne as he observed the tension between colonial officials and Batman's and Fawkner's parties, which, now that their claims to the land had failed, wanted compensation.

On the high ground of what would become Collins Street, the governor, in the "full uniform of a Lieutenant General surrounded by his staff of officers ... and a detachment of the 4th commissioned officers," proclaimed the establishment of a city. In an elaborate performance of European possession, Bourke named the city Melbourne in honour of William Lamb, Lord Melbourne, the British prime minister, and accepted the general outline of the settlement, which was planted in the middle of Boonwurrung and Wurundjeri country.[58] The ceremony was "certainly a scene by no means devoid of interest," wrote

Langhorne. The customs officers, surveyors, and Batman's and Fawkner's parties stood by, and looking on "at a respectable distance" with a "mixture of curiosity and fear manifest in their countenances were grouped about 200 Aborigines, mostly men." After the proclamation, Bourke "turned to the Aborigines and told them through the interpreter Buckley that he had sent me [Langhorne] to them and that whilst obedient to the Police Magistrate and if peaceable and well behaved they would have a friend in the Governor, all this Buckley repeated to them, and the gravity of demeanour they displayed was perhaps as much attributable to fear as to any appreciation of the promised future held out to them."[59] Langhorne thought Governor Bourke was sincere and that his efforts were "no mere courtly following of orders from home." Importantly, Langhorne made note of the governor's theory that eventually the "two races of white and black (the lower class of white) could be amalgamated."[60] This early official aspiration for amalgamation would be refuted time and again over the next two decades but was, nevertheless, prescient.

Earlier Orders to Keep Aborigines Out of Towns

The early outlaw status of Melbourne and its dependency on Aboriginal knowledge and labour meant that Aboriginal people moved in and out of the new settlement at will. It is, therefore, worth considering earlier orders to keep Aborigines out of the towns of the Colony of New South Wales. Governor Macquarie's proclamation of 4 May 1816 had prohibited Aborigines from appearing armed within a mile of any white settlement or farm. No more than six Aboriginal people were allowed to "lurk or loiter" near such places. Assemblies of large numbers of Aborigines near any settlement, "on the plea of inflicting punishments on transgressors of their own customs and manners," were banned as a barbarous custom repugnant to British laws.[61] Aborigines who desired the protection of the British government and conducted themselves in a suitable manner were to be supplied with passports or certificates signed by the governor and issued by the colonial secretary on the first day of each month. The proclamation directed "British subjects of the interior" to drive away hostile Natives by force and, if necessary, "apply to a magistrate for aide from the nearest military station."[62] The proclamation of martial law in Bathurst, Colony of New South Wales, in 1824 was used by settlers to defend the killing of Aborigines, and "witnesses described numerous armed forays to confront Aborigines in the area."[63] When European and Aboriginal violence occurred in Van Diemen's Land during the late 1820s and 1830s, Governor Arthur called for Aborigines to be kept out of settled areas such as Hobart and used border police to patrol the settlements. Aboriginal women, however, had their own reasons for not venturing into Hobart. Underscoring the point that child removal was an integral and early

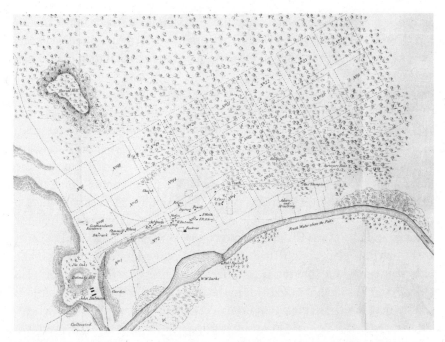

Figure 6 Detail of "Map showing the site of Melbourne and the position of the huts & building previous to the foundation of the township by Sir Richard Bourke in 1837" (surveyed and drawn by Robert Russell) on which the Hoddle grid plan is super-imposed. State Library of Victoria.

part of Aborigines' experience of colonization, Anna Haebich notes that women did not bring their children into town for fear that they would be stolen.[64]

An Imaginary City Is Auctioned

Two days before he proclaimed the foundation of the city of Melbourne, Governor Bourke rode the boundaries of the new settlement. He later wrote to his superior, Lord Glenelg: "I directed a town to be immediately laid out, which your Lordship will perceive by the map has received the name Melbourne." On the governor's instructions, Robert Hoddle plotted the city grid, which covered an area two miles long and a mile wide (see Figure 6).

The grid is represented as a modular schema of repetitious space, apparently superimposed over the natural topographical features of the landscape. As many scholars have outlined, the nineteenth-century New World city was typically created within the context of notions of the Cartesian order and associated spatially with its grids, binaries, hierarchies, and opposites.[65] Straight streets and the grid plan were defining characteristics of these cities, and they emphasized and exaggerated order, progress, and the prospects for unlimited growth. Described as a "matrix of colonization," the grid reordered the land and denied all existing social and topographical schema; it reminds us that cartography was a powerful tool of imperial discourse.[66]

Scholars have argued that the grid – a spatial signature of modernity, with its connotations of rational, ordered space – functioned as a mechanism of control and discipline both in Britain and, increasingly, its colonies.[67] By the mid-nineteenth century, concerns about the regulation of the lower orders, civility, sanitation, and disease fuelled debates on ideal or model towns in England and the growing trend of discipline through spatial and urban control. Other theorists have written about the grid as cadastral discipline.[68] The grid formation system was used in nineteenth-century New World cities in the United States, Canada, and New Zealand and was known throughout the Australian colonies as the machine plan, an inherited spatial concept used for the rapid planning of settlements in the interior. Governor Darling had prescribed the grid plan for the establishment of new towns in the Australian interior. The dimensions of allotments and streets in Melbourne were in accordance with Darling's regulations. From the date of Governor Darling's order in 1829, intensive town planning had begun in New South Wales.[69]

Although there is much archaeological evidence that reflects the Melbourne of the late 1830s and 1840s, it is now hidden deep beneath city high-rises. Very little physical evidence or built form remains visible for this early period.[70] It is Melbourne's grid plan, which continues to shape social and economic flows, that is its enduring feature. And the way the grid diverged from standard practices makes it interesting.[71] Many authors write about the cartographic hegemony of the grid and its disregard for existing topographical features. Miles Lewis, however, has noted that topography was taken into account in the layout of the grid formation in Australian towns: "Russell's topographical survey of Melbourne, whether by himself or by Hoddle, has 10 chain blocks and 1 and a half chain streets, in conformity with the Darling regulations. In other respects, its disposition, parallel with the river and between two hills, is all determined by topography."[72] Grid lines and maps were, nevertheless, drawn without reference to Indigenous peoples or their spatial orders and marked the beginning of cadastral space, the transformation of Indigenous land into European "property."

By 1 June 1837, Bourke had approved the auction of one hundred allotments of land. Amid the crazy excitement, an imaginary city was auctioned off, and many of the beneficiaries were members of the Port Phillip Association. Fawkner bought blocks on Flinders and King streets for £32 and another on Flinders Street for £25. Batman purchased allotments at the corner of Flinders and Williams streets for £75, at Williams and Collins streets for £60, and at Elizabeth and Collins streets for £23. Wedge, like his Port Phillip Association compatriot, also benefitted from the land sale. He purchased lots on Collins and King streets for £50.[73] These men helped to realize the European cadastre through their private property.

A new spatial order may have been inscribed into the landscape by Europeans in an effort to overcode Indigenous land and knowledge. But for Aboriginal peoples, this was not so. In March 1837, around the time that Bourke made the proclamation, a large corroboree, an interclan gathering, was held in the place that Europeans described as the low ground between Elizabeth Street and Swanston Street. These streets, however, belonged only in the imagination, in the realm of maps. They did not yet exist. The place, instead, was a large camp for the gathering. The Scotsman George Russell walked down to this camp with a group of friends in the evening to see the grand corroboree. In his recollections he anticipates many touristic moments for Europeans in the newly forming streetscape of Melbourne: "It was the largest and most important corroboree that I have seen. About 300 natives were present ... A large camp fire was made, and the light boughs or tops of trees were thrown upon it at intervals, giving out a great deal of flame and lighting up the camp so that everything was seen almost as well in daylight."[74] Russell saw fifty or sixty dancers, and "in a very short time the master of ceremonies, who walked about in a very dignified way, was seen in the distance mustering another party, when the same thing was repeated." Observing the dancers and their moving tableau, he wrote, "The whole scene was very striking and interesting and gave *a true picture of savage life.*"[75]

"To Get These Wanderers to Settle": "White" City, "Black" Villages

As early as 1835, when news of the settlement first arrived, colonial officials were greatly concerned with the civilization of Aboriginal peoples and with averting the violence and brutality that had occurred in Van Diemen's Land. Although no treaty would be entered into, a system of conciliation was upheld as the route to peaceable settlement.

Part of this system and a paramount concern was getting "these wanderers to settle," as Justice William Westbrooke Burton wrote to Governor Bourke. "I think a great national injustice has been done to these people in not long ago providing them with resting places upon their native soil." Burton advocated the establishment of "Black villages" outside of the town, with a portion of space reserved inside the town "for the blacks who might thus be induced to leave their wives and children and infirm people there." For these "benefits," he stated, Aboriginal people must work, and great attention would be focused on Aboriginal children. Burton insisted that "I would have these fed and clothed as Europeans so that the contrast should be as strong as possible between their treatment at school and in the bush and not only a dislike of the latter but an incapacity to even live in it be induced."[76]

Perhaps importing ideas of African social structure and colonial village making from the Cape Colony, where he had been a judge on the Supreme Court, Burton advised that they should begin by "building a hut for the Chief. I can imagine great effect to be produced by his finding himself the owner of a home in inducing him to settle and others to settle with him."[77] Just as the ideological motivations for the grid were to order and discipline colonial subjects, Native villages located outside the grid were to sequester and discipline Indigenous subjects.

Not long after, in 1836, Governor Bourke gave the newly appointed superintendent of the Port Phillip region, Captain William Lonsdale, a charter regarding Aborigines. He was to protect and conciliate the Aborigines and, importantly, attempt to "establish them in a village."[78] George Langhorne was charged with this task. Alexander McCleay, the colonial secretary for the Colony of New South Wales, gave him instructions: "So essential is the formation of such a village as introductory to all other benefits that no other labours ought for the present to subtract any portion of Mr. Langhorne's attention from this grand object."[79] He continued, "The great object will be to wean the Blacks by proving to them experientially the superior gratifications to be found in civilised life. Those who ... assemble in a village it will be necessary at first to supply with food and clothing from the public stores and by degrees they may become capable of maintaining themselves by their own labour ... by cultivation or labour to the whites." So, indeed, Kulin peoples who were "weaned" from their traditional lifestyle were encouraged to stay near the white settlement, form villages on its perimeter, and engage in the civilizing and transformative practice of labouring for white settlers. McCleay warned about the Aborigines returning to the bush or "living in idleness." He stated that "presents of food and clothing will be made in proportion to the useful labour they perform and the attention they pay to the advice of their white friends ... it should also be known that when they quit any land which had been allocated to them it ceases to be theirs during their absence."[80]

The possibility of establishing discrete black towns outside the perimeters of Hobart and Sydney had been the subject of much debate for over a decade. The village, it was thought, would not only discipline but also transform Aboriginal life ways. To the English, the village was the premier emblem of settlement. It would fix Aboriginal people on one site, arrest their wandering habits, assist in the inculcation of habits of industry, and alter their social and economic structures. The Reverend Langhorne, however, sought to temper Bourke's proposal and warned that the utmost caution should be used, as "Your Excellency is doubtless aware that a similar attempt was made with the blacks near Sydney but proved a failure [as]... inconsiderate efforts [were] made to force the natives all at once into an artificial mode of living with which they were unaccustomed."[81] Years later, in 1851, the German immigrant Carl Traugott Hoehne would write dispiritedly that in Sydney "Governor Macquarie had a settlement 'Black Town' laid out inclusive of the Aborigines, but only a few families made use of it and soon all the buildings stood abandoned and empty."[82]

The combined action of removing and sequestering Aborigines and simultaneously setting out the terms of the cadastral grid, which would spread out over Indigenous land in an act of imperial possession, was far from coincidental: it was part of the reorganization of space and the creation of private property. Attempting to contain Aboriginal peoples in villages was a counterpart to plotting the grid and establishing a white town and, in these processes, the mutual fashioning of white and Indigenous space and the rapid attempt to establish colonial order were apparent.

In 1836 Rev. Langhorne had estimated that "in this year the Aboriginal population of 30 miles around Melbourne numbered 700 men, women and children ... divided into three tribes Worrorong, the Bonnorong, and the Watorrong."[83] He hoped that an area of land "about 50,000 acres between Hobsons Bay and the Yarra to its confluence with the salt water [would] be considered" for a village and mission. Langhorne knew that the government wanted the complete isolation of the institution, otherwise it would not succeed because of the "contaminating influence arising from the close proximity to the settlement." It had been made clear to him that the land in the "vicinity of Melbourne would soon become too valuable." Langhorne also proposed that French Island in the distant Western Port Bay area be reserved for Aboriginal people. To explain his proposal, he wrote, "I have ever been convinced that nothing short of isolation of intercourse with the whites would suffice to save a remnant of the Aborigines from extinction and the event had proved I was right."[84]

Instead of the desired site between Hobson's Bay and the Yarra River, almost nine hundred acres for an Aboriginal village mission was set aside "on the south bank of the Yarra," opposite the main settlement, by a "lush swamp." The site later became the Melbourne Royal Botanical Gardens. The mission was established in 1837 and consisted of three houses and a number of Aboriginal huts. Cultivation of plots of land was encouraged, and rations were distributed. The first Aboriginal school opened in May 1837, in a "rough building erected by [Wurundjeri] tribesman paid a quarter-pound of bread per hour."[85] Children were urged to attend school, and it was suggested to Langhorne that he should "induce the attendance of the children by presents to the parents and by all other suitable means."[86] Bourke approved of this system of bribery but warned Langhorne that he should not force the children to stay or the parents to give them up. Enrolment soon rose to twenty male students.

In March 1838 Langhorne expressed the hope that the children were becoming "reconciled to their new mode of life." But this vision was not to be. The children were constantly called back to the bush by their parents, some became involved in petty crime in the town, and adults stayed only for rations.[87] Despite Langhorne's efforts, Aboriginal people continued to come and go as they pleased, depending on the level of violence directed towards them in the town and seasonal and ceremonial obligations with their own people. By June 1838 Langhorne requested that the mission be moved away from the corrupting influences of Melbourne, "where these miserable people are already sowing the seeds of disease and premature death by drunkenness and licentiousness."[88] Although he had persuaded some Aborigines to stay at the mission, "swapping four hours of field labour for three meals a day," the poor quality of the rations was no match for what could be found in town. Langhorne's inability to keep the boys at the school showed that his mission had failed, and he wrote, "I have the mortification of seeing these children running in rags and filth in the town."[89]

After loss of staff, reduced government rations, and disharmony with Police Magistrate William Lonsdale, Langhorne was in despair. In February 1839 he wrote: "The blacks scorn the idea of performing labour to be rewarded with coarse flour or a few potatoes, and nothing now will satisfy them but 'white money' to buy bread for themselves. Money they obtain readily in the town in return for the trifling services they perform, and the bakers in Melbourne assure me they are their best customers."[90] To the Wurundjeri, Wathawurrung, and Boonwurrung, the mission was, Langhorne wrote, a mere "temporary place of abode for them when weary of the town," a place "[where] they are acquiring all the low habits, pilfering tricks and demoralising practices of the lower order of Europeans."[91] Langhorne reported that Aboriginal parents used every pretext to remove their children from school and noted that the "primary object of the institution had failed with regard to the employment of the blacks and the education of their children."[92]

Aboriginal people no doubt had their own reasons for rejecting new European systems and holding on to their own culture. Despite colonial manoeuvring, Aboriginal peoples refuted imposed temporal and spatial strictures and rejected colonial attempts to engage Aboriginal peoples in schools and European labour. By March 1839 the chief protector of the Aborigines, George Augustus Robinson, had been appointed, and Langhorne acknowledged the failure of his mission. The school had largely been abandoned, and the mission closed by the end of the year. The "black village" and the attempt to spatially partition and transform Aboriginal people had failed. Yet in his reminiscences Langhorne looked back on the city of Melbourne and wrote: "The time passes rapidly away and to view the immense city, as it now stands, and to think that a few years ago that there were only on its site a few huts and canvas tents; its progress seems almost inexorable."[93]

4

First Nations Space, Protocolonial Space
[Victoria, Vancouver Island, 1843-58]

*An Indian arrowhead was recently found in a claim at Buck-eye hill
Nevada county, California, 115 feet below the surface, in solid dirt over
which had grown a tree six feet thick.*
— British Colonist, 1859[1]

*Spear head found in cave approx 11,000 years old ... on the Queen
Charlotte Islands."*
— Vancouver Sun, 2003[2]

Why is not the Indian title to Cowichan extinguished at once?
— British Colonist, 1859[3]

THE STÓ:LŌ PEOPLE of the Northwest Coast of Canada say that they have occupied their land since time immemorial.[4] Although there is no written record
of Aboriginal peoples on the Coast before contact, evidence of their continued
presence dating back approximately eleven thousand years exists in the oral
record and in the landscape.[5] The reportage of archaeological moments such
as the discovery of arrowheads metres under the ground, buried below the roots
of aged trees or in inaccessible caves, can be found in many newspapers of the
colonial period and of our postcolonial times. These reports, which point to
the long-standing presence of Aboriginal peoples on the land, often clash with
reports in colonial newspapers that call for the swift extinguishment of Native
title and, today, with reports of the legislative trajectory of Native title claims.
Archaeological finds potently symbolize the tensions between the antiquity of
Indigenous ownership of the land and the syncretism of the landscape as the
settler-colonial project constructs itself.

Archaeologists believe that early populations, ancestors of the Stó:lō, reached
the area now known as British Columbia at least 12,500 years ago. Moving
southward from Alaska, these people travelled along ice-free corridors on the
east side of the Rocky Mountains down to the Plains, made their way across
the mountains, and then journeyed west and south to the Pacific Coast. The
physical traces of people who inhabited the land known as S'ólh Téméxw can
be dated archaeologically to between ten and eleven thousand years ago. At the

time of actual contact, the diverse cultural-linguistic groups of the Northwest Coast – including Tlingit, Tsimshian, Haida, Nuu-chah-nulth (or Nootka), Kwak'w<u>a</u>k<u>a</u>'wakw (or Kwakiutl), Bella Coola, and Coast Salish – are now esti-mated to have numbered up to two hundred thousand (see Figure 7).[6] Because several smallpox epidemics preceded the actual landing of Europeans, it is dif-ficult to estimate the pre-smallpox population; however, figures of up to four hundred thousand have been suggested.

The fertile environment of the region, which was rich in natural resources, supported these dense populations and diverse cultures. In the late eighteenth century, Europeans observed that First Nations lived in villages composed of large multi-family plank houses and moved seasonally to various fishing, hunt-ing, trapping, and trading locations. In summer people moved across the land to hunt, and in winter they joined larger groups at winter villages.[7] Depicted stereotypically by Europeans as peoples who built villages surrounded by large totem poles facing the sea, these groups were in reality culturally and politically diverse, they spoke many languages, and they engaged in highly ritualized social exchanges. First Nations groups of the Northwest Coast spoke over thirty-four distinct languages. People were organized through marriage and kinship ties into sophisticated networks of "multi-band or multi-village units."[8]

There is abundant evidence of active land management, food cultivation, and preservation practices, processes that overturn the long-standing European misconception that Aboriginal peoples of the Coast did not engage in practices that resembled European agriculture. It has been proposed that a stable food surplus such as salmon required, up to 6,500 years ago, the preservation and storage of food in permanent home bases and the "establishment of a settlement pattern of permanent winter villages and seasonal resource camps."[9] Recent archaeological investigations have produced evidence of extensive mariculture; for instance, clam beds were walled in and cultivated by coastal groups, particu-larly around the Broughton Archipelago, southeast of Queen Charlotte Strait.[10] Archaeologists have identified fourteen kilometres of retaining walls for terraces, or clam gardens, in this area, which proves that the Kwak'w<u>a</u>k<u>a</u>'wakw people practised an "extensive and elaborate" form of mariculture. Kwak'w<u>a</u>k<u>a</u>'wakw Elders, who hold the memory and the received oral history of the ancient clam gardens, have provided corroborating evidence of the practice of clam farming. There is also pre-contact evidence and historical descriptions of other food cultivation practices such as the tending and harvesting of wild roots and bulbs in the southern Interior and on Vancouver Island, the cultivation of cinquefoil and clover, and the burning of the landscape to stimulate plant growth.[11]

Lekwammen people lived at the southeastern end of Vancouver Island. They belonged to the Northern Straits language group of the Coast Salish family, a

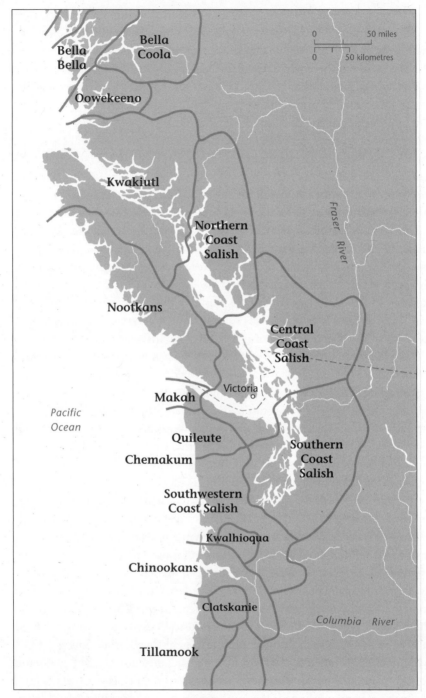

Figure 7 Cultural-linguistic map of the Pacific Northwest.
Cartography by Eric Leinberger

group that in the nineteenth century comprised around six identifiable tribes of differing dialects. The Lekwammen had several villages in and around Victoria.[12] For the greater part of the nineteenth century, Europeans defined the "Songhees" as a collection of family groups that spoke the Lkungeneng dialect of Straits Salish. With the passing of the Indian Act in 1876, however, the Lekwammen were split into three bands – Esquimalt, Discovery Island, and Songhees – by "tying each group to a reserve and defining an Indian band to be a group of Indians for whom land had been allocated." The Songhees and Discovery Island bands were later combined.[13] This making and remaking of First Nations identity through colonial and federal legislation was, as we shall see, an ongoing feature of Northwest Coast history, and it reflects shifting racializations that were performed in the service of state goals.[14]

The Lekwammen, like other Northwest Coast groups, were organized through marriage and kinship ties into multi-band or multi-village units. The potlatch and other gift-distribution ceremonies were among the most important reasons for accumulating wealth in this prestige-based society.[15] Fishing at family-owned reef-net sites and harvesting the camus bulb in specially cultivated fields were two vital subsistence practices that shaped the Lekwammen's social and economic relations. These aspects of their livelihood ultimately came to be a chief source of contestation between the Lekwammen and European immigrants.

The history of the Lekwammen since contact has been described as a series of dispossessions and repossessions of land, as a series of contestations and negotiations for space.[16] It is clear, however, that prior to European settlement the land of the Coast Salish was Aboriginal space. Despite nearly fifty years of maritime and land-based fur trading with Europeans, First Nations peoples remained largely in control of their land. Once the mercantilist economics of the fur trade began to initiate an industrialized resource-extracting economy based on mining, forestry, fishing, and food processing – industries that brought European settlement – Indigenous links to the land were radically transformed. Aboriginal space was increasingly regulated and litigated by the colonial system. This spatial contestation, especially in emerging towns, took on a particular and charged character. Victoria shifted from a fluid, hybrid town to a place in which the harsher racializations and segregations of the 1860s were enacted and in which the boundaries of whiteness were spatialized and litigated in the crucial transformation from Indigenous land to the colonial order.

"A Perfect Eden": Mapping Desire

The planting of Fort Victoria in the middle of Indigenous territory laid the groundwork for the region's transformation to a settler society and to the emergence of the town of Victoria. The selection of the site for the fort and the earliest imaginative and spatial processes through which this new Hudson's Bay Company space was made justified the possession of New World terrain on the Coast, for just as European possession of the landscape was concerned with survey and allotment, it was also preoccupied with mapping imperial desire. Geopolitical tensions in the early nineteenth century between the United States and Britain over the location of a border on the Pacific Northwest Coast provoked the Hudson's Bay Company to search for a new and more northern commercial centre. As early as 1835, George Simpson, the governor of the Hudson's Bay Company, requested that a new site be found for operations. By 1842, negotiations between Britain and the United States threatened to leave Fort Vancouver, the Hudson's Bay Company's primary fort, in American hands.[17] As representatives of the Colonial Office stressed, it became urgent for the company to "select an advantageous situation for carrying on the company's trade in the event of any portion of the territory north of the Columbus River falling under the dominion of the United States."[18] Like other forts on the Coast, the new fort was to be a centre for the fur trade, but it was also supposed to develop its own industry, reshape the land, and, ultimately, encourage settlement within British-controlled space. In this sense, the Hudson's Bay Company fort, operating as a protocolonial force of considerable influence, would play a central role in the expansion of empire.

The southern end of Vancouver Island was considered the best site for the new fur trade centre, because its placement there would "strengthen Britain's claims to the whole of Vancouver Island."[19] After much deliberation and four reconnaissance expeditions, Chief Factor John McLoughlin, the second in command at Fort Vancouver, selected James Douglas to choose the exact site, safe within British territory. In 1842 Douglas reported to his superiors that the site for Fort Victoria had one of the best harbours on the Coast and noted that

> there is a pleasant and convenient site for the establishment within fifty yards of the anchorage, on the border of a large tract of cleared land ... Being pretty well assured of the capabilities of the soil as respects the purposes of agriculture, the climate being also mild and pleasant, we ought to be able to grow every kind of grain raised in England ... We are certain that potatoes thrive and grow to a large size, as the Indians have many small fields in cultivation, which appear to repay the labour bestowed upon them, and I hope that the crops will do as well.[20]

The Lekwammen people had several winter villages in and around the Victoria region. On a second visit in 1843, James Douglas was accompanied by a missionary, Jean B. Bolduc, who estimated that 525 people were present at one of the two villages near the site. A few days after this estimate more than twelve hundred people were assembled at the site, although many may have travelled from other areas. John Lutz estimates that the pre-contact population for the Lekwammen was around sixteen hundred.[21]

Despite his written recognition of the presence and farming practices of First Nations in the area, Douglas neither acknowledged nor discussed Lekwammen rights in land. Instead, he wrote to his friend James Hargrave to discuss the selection of a plain that had the appearance of being a cleared and manicured site: "The place itself appears a *perfect Eden,* in the midst of the dreary wilderness of the Northwest coast, and so different is its general aspect from the wooded rugged regions around, *that one might be pardoned for supposing it had dropped from the clouds.*"[22] These men of empire sought to possess the new landscape, first, by imaginatively producing a space that could be appropriated. James Douglas' "perfect Eden" was akin to Robert Burnaby's "land of promise," which he encountered fifteen years later on his journey from England to the sites of the gold rush.[23] Utopian descriptions remind us of the spatial and imaginative qualities of imperial endeavour and that these metaphorical destinations were charged with a divine destiny. Yet unlike the godlike John Pascoe Fawkner, who wrote "I made up my mind to venture across the straits and commence the world again" as he travelled to Port Phillip,"[24] Douglas wrote that Eden had dropped from the clouds, presenting itself fully formed and prepared, it seemed, by Providence. Like land surveyed in southeastern Australia, the countryside of the Pacific Northwest appeared to British eyes as a gentlemen's park, prepared by Providence for the taking and framed by European artistic and cultural notions of the picturesque. Writing to Chief Factor John McLoughlin, Douglas described the future site of Victoria as "the most picturesque and decidedly most valuable part of the island that we had the good fortune to discover."[25]

George Vancouver, in the course of his surveys in 1792, had likewise observed the "stately forests ... presenting in many places, extensive spaces that wore the appearance of having been cleared by art."[26] As Lutz has shown, European sensibilities towards the land as a natural park were also present in the observations of Berthold Seeman, a naturalist who arrived aboard HMS *Herald.* In June 1846 he wrote: "In walking from Ogden Point round to Fort Victoria ... we thought we had never seen a more beautiful country; it quite exceeded our expectations ... It is a natural park; noble oaks and ferns are seen in the greatest luxuriance ... One could hardly believe that this was not a work of art; more particularly when finding signs of cultivation in every direction – enclosed pasture-land, fields of wheat, potatoes, and turnips."[27] Like travellers in Australia Felix, Seeman described the wilderness of the island as a providential work of art, as a noble park, ready for possession. Crucially, he counterposed the wilderness with the outcome of European progress and industriousness: cultivated, enclosed fields. His descriptively stadial account, like that of landscape painting, captured two modes of subsistence – the uncultivated inviting land and the land transformed by European agriculture.

These early spatial imaginings of the Victoria region were spatial strategies that worked together with cartographic practices to transform physical space into a "symbolic object whose properties were as much historical as geographical."[28] The marginalization of Aboriginal peoples, who were configured in stadial theory as undeserving of the land, accompanied these strategies. The picturesque in both visual and literary culture therefore bolstered British identity at the far-flung reaches of empire and facilitated the possession of the landscape. Furthermore, as Lutz observes, the "astonishment of these European visitors that such a picturesque country existed independent of human manipulation was related to their discursive and cartographic emptying of the land."[29] The picturesque was, thus, a harbinger of settlement. As Paul Carter writes, "picturesque meanings multiplied around settlement and the promise of settlement ... for the essence of the picturesque was that it drew the traveller on: It *led him* to settle."[30]

In "Preparing Eden" Lutz demonstrates that these seemingly untouched plains – which Vancouver, Douglas, and Seeman so admired and thought of as prime agricultural land – had in fact been husbanded and cultivated by Aboriginal women for generations. Although salmon was the main source of food for the Lekwammen, the bulb known as the camus root provided their staple diet of carbohydrates. The open prairies that European immigrants wrote of were in fact part of a vast territory for the consumption and trade of camus. The open meadows in which the camus grew were managed through annual firing, or fire-stick farming as it is known in Australia, which created the appearance of open, almost manicured, parks or savannas. Lutz asserts that Douglas' Eden was *Meequan,* as the local people knew it, one of the Pacific Northwest's prime camus fields.[31] Wherever Europeans sought to settle on the islands of the Puget Sound, they looked for these open meadows and noble parks, these fields that in fact had been cultivated by Coast Salish peoples.

On Planting a Fort: Protocolonial Space

First encounters are always worth exploring, and although we can only judge such events through the lens of European sources, they can give us a sense of the mutual expectations of both parties. When he first reached the new site, James Douglas expected the Lekwammen to be numerous, daring, and barbarous. Instead, canoes surrounded Douglas' steamboat,[32] "all shook hands," and the leader of the Aboriginal group took Douglas' party inland to look for the best site for a fort. Bolduc noted that Douglas "informed them [Aboriginal people] of our intention of building in this place which appeared to please them very much and they immediately offered their services in procuring pickets for the establishment."[33] This was a seemingly easy conquest; a trading relationship was established in which land, at least ostensibly, was not the primary object. Fourteen years later, in 1860, during a period of accelerated settlement, the young English businessman Gilbert Malcolm Sproat would force the Aht peoples of the island's west coast to sell their land "under the fear of loaded cannon pointed towards their village."[34] During this period it was possible to dispossess Northwest Coast peoples of their land by force. Later, as Cole Harris contends, land was taken from them in "more formal and institutionalized ways as government officials laid out Native reserves across the province."[35]

In his reminiscences Dr. John Sebastian Helmcken wrote of the new fort: "There was nothing else to be seen save land, water, canoes and Indians. It did not seem very inspiriting – it looked like York factory – about as solitary."[36] Building of Fort Victoria – a typical wooden palisade in the form of a quadrangle, with three or four guns mounted on towers – began in 1843.[37] By the following year, around five acres were under cultivation and the Lekwammen had moved their villages to form a substantial settlement adjacent to the new fort on the inner harbour, no doubt to monopolize the trade that they knew "their" fort would bring. James Douglas observed that the Lekwammen "considered themselves to be specifically attached to the establishment."[38] Unlike Kulin peoples in Melbourne, who were quickly removed to the other side of the river, the Lekwammen established themselves as crucial middlemen who brokered trade between Europeans and other Aboriginal groups. The distinction between the early pastoral settlement of Australia and Victoria's fur trade economy is clear: the differing economies positioned Indigenous people differently and required different things of them.

The Lekwammen freely proffered their labour to construct the fort and were paid one blanket for every forty pickets of 22 feet by 36 inches that they could provide.[39] This type of exchange would set the tone for a long time to come. Bolduc relates that almost all the "Songhees men were working to cut stakes for the new fort," but they also provided ongoing labour and provisions such as "pickets, firewood and salmon, berries and other foodstuffs" to the traders, "all without need for training or coercion."[40] Why were the Lekwammen so eager to be pulled into the fur trade economy? And to what extent did it affect their subsistence? The Lekwammen clearly chose to benefit from exchanging goods and labour with the newcomers. Blankets, for example, were of great value within Lekwammen society. As Lutz notes, the swapping of blankets for pickets was not merely an exchange, it was a transformative process that connected two value systems.[41] Robin Fisher's central thesis – that the fur trade at this time was based on mutually dependant relations for Aboriginal peoples and traders – is pertinent here, as is the possibility that the Lekwammen allowed the fort to be built there. Aboriginal agency and the traders' susceptibility to being overwhelmed by a far larger Aboriginal population also needs to be taken into consideration.[42] Compared to the Native-newcomer relations at Port Phillip, the mutuality of the situation in British Columbia seems clearer, at least at this early point in time, and is better documented in the archives.

The Hudson's Bay Company's planting of a fort on Aboriginal land, however, was not without conflict. The balance soon tipped in favour of the newcomers as the gradual encroachment of fields for cultivation, the grazing of livestock, and the allotment of lands pushed Lekwammen people off their lands and threatened the camus bulb fields on which they subsisted. A growing cadastre of European-style fields began to overcode Aboriginal land. As Lutz writes, the Lekwammen "although wanting to benefit from exchanging goods and labour, which the new settlement opened up, resented the appropriation of their camus fields." Gradually losing their land base, the Lekwammen "retaliated against the invasion by harvesting the settlers' cattle."[43]

In 1844 the Lekwammen were accused of killing an ox that had been grazing in open country near the fort. A dispute followed, and the Lekwammen threatened to attack the fort with aid from other tribes. The Hudson's Bay Company fired a cannon into a chief's house (which was empty of people) as a demonstration of might.[44] Sheer firepower subdued the local Aboriginal population, and this tactic of violence would be used repeatedly in Victoria and the surrounding area to elicit co-operation from local peoples. The military tactics of the Hudson's Bay Company should not be underestimated when evaluating Aboriginal-newcomer relations in this period. Fur trader hegemony, maintained through a combination of coercion and consent, explains relations at this time.

In his reminiscences Roderick Finlayson, the commander or chief factor of the fort, who would later become a landowner, recounts similar spatial contestations when he tells of a fire that began near the fort and Johnson Street around 1844. Following the fire, the Lekwammen were pushed to move to the other side of the harbour, which they at first refused to do. They claimed the land was theirs. Finlayson recalls that, after some argument, it was agreed that "if I allowed our men to assist them to remove they would go, to which I consented. This was the origin of the Indian Reserve.[45]

This was the first of many manoeuvres to segregate First Nations and the European inhabitants of the new fort town. Placing the Lekwammen settlement across a body of water, on the other side of the harbour, was similar to events that occurred in early Melbourne. In the incremental displacement and confinement of Aboriginal peoples, these officers were making a fort space, a place of trade and settlement; they were, simultaneously, remaking Aboriginal space. Spatial conflicts and the tightening of European possession through mapping and naming continued. By 1846 two survey ships, the *Fisgard* and the *Pandora*, were mapping the harbours of Victoria and Esquimalt, and the captains were naming features of the landscape after their European colleagues.[46]

Despite trader encroachment on their camus fields, Aboriginal people were clearing the fields, building the town, and making the roads. Once the fort was built, Chief Factor Finlayson used his Hudson's Bay Company men to clear the land. The fort settlement continued to grow. Soon the Lekwammen were filling a range of roles, clearing land, ploughing, shearing sheep, working in dairies, and making pickets and shingles.[47] In his *Reminiscences* Dr. Helmcken writes of building his house and garden, with "Indian's clearing out the stumps," and mentions that "we had our Indian servants."[48] During this time the Hudson's Bay Company did the bulk of its trade with the Lekwammen, who, in addition to their valuable labour, provided the fort and growing community with food and goods such as potatoes, clams, oysters, lathes, and baskets.[49]

In 1851 James Douglas wrote that there were "about 100 Indians employed in clearing brush and trees and bringing new land into cultivation." Two years later he observed that "a great part of the agricultural labour of the colony is at present preformed by means of the Natives, who though less skilled and industrious than the white men, work at a comparatively cheaper rate, so that on the whole they are exceedingly useful to the colonists."[50] Not only had these new immigrants used Aboriginal space, they had also productively availed themselves of Aboriginal people's labour and subsistence systems.

The Hudson's Bay Company's Grant and Making Colonial Space

The growth of the fort settlement was recorded in the extracts of a letter written by Captain Courtney, on board HMS *Constance,* in September 1848 and passed on to the Colonial Office: "The HBC settlement of Fort Victoria is only three miles from Esquimalt, so that we got our daily supplies of beef ... The company have 300 acres under tillage there, and a dairy farm of 80 cows, together with numerous other cattle, twenty four brooding mares ... under the superintendence of a civil but hard Scott named Finlayson who had about thirty people of all descriptions under him. They are likewise building a sawmill at the head of Port Esquimalt."[51] In the same year, the *Illustrated London News* published an article that reported on the "very striking debate" in the House of Commons regarding the grant of Vancouver Island to the Hudson's Bay Company (see Figure 8).[52]

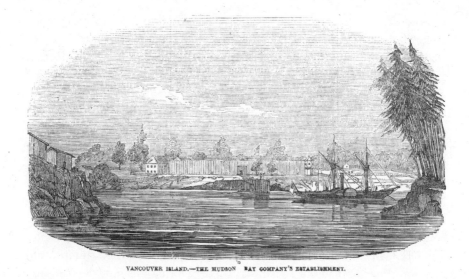

VANCOUVER ISLAND.—THE HUDSON BAY COMPANY'S ESTABLISHMENT.

Figure 8 "Vancouver Island – The Hudson's Bay Company's Establishment,"
Illustrated London News, August 1848. State Library of Victoria.

Discussions about the grant to the company of the British territory lying west
of the Rocky Mountains, particularly Vancouver Island, had been made possible
by the 1846 Oregon Treaty, a negotiated settlement between Britain and the
United States. With no discussion of Aboriginal rights in land, Britain assumed
sovereignty over the mainland north of the forty-ninth parallel and Vancouver
Island. As Harris writes, the British Crown was thus at liberty to make proprietary grants within its territories, and did so in 1849, when it granted Vancouver
Island to the Hudson's Bay Company for a period of years and under certain
conditions.[53]

During the House of Commons debate of 1848, the colonial secretary, Earl
Grey, had favoured the application of the grant of Vancouver Island to the
Hudson's Bay Company and justified it as follows: "The island in question has
not advantage enough to ensure its voluntary colonisation, and that if we did
not make provision for occupying it in some manner or other, we should probably be anticipated in such proceedings by parties ready to avail themselves of
it."[54] British ambivalence about the territory was clear; nevertheless, a scramble
for the Northwest Coast between the empires prevailed. Britain's apprehension
regarding the expansion of the United States northward was powerful, even
after the Oregon boundary settlement.[55] One member of the House, William
Gladstone, called for "investigation, deliberation and caution" before the confirmation of the charter, but the motion for an address to the Crown to stay the
grant did not pass – fifty-eight were in favour and seventy-six were opposed.[56]

As the *Illustrated London News* saw it, the "importance of the island as a field for colonisation" was "geographically illustrated by more than one speaker." Trade and crucial geopolitical considerations were key objects of the House. Vancouver Island was "the sentinel of the Pacific Ocean," stated one member. The *Illustrated London News* explained his position: "Its [British Columbia's] local position, with reference to China, Australia, New Zealand, and other important places, made the possession of it a matter of great moment ... and the time he believed, was not far distant when Vancouver's Island would command trade with China." Objections were raised. One member noted that "it was lamentable ... to think that anxious as we were to promote colonisation by self-governing settlers, we should surrender such an opportunity to this company." At the close of the debate, it was announced that the grant of the island would be accompanied "with certain conditions, which would make it imperative upon [the company] to do all in their power to promote colonisation."[57]

In an attempt to create a colony of British subjects, the British Colonial Office chose to amplify British strength in the area through the agency of the Hudson's Bay Company. As James E. Hendrickson observes, although the Hudson's Bay Company had both an "interest in and knowledge of the area as well as the requisite capital resources to undertake a project of this magnitude," it was, nevertheless, a "fur-trading monopoly, whose activities were inherently opposed to large-scale settlement."[58]

The colonial period, as it is traditionally known, began with the establishment of the Colony of Vancouver Island by royal charter on 13 January 1849. Richard Blanshard was appointed as the first governor, and he arrived on 9 March 1850. A royal commission and instructions issued to Blanshard formed the constitution of the new colony.[59] The instructions made the Hudson's Bay Company the "true and absolute lords and proprietors of the ... territory" and gave the company the exclusive privilege to trade with First Nations. Furthermore, the instructions stipulated that if the company did not create a "settlement of resident colonists" within five years, the lands could be revoked.[60] These were the certain conditions that made it an imperative for the Hudson's Bay Company to do all in its power to promote colonization. First Nations were not mentioned, except for in one statement: "And ... it would conduce greatly to the maintenance of peace, justice and good order, and to the advancement of colonisation and the promotion and encouragement of trade and commerce in, and also to the protection and welfare of the native Indians residing within that portion of Our territories in North America, called Vancouver's Island if such Island were colonised by settlers from the British dominions."[61] The scant mention of Indigenous peoples was deliberate, observes Cole Harris. The colonial secretary of state, Earl Grey, had in 1844 been the chair of the House of Commons Select

Committee on New Zealand. Despite the Treaty of Waitangi, which had been signed four years previously, the committee had endorsed the view that "Maori rights in land extended only to village and burial sites and to cultivated fields." The Colonial Office, however, objected to this and held that the Treaty of Waitangi was binding. On the Northwest Coast, the Colonial Office was reluctant to make any policy that would inhibit future colonization and, as Harris surmises, "claimed to have little knowledge of the people of the Northwest Coast, and preferred to leave the matter of Native land policy to the Hudson's Bay Company." The Colonial Office "simply did not know to what extent British sovereignty on Vancouver Island was burdened."[62]

Over a decade earlier, in 1835, the Port Phillip Association's treaty with Indigenous peoples had been promptly declared null and void. As noted, the treaty was considered a threat to the notion of Crown land because it gave implicit acknowledgment of Indigenous rights in land. A small party of mercantilists was, thus, prevented from subverting the land policy of the Crown. In contrast, and because of strikingly different regional circumstances, the British Crown ceded control of Vancouver Island to its proxy, the large Hudson's Bay Company. The scramble for space on the Northwest Coast and the threat of other nations prompted the Crown to act before "parties ready to avail themselves of it" took action and occupied the territory. A large and powerful mercantilist company with an established foothold throughout the region was made a colonizing power by proxy. Moreover, the company was handed control of Native land policy. With this power went the right to create "so many Counties, Townships, Parishes, Cities, Boroughs, and Towns as you shall judge necessary."[63] The key proviso – which, clearly, was to induce colonization – was to make settlements within five years. Whereas Melbourne was a renegade settlement with European inhabitants deemed trespassers on Crown land, Victoria was a trader fort with a company sanctioned to take control of the lands, direct the lives of First Nations, and create conditions for settlement.

Unlike Port Phillip, with its rush of entrepreneurs eager for land, European settlement came slowly to the Northwest Coast. Few settlers had arrived before Governor Blanshard in early 1850, and James Douglas, as chief agent of the Hudson's Bay Company, had jurisdiction over the majority of the population, company employees, the sale of land, and the enactment of public works. In 1852 there were only 435 immigrants in the colony. Only eleven had purchased land, and another nineteen had applied for it.[64] James Douglas reported in 1853 that the population of Victoria was "254 people, comprising 11 men, 5 women, and 93 children."[65] To agricultural settlers, the attractions were slim. The landscape did not immediately lend itself to pastoralism, as did the lands of Port

Phillip Bay. Another disadvantage was the high cost of land, which was a deliberate policy designed to attract the right kind of settler. There was also constant tension between a small group of free settlers and company people. A dispute that lasted several decades ensued over who could control the town in terms of civic and property relations. Several bodies – including the Hudson's Bay Company, the Crown, the colonial government, and, later, the municipal council (i.e., the town council of Victoria) – vied for control. In addition, Vancouver Island would always be starved of British support and judged as a distant, rather inconsequential colony.

Early Racializations

The Pacific Northwest Coast and the Columbia Plateau were densely populated by Aboriginal peoples who were linguistically, culturally, and politically diverse.[66] Aboriginal people were neither a homogenous nor a monolithic group. So, too, Hudson's Bay Company fur traders and other newcomers were not a homogenous "white" group, and they were at times both the subjects and agents of imperialism.

The labourers whom Finlayson used to clear the land were not white men. As Dr. Helmcken himself observed, "Most of the men in the Fort were either French Canadians or Kanakas – an Iroquois or two."[67] As at Fort Langley, a fort on the Mainland whose small society was polyglot and multiracial, the superior officers at Victoria were Scottish, and most of the men were French Canadian, Métis, British, Iroquois, or Hawaiian. French and, later, Chinook were spoken. The majority of women were First Nations. Some came from the Columbia River, but, writes Harris, most were from the area around Fort Langley.[68] Helmcken's observation is important to note, since it overturns easy presumptions of a binary tension between white and Aboriginal that so many studies trade in – it problematizes the idea of a fixed white or British identity. Early Fort Victoria was a hybrid, mixed place. Without understating the power of the Hudson's Bay Company's protocolonial agenda, its appropriative charter, and the fact that most high-ranking company officers were of Scottish-Presbyterian origin, it is important to recognize the partial and particularized nature of this protocolonial mercantilist project. In Victoria, imperial discourses were refracted at the local colonial level, and imperial subjects were likewise refashioned in this environment. James Douglas was one of these subjects; he was an imperial subject as much as an agent of imperialism. Douglas, chief factor of Fort Victoria and later governor of the Colonies of Vancouver Island and British Columbia, had been raised in British Guiana by a Creole mother and a Scottish father and was described as a "Scotch West Indian" and, more derogatively, as a "mulatto."[69]

The Hudson's Bay Company men and their wives who arrived at their chosen site may have possessed imperial eyes that scanned the landscape for resources that could be appropriated for profit, as John Lutz, using Mary Louise Pratt's famous notion of imperial eyes, has observed.[70] And, ultimately, they may have attempted to transform "Victoria into an English village."[71] Douglas most certainly possessed an "imperial vision" and carried out its mandate, but in light of his background, he was also created by British imperial endeavour. Douglas' mixed background informed his governance and policies with respect to First Nations, immigrants, and issues of race in the town of Victoria. In this early period, notions of whiteness were not fixed or stable but permeable and shifting.

Racialized Indigeneity

From the time of first contact, Europeans offered particular representations of Indigeneity on the Northwest Coast. John Lutz has traced the making of the category "Indian" in colonial and post-Confederation British Columbia, noting that how settler society defined the term *Indian* was integral to the place of First Nations in the historical literature, in society generally, and in the capitalist market economy in particular. Importantly, he noted that changing racializations become most apparent when "comparing the different construction of 'Indian' in the fur trade, colonial, and confederation periods."[72] Lutz's matching of particular racializations with the historical periods of European occupation and economy on the Northwest Coast is insightful. Changing racializations reflected how First Nations were discursively positioned in the colonial economy according to its particular requirements at a given moment. At times these overlapped, giving rise to competing, seemingly contradictory discourses on Indians. Indians were at once indolent and hard-working, to the point of taking white men's jobs.[73] The opportunistic shaping of the Aboriginal subject, the making and remaking of Indigeneity to suit the particular historical and economic requirements of the colonial economy, is significant.

In "The Image of the Indian," a chapter of *Contact and Conflict,* Robin Fisher charts the varying European representations of First Nations, noting that because land-based fur traders lived among First Nations, they were more objective and less prejudiced than settlers.[74] He argues that settlers' images of First Nations were often the result of events and currents of thought in the metropolis, whereas traders' attitudes were based on their lives on the frontier. "Generally traders reacted to what they saw, while settlers tended to react to what they expected to see."[75]

During the Age of Exploration, European nations avidly assessed Indigenous peoples; they ranked them for their manners and customs and sent this information back to Europe. Many descriptions of the peoples of the Northwest Coast in the emerging ethnographic practice of the late eighteenth and early nineteenth century are now considered predictable and common in European exploration literature. Speculation about cannibalism, the physical difference between Europeans and Indigenous peoples, and Indigenous women as the barometers of civilization were prevalent and circulated in tandem with descriptions of savagery and debates about whether New World peoples were indeed part of the same human family as Europeans.[76]

Along the Northwest Coast, First Nations societies confounded European notions of gender because the more northern groups were organized along matrilineal lines, while the southern groups were organized along patrilineal lines. First Nations women's active involvement in trade and bartering was a particular site of European speculation. Gambling, mourning ceremonies, and head flattening were also areas of great interest, as if the European practice of similar customs and body modifications was natural and not equally curious. In 1848, in a letter describing Fort Victoria, Captain Courtney commented on the Lekwammen. He remarked, "The Indians inhabiting Vancouver Island and the neighbourhood area are a dirty, wretched set of people, without fixed habitations, but many of them have handsome features, particularly the women. I was agreeably surprised to see that they are not as thievish as represented, scarcely a single instance of dishonesty occurred during our intercourse, but they will not do you a handswork or give you a drink of water without payment."[77] Courtney's comments about the Lekwammen did not conform to the entirely negative stereotypes of Aboriginal peoples as lascivious and dishonest that were common among maritime fur traders, but he did make particular mention of Aboriginal people's handsome features and keen abilities in bartering and trading for their labour.

Land-based fur traders, who were more attuned to tribal differences than their maritime counterparts, developed racialized and hierarchical representations of First Nations along the Coast. European men, for instance, tended to have relations with or marry women from the northern rather than the southern tribes. The perceived superiority of northern groups such as the Haida and Tsimshian over more southern groups such as the Coast Salish was due to the notion that northern groups were less degraded by Western contact and were a greater military threat.[78] Several authors have speculated that the preference for peoples of the northern coast was based on the characteristics that these groups shared with Europeans.[79]

Europeans tended to rank Aboriginal modes of subsistence according to their own entrenched notions of material and social development, which were encapsulated in stadial theory. Fisher traces a wealth of commentary by ethnographers and travellers who privileged the perceived nobility and strength of the more northern hunting societies over the lesser, more "lazy" fishing societies of the Coast Salish. The perceived difference also had an economic basis. Because the Coast Salish had participated with Europeans in the fur trade for years, they were perceived as dealers rather than hunters.[80] In addition, the Coast Salish were often considered wretched because they did not conform to images of the noble savage, the warrior-like Indian of the Northern Coast or the Plains who was deemed more authentic because he was less degraded by contact.

Travel writing indicates that by the late 1850s, when the gold rush caused increased European settlement, the Lekwammen were detested. Many settlers in the 1850s and 1860s brought with them hardening attitudes about race that were developing in Britain, attitudes that not all fur traders shared.

Tender Ties, Transglobal Ties: Fur Trade Families

Victoria's early years were shaped by the military-style governance of the Hudson's Bay Company, whose officers had common law wives who were often high-ranking Indigenous women or women of mixed descent. Mixed relationships were an important feature of many trader forts, and they set the social and spatial relations of Victoria well into the late nineteenth century. Census material and cemetery records provide insight into Victoria's social and spatial demographics by providing information about early families and others who lived and worked in its streets.[81] The census of Vancouver Island in 1854 lists the number of settlers as 774. Of the 416 individuals who were older than twenty years of age, "307 were men and 109 women."[82] Some may presume that those counted were white settlers, but this was not the case.

Sylvia Van Kirk's *"Many Tender Ties": Women in Fur-Trade Society, 1670-1870* (1980) was influential for its reassessment of the economic and cultural role of First Nations women in the fur trade and the vital linkages they fashioned in their marriages to men of fur-trading companies. The study brought attention to the intimate, human relationships through which the fur trade, a mercantilist and protocolonial project, operated. Van Kirk was primarily concerned with relationships on the Prairies, particularly at Red River, but she also addressed relationships on the Coast. She outlined the agency of Indigenous women and traced the positive aspects of their alliance with male fur traders, observing that within tribes these women often fostered trade with Europeans.[83] First Nations women taken as marital partners by traders were an integral part of fur trade society; they often took the initiative in securing husbands and became women in between two groups of men, "a situation which could be manipulated to advantage."[84] Although women's position in the fur trade eventually declined,

Van Kirk argued that First Nations women must be viewed as "active participants in the developing complex of Indian-white relations."[85] Contrary to the stereotypical images of First Nations women as prostitutes and purveyors of vice that circulated in Victoria, many First Nations women became translators, guides, consultants, and traders. By contrast, although mixed marriages were not illegal in Port Phillip in the 1840s, there was no long-standing tradition of publicly accepted unions between Aboriginal women and European men. On the Pacific Northwest Coast, marriages *à la façon du pays* set in train very different social dynamics.[86] Yet these unions profoundly affected, in very different ways, the socio-spatial politics of the cityscape in both places.

Many of the fur traders' Aboriginal wives were from farther up the Coast, and it is important to distinguish between the differing imperial racializations of First Nations. Hudson's Bay Company officers married Plains women or women from Red River (present-day Winnipeg), not Lekwammen women. By the 1860s, however, these common law marriages, as Adele Perry has shown, were increasingly derided, and these partnerships were later encouraged to meet European standards of acceptable union in the form of church marriage.

In Port Phillip short liaisons and the sexual abuse of Aboriginal women on the frontier were commonplace. Similar behaviour was also widespread on the Northwest Coast. As Perry writes, "for some white men, casual connections with Aboriginal women were a part of the travel experience."[87] The casual and transient nature of such relationships, she argues, "probably legitimated the ease with which white men abandoned their Aboriginal partners."[88] By problematizing the agency of First Nations women that Van Kirk established in "*Many Tender Ties,*" work such as Perry's confirms the easy use and abuse of First Nations women and the hardening ideas of white observers who believed that "mixed-race relationships were necessarily degraded ones."[89]

In a more recent article, Van Kirk traces five elite fur-trading families, all headed by high-ranking officers of the Hudson's Bay Company – John Todd, William Henry McNeill, Charles Ross, James Douglas, and John Work – who had married women of First Nations or mixed descent and who had a monopoly on the best land around Victoria in the late 1840s, 1850s, and 1860s.[90] The affectionate aspects of such partnerships cannot be discounted. Yet as racist attitudes hardened as new settlers arrived, these men went to great effort to Anglicize their families "at all costs."[91] James Douglas, for instance, enjoyed a long marriage to a woman of First Nations descent, who, when he became governor, famously became Lady Amelia Connelly Douglas. Several authors have commented on the image of white, bourgeois, and Victorian womanhood that she presents in her photographic portrait.[92]

It therefore cannot be presumed that all those counted in the census for 1854 were white. Victoria's early cemeteries likewise highlight mixed marriages that the census perhaps does not reveal. Cemeteries are material artifacts that reflect the historical socio-spatial relations of the city in which they reside. They reveal battles over demarcation between religious denominations and reflect a site hierarchy based on class, race, and religion. Cemeteries are, thus, a spatial schematic or microcosm of social relations as they were embodied by the city at a given period of time. Nevertheless, they must be used in tandem with other sources. Matching Van Kirk's five families with census and burial records reveals a great deal about the early character of Victoria.

Unfortunately, spatial records such as maps that show the location of burials in Victoria's early cemeteries and the location of the Douglas-Johnson Street and Quadra Street cemeteries were destroyed when the new Ross Bay Cemetery was established in 1874 farther away from town.[93] However, extant burial records from the Catholic and Anglican denominations reveal a great deal of information about burial demographics, particularly in regard to race, and give a snapshot of the mixed social history of the streetscape in the trader town. If a First Nations person had converted to a particular faith, he or she would often be buried in that section of the cemetery. Local Lekwammen peoples, however, were buried in traditional places such as Dead Man's Island or Hycatt Island or on other smaller islands in the area.

A qualitative examination of Anglican burial records for Christ Church Cathedral between 1849 and 1858 provides a snapshot of the constitution of the town, including mixed marriages, and a record of the burial of many infants and other members of the five families.[94] For instance, records for 1849 show that Rebe Douglas, who was only eight months and nine days old, was buried. In 1855, amid listings of persons from various parts of the British Isles, are listed two unidentified Hawaiian men, or "Kanakas," who were employees of the Hudson's Bay Company. An infant listed as "Nahona," Kanaka, was also buried in October 1855, as were John Bull, Kanaka, who was forty years old, and Thomas Mauho, Kanaka, who was twenty-eight years old. In June 1856 Henry Work, a ten year old, was buried. In 1858, amid the burials of men from HMS *Satellite*, the steamship *Otter*, and HMS *Plumper*, was the burial of Cecelia Nahona, a thirteen-month-old infant, on 2 February and, on 5 February, "the wife of Doctor Kennedy an Indian woman." On 10 March 1858, "Mary Anne an Indian girl," who was a "native of Queen Charlotte Island" and whose abode was on the "hillside near Victoria" was buried.[95] Eight days later, the infant Margaret Jane Helmcken was buried.

Within the span of nine years, therefore, the infants or children of several of the families that Van Kirk selected, such as Douglas and Work, who were all of mixed or Aboriginal descent, were buried within the Anglican church grounds. This is unsurprising, as it reflects the social dominance of the elite trader families and their forging of a mixed community that would become increasingly Anglicized. The burial registers record under which denomination a person was buried, but they do not reveal the location of the burial. A Hawaiian, or Kanaka, company employee, for example, may have been buried by an Anglican minister but in the Kanaka, rather than the Anglican, section. There is no way to know, since the actual spatial records of physical placement have been lost. It is probably true to say that Aboriginal women – especially the wives of mixed descent who were Anglicized, married, baptized, and accepted as part of the community – would have been buried beside their husbands in plots within their own denomination. In other words, these women and their children were not outside the pale simply because they were non-white.

The burial register of St. Andrew's Catholic Church for the same period, from 1849 to 1858, likewise reflects the prevalence of mixed marriages between Métis and First Nations peoples and other Hudson's Bay Company employees.[96] The parents or origins of the person are often listed. In 1849 Honore Anhem, a "Northern Indian," was buried on 25 September, and the "wife of Pahia ... of the Manhouis nation" was buried on 27 October. Catherine Oahis, an infant of ten months who is described as the "daughter of George Oahis from the Sandwich Islands," was buried on 25 July 1850. A woman known only as "Louise, wife of Ignace, Iroquois" was buried 23 August that same year, and "Jean Baptiste Kiaret Oahis ... son of L. Kiaret Oahis" was buried on September 20. The marriage of many Métis and First Nations people to Europeans has been documented, but there is less research on unions between Polynesian and Métis people. Jean Baptiste Kiaret Oahis, was, judging from the name, a Kanaka or Polynesian and a Métis person. On 26 October 1851, "Simeon ... the hundred year old grand Chief of the Cowichans was buried." On 23 December 1853, the burial of Piere Vatrin, son of Jean Baptiste Vautrin and Isabella, "a Tsongas woman," is recorded. And on 27 July 1855, "Agnes Falardeau ... Stetkin woman, wife of Louis Falardeau," who was thirty years of age, was also laid to rest at the cemetery.

This survey of Anglican and Catholic burial records reveals the plurality that existed at this edge of empire before the gold rush. It also points to a growing diaspora of Pacific peoples along the Northwest Coast. The fur trade created mixed relationships between Aboriginal women and Hudson's Bay Company men that altered socio-spatial dynamics and living and burial arrangements, but the trade also – even before the gold rush – created transglobal ties. The multi-ethnic crossroads that became Victoria only amplified these relationships and ties.

By the summer of 1858 and the beginning of the gold rush, Aboriginal, French, and Polynesian names were listed alongside the names of Catholics from South America and Ireland. On 23 July 1858, "Thomas Riley ... a native of Country Craven, Ireland" was buried, and on 10 August "Tiburcio Montealegra, 21 years ... native of Gaupapa [sic], Mexico" was put to rest. By 15 June 1859, "Michael McDonald ... 20 yrs ... native of Oxford" and "George Beard, 33 yrs ... native of New Orleans" had also come to rest in the Catholic cemetery.

Although taking ethnicity and gender into account is important, differentiation in cemeteries lay primarily along a denominational axis. If a person was part of a certain denomination, then the minister or priest of that denomination would bury him or her, regardless of his or her ethnicity.[97] Later, by the time that the Ross Bay Cemetery was built in 1874, a separate section, which was marked "N," existed for "Aboriginals and Mongolians"; however, if an Aboriginal person was of a particular denomination, it is quite likely that he or she would be buried in the separate section or in sections set aside for particular denominations.[98]

Burial registers for the two earliest cemeteries in Melbourne, the Flagstaff or "burial hill" cemetery and the larger northern cemetery, now underneath the Queen Victoria Market, do not exist. However, a map of the northern cemetery in around 1920 does exist, and it reveals that Aborigines and members of the Society of Friends were, literally, outside the pale. When this cemetery was re-claimed as commercial land, it was the Society of Friends and Aborigines plots that were the first to be covered.[99] Lack of burial records makes it difficult to trace peoples of mixed descent. The Melbourne General Cemetery on Lygon Street, established in 1854, was a modern cemetery with more distinct denominational areas. The major churches – the Church of England, the Presbyterian Church, and the Roman Catholic Church – were allotted 1 hectare each, while Independents, Jews, Baptists, and Wesleyans were allotted 0.4 hectares each. Aborigines and Quakers were jointly allotted 0.2 hectares.[100]

The highly mixed character of British Columbian society in the mid-nineteenth century challenged the normative racial and gender standards expected of Anglo-American social life, as Perry has amply demonstrated.[101] While censuses from the 1860s and 1870s show the "expansive definition of whiteness" in Victoria, cemetery records from this earlier period amply reveal its roots.[102] Furthermore, racial pluralism extended well beyond fur trade marriages. As Perry shows in her survey of church marriage records, in many cases the grooms had "working-class occupations characteristic of a coastal resource economy, they were sailors, miners, and building, industrial and retail workers."[103] In contrast, while the rough and unruly character of Melbourne society also challenged conventions, there was, nevertheless, a social binary between Indigenous peoples, who formed a minority, and Europeans largely from Anglo-Saxon backgrounds. This binary would not shift until the gold rush period.

Seasonal Migrations to See the White Town

The Fraser River gold rush was a watershed in Victoria's economic and cultural history. It transformed the site into a cultural crossroads as thousand of miners from distant places made their way to the region. But the growing seasonal migration of many First Nations groups to the town in the early 1850s also proved to be enormously significant to its spatial and cultural transformation. Trading visits from these groups had occurred since the fort was founded in 1843; however, mass migrations on a seasonal basis began only in the summer of 1853.[104] As Lutz relates, in 1853 James Douglas wrote that three thousand Aboriginal people had congregated as guests of the Lekwammen for a potlatch on the harbour across from the fort.[105] In 1854 Douglas again recorded that First Nations from "all parts of the mainland coast south of Cape Spencer" had come not only to potlatch but to see Victoria and its curious new inhabitants. Lutz writes that "from 1853 through to the 1880's, 2,000 to 4,000 Aboriginal peoples canoed up to 800 miles to spend part of the year in Victoria."[106]

Trade (both between First Nations groups and with the fort's residents), the high price paid for labour, and the spectacle of seeing newcomers were great attractions. Increasing numbers of First Nations arrived to obtain work from Europeans, and they traded with one another throughout the early 1860s. Victoria at this time has been described as a vast "Native emporium," as Aboriginal people from the northern coast and Queen Charlotte Islands flocked to the town in canoes.[107] The vast majority of visiting First Nations were loosely termed "Northern Indians" to distinguish them from the local Lekwammen people.

The census for 1854 notes lists 774 non-First Nations peoples but "34,000 or so inhabitants of the colony of Vancouver Island and its adjacent islands and shores."[108] First Nations vastly outnumbered the tiny trading enclave. Settler fear prevailed. The minutes of the Council of Vancouver Island contain repeated warnings of "Northern savages" visiting the small colony, which was "destitute of any military force." On 27 February 1856, the council resolved that a company of thirty men – one lieutenant, one sergeant, two corporals, and twenty-six privates – should be "immediately raised and maintained at the publik [sic] expense until the Northern Indians leave the settlements."[109]

Later that year, with the appointment of the first elected Legislative Assembly, Douglas gave an address. He noted that Vancouver Island was a self-supporting colony, "remote from every other British Settlement." He spoke of the poverty and underdevelopment of the colony, yet he rightly predicted that coal, timber, and the fisheries would "assume a value before unknown." He noted that fears of "Northern Indians" had "excited not an unreasonable degree of alarm" and that the naval frigate *President* had been called to defend Vancouver Island. With such imperial might behind him, Douglas then pledged to continue to conciliate the goodwill of First Nations: "By treating them with justice and forbearance, and by rightly protecting their civil and agrarian rights ... We know from our own experience that the friendship of the Natives is at all times useful, while it is no less certain that their enmity may become more disastrous than any other calamity."[110]

5

The Imagined City and Its Dislocations: Segregation, Gender, and Town Camps
[Melbourne, Port Phillip, 1839-50]

> *Metropolitanism creates an imaginary city of heightened possibilities that interact with the space of lived experience to produce dislocations.*
> — ROBERT ROTENBURG, "METROPOLITANISM AND THE TRANSFORMATION OF URBAN SPACE"[1]

ON ROWING UP the Yarra River in 1842 in a small boat at night by the light of a beautiful moon, David Monro wrote, "We could see the lights of Melbourne on rising ground ahead." Looking across the water at the "huts of very primitive construction," he thought them "comfortable with the red light of fires and candles radiating from the doors and windows." Peering in on the nightlife of the new town, Monro observed that the local Europeans seemed savage enough, for he heard "crass peels of laughter," and in the cottages he saw many "devoted to the service of Bacchus." In this society, Monro pondered, "refinement was in an exceedingly small portion to mirth." Reflecting on this first night, he wrote, "I felt exceedingly disappointed and began to think that I had come to the other side of the world to very little purpose."[2]

Like the hopes of so many visitors from Europe, David Monro's expectations for the colonial city were countered by the reality of the frontier streetscape. In this chapter, I look at the imagined city and its dislocations to examine the disjuncture between heightened ideas of regulated town space, colonial order, and notions of racial purity and the lived actualities of an urbanizing empire. The spectacle of the colonial streetscape is considered alongside European attempts to survey and control Aboriginal peoples and mixed-race relations. In turn, the experiences of Aboriginal people, who refuted and subverted this often violent colonial order, are taken into consideration.

Spectacle and Racialization in the Streetscape

In 1838 Melbourne's European population was around eighteen hundred, and it had around three hundred European buildings. Three years later, because of an influx of hopeful pastoralists, Melbourne could boast "upwards of a thousand dwellings" and six thousand European inhabitants.[3] George Arden, who published a booklet, *Recent Information Regarding Port Phillip*, in 1841 in an effort to attract immigrants, declared that the town was "populated by the experienced capitalists of neighbouring colonies" and was important as a "sea port of a country fertile and extensive." The total value of property in Melbourne, he exclaimed, was "one million four hundred and seventeen thousand!!!"[4] This New World settler-colonial city was a canvas onto which optimistic town promoters could project their desires for imperial glory and commerce. An influx of immigrants was drawn to Melbourne, a hub of pastoralism, in the hope of making their fortune. In the middle of this rapidly expanding European population were several hundred Wurundjeri and Boonwurrung people, who often camped at the edges of the town grid. The largest camp was located on the opposite side of the Yarra River, near the mission and behind the town brickworks.

By the early 1840s, constructed representations of Aboriginal people in and around Australian towns were recounted and portrayed in travel books, brochures, and pamphlets, serving genuine European curiosity and empire's need to manage ideas about colonized peoples. Newly arrived settlers would often seek out pamphlets in an effort to acquaint themselves with the new town and the Aboriginal peoples who became the objects of their curiosity. Once they landed in Melbourne, new immigrants often walked down to the Native camp to watch a corroboree. William Kyle, who arrived with his family in Melbourne in 1841 at the age of nine, remembered that "at the time of our arrival in Melbourne there was a fairly large black population." The Yarra Yarra "tribe," he recalled, "camped on the site now occupied by the Melbourne and Richmond cricket ground where they held numerous corroborees of much interest to the white people."[5] Viewing fights between Aboriginal groups was a source of entertainment and a spectacle for newly arrived Europeans. George Frederick Belcher, who later became an official in Geelong near Melbourne, waited eagerly for a conflict to begin near the present site of Government House: "Nor had I an hour to wait and the fray had commenced. Boomerangs and spears were soon flying about and rather too close for comfort so I moved some distance away and looked on. One old fellow was speared in the ankle and carried into camp. When the fight was over no lives were lost.[6]" Corroborees and fights were thrilling performances for newcomers who were expecting to see savagery on display.

At times Aborigines were handed rum and encouraged to fight one another.[7] At other times local Aboriginal people participated in dance or athletic performances in town fairs, which were sometimes presented as entertainment for visiting dignitaries. Recalling the visit of Lady Franklin in 1839, Belcher wrote about Melbourne celebrating its "first illumination." The celebration, "accompanied by fireworks, took place in the evening ... the natives in honour of the occasion held a corroboree or dance, on the site now occupied by the Houses of Parliament, her Ladyship was present for a short time, and reviewed over five hundred blacks, who had formed a camp where St. Peter's Church now stands."[8] Sometimes, however, Aborigines were not willing participants in festivities. In that same year, 1839, a feast in the town was proposed by George Augustus Robinson, the chief Aboriginal protector, to conciliate Aboriginal people at the government's expense. Those who were there observed that it was a "fair show": "In fact all looked very fine, almost all of the gents introduced their Ladies, it was a regular holiday." There was a darker side, however, to this festivity. Aborigines feared whites and thought "the government was only inviting them to take them all prisoner like Mr Robinson had done to them in Van Diemen's Land."[9] News circulated quickly among Europeans in the colony, but Aboriginal people in town received their own news from the frontier. Circuits of Aboriginal knowledge, of which we can only catch glimpses, clearly existed. Aboriginal people feared that the food had been poisoned: "The poor fellows unwillingly drew up to the feast, and I was almost forcing them in and when appeared afraid to eat, however, after an hour or so they increased in confidence. Gents were giving them money and handkerchiefs for throwing spears, running, and getting up a greasy pole for a shirt ... they enjoyed it themselves."[10] Later, and perhaps unsurprisingly, Aboriginal people "could not be prevailed upon to corroboree."[11] In 1843 Sara Bunbury wrote to her father from the settlement of Williams Town, which was further west around Port Phillip Bay from Melbourne: "Two tribes of Blacks were encamped at the mouth of the river about a mile from us last week, and at last I have seen a coroberree [sic] ... and it was well worth seeing."[12] She continued:

It was exactly like a scene in a play ... the night was very dark, but the large blazing fires that they have at the front of each my my [mia mia] threw light on the dancers, and on the old men, women and children who sat looking on. The dancers were very nearly in a state of nature as to garments, but the white paint with which they ornamented their bodies, gave them a clothed appearance. They made the most hideous faces whiles dancing and more fiendish looking creatures it would be difficult to imagine ... I was quite delighted ... [they were] like opera dancers on a stage. They kept the most perfect time, and they make every limb quiver in the most extraordinary manner. It looked like machinery.[13]

Like Sarah Bunbury, many Europeans viewed the urbanizing colonial frontier as a stage upon which the shifting performance of civility and savagery was being played out. When George Russell watched a corroboree in the yet-to-be-formed streets of Melbourne and noted that "the whole scene was very striking and interesting and gave *a true picture of savage life*," he evoked ideas about spectacle and sought out a preconstructed primitive authenticity.[14] The nineteenth-century spectacle embodied the idea of the world as stage, a trend that can be detected in much travel writing of the period. The "rendering of things up to be viewed" and the impulse to order and represent foreign places and peoples were part of a particularly Western phenomenon.[15] It was part of bourgeois, European self-fashioning, and it reflected growing imperial confidence about the power of western Europe to represent and control the colonized Other. It reflected, for Britain, the growing political certainty of a new age, which would reach its peak in the late nineteenth century.

Some of the earliest photographic images of Australian Aboriginal people were taken by Douglas T. Kilburn, an Englishman who opened Melbourne's first commercial photography studio. The striking daguerreotype "Victorian Aborigines" (see Figure 9) shows two Kulin men and a boy. The Kulin men appear composed, dignified, and perhaps curious. They wear traditional incised possum-skin cloaks. By 1847, however, around when this picture was taken, it is likely that many Kulin people, especially those in the immediate Melbourne area, would have possessed some European garments and objects. Other works by Kilburn show that he had an eye for the desired visual lexicon of the time and sought to capture markers of difference and savage authenticity.[16]

Yet Aborigines also came to town, often travelling long distances, to look at Europeans. For some members of the Kulin Nation, coming into Melbourne was a new experience; many had never seen a European town. It is possible that the men in Kilburn's daguerreotype were from a group farther out from Melbourne and that these are, indeed, their own garments. In 1840 Chief Aboriginal Protector George Augustus Robinson recorded a long conversation he had with visiting "Dardowerong natives" (Djadjawurrung) about their country in which he reported watching the Port Phillip Aborigines making a large amount of smoke on a fire to "signal to the natives in the country" to come into the town.[17] Clearly, spectacle could run both ways, and Aboriginal people were witnesses to the development of the white townscape.

Entertainment was one thing. The continued presence of Aborigines in and around colonial towns and cities created much anxiety among Europeans, as evinced in reportage, artwork, and cartoons in which fears of mimicry, mendicancy, and the cross-contamination of cultures prevailed. Edmund Finn's derogatory reminiscences of the 1840s are but one example: "At almost every turn one met with the Aborigines, in twos and threes, and half dozen – coolies, gins, lubras, and piccaninnies – the most wretched-looking and repulsive specimens of humanity that could be well found. The men half naked with a tattered o'possum rug, or dirty blanket thrown over them, as far it would go; and the

Figure 9 Victorian Aborigines, ca. 1847, daguerreotype (photographer, Douglas T. Kilburn, 1811-71). National Gallery of Victoria, Melbourne, PH407-1983.

women just as nude except when an odd one decked herself in some cast away petticoat or ragged old gown."[18]

Upon landing in Sydney in 1844, Louisa Meredith was clearly not averse to a little patriotic British spectacle herself. In her notes and sketches, she wrote, "My joy was complete ... seated in a slung chair ... wrapped in the British flag, I gladly bade adieu to the good ship that had so long seemed to me a weary 'prison-house' ... and with a delight that must be felt to be understood, stepped again onto *land*."[19] Mythologizing her arrival, Meredith wrote that her ship had passed through the gigantic heads of Sydney Harbour, "as through a colossal gate" into the Antipodes. Her self-adornment with the British flag was a gesture full of patriotic nationalism and spoke of the power of empire, but it was also about racialization. In one dramatic moment, Meredith flaunted her Britishness just as she came ashore to a foreign space. Once in the streetscape, like any tourist, she began pointing out differences, and spectacle was implicitly linked to racialization.

In the streets of Sydney, Meredith witnessed "the noblest specimens of 'savages.'" As a Maori chief walked along, with his wife following him, she mused on the "majestic demeanour ... of this untutored being, with his tattooed face and arms," who "might put to shame many an educated but less civilised European." Although Meredith did not mention the presence of Australian Aboriginal people in Sydney, when she visited the inland town of Bathurst she noted, "The natives in Bathurst were less ugly and better proportioned than I had expected." Yet, following conventions circulating in the colonies, she then outlined some of their supposed ignoble cultural limitations: "[They are] polygamous, female children [are] promised in infancy, the women are treated brutally and like slaves, and although they appear to treat their children kindly, they commit infanticide." About the Maori however, echoing prevalent European rankings of peoples in the Pacific, she wrote that they were "immeasurably superior to the natives of New South Wales in everything but the melody of their song."[20]

Meredith was giving voice to a notorious feature of colonialism in the mid-nineteenth century: the deployment of a pervasive racist discourse. Broader metanarratives of race, which circulated between the colonies and the metropole, were constructed around theories of degeneration, monogenism, or polygenism.[21] Margaret Jolly notes that ideas about race in this transitional period had not yet become the firm "hegemonic ideologies of evolutionism or Social Darwinism" that suffused science and the "popular ideologies of Europeans at home and abroad" after the publication of Charles Darwin's *On the Origin of the Species by Means of Natural Selection* in 1859.[22] Before Darwin, Europeans had increasingly applied ideas about the ranking of types to the peoples of the Pacific, and European colonial powers graded these societies according to their degree of civilization, which was based on how closely their social and political structures resembled those of Europe and, thus, were suitable for various European styles of governance. From the 1770s onward, Europeans contrasted Polynesians with Melanesians, and the latter attracted descriptors such as "darker," "more primitive," "hostile," "suspicious," and "ugly." In contrast, Polynesians such as Fijians were regarded by the British to be less warlike and more advanced than the Papuans or the Solomon Islanders. Meredith's Maori chief, with his "magnificent demeanor" and "true gentlemanly bearing," was likened to a European. By contrast, Aboriginal Australians were thought to represent "the lowest rank of humankind."[23]

In 1834 John Dunmore Lang provided another an example of the application of a classification system when he responded to Thomas Foxwell Buxton, the chairman of the Parliamentary Select Committee on the Aboriginal Tribes (British Settlements). Lang outlined prevalent ideas about ranking and classification, as well as the impact of colonization on Aboriginal peoples:

> The Aborigines of New South Wales are ranked by physiologists of the class Papuan Negro – they approximate the African in colour – texture of hair, sometimes woolly, wiry and often a compound of both in the thickness of the lips, cast of their eyes, [and] in the formation, thickness, and strength of their skulls ... they are divided into infinity of tribes speaking infinity of barbarous tongues, subsisting on whatever the river or forests spontaneously produces without clothing or houses, ignorant of manufacture and agriculture generally in a state of warfare with each other, in several of the groups of the Western Pacific they have mingled ... in general they are abject in the extreme, degraded in mind, and feeble in body. They are neither devoid of intelligence or destitute of capacity nor strangers to enjoyment ... they seem to have no idea of creator or Governor of the Universe ... Their state is made wretched by their hunting grounds being seized by Europeans ... they have been turned into a race of paupers and taught to beg their bread.[24]

George Arden, writing from Melbourne in 1841, also harshly racialized Aboriginal people, noting that "in comparison with New Zealanders or other foreign savages ... [Aborigines] can only be placed in the great animal family as one degree above the brute creation." The women, he wrote, "as in most savage nations, are considered beasts of burden; great restrictions are placed upon their movements, and none are allowed to participate in either the festivities or ceremonies of the men."[25]

By contrast, early European perceptions of Aboriginal people in British Columbia were far more generous. Early traders praised Aboriginal people's intelligence and acuity in trade, because, of course, they depended on it. In 1820 naturalist John Schouler, an employee of the Hudson's Bay Company, judged that Aboriginal peoples "especially the coast tribes, have made considerable progress in the rude arts of savage life ... their canoes are constructed with much skill; their houses being for permanent residence, have been erected with forethought and attention to comfort." Terms such as *abject* and *wanders* were not often applied, at least in the early fur trade period. Instead, Schouler valued

Aboriginal people's apparent permanency and material culture such as "fishing apparatus and articles of domestic economy."[26] As Stuart Banner has noted, one missionary paid people of the Northwest Coast the highest compliment when he declared that they were "superior to most other civilized nations"; indeed, the people of the Queen Charlotte Islands were "physically and mentally regarded as fine as a race of men can be met with." The missionary concluded, "They may be truly styled the 'Anglo-Saxons' of this coast."[27] As settlement and contact increased on the Northwest Coast, however, negative portrayals of Aboriginal peoples increased.

In Melbourne and Sydney, public debates about the Aboriginal question and the abolition of slavery in 1833 were peppered with meditations on the scientific status of Aboriginal people and questions about difference. Were Europeans and Aboriginal peoples of the same species? Debates about monogenism versus polygenism and about the idea of degeneration constituted a broad discourse on race – the race thinking that shaped thought in the first half of the nineteenth century. Amid Christian entreaties to admit the Aborigine into the fraternity and to treat him as a fellow man, opposing calls posited Aboriginal people as a dying race.

These may have been the theoretical and spiritual contours of the debates, but in the developing frontier townscape of Melbourne, the proximities and separations of the contact zone between Aboriginal people and Europeans were complex. Rather than hard segregations, there were fluidities and mutual dependencies that gave rise to a complex system of interactions and boundary demarcations. Aboriginal Protector William Thomas, a deeply Christian man, within his first few weeks in Melbourne, "where God had mercifully brought me," was ordered by Chief Protector Robinson to camp and travel with Aborigines from the Melbourne area in order to protect them. Immersed in the newness of his situation, Thomas hesitated. As Thomas recorded in his diary, on his "first night with the Aborigines," although an Aboriginal man had seen his thirst and hunger and brought him water and bread, he worried that it was "a black's pannikin, black's water ... I little thought that I should soon be glad to eat and lay down with the savage."[28] That night Thomas did not sleep but stayed up all night by candlelight. Nevertheless, over the next two decades Thomas would learn the Wurundjeri language (Woiwurrung) and become a constant advocate for Aboriginal people in and around Melbourne as he moved between the various camps that formed around the Melbourne grid. He, too, would become transculturated and refashioned by the contact zone.

In public discussions about the difference between Europeans and Aboriginal peoples, Aborigines were the raced subjects in colonial relations; their appearance, language, and behaviour were at all times the sites of scrutiny. But whiteness is also a racialized condition.[29] Current theory on whiteness asserts its invisibility. Yet the close attention to ranking that was paid in the nineteenth century reveals that there was, indeed, great self-conscious and rhetorical consideration of what constituted the Caucasian or Anglo-Saxon racial type, his (or her) physiognomy and habits.[30] In this first half of the nineteenth century, particular constructions of Anglo-Saxonism and Britishness in Australia, although naturalized and not subject to the same level of scrutiny as Aboriginality, were, nevertheless, promoted and set as the racial ideal. Whiteness was constituted first and foremost through not being Aboriginal, and, not surprisingly, it was an identity largely constituted as male. Louisa Meredith's public declaration of her Britishness was, thus, a rare moment.

In Melbourne, John Cotton, like many other colonists, listed superiority and industriousness as being the marks of the British, white race and declared that invasion was natural and just. Articulating the dynamic of displacement and replacement that is the keystone of settler colonialism, Cotton believed that Europeans were fulfilling nature's law by "replacing an inferior 'race' with their own superior kind." Celebrating this idea, he claimed that the "indolent savage has been supplanted by the industrious Briton." His descriptions of Aboriginal men were at times feminized. He note that "in general, [their] well-moulded forms are enveloped in a blanket, kangaroo or opossum rug, which some of them wear very gracefully ... I have seen some of the blacks walking the street of Melbourne who might have been termed the native dandies in town."[31]

Cotton's view of Aboriginal women was less harsh than that of some Europeans, notwithstanding his gaze as a European man: "The women ... are invariably attended by a considerable number of half-starved mongrel dogs, of which they appear to be particularly fond; the children or piccaninnies caress and play with them. There is great beauty in the well-moulded limbs and forms of the young native, and as they often have the right arm and shoulder bare, with the blanket folded around their bodies, there is a rude elegance in their appearance which is for me more pleasing to the eye than the fitted suit of the European."[32]

Spectacle and racialization in the streetscape were foremost about European titillation and self-fashioning. Despite occasionally sensitive observations, many travel narratives of the city portrayed Aboriginal people as misplaced and ridiculous. Such writing increasingly depicted the presence of Aboriginal people in cities as unnatural and illegitimate. In 1843, after he had seen an Aboriginal man and woman in the street, William Adeney noted in his diary, "Met two of the poor Aborigines looking almost like the inhabitants of another world."[33] When the spectacle was over, many Europeans saw Aborigines in towns as nothing more than nuisances. *The Australian* described them as "vagabonds ...

wandering through our streets, exhibiting symptoms of debasement and degradation ... whilst they have lost the unadorned simplicity of nature they have gained nothing of the refinements of civilisation."[34] The constant rendering of Aboriginal people as vagabonds, nuisances, or objects of ridicule made their presence in "civilized" urbanizing districts seem anomalous and prevents alternative readings of the urbanizing frontier in the present. For some writers the clear implication was that Aborigines could not survive the impact of urban European contact. This idea was a classic narrative of the settler-colonial society, whose goal was to replace Indigenous people on the land

   The emergence of settler-colonial cities involved the rapid reorganization of bodies and spaces. Aboriginal people were dislocated, rendered anomalous, and, hence, extraterritorialized as vagrants, but so too were Europeans at this edge of empire. Yet Europeans arrived by choice as tourists or settlers. As Zygmunt Bauman has observed, the tourist and the vagabond are "two halves of postmodern society. Both move through other's spaces"; both are "extraterritorial: the tourist by choice, the vagabond not. The vagabond is the alter ego of the tourist."[35] When Europeans saw Aboriginal people as vagrant or degraded, they were witnessing people transformed by colonial relations, just as they were also in the middle of transformation. As the majority of Europeans thrilled to the spectacle of the frontier town, others paid close attention to and lamented the bitter realities of the streetscape for Kulin peoples.

Spectacle to Surveillance: To Resist or Survive the Lure of the City

The "miam miam or huts," wrote Chief Protector Augustus Robinson, were "scattered over a beautiful eminence at the north-east corner of the township."[36] In 1839 Aboriginal people moved in and around the town of Melbourne; they had not remained on the south bank as officials had entreated. Although the main camp was on the south bank of the Yarra River, near the mission reserve land (now the Royal Botanic Gardens Melbourne), there were several camps that shifted frequently. Aborigines moved their camps between the northeast corner of the town, back across the river, and the northwest end of the city, behind Flagstaff Hill. The Wathawurrung often camped at this site, away from the Wurundjeri. In 1839 William Thomas, the newly appointed assistant protector of Aborigines in Melbourne, estimated that the Wurundjeri and Boonwurrung clans around Melbourne comprised around 230 people.[37] This was a significant drop from Langhorne's estimate three years earlier of "700 men, women and children," although this figure also included the Wathawurrung.

   By 1840 newspapers were announcing the rapid allotment and sale of land in triumphal tones, with the *Port Phillip Herald* noting: "The voice of the world has stamped Australia Felix as the most rising and prosperous colony of the globe. The daily, rapid, and astounding increase of the value of Town allotments has caused a general outcry that the township was not formed upon a scale sufficiently large. This defect, however, comes with its own remedy. The suburbs nearest the Town are now becoming part and parcel of the Town, and in a year these will really be the centre of the Town, possessing every advantage that nature and art can bestow."[38] The creation of a new settler-colonial space involved a ritual invocation of the future, the calling into being of a new and culturally distinct space of progress. As the *Port Phillip Patriot* put it in 1840, "Let Melbourne flourish! Still in grandeur rise – And rear her stately Buildings to the skies!"[39] But the swift spread, in both the imagination and geographically, of the cadastre was more than a one-way movement. European land grabbing pushed back Aboriginal clan lands, upset traditional boundary agreements, and caused intense strain on food resources, all of which led to disputes and conflict between Aboriginal groups.

Melbourne's urbanizing frontier must also be viewed against the backdrop of frontier violence and resistance. While town promoters were invoking "stately buildings rearing to the skies," the Kulin Nation and groups in outlying areas were engaged in sustained and at times effective guerrilla warfare throughout southeastern Australia.

The use of guerrilla warfare reached a peak in the Western District in the 1840s. Throughout southeastern Australia, from the Western district to Gippsland in the east, Aboriginal groups made surprise attacks on shepherds' huts and squatters' homes, sometimes burning them and taking goods. They often killed hut keepers, especially those who were known to have abused Aboriginal women.[40] Throughout central and northeast Victoria, Kulin groups carried on an equally extensive campaign.[41] They disrupted stock routes and drove off flocks of sheep; in some cases, they, like Europeans, fenced the sheep to use them for food. They often broke the legs of sheep and cattle to send out a clear message to the invaders, who were seeking to take Indigenous land and overrun it with stock.

European reprisals were often swift and vicious. After a visit to outlying stations, Charles Sievright, assistant Aboriginal protector for the Western District, related the sense of ominous violence to William Thomas: "The state of society in the interior towards the poor Aborigines is awful, out of sixteen stations ... but one (Mr. Airy) [was] humanely disposed to the Aborigines, 2 out of 16 ... visited had skulls of Aborigines placed over the door of their huts."[42] In the Port Phillip area, an estimate of all officially recorded conflicts between 1836 and 1844 stated that "40 whites and 113 Aborigines had been killed."[43] Yet officials routinely tried to obscure the high rate of Aboriginal deaths. As one police magistrate remarked in 1839: "A murder committed by the black is paraded in the papers, and everybody is shocked; but there have been hundreds of cold-blooded murders perpetrated by the whites on the outskirts of the Colony, which we have never heard of."[44]

Historians have recounted the prevalence of frontier violence and the regulation of Indigenous peoples in British Columbia. The frontier of southeastern Australia was likewise characterized by unrelenting violence against Aboriginal peoples, but it was of a much greater magnitude.[45] In British Columbia an early tradition of trade, interdependency, and mixed marriages mitigated some violent action. On the Australian pastoral frontier, land grabbing and settlement, which went virtually unchecked, led to rapacious violence.

In Melbourne rumours of frontier violence and concerns regarding the "Aboriginal problem" circulated constantly. There was intense concern and trepidation among Europeans who were hoping to "take up runs" in the new pastoral lands and among humanitarians and missionaries who held grave fears for the plight of Aboriginal peoples. Public meetings were held in churches and other venues to discuss the problem. William Adeney shared the concerns of both groups. Recently arrived from England and a church-going young man, he was not yet encumbered by the bitter prejudices against Aborigines held by those on the outer frontier. Yet, like many other eager speculators, he hoped to go up country to find a pastoral run. After attending a meeting in town with Wesleyan missionaries, Adeney wrote: "The reports of the natives' conduct are very bad and everyone seems at a complete loss what to advise for the prevention of these evils or the benefit of these unfortunate beings. There were tho' [sic] expressions I heard regarding their state at the Wesleyan Missionary meeting tonight. The attendance was small but the audience was attentive."[46] The tensions on the outlying frontier, between colonists who wanted fast access to pastoral lands and felt that "the life of Aborigines was nothing against the safety of stock and property" and those with humanitarian sentiments, would play themselves out in the townscape.[47] Partitions between the urbanizing and the pastoral frontiers in many historical accounts are artificial and overstated. Information and people circulated between the two frontiers, and the urbanizing frontier could be, for Aboriginal people, as violent as the pastoral frontier.

William Thomas and George Augustus Robinson, the Aboriginal protectors, had been sent to Port Phillip following the humanitarian campaign by evangelical Protestants at Exeter Hall and were "regarded with wariness by colonial authorities."[48] Suffering from a lack of government support and funds, and little or no assistance from the police, the protectors suffered constant frustrations. Opponents described the protectorate as a waste of government funds, and journalists frequently derided the protectors. The *Sydney Morning Herald* described them as "the whining crew who infest the colony" and noted with disdain that the "aborigines are not worth saving."[49] George Arden, voicing his hostility to the protectorate system, believed that "only a systematic separation of the child from their parents can ever promote the chance of a civil and religious education which must in itself be founded *upon habits of industry*." He also called for the spatial partition of Aboriginal peoples.[50]

As Jessie Mitchell surmises, protectors were charged with the task of "aggressively promoting British civilisation to Aboriginal people, whilst feeling out of place and morally besieged within white society." These contradictions were only heightened when protectors attempted to remove Aboriginal people from the town.[51] As racial antagonism increased on the pastoral frontier, the urban frontier was beset with tension and violence. The thrill of the spectacle may have been the privilege of recently arrived European tourists, but for Aboriginal people increased surveillance was the order of the day. The police magistrate and constables often refused to assist in the policing of crime against Aborigines and deferred all issues to do with them, as Aboriginal affairs, to the protectors. If, however, Aborigines committed infractions in town, John Cotton observed that "the police are active and they are sure to suffer.[52]

The archival records of the Port Phillip Aboriginal Protectorate, which was active between 1839 and 1849, are a rich source of information and provide a window on transactions in Melbourne between Aborigines and Europeans.[53] Letters between Protector Thomas, Chief Protector Robinson, and colonial officials reveal the continual movement of the Wurundjeri and Boonwurrung and other Kulin groups in and out of the growing Melbourne precinct. Although protectors repeatedly entreated them to stay out of Melbourne, Aboriginal people were strongly attracted to the town.

The Wurundjeri and Boonwurrung clans ventured into Melbourne to barter, buy munitions, exchange their labour, and sell goods such as skins and lyrebird feathers. In 1839 letters passed between the Aboriginal protectors and Charles La Trobe, superintendent of the Port Phillip District, regarding the sale of mission land adjacent to the town and its division into ten acre lots. As the town grew and filled rapidly with European immigrants, land was deemed to be too valuable and too close to Melbourne to be reserved as an Aboriginal Station.[54] When the Yarra River flooded in December 1839, Robinson saw it as a "fortunate occurrence," for he hoped that it might "prevent the folly of forming the town on the south side of the Yarra."[55] The protectors believed that Aboriginal people's contact with the vices of white settlers would morally degrade them; therefore, their exclusion from Melbourne was imperative to protect them and for humanitarian reasons. Yet fears among officials of cross-contamination or two-way pollution were also apparent. Thus, tensions moved both ways. While protectors tried to keep Aborigines out of the townscape, merchants, especially those selling munitions and alcohol, encouraged their presence in town. Civilizing Aboriginal people was part of the protectors' mandate but above all it seems that the surveillance and removal of Aborigines from Melbourne was the task that colonial officials pressed them to perform.

Disease and Violence

Aboriginal people in the vicinity of Melbourne suffered a radical interruption to their lifestyle and were frequently reported as being ill and starving. European diseases, particularly syphilis, passed from white men to Aboriginal women and took an enormous toll on the Aboriginal population. The Aboriginal camp on the south side of the Yarra River was beset with illness. On 4 May 1839, Robinson recorded that five Aborigines had died from dysentery and that "one little girl of tender years, supposed eight years, was grievously afflicted with venereal."[56] After visiting the camp the next day, Robinson compared the state of dispossessed Aboriginal people with that of Europeans who were benefitting from escalating land prices in town:

> I found them in a deplorable state of disease and wretchedness. Six deaths had taken place within a few days ... I visited each abode of misery and famine and was intensely excited at the scenes of misery I beheld, particularly when I contrasted it with the appearance possessed by the Europeans derived from their lands and the sale of their lands. Land has sold in Melbourne for £1200 per acre, 90 and 100 percent is also the acreage return for flock masters and yet the original occupiers of the soil are perishing with disease, want and the extreme of wretchedness. This is a disgrace to humanity. How much more reprehensible for a British government and for a Christian people to depict the languishing look, the outstretched arm of the patient to examine the pulse.[57]

Walking around town in August that same year, Robinson saw an Aboriginal family and summoned the doctor. "A man, his wife and a little boy. The man was extremely ill and had the venereal, the boy was dreadfully afflicted with ... hawse."[58]

Colonial commentators such as William Westgarth viewed Aborigines as beggars and thieves and recalled their "non-conformity of attire ... their temptation from offers of drink by thoughtless colonists, and their inveterate begging," which made them "a public nuisance."[59] To prevent begging and public nuisances, protectors made constant entreaties to Aborigines to stay out of town. In October Robinson wrote to assure Governor La Trobe that "I have much satisfaction in stating that the Aboriginal natives are retiring from the environs of the township ... they have been apprized [sic] that their coming to Melbourne is against the wishes of the Government and that a reservation of land will be shortly set apart for their use in the interior, where they can have provision, provided they give an equivalent, ie labour, for the same."[60]

Settler fear ran high, particularly when Aboriginal people were seen to accumulate firearms. Indeed, as was the case on the pastoral frontier, Aborigines in town obtained ammunition and firearms whenever they could. In October 1839 Thomas asked for police assistance in the Aboriginal camp, not only to remove drunken European men but also to help confiscate weapons, a duty he was required to perform. "I found 31 stand of arms among the natives and thought it my duty to deprive them of the same."[61] A constant refrain of the newspapers was that Aborigines should not have firearms, and Governor La Trobe frequently expressed his opposition to Aborigines possessing guns. He wrote to Robinson, "you have doubtless, in common with myself and the whole of this neighbourhood, remarked on the recent discharge of firearms, by day and night in the black encampment on the left bank of the Yarra Yarra."[62]

Protector's reports show that Aboriginal people were attacked repeatedly in the town for behaviour that Europeans perceived as begging. For example, in 1839 a young Aborigine known as "An.note" complained to Robinson that a "white man had struck him and knocked him down with his fist near MacNall's, the butcher, because he asked for bread."[63] While Robinson was in the street, an Aboriginal man came to him to complain that a "white person" had assaulted him by "striking him with a stick and kicking him." Later, an Aboriginal woman who had been begging for bread with her children came to Robinson with a note. "Some blackguard," wrote Robinson, "had given this to the poor creature as her request for bread. It read, 'Mr. Baly, give the bearer a good licking, Bill Cheeks, Esq.'"[64] Nunupton, an Aboriginal man, was tied up and flogged in the street by Dr. Farquhar McCrae (the brother-in-law of the painter and diarist Georgiana McCrae), who claimed that Nunupton had robbed him.[65]

William Thomas recounts a similar event that occurred that same year. Karngrook and Bulbegunner, two Aboriginal women, were near the butcher's on Little Collins Street. It is likely that they were hoping to get some meat. Aboriginal people regularly lined up at the abattoirs to do this. "Thomas Whitehead, the butchers assistant, set a large dog on them." Thomas continues, "Two highly respectable gentlemen Mr Gordon MacArthur, & Mr Henty were passing at the time ... had it not been for the humane exertions of these gentlemen, the poor women must have sustained great injury, the two gentleman willingly offered to appear and give evidence against the brutal conduct of the man." The police magistrate, however, "refused to grant a summons, stating that he would have nothing to do with Aboriginal affairs." Thomas wrote out a legal summons and served it himself. His calls for constabulary assistance to defend Aboriginal people in the street were regularly ignored.[66]

Despite town violence, there was a strong desire on the part of Aborigines to come into town, where they could obtain food and ammunition by whatever means. Thomas wrote the following to Robinson from an encampment at Arthur's Seat, which was around the bay and southwest of Melbourne:

> The Native encampment is much ruffled owning to the desire to visit the settlement ... and that the white people at Melbourne say where is Mr. Thomas and the other Blackfellows ... I learn further that the [women] are sent in daily and that they are encouraged by the whites to bring in the men, also that the women are supplied with powder and shot, and convey it to the men. I am now fearful that the Blacks will break up the encampment as they now have [the] idea that Melbourne is flowing with milk and honey.[67]

Aboriginal incursions into settler space were frequently reported in newspapers and expressed in the language of fear. Aboriginal "bands" that ventured into farms or gardens suffered violent reprisals. The *Port Phillip Herald's* hyperbolic reportage included an account of the "notorious Jacky Jacky" and his "strong party of armed blacks," who committed "depredations" on settlers near the Yarra River. According to the account, they dug up a farmer's field of potatoes with sticks during the night. For this crime, mounted and border police followed them for several days and around ten miles up the Yarra River. Several gun battles ensued.[68]

The raid may have been an act of guerrilla warfare, but it was also a necessity: Aboriginal people in the region were starving because many had been pushed off their traditional lands. Thomas wrote about the scarcity of food in the main camp and how colonization had interrupted traditionally gendered food-gathering roles: "Almost all men and women and children off to catch mussels. Quite an uncommon occurrence for men, they complain of being plenty hungry."[69] It was the same on the pastoral frontier, where Protector James Dredge wrote of the Daungwurrung peoples of the Goulburn River region, which was northeast of Melbourne, being so hungry that they would "part with anything for a trifle to eat or drink."[70]

Aboriginal women were sent by Aboriginal men into town to collect provisions and ammunition. In the push and pull of public space, Aborigines monitored tensions and the level of European hostility towards them, and they sensed when it would be safe to venture into the streetscape. As the *Port Phillip*

Herald noted after the "affray with the notorious Jacky Jacky," few Aborigines from this group had come into town. However, "about the middle of last week the women and children belonging to the Melbourne tribe came into town, evidently being sent as pioneers to feel the way and to ascertain whether the excitement ... [had] abated to allow the males of the tribe making their appearance without risk."[71]

There was little official tolerance for the formation of Aboriginal camps in or near town. When, in April 1840, six or seven hundred Kulin peoples collected in one camp for regular ceremonial meetings, their mia mias were burnt, the camp was dismantled, and Thomas persuaded the punt men to "stop all other traffic and carry them over to the south side of the Yarra."[72] Thomas wrote, "Confusion in the camp, many afraid, the camp consisted of Woiwurrung and Boonwurrung 203, Mount Macedon 87, and Barrabools, 95, and Goulburn 496." Aborigines were put on the punt and forced back to the south side of the river. Registering the distress and the spectacle of the scene, Thomas wrote, "There was one punt load of 187 men women and children and it was a curious sight, all spears up, to behold the owners of the soil wretched, diseased."[73]

Under the governance of La Trobe, who arrived in Melbourne on 3 October 1839, Aborigines who continued to come into Melbourne to beg and to buy munitions were less welcome. As a frustrated La Trobe would write to Robinson in September 1840: "A number of the Blacks had again made their appearance in the streets of the town and requesting that you would take measures to induce them to remove – since that their numbers have been evidently on the increase ... I find that the utmost exertion of the constables and of the policeman ... your exertions and influence ... is quite insufficient to keep them out of the town boundary."[74] La Trobe complained that Aborigines were encouraged to come to town, particularly by vendors of arms and ammunitions, "in whose shops they are seen not only by day but even after dark."[75] Despite La Trobe's previous colonial administrative experience in the West Indies – where he adjudicated education systems for recently emancipated slaves – and his reputation as an effective administrator who created prosperity and good governance for the Port Phillip region, he was harsh towards Aboriginal people around the town precinct and deployed the military and police to remove them.

At dawn on 11 October 1840, for instance, Major Samuel Lettsom, a mounted Army Corp, and fifty-eight soldiers and police rode into the Aboriginal camp, which is on the site of the present-day Melbourne Cricket Ground. Four to five hundred Aborigines – the Wurundjeri, Boonwurrung, and Daungwurrung – were aggressively "rounded up."[76] The Aborigines had gathered in the town for traditional ceremonial purposes. That a relatively small group of Aborigines could make a town of around five thousand immigrants so anxious reveals the level of the settlers' fear and Governor La Trobe's impatience with Aboriginal people.

Lettsom's party had followed the Daungwurrung, Aboriginal people from the land northeast of Melbourne around the Goulburn River valley, to Melbourne after an attempt to apprehend Aboriginal leaders thought to be responsible for attacks on settlers' huts in this region. The Governor of New South Wales, Sir George Gipps, had directed Lettsom and a detachment of soldiers to apprehend the leaders. When Lettsom demanded that Thomas "hand over a number of the more 'troublesome' Aborigines," Thomas objected because there were no warrants for the men's arrest. The Daungwurrung may have sought protection in Melbourne, but on 10 October, while Thomas was away, La Trobe granted permission for Lettsom to march on the Aboriginal camp and apprehend the Daungwurrung men.[77] La Trobe may have wanted to teach the Aborigines a lesson and inculcate fear of British military strength, but he was aware that "no tragedy of such dubious legality" could occur under his watch. He warned Lettsom "that nothing but extreme and imperative necessity can palliate the shedding of blood."[78] La Trobe endorsed this display of British military power and discipline.

Aborigines were marched into town, pricked with soldiers' bayonets, and beaten with the butt end of muskets. One Aborigine, Windberry, who resisted arrest was shot, although no command had been given to fire.[79] When Protector Edward Stone Parker visited the corralled prisoners, they were terrified and asked, "why had they been driven like sheep into this place?" Aborigines feared they were to be "sent in a big ship to Sydney." Protector Parker assisted in freeing "all but 30 of Goulburn Aborigines." Later that night one of the remaining Aborigines was shot and another was wounded as they attempted to break out of the storehouse in which they were imprisoned.[80]

By this time the Port Phillip press was decidedly anti-Aboriginal in sentiment. When the *Port Phillip Gazette* reported the incident, it stated that it was "indubitable ... that very many allowances" should be made for "the black passions of the black marauder" but warned against any sympathy that settlers may have for the captured Aborigines. According to the report, those who "assert the harmlessness of the native ... compromise their own safety by a liberal abuse of the whites." The author called to "set at rest ... maudlin sympathy for the natives" and announced that "any settler who has suffered from their ferocious and treacherous habits to ride into town now and identify the transgressor!"[81]

Hanmer Bunbury, who recalled a private conversation with La Trobe following the Lettsom incident, noted that officials feared that the numbers of

Aborigines had "become quite alarming, between 4 and 500 fighting men having mustered at one of their residences." He believed that "some of the black servants employed in the town" had alerted whites that the "tribes" would "attack the town in the night and make a general massacre."[82] Merely a month after the Lettsom incident, the Aborigines, asserting their presence on their own land, insisted on camping around the Melbourne precinct. Thomas complained in his journal: "From sunrise to sunset spent arguing, reasoning and persuading the Natives – They declare they will not remove and persist in going to Melbourne ... I again tell them that they make Willums [huts] on White mans ground, and cut down trees and cut off bark, make White Man sulky – they say no White mans ground, Black mans."[83]

Double Vision along the Yarra: Bifurcated Space and Gaps in the Grid

Throughout the 1840s Aborigines moved in and out of town space and camped all along the Yarra River. Yet Sarah Bunbury could walk the same river in 1841 and see an entirely different cultural space. "I am charmed with Australia dear Mama and Papa," she wrote in a letter home. Bunbury described the houses of Europeans along the banks of the river as "very pretty English cottages," and she wrote that "at the back of the house was a pretty plantation of gum trees and mimosas ... thinned out enough to make it look like an English park."[84] Although Bunbury's husband, Hanmer, freely registered his own hostile adjudications of Aboriginal people, until she viewed a corroboree in 1843, Sarah never mentioned in her many letters home either seeing or encountering a single Aboriginal person.

White women settlers were significant actors in the process of settlement and complicit in the dispossession of Aboriginal lands. Yet, as residents of the private sphere, white women's contact with Indigenous peoples was often limited or brokered by white men.[85] Nevertheless, some white women were keen, if partial, observers, and they sometimes defied Victorian conventions. The diarist and painter Georgiana McCrae, for instance, commented on Aboriginal people lining up for meat at the abattoirs in Melbourne. She also wrote about crossing the Yarra River on a punt with two Aboriginal men and an Aboriginal woman and about her own children playing with Aboriginal children camped along the Yarra River. McCrae's writings on Aborigines, however, were scant and remained within the bounds of gentility. She did not mention that her brother-in-law, Farquhar McCrae, had tied and beaten an Aboriginal man in the street, nor did she chronicle the nefarious activities of white men in the Native camp.[86]

If Aborigines barely existed for some Europeans, others wrote much about their presence. This double vision, the strange bifurcated space of the colonial

Figure 10   Native Encampment on the Banks of the Yarra, ca. 1845, watercolour (artist, John Cotton). State Library of Victoria.

encounter, was one in which Aborigines were at once absent and present to the colonial eye. It tells us of the intimacy and distance of the colonial encounter, although the intimacy was sometimes forced and the distance sometimes willful.

As the cadastral spread of private property moved outward into Indigenous lands, it was in unallotted spaces such as riverbanks, road reserves, and swamps that the Wurundjeri and Boonwurrung remained safe. Denis Byrne has observed that because the cadastral spread halted at shorelines, rivers became zones of freer movement for Aboriginal peoples, who had boats or canoes. "Water was a neutral unsegregated zone, and from an Aboriginal point of view a gap in the cadastre."[87] The Merri Creek and the Yarra River became, therefore, sanctuaries in an increasingly allotted network of private property in the town and an uneven but burgeoning cadastre of fenced paddocks in the surrounding pastoral lands. Many images and accounts exist of Aborigines camping along the Merri Creek or the Yarra and Maribyrnong rivers (see Figure 10). William Thomas regularly recorded his visits to various small encampments up and down the Merri Creek. In 1841 he visited the camp near Darebin, where there were "68 people of the Yarra and Goulburn with eight young Western Port men."[88] Two white women, he wrote, were very frightened at the sight of the large group of Aborigines with spears in hand, and local "settlers all came to watch a corroboree at night."[89]

Spaces along the creeks were transitional within the process of colonization; they were nervous spaces that were not yet property. Even as Aboriginal people lived along its banks, the Merri Creek was being auctioned off lot by lot. In 1840 the *Port Phillip Gazette* printed announcements for the public auction of 150 acres.[90] To the "capitalist and speculator of land," it exclaimed, "very little need be said of the profits of such a speculation ... [as] the smiling faces and well-lined pockets amply testify." The advertisement appealed to settlers, tradesmen, yeomen, and others in Port Phillip, and it assured them that they would be "laying the stepping stone of a fortune for their offspring."[91] The processes of invasion and colonization swiftly reordered bodies and spaces. New spaces were forming, and Indigenous and non-Indigenous lives were altered in the transactional contact zone.

The rapid conversion of Indigenous lands into property created land mania in Port Phillip. A cycle of boom was followed, however, by a financial bust, which impoverished many Europeans. The state of false opulence that prevailed in Melbourne in 1841 was evoked vividly in the writing of Hanmer Bunbury, who described a "castle in the air" and the "imaginary state of wealth and prosperity" caused by the uncontrolled sale of land. While women dressed in the "richest silks, satins, and velvets," which "swept the dust and mud of Melbourne," a property collapse was occurring.[92] This intense cycle of property speculation only intensified the rapid dispossession of Aboriginal peoples. The settler-colonial city was, thus, less a site than a *process* by which Indigenous land was quickly converted to individual property allotments. As settler-colonial towns became incorporated and commodified spaces, as they shifted from the more fluid places of mercantilism to nodes in an increasingly industrialized economy, legislation that upheld the new spatial order was designed and enacted by town officials to regulate Aboriginal peoples and segregate them from the white population.

The Town Council

The settlement of Melbourne was incorporated in 1842 and administered by the Melbourne Town Council (which would become the Melbourne City

Council in 1847).[93] The council was a tight-knit group of men, mainly over-straiters from Van Diemen's Land, who ran the town "in defence of the corporation."[94] The council was the administrative apparatus that shaped the town into a civilized, ordered cognate of mid-nineteenth-century British urban space.

The Melbourne Town Council addressed the demarcation of wards or precincts, the building of roads and drains, the administration of Crown Lands, the establishment of town rates, the protection of the water supply, and the erection of bridges and public buildings. Council members envisaged Melbourne as a place of civilization and control. The high productivity of these city shapers in the month of September 1843 shows just how profound the effects of incorporating social space could be. On 12 September councillors dealt with a reply to their letter "requesting the removal of all prisoners of the Crown from their district." At the same meeting, they "resolved that ... a committee be appointed to consider the best means of ridding the town of the nuisance of the mangy dogs which follow in the train of the Aborigines."[95] The regulation of dogs in the settlement was a device white settlers used in the continued surveillance of Aborigines. In 1844 a bylaw was passed that allowed them to do so.[96] During the September 1843 meeting, the council also resolved that the town surveyor "lay a portion of a street or streets with wooden pave similar to that recently adopted in the City of London."[97] Thus, in its attempt to fashion an urban environment with spatial signatures that were bourgeois and British, the council gradually cleaned up Melbourne town. Attempts were made to eradicate rubbish, offal, dogs, nightsoil, noise, convicts, and Aborigines from the urban landscape through surveillance, bylaws, and fines. Even street noise would come to be viewed as barbarous, and a bylaw was passed to regulate excessive noise.[98] The council addressed the social and cultural aspects of town life by seeking to create an education system. As early as 1843, it marked out a site in the city for the instruction of urban subjects through science, education and industry. Batman's Hill, when compared to "any part of the globe," was deemed a site "in every way eligible" for a "superb botanical gardens" and marine and fresh water aquariums, which would "promise such advantages in a scientific and practical point of view for developing the resources of the province." Such an "object," the minutes noted, would be "intimately connected with the health, comfort and amusement of the inhabitants."[99]

These developments represented incipient bourgeois metropolitanism in the colonies. Robert Rotenburg has described this trend of the eighteenth and nineteenth centuries as it occurred in European cities, where such a movement was a transnational effort to refashion cities in a bourgeois image and through a capitalist process of investment. The transformation, reordering, and rationalization of cities included the reconstruction of London and Paris, which incorporated ideas about rational space, open boulevards, private property, sanitation, and central civic buildings.[100] All of this activity relied on capital from a colonial economy: transnational colonialism financed metropolitanism. Financial and cultural circuits of empire ensured that metropolitan and colonial cities co-produced one another, just as European and Indigenous subjectivities were mutually imbricated in the colonies and the metropole. Just as the metropolitans of London, Paris, and Vienna made money and built prestige from the colonial economy, a new class of wealthy metropolitans emerged in the colonies. The discursive similarities between James Silk Buckingham's treatise on model towns and the contemporaneous colonial work *Melbourne As It Is and Ought to Be* reveal the transimperial circuits of nineteenth-century city shaping.

Yet there were tremendous tensions between the imagined bourgeois city and the *lived* city. Rotenburg writes, "Metropolitanism creates an imaginary city of heightened possibilities that interacts with the place of lived experience to produce dislocations. This lived experience was one of severe housing shortages, disease epidemics, political uncertainty, rapid population growth, and an informational explosion."[101] The cities of Britain and Europe did not, however, contain expropriated Indigenous populations. Tensions between the city of the bourgeois imagination and the lived colonial city were much more dramatic.[102] The Melbourne Town Council laid pave to enhance its similarity to London; for the same reason, councillors sought the removal of Aborigines and criminals and, later, objected to "coolie and cannibal" labour.[103] The Melbourne Town Council was building a city and shaping a desirable colonial polity that was classed and racialized.

The "Inconvenience and Immorality of Aborigines in Town"

Throughout the 1840s the surveillance and regulation of Aboriginal people in the developing town space was an issue of intense concern. This "problem" was often left to the Aboriginal protectors, but the "evils" of Aboriginal people's presence in town were raised intermittently in town council meetings. In May 1845 it was moved that the "Mayor be requested to address his Honour the Superintendent William Lonsdale and the Chief Protector of the Aborigines, on the increasing inconvenience and demoralisation attendant on the presence of the Blacks within the Town."[104] Later that month a letter was read to the council "from His Honour the Superintendent in reply to the Mayor's communication on the evils resulting from the presence of the Aborigines within the Town. Letter ordered to be considered and the next Council meeting." The index of the council minutes lists the "Inconvenience and Immorality of the Blacks being in the town" and notes that "Bathing within prescribed limits by Aborigines – disallowed."[105] Council proceedings and bylaws of the mid-1840s reveal developing colonial manoeuvres to shape the city and regulate its inhabitants, especially Aborigines, at the day-to-day level.

In town, shared amenities such as the punt, water pumps, and bathing areas increasingly became contested sites. In 1844 the punt man reported the "bad conduct of the Aborigines" and deposited a long report with authorities.[106] Newspapers complained about the "hordes of mangy dogs" in the train of Aboriginal women and the "inconvenience" of their habit of washing their dogs at water pumps. The *Port Phillip Gazette* reported that the "chief constable complained to the bench that the aboriginal women were constantly in the habit of taking their wretched mangy hounds to the banks of the Yarra" close to the pumps, to the "infinite annoyance of the inhabitants." The police magistrate directed that "if any of them should be found so offending ... they should be taken into custody."[107]

Newspapers frequently complained about "diseased quadrupeds" being brought into Melbourne, and the town council's Mangy Dog Committee used bylaws to eradicate streets dogs. This was also a way to regulate Aborigines in the streets. The *Port Phillip Gazette,* recounting the proceeding of the Mangy Dog Committee, noted Alderman Russell's comment that "the numerous mangy dogs in the town are an insufferable nuisance." Russell was, the article reported, "equally anxious that mangy bipeds should be got rid of, but that was a more difficult achievement."[108] The Dog Act ensured that diseased dogs, if unregistered, were routinely killed in the streets. They were "tailed," hung from trees, and beaten to death. "Each police constable received 2s. 6d. for every tail brought to the police office.[109] William Thomas wrote in his journal that Aboriginal women in one of the town camps "cried for their dogs," but the women, unobserved by the constables, were later given meat by the butchers. A week later the Aboriginal group left the settlement "on account of their dogs being killed."[110] Incorporation and early efforts at sanitation were used in the surveillance and segregation of Aboriginal peoples. As will be shown later, segregation in British Columbia reached greater regulatory heights through the application of direct bylaws, violence, and organized sanitation drives.

In Melbourne, foot police and the constant violence of settlers were used to move Aborigines outside of town limits. The minutes of the Melbourne Town Council increasingly described Aboriginal peoples as inconvenient wanderers or nuisances, as impediments to the development of urban space. What does it mean to be described as inconvenient or to be a nuisance in the colonial townscape? In a sense, these categories were synonymous with vagrancy. Karl Marx's words on vagrancy in Britain after the Enclosure Acts are illuminating. Marx wrote of "the forcible expropriation of the people from the soil ... these men suddenly dragged from their wonted mode of life, could not as suddenly adapt themselves to the *discipline of their new condition* they were turned *en masse* into beggars, robbers, vagabonds, partly from inclination, partly from stress of circumstances."[111] This is not to say that Aboriginal people were an expropriated proletariat. Rather, I draw attention to the expropriation of Indigenous land and, importantly, the new regime to which Indigenous peoples were exposed, the "discipline of their new condition," that is, an emerging colonial modernity. The settler-colonial order, which made them landless, also constructed Aboriginal people as inconvenient, anomalous, and vagrant. As Judith Butler asserts, bodies were produced *materially* and "tend to indicate a world beyond themselves."[112] Settler colonialism, as a transformative structure, produced Aborigines materially as nuisances and vagrants in the urbanizing landscape. The 1837 report of the Parliamentary Select Committee on the Aboriginal Tribes recognized this and sought to overturn the very conditions that had created Indigenous "vagrancy" – that is, the loss of land – and advised that "no vagrancy laws or other regulations should be allowed, the effect of which might be to cripple the natives by preventing them selling their labour at the best price, and at the market most convenient for themselves."[113]

One of the internal paradoxes of colonialism was that Aboriginal people were described repeatedly as vagrant, but the law at that time could not constitute them as such. The Vagrancy Act could not, in fact, simply be applied in Port Phillip. Legislation to prevent vagrancy in the Colony of New South Wales, for instance, was aimed specifically at non-Indigenous people. It stated that

> every person not being a black native or the child of any black native found lodging or wandering in company with any of the black natives of this Colony shall ... give a good account to the satisfaction of such Justice that he or she hath a lawful fixed place of residence in the Colony and lawful means of support and that such lodging or wandering hath been for some temporary and lawful occasion only and hath not continued beyond such occasion ... shall be deemed an idle and disorderly person ... and it shall be lawful for any Justice of the Peace to commit such ... to His Majesty's nearest gaol or house of correction there to be kept to hard labour for any time not exceeding three calendar months."[114]

The particular qualifier that Europeans who were "found lodging or wandering in company with any of the black natives" were to be especially targeted is of interest. The legislation appears to have been used partly as means to curtail the mixing of European and Aboriginal people.

Kulin peoples had fulfilled a crucial role in the Port Phillip settlement since 1836, because the district was "without benefit of any description from convict labour."[115] Recruited as servants and used opportunistically as itinerant labourers,

Figure 11   View of Melbourne, Port Phillip, 1843 (artist, W.F.E. Liardet).
State Library of Victoria.

Aborigines chopped wood, made and bartered brooms, carried water, and sold goods such as skins and lyrebird feathers. In addition, some young Aboriginal boys and men entered labour contracts. Aboriginal labour was a necessary part of the early settler town and the local colonial economy.

In 1837 the Select Committee recommended that Aboriginal labour contracts should not exceed twelve months and "the servant should be in the fullest sense of the term free to abandon or to continue service at his discretion." Every contract, it noted, "should be made in the presence of the officer specially appointed for that purpose."[116] In the early years of the settlement, William Thomas had often negotiated labour contracts for employment in town on behalf of Aborigines. Casual and contractual labour agreements ensured that Aborigines and Europeans were closely acquainted. Wurundjeri and Boonwurrung people well understood the nature of "white money" and the terms of contractual labour. While many Aborigines may not have wished to engage in the colonial economy, some, orphaned by violence on the frontier, found themselves at a young age working in white homes as servants. Aboriginal men asserted their right to a contractual agreement when they could. A man known as "Pigeon" complained to Robinson that he had not received wages for his labour from his erstwhile master, the "founder" of Melbourne, John Batman.[117] As the European immigrant population grew, however, Aborigines were not required as labourers.

Representations: View of Melbourne, Port Phillip

In the settler-colonial cities of the mid-nineteenth century, racialization was mobilized in tandem with bourgeois metropolitanism in powerful ways. In the streetscape, bourgeois power was constituted through far more than property relations and the surveillance of people. Bourgeois power, as Rotenburg writes, shifted from a mere hold on property to "participation in the cultural performances in the representational space of the central district, and separation from the excluded colonial classes."[118] In Melbourne, city and colonial officials attempted to control physical and imaginative space in just this way. Partition was expressed and maintained through representations of Aborigines in paintings, cartoons, and sketches of the urban landscape to bolster colonial myths of settler-colonial space and the public order.

In 1843 the Melbourne Town Council responded to the painter W.F.E. Liardet's request to buy his painting of the town. They responded that the "painting was inspected by the Council, but as it appears to be unfinished in some particulars they deferred complying with Mr. Liardet's request until the painting was complete."[119] The painting was the panoramic *View of Melbourne, Port Phillip* (1843) (see Figure 11), which remains an iconic representation of early Melbourne. In the foreground a dramatic scene takes place. Charles La Trobe, the superintendent; Henry Condell, the mayor; and Major St. John, the police magistrate gallop on finely bred horses to a camp of Aborigines on the south bank of the Yarra River. The Aborigines fight one another and throw weapons in classicized poses.

The Melbourne Town Council had the final jurisdiction over this image of the new settler-colonial space. Many have interpreted this painting a being a mere panoramic vision of 1843. The theatrical action in the foreground, however, highlights the triple exercise of power by the government, the council, and the police over the management of Aboriginal peoples and the maintenance of the colonial order. Tony Birch was correct when he observed that "control of the Australian landscape [was] vital to the settler psyche."[120] Narratives of the urban landscape were as important as its physical control.

Despite many attempts to partition Aboriginal people from the town, small camps of Aboriginal people continued to shift around on the outskirts of the growing town grid until the early 1850s. In 1845 William Thomas visited seven encampments. Figure 12, which is based on Thomas' notes, shows the placement of the camps. According to Thomas, there were 72 Yarras at the east camp, 130 Barrabools and Western Port at the south camp, and 36 Barrabools at the north camp. Another camp north of the grid held 176 Mount Macedon and Bonnyongs, while two more camps to the east held 138 Mogoollumbeek and Devils River Goulburns and 62 Goulburns.[121] Farther out, Aborigines continued to camp along the Merri Creek at St. Kilda and up beyond Sydney Road at Keilor.[122]

Thomas regularly made rounds of the camps to check on Aboriginal people, attend to the sick, serve as their advocate when they were ill or in jail, negotiate with police, and translate in court on their behalf. The "poor Aborigines," wrote Thomas, "are now compelled almost to shift at the will & caprice of the whites."[123] By 1849 the growth of Melbourne was so great that Thomas recorded that there were two main camps, one at St. Kilda and the other three miles southeast of the Yarra River, and that Aborigines were moving farther from Melbourne as the city's cadastre spread. That same year the punt men were ordered not to allow Aborigine people across the Yarra River, and La Trobe asked missionaries to "keep the Aborigines totally out of Melbourne."[124]

In 1850 German immigrants Johann and Carl Graf wrote home and noted that there were few Aboriginal people in Melbourne. This is what newcomers to Melbourne encountered, and it may have appeared natural, but the segregation of Aboriginal people was due to the constant surveillance of William Thomas. In the early 1850s, Thomas spent large amounts of his time travelling by horse between the various camps to urge Aboriginal people to stay out of Melbourne.[125]

By 1850 imaginative visions of Melbourne had become thoroughly racialized. Writers such as the author of *Melbourne As It Is and Ought to Be* articulated a

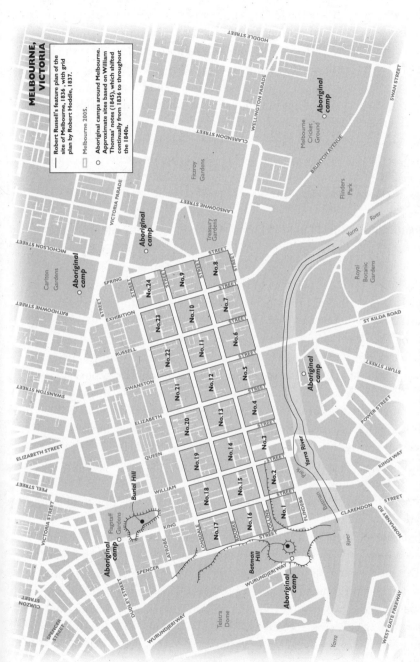

Figure 12 A comparative view of Melbourne based on Robert Russell's feature plan (1836) and a contemporary map of metropolitan Melbourne (2005). Aboriginal camps are marked and are estimates of locations mentioned in William Thomas's journal entry of 1845. Cartography by Paul de Leur.

vision of Melbourne shaped by bourgeois metropolitanism, but its disjunctures were markedly apparent. As David Hamer has observed, the more extravagant the optimism preached by the promoters, and "the more determined they were to focus attention on the certainty of the great and glorious future for their city, the more likely it was that they were seeking to draw attention away from a present that was characterized by confusion, division and doubt."[126] With an aim to promote unqualified optimism, promoters and town officials rarely mentioned poverty or the expropriated Aboriginal population and its constant segregation and surveillance in the streetscape. Yet heightened ideas of a regulated town space and notions of racial purity were offset by the lived actualities of empire. The refutations of Aboriginal peoples produced tensions and disjunctures in a nervous landscape.

The Intimate Urban: Town Camps, Unwholesome Places, and Other Spaces

In the midst of town creation, violence, and attempts to regulate urban space and impose colonial order, other spaces formed. Aboriginal camps at the perimeters of town were countersites to increasingly regulated city space. The Aboriginal camp on the south side of the Yarra River was an unpoliced site that lay outside of the emerging city grid, and it was perceived by Europeans as a place of entertainment, drunkenness, gunfire, violence, and interracial sex.

Aboriginal camps at the edges of Melbourne were visited constantly by prying visitors throughout the 1840s. Europeans ventured by the punt or by boat across the Yarra River to the south bank to view the main camp near the mission tents either for amusement or for far more pernicious reasons. Sailors, anticipating drunken festivities, often went to the camp at night, and other men, seeking sexual relations with Aboriginal women and girls, appeared regularly at night or during the day. Aboriginal camps were far more than spectacle – to Europeans they were spaces of powerful allure.

Strolling through the Aboriginal encampment was akin to a titillating tour of the dark slums of London, where the inquisitive middle-class observer could be thrilled and appalled by the daily lives of the lower orders. The Aboriginal camp was a lure for whites, just as the white town was a lure for Aboriginal people. Despite the attempts by authorities and vagrancy laws that were specifically aimed at partitioning whites and Aborigines, it was impossible to stop contact between the two groups. In 1844 William Thomas wrote despairingly about the main camp across the Yarra River in his journal: "So many whites in the camp today it was like a regular promenade."[127]

The imagined city and its dislocations are clear. British imperialists were confident in this spatial order, which was manifested in the grid and built form of the city and its power to both produce and discipline subjects. Yet monolithic projections from the metropole simply did not bear out in the urbanizing spaces of the empire's periphery. Instead, mixed, uneasy, and transformative spaces formed, and they were shaped as much by Indigenous people as newcomers. How can we understand and give political meaning to these emerging colonial spaces? New forms of conceiving social space inspired by ideas about contact zones, heterotopias, other spaces, and hybridized spaces are perhaps more productive ways of understanding the lived, local socio-spatial relations of the colonial city. Foucault's heterotopia, or other space, has been described as a way forward in the apprehension of "contested heterogeneous social space."[128] As Foucault noted, these sites have the "curious property of being in relation to all the other sites in such a way as to suspect, neutralise or invert the set of relations that they happen to designate, mirror or reflect."[129] They are not necessarily sites of resistance. In the case of colonial Melbourne, I suggest that Aboriginal camps were powerful heterotopias or other spaces that transgressed and undermined the imaginary coherence of the British settler-colonial city.

The main Aboriginal camp on the south bank of the Yarra River was next to a large swamp. Swamps are designated in the European imagination as representing all things bad. They are seen as liminal, dystopian spaces that are neither picturesque nor useful: they are wasteland. In his exploration of the iconography and phenomenology of wetlands, Rodney Giblett notes their description as "black water," which has "incipient racist associations."[130] Swamps cannot be transgressed, measured, or allotted easily. Nor can they easily be converted into propertied, commodified space. Giblett reminds us of the way swamps, or black waters, have been seen as horrific places, as places associated with death and disease.[131]

Yet swamps were a place of plenitude, a great source of food, for Aboriginal people. No matter how they were configured in the European imagination, the camps – which were created through colonialism, however temporary or violent – were the homes of Aboriginal people. Sitting unsettlingly at the edges of the Melbourne town grid and across the river, the Aboriginal camp was for Europeans the equivalent of the demimonde. Such places were sites of desire, but they were also required by the settler-colonial project. In this sense they cannot be read simplistically as sites of resistance or as part of an underworld. The Aboriginal camp was not a "natural" entity, it was constituted in relation to other spaces of colonization.

In Melbourne the south bank of the Yarra River near the swamp was not only reserved for Aboriginal people, it was also designated as place for the lower orders. The site of "tent city," where excess populations of immigrants were placed, highlighted the mutual processes of colonization and immigration in the development of settler cities. In October 1839 Protector Robinson wrote about the latest group of immigrants, "all Scotch," who had arrived on the *David Clark*. Robinson noted that 250 people camped in 50 tents and that the "natives are camped next to them."[132] At night large parties of newly arrived immigrants congregated near the camp to watch corroborees. The immigrant camp was a transient space for dislocated Europeans; it was also a countersite to the permanent allotments of the propertied town space. Aboriginal people had nothing except displacement in common with these boatloads of newcomers.

The spectacle of the camp resonated through colonial culture in multiple ways. Sketches and pamphlets describing Aboriginal people were sold to new arrivals (often circulating back to the metropole) or were included in colonists' accounts of their journey to Australia Felix. As late as 1849, several Aboriginal camps continued to shift location around the edge of Melbourne's grid. That year Ernst Bernhardt Heyne wrote home to Dresden, "I can relate something about the Aborigines of the district, because I have succeeded not only in getting some brochures about them, but also because there was a large camp of them quite close to our park. I visited them nearly every night. Probably there is scarcely a more miserable folk living on the earth than these."[133]

The allure of the Aboriginal camp was based on the promise of spectacle, but its allure was also about the attraction of otherness, contact, and interracial sex. As scholars studying gender, colonialism, and space have demonstrated, the settler-colonial frontier was not an outward-moving linear abstraction, it was often domestic, local, and personal.[134] In Australia's urban landscape of the mid-nineteenth century, such frontiers were hidden spaces that either went unmentioned in official archives or accounts or were spoken of only in euphemistic terms. Astoundingly, Beverley Nance's article on interracial violence in Port Phillip, which was published in 1981, asserts that "personal relations between white and black were almost non-existent."[135] Nance focused her study on "official" incidents of violence or combat. Her account, like many, however, was composed overwhelmingly of incidents of male-to-male violence and represented the frontier as a linear and external space, rather than as transactional space that was internal, sexual, and psychic.[136] Studies of frontier relations in Australia have only begun to address that Aboriginal women were historical actors and that sexual relations were a crucial contour of the frontier. As Adele Perry writes about nineteenth-century British Columbia, the "contact zone ... was explicitly gendered, bringing together men and women rather than ungendered racial subjects."[137]

So, too, Melbourne's urbanizing frontier was explicitly gendered and sexualized in the contact zone. Yet Aboriginal women in Australia's colonial cities typically received little more than fleeting mentions in the visual and literary material of the period. Ann Stoler, commenting on the increased attention that scholars have paid over the last two decades to the intimacies of empire as vital political sites, notes that "intimate matters and narratives about them figured in defining the racial coordinates and social discriminations of empire."[138] Aboriginal camps were places where men sought sexual liaisons with Aboriginal women; they reveal much about sex, race, and space in colonial Melbourne.

When considering Aboriginal women in the colonial streetscape, the widespread sexual abuse of Aboriginal women on the wider frontier (a theme that a range of authors have addressed) needs to be kept in mind.[139] The association between lands to be colonized and Aboriginal women's bodies has long been established.[140] The extreme imbalance between European men and European women in colonial Melbourne and the perception of a lack of a "good" society regulated by the presence of bourgeois, white womanhood was apparent. Larissa Behrendt has observed that Aboriginal women were represented as "easy sexual sport" in all of the Australian colonies.[141] Aboriginal women were frequently portrayed as "cheap or low class prostitutes." Furthermore, Berhrendt notes that European men felt shame upon sleeping with a black woman and held the notion that "lying with a black woman would eventually lead to a white man's impotence with white women" – that is, interracial sex would lead to the emasculation of the white man.[142] For white men, the colonies provided new and heady freedoms. Nikki Henningham has evocatively recorded the attitudes of young men who wrote home to Britain from the Queensland frontier and reported that they were "picking up colonial experience," which was often a euphemism for the sexual exploitation of Aboriginal women.[143]

William Thomas frequently recorded in his journals instances of European men going to the main Aboriginal camp on the south bank of the Yarra River: "Found a gentleman in an Aboriginal woman's tent," he wrote.[144] On a night visit to the camp, Protector George Robinson likewise recorded that he "gave two frocks to two little girls. On going away one of the girls said 'good night my dear.' [I then] ... turned a drunken man away from them."[145] Highlighting the prevailing idea that Aboriginal women were synonymous with prostitution, Thomas recorded his journal: "Just as I was getting to bed I was interrupted by another apparent gentleman, who came boldly up to one miam [bark hut] saying 'I want an [Aboriginal woman], here's white money.' I despatched him, who said that a black [woman] had a right to be a whore as well as a white one, and I am sorry to say that the blacks are willing to accommodate him. What can be done with these people under such circumstances and what power have I? None."[146]

Behrendt has observed that Aboriginal women lack agency in archival material and that their "assent to sexual relations [was] perpetually assumed" on the frontier.[147] As the night visitor to the Aboriginal camp perversely opined to suit his own ends, prostitution was the "right" of Aboriginal and European woman alike. Furthermore, many authors also deemed venereal disease, which was given to Aboriginal women through sexual contact with white men, to be evidence of the wantonness of Aboriginal sexuality. Patricia Grimshaw and Andrew May have noted that even the Aboriginal protectors, who were clearly aware of the conduct of white men, "presented [Aboriginal] women as contributing to their plight because they appeared to have within their own cultural system sexual practices which deviated from those of British Victorian practices which the protectors upheld as proper behaviour."[148]

But not all women were willing to accommodate such intrusions. Another night at the camp, as Thomas was about to go to bed, he heard an Aboriginal woman cry out "'oh oh, hurt no hurt' [and] ... heard a white man say 'Be quiet, white money.'"[149] Thomas investigated and found that it was the white man who had several days earlier pleaded that his stay in the camp was innocent, that he had come over to the camp to see the corroboree and missed the last punt back.[150] Sexual violence and physical attacks on Aboriginal women by European men were frequent occurrences. On another occasion Thomas recorded that "in the afternoon a drunken fellow came into the encampment and commenced in the most brutal manner insulting the [Aboriginal women]. He knocked one [woman] down with an infant in her arms. We took him and I clapped him in the watch house, where he had to remain till Monday." Later, Thomas went to the police office and identified the drunken man who had assaulted the women. He wrote, "As the assault was seen only by blacks ... he was acquitted of assault and fined five shillings for being drunk. The blacks got 2s 6d of it, which pleased them very much."[151]

Attempts were made to curtail the mixing of Europeans and Aboriginal people. The Vagrancy Act was applied not to Aboriginal people but to Europeans. Although Thomas observed the tenderness that Aboriginal wives had for their husbands and children, he also noted that Aboriginal women were the victims of violence by Aboriginal men. He reported, "a black man had beaten his wife and her life was despaired of."[152] Aboriginal men also traded their wives' sexual favours to white men. In 1841 Thomas wrote, "Found that Jack Weatherly was lending his to the Splitters &c who are scatter'd about & inviting them to encampment at night."[153] Aboriginal women may also have brokered these relations on their own terms. Often starving and in search of "white money," women traded sex for food and cohabited with white men in town. Thomas wrote of a young man who lived with two women who "often entic'd [other] young [women] to his home." Aboriginal men in the camp complained to Thomas about their wives being in white men's beds.[154]

When they were outside of towns on pastoral runs, European men and women frequently turned a blind eye to the unrelenting sexual abuse of Aboriginal women. In town it was little different. In settlements European men were certainly open to far more scrutiny from humanitarians, such as the Aboriginal protectors, if not the law. And notions of civility and gentility may have prevailed in "civilized" urban company. Therefore, sexualized relations in towns may have appeared to be more restrained, but in reality attitudes towards the sexual abuse of Aboriginal women differed little between the pastoral and urbanizing frontiers. Aboriginal camps were far more than mere spectacle; for many Europeans they were spaces of powerful sexual allure, where many men "picked up colonial experience." Settler colonialism may have been a project of extraterritorialism, but it was also a rapacious project of gendered territorialism.[155] Both processes occurred simultaneously, revealing the twin operations of the settler-colonial project: the removal of Indigenous peoples and their replacement through the bodies of Indigenous and non-Indigenous women. These processes were writ large in the colonial city.

These sexual and violent relations presented a disjuncture, or dislocation, from bourgeois metropolitanism and its fictive ideas of racial containment, purity, and white space. These socio-spatial relations produced new "mixed-race" colonial subjects. Thomas wrote about a white man who returned his mixed-race child to the camp in 1844, noting a "white Settler allowed his illegitimate child to live with her mother and the Aborigines."[156] Yet such incidents are rarely mentioned in the official records of the colonial city. On this issue William Westgarth opined in 1846: "There are *no instances,* the Newcastle bench *states,* of the union of whites with the female Aborigines, but the labouring classes are in the constant practice of cohabiting with these females, and there appears to be no repugnance on either side."[157] These relations were barely spoken of in genteel company, and the urban archives are often silent about them. Yet the allure of the Aboriginal camp certainly shaped social mores in the streetscape and had an impact on the behaviour of European men and the daily lives of Aboriginal women.

Amid harsh and skewed constructions of gender and the violence of the intimate urban frontier, the presence of Aboriginal women in the colonial streetscape should not be overlooked. At times Aboriginal women aligned themselves financially and sexually with European men for obvious strategic reasons. Attention to the presence and action of Aboriginal women brings to light not only the intimacies of empire in the colonial city but also the making of social spaces in which Aboriginal women negotiated their own meaning within a difficult and rapidly changing frontier.

Throughout the 1840s the Melbourne Town Council made moves to regulate and frame bylaws "to suppress and prevent *certain nuisances* which now may or may hereafter exist by reason of *certain places* within the town which are or may become in an *unwholesome state.*"[158] Were these "certain nuisances" and "certain places of an unwholesome nature" the Aboriginal camps? During the same period, "canvas town and tent nuisances" and the "removal of canvas town" were listed as items for discussion in council minutes.[159] It was "resolved ... that the mayor be requested to enforce as stringently as possible the various provisions of the town's Police Act, and use every endeavour to have the masses of filth and offal which disgrace many portions of the city removed." Later, in line with Victorian fears of disease borne by breezes and noxious miasma, and referring to the area between the beach and town (the swampy area where the main Aboriginal camp was located), the councillors "resolved ... to write to his Excellency the Governor suggesting the necessity of clearing the land of trees between the City of Melbourne and the beach so that the obstructions of the free access of pure sea air may be removed."[160]

The Boundaries of Whiteness: Race, Space, and the Law

In "Nervous Landscapes," Denis Byrne asks, how do people live in a cadastral grid in which they have no proprietary state?[161] In New South Wales, Aboriginal people maintained detailed mental maps of the colonized landscape. These maps, writes Byrne, were composed of "detailed knowledge of the mosaic of friendly and hostile white landowners and the routes which enabled safe movement through this mosaic."[162] They were part of a survival kit that enabled Aboriginal people to operate safely in a segregated landscape and maximize the "possibilities of movement through it," partly by exploiting incompletely colonized areas such as swamps, river banks, stock routes, road reserves, and patches of uncleared bush that were "gaps in the grid."[163] As the mosaic of allotments closed around them, Aborigines were transformed into trespassers on their own land and had to exploit these incompletely colonized areas. In his article Byrne calls their activities "tactical transgressions of segregation's mostly invisible boundaries." "In theory," writes Byrne, "the colonised were gridlocked by the cadastre but there were always ways through it and ways of subverting it."[164]

For Aboriginal people residing in this anxious empire, however, life was more than merely living in the gaps or negotiating vestigial spaces. There was also the possibility of acts of clear resistance to the burgeoning spatial hegemony, moments that Byrne compellingly calls "fence jumping" or "anti-cadastral activity."[165] This concept, which is both physical and psychic, helps us to reread Eurocentric accounts of the formation of settler-colonial urban and cadastral space and illuminates other facets of the urbanizing frontier. In the late 1830s and 1840s, during the frontier period of southeastern Australia, attacking sheep was an assault on the prime asset of pastoralism. Fences were the cadastral grid materialized, and Aborigines jumped fences that had been erected around Melbourne to partition the land and hinder Indigenous peoples from food gathering and other life ways. Kulin people pulled fences – barriers that stopped them from moving across the land to ponds that provided seasonal food sources such as eels – down. They routinely burned fences for firewood, camped in wheat paddocks, and crossed fields, to the constant complaints of farmers. In 1846 Edward Curr complained to Governor La Trobe that "the Blacks have formed an encampment ... about 4 miles from Melbourne," and he noted that his "farm &c is in peril from their lighting of fires."[166] All through the 1840s and into the 1850s, there were constant complaints of Aborigines entering fenced paddocks and "trespassing" with their dogs on private land – transgressions of the closing cadastre.

Clearly, Aborigines were not passive historical subjects; they negotiated increased incursions onto their lands by sometimes sharing these spaces and, at other times, by subverting them. Paying attention to certain spatial crimes and infringements pertaining to public order in the streetscape is a productive lens through which to understand the iniquitous and racialized politics of the settler-colonial streetscape. The law and its application and the breaking of the law, or crime, adumbrate the boundaries of society and public order. The application of laws against vagrancy, disorderly conduct, drunkenness, assault, theft, trespass, and property damage reveal how Aboriginal people were disciplined in the streetscape and the expanding cadastre of private property. Comparative studies of setter-colonial societies often tend to overstate the power of the colonial state and overlook Indigenous actions. Yet crimes or spatial infringements, which were defined by and adjudicated by the state also reveal moments when Aborigines refuted, as a response to European control, the boundaries of white spatial regimes. As Gillian Cowlishaw states: "Crime is politicised in that it functions as a means of defining the impropriety of Aborigines' customs. Public order offences represent political activity in the sense that they are an active response to control, and an assertion of the right to protest."[167] It is now widely accepted that the law is not neutral or culturally unbiased. The Australian legal system, inherited from the British legal system of the eighteenth and nineteenth centuries, made inherent assumptions about whiteness.[168] It was axiomatic, therefore, that the British would interpret Aboriginality, Aboriginal crime, and other spatial infringements through the whiteness of British law. Thus, racialized crime adumbrated the boundaries of whiteness, white behaviour, and public order in the townscape. As is suggested provocatively by Byrne's term *anti-cadastral activity,* certain spatial activities and crimes by Aboriginal people can be read as subversive responses to the law. I interpret certain spatial crimes and infringements as an aspect of anti-cadastral activity.[169] In Melbourne, the punt, the water pumps, and the bathing areas increasingly became contested sites. But a wealth of spatial infringements and other crimes such as theft, holdups, trespass, and the refusal to move on were also found in the archive.

Petty theft and violence by Aboriginal people was a constant complaint. In 1839 the *Port Phillip Gazette* called on the protectors to remove Aborigines from Melbourne because "their vagrant and pilfering habits" were rapidly become "a perfect nuisance."[170] In 1842 Aborigines told William Thomas in a rather effective quid pro quo that they would continue to conduct armed holdups around the edge of town to get food, since "the Kangaroo and roots" that they had traditionally eaten had all been destroyed and replaced with sheep and cattle, "which they were not permitted to touch."[171] As violence towards Aboriginal people in the streets increased, so too did crimes by Aboriginal people in town. Robinson noted that "today Captain Lonsdale complained against five drunken natives. George Hawes said they burst open his door and demanded bread. His wife said she had none, when they said it was one big lie and that they would kill her if she did not give it to them. John Loxton said five drunken natives came to his hut and asked for tobacco, said they would kill him if he did not give it."[172] Alexander Southerland wrote of Aboriginal highwaymen with guns, who took up positions on the main roads and demanded sixpence from passersby "with a saucy and sometimes menacing air."[173] The *Port Phillip Gazette* reported that a white man, on his way to Melbourne, had been accosted by a band of Aborigines on the road and "stripped of every garment he had." He was later picked up, "travelling alfresco," by another settler. The newspapers reported that Aboriginal women in the street were "becoming very troublesome in the environs and increasing in perfection at committing larcenies."[174]

These activities were more than mere fence jumping or exploiting gaps in the grid: they were clear acts of refutation. Describing every activity as an act of anticolonial resistance is, of course, simplistic. Yet Aboriginal people, dispossessed and starving, were clearly negotiating the urbanizing frontier and the weight of the law when they could. In this way their crimes did adumbrate the boundaries of public order and emerging white space.

In September 1840 three Aborigines beat and stole money from a white boy. The *Port Phillip Gazette* again stressed that "a reserve should be set aside for Aboriginal visits to the vicinity of Melbourne, so that they could be effectively prevented by the Protectors from entering the township." The article continued: "The Aborigines' system of begging, thieving, their indecent exposure of person, their fulsome appearance and savour, all demand some wholesome restrictions in their actions."[175] By contrast, when Korum, an Aboriginal man, was brutally attacked in the street, Aboriginal testimony was not permitted. Thomas was outraged that Korum had been prohibited from giving evidence in court. In addition, his European attacker had been arrested, but because no European man would stand as witness against him in court, he had been released. Thomas wrote to the Crown solicitor about the need for Aboriginal testimony in court. The Crown solicitor's response was that "in no case whatever can the deposition of an Aboriginal be taken unless so far civilised as to understand the nature of the oath as by law established and ... to a sense and knowledge of the Supreme Being, not even in common assault."[176]

Although vagrancy laws could not be applied to Aborigines in the townscape, there were other ways to control Aboriginal people, and such control was often at the whim of the police constable on duty at the time, which raises questions about police discretion that are still pertinent to the postcolonial city. The charge of being drunk and disorderly was applied liberally and was often used to discipline Aboriginal peoples, even if all of the Europeans around them had also been drunk. The selling of alcohol to Aborigines by whites was prohibited. For the police magistrate, this was a problem.[177] There was constant confusion in British policy about Aboriginal people's status as British subjects. "By orders from London [Aboriginal people] were supposed to be equal to all other British subjects before the law. In other words, they should have enjoyed the same freedom as white men to drink."[178] Under pressure from European residents, William Lonsdale's solution was "to administer peremptory punishments to Aborigines who drank excessively and caused serious disturbances." A common punishment was several hours in the stocks located outside the police office.[179]

Chris Cunneen has rightly argued that Aboriginal resistance to the process of colonization was criminalized. Cunneen also contends that "in practice Aboriginal resistance was often seen as falling between criminal activity and resistance to invasion. However, the view of the law was that these activities were criminal *without political content*."[180] In early Melbourne acts of resistance were clearly recognized by colonial governance as political acts that threatened to destabilize the colonial order, and they were punished as such. Although public executions of Europeans had ceased in most colonies by the 1860s, public and semi-public executions of Aborigines continued in Australian towns and cities well into the late nineteenth century.[181] John McGuire, basing his work on Foucault's perspective on power, argues that public executions had didactic power and were symbolic acts that can be interpreted as fulfilling a clear political function by reasserting the power of the sovereign over the subject. Colonial officials designed these exercises in terror specifically for Aboriginal people. Through executions, varying messages were communicated to Europeans and Aboriginal people in a "complex interplay of ... deterrence, retribution and social defence."[182] The spectacle of the Aboriginal execution possessed performative currency well into the late nineteenth century.

Guerrilla attacks, moments of anti-cadastral activity, hold ups, acts of theft, and other crimes necessary for survival were often difficult to conduct close to Melbourne, where Europeans overwhelmed Aborigines. The most sustained campaign of guerrilla attacks was led by five Tasmanian Aborigines who, ironically, had been brought from Flinders Island by George Augustus Robinson to help civilize Aborigines at Port Phillip. Instead, they persuaded local Aborigines to help them in a series of raids.[183] Timme (Robert Timmy Jimmy Small-Boy), Jack Napoleon (also known as Peevay or Tunnerminnerwait [waterbird]), and three Aboriginal women (Trugernanner, Matilda, and Planobeena [Fanny]) visited four stations and killed four whites. Timme and Tunnerminnerwait, thought to be the leaders of the group, were hanged for the crime, and the rest of the Tasmanians were sent back to Flinders Island. Judge John Walpole Willis, who had come from Upper Canada, hanged Timme and Tunnerminnerwait on 20 January 1842.[184] It was the first public hanging in Port Phillip and occurred in the centre of town as a lesson in British justice and its spatial and legislative control. The two men were executed in front of a crowd of six thousand Europeans on Melbourne's eastern hill. Kulin people sat looking on from trees on the perimeter of the scene. The hanging was an object lesson in British justice meant to deter and terrorize local Aborigines who might participate in any kind of attack or act of violent resistance.[185] It was an act that sought to maintain the notion of civil space and public order.

For some Europeans the presence of Aboriginal people in the newly formed streets of Melbourne was a curious spectacle, a "true picture of savage life" in the remote parts of Australia's southeastern colony.[186] But as the town grew curiosity turned to surveillance and efforts to segregate Aboriginal people. Rather than effecting segregation through elusive conventions, Europeans used a range of strategies to defend and control urban space. An examination of outright violence, municipal bylaws, policing and the defence of property, missionary entreaties, and Indigenous crime reveals how racialized segregation operated in colonial Melbourne. Despite these efforts, the city as it was imagined – as a city of controlled, contiguous British space – and fictive ideas about racial purity were contested in the growing colonial city, with its contact zones, Indigenizing spaces, and Native camps, which created displacements and dislocations. While white women such as Sarah Bunbury chose to see only a transformed landscape of pretty English cottages and parks, Aboriginal peoples asserted their presence in the city, resisted settlers and the expanding cadastral grid over their lands, and continued to use lands in the urbanizing frontier.

6

Narratives of Race in the Streetscape: Fears of Miscegenation and Making White Subjects
[Melbourne, Port Phillip, 1850s-60s]

IN 1849 THE PORT PHILLIP Aboriginal Protectorate was dismantled on the advice of a select committee. William Thomas was the only protector kept on and was given the title Guardian of the Aborigines. Although Thomas' statement of duties was detailed, one of his major roles, which was at the behest of Governor Charles La Trobe, was to ride the boundaries of Melbourne and provide free rations to Aboriginal people to keep them out of town.[1] In the mid-nineteenth century, policies towards Aboriginal peoples in southeastern Australia became laissez-faire, and this approach readily suited the colonial administration, given the decreased humanitarian influence of London's Exeter Hall and an apparent reduction in frontier violence, at least in the southeastern colonies. The 1850s have been described as a period of almost complete government neglect of Aboriginal peoples.[2] While they were overlooked by government during this time, Aboriginal people also suffered further cultural devastation because of the massive transformations that accompanied the Victorian gold rush.

The discovery of gold in the Colony of New South Wales in 1851 spurred tens of thousands of immigrants to travel to southeastern Australia. In the years prior to this, some finds had been reported. In 1851 Edward Hammond Hargraves returned from the California goldfields to the colony and discovered payable deposits of gold near Bathurst. Some months later Port Phillip separated from the Colony of New South Wales and the new Colony of Victoria was formed. It also became a site of gold rush fervor. Within a few years, gold seekers swelled Melbourne's population. By 1852 thousands of Vandemonians, South Australians, and others had flocked to Port Phillip upon hearing that gold had been discovered.[3] Britons, Europeans, Americans, and Chinese also flocked to the gold rushes of Australia Felix. Many had been to the goldfields of California. In 1855 William Howitt observed the multi-ethnic nature of the newly transformed streetscape; he noted that Americans, Persians, and Chinese, "Turks, Lascars, and Negroes," appeared in their own "strange" dress.[4] The vast majority of immigrants were from the United Kingdom, however, and they were overwhelmingly male. Andrew Markus notes that 290,000 Britons migrated from the British Isles to the Colony of Victoria between 1852 and 1860, compared to "less than 15,000 non-British Europeans and 18,000 from the United States."[5]

The gold rushes of California, Australia, and British Columbia in the late 1840s and 1850s radically altered the demographic, economic, and cultural balance of each region. In 1848 California, a recently conquered region of the United States, produced 41 percent of the world's gold. Gold seekers increased the population from fourteen thousand in 1848 to one hundred thousand by the end of 1849 and three hundred thousand by the end of 1853.[6] Between 1851 and 1860, the Australian gold rush produced 39 percent of the world's gold, and much of it was from Victoria. The Port Phillip District was transformed rapidly from a small pastoral settlement to one of the most celebrated British colonies.[7] The European population of Melbourne in 1840 was estimated to be around 5,538. By the first year of the gold rush, the city had a population of between 23,000 and 29,000 people, and by 1861 it had increased to between 125,000 and 140,000 people. The colony's population tripled to 237,000 by 1854, and it more than doubled again by 1861.[8]

By contrast, in 1858 on the Pacific Northwest Coast, around thirty thousand immigrants made their way to the British Columbian mainland. The population drawn to the town of Victoria by the 1858 Fraser River Gold Rush peaked at around 6,000, which was a significant increase from the 435 "Europeans" who were listed as inhabitants of the Colony of Vancouver Island in 1852.[9] The influx of immigrants to Melbourne, the gateway to the gold rushes of southeastern Australia, was far greater. By the mid- to late 1850s, aspiring to gold rush prosperity, British Columbia looked to Melbourne and San Francisco as visions of its possible future. The *British Colonist* exclaimed that the gold rushes were a gift from Providence, proof of the imperial destiny of the Anglo-Saxon races: where "the finger of Providence was manifest the discoveries of gold had ... planted a new centre of light and civilisation on the Pacific."[10] W.C. Grant's comment that "the two distant extremities of the British empire might thus be made to join hands, with mutual benefit to each other" represented his aspirations for Vancouver Island.[11] Yet the Colony of Victoria and the city of Melbourne rarely looked to the Northwest Coast for inspiration. This gold rush society became largely self-possessed and confident in its destiny. Colonial confidence was, however, deeply threatened by the thorny issue of race.

Thousands of new immigrants clustered first in Melbourne, a port and service centre for various gold rushes, before making their way to the Plenty and Yarra valleys northeast of the settlement (lands of the Wurundjeri and Boonwurrung) and then to lands to the northwest (lands of the Djadjawarrung). The segregation of Aboriginal peoples from the townscape, and Aboriginal peoples' increased demands for land of their own, led, in 1852, to the granting of two reserves twenty-five kilometres from Melbourne. The Wurundjeri were given 782 hectares on both sides of the Yarra River at present-day Warrandyte. The

Figure 13   St. Kilda Beach, 1854 (artist, William Blandowski) This drawing was photographed and appeared in *Australien in 142 photographischen Abbildungen* [Australia in 142 Photographic Images], published in 1862. The image is based on sketches or possibly rendered from photographs made by Blandowski in Melbourne in the mid-1850s. The image was then commissioned by Blandowski and painted by Gustav Murtzel in 1861. Haddon Library of Archaeology and Anthropology, Cambridge.

Boonwurrung selected 340 acres on Mordialloc Creek. As Michael Christie notes, however, with little incentive to stay, no means to cultivate the land, and no supplies, few Aboriginal people remained on the reserves for long, and Europeans appropriated the areas.[12] But there were Aboriginal groups that camped farther south along the Port Phillip Bay area, including at St. Kilda Beach and Brighton. The natural scientist William Blandowski photographed an Aboriginal man fishing with a spear on the bay near the city in 1854 (see Figure 13).

In the early 1850s, hopeful gold seekers inundated Melbourne. In a mere four months in 1852, for example, 619 ships, carrying 55,057 passengers, arrived in Hobson's Bay. Melbourne, however, was already a town of about twenty-nine thousand residents and was far more developed than, for example, San Francisco, which at the time of the discovery of gold had only about one thousand residents.[13] A tent city, known as "canvas town," sprang up in south Melbourne and then on the south bank of the Yarra River, the place where many Kulin people had camped. The face of the city was radically transformed by the gold rush, which created a new hierarchy and new fears. In 1853 Carl Traugott Hoehne wrote about the rough and thievish tenor of the Melbourne streets and the savagery of Europeans and other miners: "So much swindling and stealing occurs. In the middle of the town, people were assaulted by street thieves and beaten half dead. Generally, one would probably not come across anywhere a rougher nation than one finds in the Australian towns and on the goldfields. The Aborigines are not so bad as the whites."[14] Hoehne, however, went on to quote long passages taken directly from German pamphlets on Aborigines that were circulating in the colony. The pamphlets outlined Aboriginal people's "habits" in derogatory terms and forecast their imminent extinction due because of the polluting influences of civilization: "At all events the Australnegros are the only race on earth that has never risen to the consciousness of being a people ... Now little more will be remaining of the inhabitants of the eucalyptus forests before we enter into a new century, undoubtedly they are approaching extinction and quickly. Like all savage nations at the side of more civilised ones, the Australians also become extinct beside the Europeans, because the necessary time for their development is too great in order not to destroy them by the disadvantages of civilisation that spread faster than the advantages."[15]

The discovery of gold in central Victoria had a devastating impact on the Aboriginal population, which had already been affected adversely by pastoral expansion and contact with Europeans. The influx of gold diggers, especially into the lands of the Wathawurrung and Djadjawurrung peoples, disturbed wildlife and, therefore, food sources. Gold seekers took over the camps of Aboriginal peoples and disturbed sacred sites. As David Goodman has commented, "It is difficult to imagine any other event which would have sent the invaders so rapidly and so single-mindedly into the interior." These disruptions led Kulin people to gather again in and around Melbourne. William Thomas, Guardian of the Aborigines for the Melbourne region, reported in 1854 that the condition of the Aborigines had "lamentably deteriorated," because "the discovery of gold has greatly affected their moral condition"; they were only "with great difficulty kept from the town itself."[16] Ideas about the imminent extinction of Aboriginal people had been firmly in place in the settler imagination since the 1820s, and in the face of gold rush transformations and accelerated immigration these notions were only heightened.

Extinction narratives may have been irresistible, for they were driven by the syntax of the four-stages theory of human development, which provided a culturally and conveniently naturalized explanation for the demise of Aboriginal peoples. In 1855 William Howitt invoked familiar narratives of stadial development to query the fate of Aborigines. Their degraded condition, he argued, was reminiscent of the "biblical distinction between the hunter races (the accursed sons of Ham) and the tillers of the soil (the sons of Japhet)." The former were destined to disappear, wrote Howitt, because "they possess no organ of imitation, no emulative principle or faculty of constructiveness and progression."[17] Yet many Europeans also recognized the desperate state of Aboriginal people, who sometimes camped on the fringes of the goldfields and who, at times, were the victims of violence, sexual abuse, and drunkenness. Edward Stone Parker, Aboriginal protector of the Loddon District in Central Victoria, did not deny the violence directed towards Aboriginal people, but he did believe in their survival and transformation. On violence, he stated publicly in 1854 that "the truth must and ought to be told." He argued passionately, "Let us not for one moment be supposed that there are any intellectual obstacles to the Christianisation and civilisation of these people"; the only obstacle, he believed, was moral, and religious instruction alone would "place the foot of the aborigine on a higher step in the social scale."[18]

The gold rush created extensive disruptions to Aboriginal cultures and land. However, Aboriginal peoples have been long overlooked as active participants in these developments. Throughout southeastern Australia, Kulin people worked in the goldfields, sometimes as miners but also as police, guides, and gold finders, as wives and sexual partners, and as farmers and entrepreneurs who traded cultural items and food. On pastoral stations they also worked as house servants, shepherds, stockmen, station hands, and harvesters as European men abandoned their jobs for the goldfields. In fact, the labour of Aboriginal people ameliorated the worst effects of the labour crisis that the gold rush precipitated.[19] Figure 14 shows Wathawurrung people in European-style clothes in Geelong in 1852.

Coupled with ideas of imminent extinction was the notion that the frontier had closed. In 1853 Thomas wrote to the colonial secretary and informed him that Aboriginal resistance in the Colony of Victoria had come to an end. "Weapons of opposition had been laid aside," armed police were no longer required, and loopholes in settler's huts were no longer needed. Aborigines, he continued, were engaged mainly in European employment and had abandoned their "erratic habits." Nathan Wolski argues that Thomas was articulating a European perception that the frontier was now closed. Basing his work on more recent postcolonial readings of resistance, Wolski problematizes this narrow conception of the frontier, which is based on a limited dispossession-resistance model.[20] The internal, continuous, and psychic contours of settler colonialism and the administrative violence that came to bear on Aboriginal people through surveillance and eventual missionization must also have been considered.

In the mid-1850s Melbourne, flush with gold rush money, was heralded as a great new imperial city; by the 1860s it would be further likened to Britain's

Figure 14   "Aborigines in Geelong," 1852. State Library of Victoria, H3406.

metropolitan spaces. The new Colony of Victoria in the 1850s, was, as Christie writes, "a flourishing, colourful self-satisfied colony."[21] Melbourne was described as a nodal point in the network of empire, and utopian ideas about contiguous imperial space – gridded, allotted, and fashioned culturally and legally across empire – prevailed. "Melbourne is London reproduced; Victoria is another England," remarked James Ballantyne.[22]

The illusion of British cognate space may have become more convincing in Melbourne as Aboriginal peoples were segregated from the city; however, the city was built on Indigenous land. In 1856 Edward Wilson, owner and editor of *The Argus,* a newspaper, recognized this fact. He wrote that in the five years since Victoria had become a separate colony, "the government had sold Aboriginal land worth four and a half million pounds, that gold to the value of thirty-five million sterling had been taken from that land, and that millions more had been made from the sale of beef, mutton, and wool." In return the government had appropriated "the contemptible sum of 1,750 [pounds] for the Aborigines" benefit.[23]

Dystopian Fears of "Mongolian Melbourne"

By the 1850s, however, settler-colonial relations rarely conformed to an exclusively Indigenous-European dynamic. In the new hierarchy of the streetscape, racial fears settled on Chinese immigrants and were used to promote ideas about Aboriginal extinction. Furthermore, the increased circulation of ideas about civilization and savagery and mimicry and miscegenation occurred at the very time that there were few Aboriginal people permitted in Melbourne's streetscape.

In early 1854 a census recorded two thousand Chinese gold miners in the Colony of Victoria. Between July 1854 and June 1855 that number jumped to fifteen thousand, and between January and June 1857 another fourteen thousand Chinese immigrants arrived. By 1858 the Chinese population of the colony was approximately forty thousand.[24] In response, narratives of race in the Melbourne streetscape began to shift, and racial fears quickly settled on Chinese immigrants. A cartoon titled "Celestial Happiness," which was published in *Melbourne Punch* in 1856 (see Figure 15), reveals European fears that an inversion of racial norms was occurring in the Melbourne streetscape: the Englishman is brought to his knees to shine the shoes of a large, superior, smiling Chinese man. Such cartoons expressed fears that Anglo-Saxon dominion would submit to the power of new immigrants, such as the Chinese.

Social relations in Melbourne in the 1850s and 1860s were characterized by these racial tensions but also by cross-cultural contact between the Aboriginal, European, and Chinese populations. Examining this triangular relationship unlocks the polarized positions of racial identity that tend to dominate many studies.[25] Christie argues that settlers by this time could afford to hold magnanimous attitudes towards Aborigines, because the only threat that Aborigines posed was to the settlers' "image of themselves as Christian civilised people imbued with British ideals of justice and fair play."[26] The play between ideas about the Chinese as new, ruthless colonizers and laments or imperial nostalgia

CELESTIAL HAPPINESS.

Figure 15   "Celestial Happiness." *Melbourne Punch,* 1856.

for the fate of Aborigines can be seen in and served to obfuscate the colonizing actions of settlers. In a pamphlet titled *A Plea on Behalf of the Aborigines of Victoria,* which was published in *The Argus,* the author asked, "Have the Chinese a claim on our sympathy superior to that of the Aborigines?" Why, the author demanded, were the churches setting up missions to the Chinese in the goldfields but not attending to the Aborigines? The Chinese, he continued, "were aggressors on our territory ... they come here from mercenary motives, dig up our gold, and take it from the country"; with them came the "most disgusting and loathsome vices that can degrade humanity," whereas the "worst vices of the black man are those we have taught him."[27]

By 1855 taxes and immigration restrictions had been placed on the Chinese, and a system of surveillance was created for the goldfields, where Chinese were placed in separate mining villages and supervised by salaried protectors. Indeed, the Chinese miners needed protection, because violence against them was frequent. Ironically, by this time John Pascoe Fawkner, who had invaded Indigenous land to "make the world again," had become a member of the Legislative Council of Victoria and was described by Charles Price as "one of the old guard restrictionists."[28] Fawkner objected to the numbers of Chinese in Victoria and pushed for the formation of a select committee to fashion legislation that would "effectively prevent the goldfields of Australia Felix from becoming the property of the Emperor of China and the Mongolian and Tartar hordes of Asia."[29]

Melbourne As It Is and Ought to Be, published anonymously in 1850, was an exercise in bourgeois metropolitanism, by which the developing cityscape was inscribed with a European vision of imperial classicism, encoded male and white. By comparison, "Imaginings of 'Celestial' Melbourne 2000 AD," a satirical and racist letter purportedly from the year 2000 that was published in *Melbourne Punch* in 1856, was another racialized vision inscribed into city space. It presented a chilling racial dystopia. According to its British author, descendants of the Britons would become slaves to 75 million Chinese people in "Mongolian Melbourne," a city in which only seventeen Aborigines survive. The author's vision suggested that the treatment of Aborigines was a barometer of civilization, and the Chinese – super economic beings and new, brutal invaders – had performed the worst.[30] Finally, "Imaginings of 'Celestial' Melbourne 2000 AD" delivered up the greatest symbolic shock of all: it announced satirically that the "new [royal] pagoda on Batman's Hill ... is to be opened on Monday next."[31] Thus, in the settler imagination, Batman's Hill, named after one of the erstwhile founders of Melbourne, became a highly symbolic and coded racial focal point in the landscape. In 1843 members of the Melbourne Town Council had envisaged the hill as the future site of "superior" aquarium and botanic gardens, symbols of scientific learning and civilization. Seven years later, in 1850, the author *of Melbourne As It Is and Ought to Be* imagined the site as sacred settler place, where white classical imperialism was enshrined with the "busts of great men."[32] One year later the vision of a giant Chinese pagoda on Batman's Hill localized racial fears by symbolizing the desecration of a key settler-colonial site. Batman's Hill became a shifting racialized space, a canvas onto which celebrations of identity and anxieties of difference were projected.

Throughout the nineteenth century, racial anxieties continued to play themselves out in Melbourne's streetscapes. By the close of the century, Little Bourke Street would come to be known as the Chinese precinct, a maze of laneways sensationalized for its opium dens and dark vices. Non-Chinese judged this place as one of the country's "festering sores and a disgrace to civilisation in Australia."[33] But was any colonial city in this period wholly British or white? Despite attempts to create British or white spaces, refutations of the spatial hegemony of the streetscape, mixed-race relationships, and the creation of new hybrid spaces through the dual forces of colonization and immigration meant that Melbourne was not – at least in the 1840s, 1850s, and 1860s – London reproduced. Instead, Melbourne was a mixed New World place. Its metropolitan counterpart, London, had likewise, over some several hundred years, undergone a radical shift as new people from around the globe came to its streets through the recursive relations of empire.

Because Aborigines were farther out of sight than new immigrants, representations of Aboriginal people shifted between images of degraded beings facing extinction and romanticized images of noble savages in white, toga-like apparel (in reality these were government blankets). The *Newsletter of Australasia,* "a letter to send to friends," featured this type of drawing on its cover in March 1857. It noted in an elegiac tone that the "illustration this month consists of portraits of two well-known Aborigines who have frequently visited Melbourne. The gradual declension of these people must give a singular interest to every faithful record of them."[34] That same year a census titled *Statistical Notes on the Progress of Victoria* showed that only 1,786 Aborigines survived in the Colony of Victoria.[35] It is likely, however, that the figure and others like it did not include people of both Indigenous and European parentage and, consequently, were used deliberately to bolster ideas about Aboriginal people's imminent extinction.

In 1858 the Governor of Victoria established a committee, consisting of seven members, three of whom were members of Parliament, to investigate the living conditions of Aborigines in the Colony of Victoria. The committee's finding led to the establishment in 1860 of the Central Board for the Protection of Aborigines, which was to provide "sanctuaries" for Aboriginal people – that is, "permanent reserves" were to be established for the "protection of Aborigines."[36] In 1859 leaders of the Kulin Nation also approached William Thomas and told him that they wished to create a community of their own. Acheron Station was selected, and in 1859 many Aboriginal people from the Melbourne region moved there.[37]

Problems continued for Aborigines, however. A squatter, Hugh Glass, forced their removal to a colder site at Mohican Station, a site that was unsuitable for agriculture and later abandoned.[38] Tired of waiting for the government to select another site, in March 1863 the group selected a traditional camping site at Coranderrk, which was over the Great Dividing Range. The government approved the site in June, when a deputation of Aborigines attended the governor's levee in Melbourne. The Kulin considered the "gazettal of 931 hectares of reserve land to be a gift from Queen Victoria 'the Great Mother Queen.'"[39] A government census of 1863 recorded only thirty-three Aboriginal people in the Melbourne district.[40]

Similar small reserves, tiny remnant pieces of land, had been gazetted for Aboriginal people throughout Victoria. Richard Broome notes that seven reserves (also known as stations and missions) and twenty-three small camping places and ration depots were in place by 1863, creating the most comprehensive reserve system in nineteenth-century Australia.[41] In 1869 the Aborigines Protection Act was passed. This piece of legislation gave the Central Board for the Protection of Aborigines far greater powers over Aboriginal employment, residence, and children. Under the Act, the board could prescribe where Aboriginal people would live – and that was the six reserves in existence at the time.[42]

Anxious, Intimate Empire: Mixed-Race Relationships

Although there were few Aboriginal people living permanently in Melbourne by the 1850s, public narratives of race in the streetscape were heavily weighted with anxieties about mimicry and mixed-race relations. In 1852 Thomas Warre Harriet, drawn by the promise of the gold rush, arrived in Melbourne. His sketchbook documents life in Port Phillip and the goldfields and contains a series of comic and not so comic images. The cartoons tell of the fate of a foppish young man, "The Ex Assistant Surgeon, pill roller ... [who] failing to find immediately on landing the young lady with 2000 [pounds] a year, who is supposed to be anxiously awaiting his arrival at Port Phillip[,] resolves to have a turn at the diggings – before he sacrifices himself to connubial bonds."[43] Harriet's asinine protagonist tries his hand at the gold diggings and does poorly. He is robbed on the road from the diggings and limps, penniless, back to Melbourne, where his dreams of finding a young English woman, a "lady with 2000 a year" comes to naught. Instead, he fancies an Aboriginal woman he sees in the Melbourne streetscape and marries her (see Figure 16). The series of comic images plays on ideas about masculine failure, or emasculation, in the colonies and the inversion of the racial order through the spectre of miscegenation. Unlucky in love, and missing his (white) lady with two thousand pounds a year, the protagonist resorts to the so-called charms of the Native enchantress. Later, "He enjoys domestic bliss and buttered toast – his gin proves a domestic spirit – and he has a prospect of several dusky apprentices of his own begetting" (see

Smitten with the charms of a native Enchantress – he smiles on her

Figure 16 "Smitten with the charms of a native Enchantress – he smiles on her."
From Thomas Warre Harriet, "Sketches on Board the Barque Mary Harrison and Ashore
in Australia, 1852-54," New South Wales State Library.

Figure 17). The second image satirizes the intimate and genteel setting of the
middle-class, British drawing room. It could be London, but it is the antipodean
colonial frontier. The Aboriginal woman, dressed in the finery of a Victorian
matron, sips tea like a true lady, her "dusky" offspring at her side. The satire
pivots on the subversion of received ideas about civility and savagery, but it also
reflects anxieties about mimicry and miscegenation and the crossing of social
taboos on the colonial periphery.

The mass emigration of men from Britain to the Colony of Victoria in the
year 1852, following the beginning of the gold rush, was described as a national
epidemic. The sharp increase in male immigration during this period was a
cause for concern, and there was public desire for equilibrium of the sexes. In
addition, immigrants were not paupers, but often members of the middle class.
Harriet's anti-hero is an ex-assistant surgeon, a professional man who ideally
seeks a British lady of some means. In many ways Harriet's narrative hinges on
the absence of suitable white women, which was a feature of a gold rush society
in flux at this time. Harriet's protagonist submits to the "charms" of an Aboriginal women; he thus represents the fears that the colonies held for many – without the presence of marriageable white women, British men would fall to the
lure of mixed-race relations.[44]

By 1850 adult men largely outnumbered women in most Aboriginal groups
in the Colony of Victoria.[45] As Katherine Ellinghaus notes, although in many
instances in the various Australian colonies the marriage of an Aboriginal woman
to a non-Aboriginal man could be granted only by a government official, "no

Figure 17 "He enjoys domestic bliss and buttered toast – his gin proves a domestic spirit – and he has a prospect of several dusky apprentices of his own begetting." From Thomas Warre Harriet, "Sketches on Board the Barque Mary Harrison and Ashore in Australia, 1852-54," New South Wales State Library.

express laws prohibiting interracial marriages were ever passed." Indeed, there were no explicit laws against a European man marrying an Aboriginal woman in Victoria in the 1840s, and Aboriginal women married men of the lower classes.[46] Ellinghaus' study, which examines the marriages of white women to Aboriginal men in the latter part of the nineteenth century, reveals how class shaped these marriages. Women of the lower classes, such as Irish women, tended to marry Aboriginal men. Harriet's ex-assistant surgeon was, therefore, also crossing a class divide. The occurrence of affectionate and shared relations should not be ruled out. There was, nevertheless, popular belief that interracial marriage was degrading for the white partner and that a white man's sleeping with or marrying an Aboriginal woman was emasculating and caused loss to his racial status as white. In addition, there were often severe consequences for men who established long-term relations with Aboriginal women. As Nikki Henningham writes of northern Queensland in the nineteenth century, formalized relationships were considered to be threatening because they "disturbed the delicate balance of power ... by blurring the boundaries between colonized and colonizer even more."[47] The fear of de-racialization was also a feature of British Columbian society. As Adele Perry has noted, mixed-race relationships were often equated with backwardness, and men "ceased to be white" when they cohabited with Indigenous women. They lost their "general racial status and the particular hallmarks of the Anglo-Saxon race."[48] Here lies the unstable stretch that unsettled the heart of settler-colonial society – mixed-race relationships and the product of mixed subjects and inverted spaces.

Cartoons and satirical images such as Harriet's were not uncommon. They belonged to the same popular visual and comic lexicon as all racialized cartoons published by the nineteenth-century British and North American press. Although emancipated slaves living in London were quite different from colonized Indigenous peoples in southeastern Australia, the importation and circulation of drawing-room satire was similar. Those coming from Britain to Australia Felix were no strangers to the presence of "blacks" in major cities. Londoners were accustomed to high levels of curiosity and prejudice in the streetscape based on the coordinates of colour.[49] This invisible luggage – racialized thinking – had always been part of English culture. Race, as Catherine Hall has argued, "was deeply rooted in English culture ... a space in which the English configured their relation to themselves and others ... foundational to English forms of classification and relations of power."[50]

The language of race moved recursively between metropole and colonies, and ideas about race were only amplified after 1859, with the publication of Charles Darwin's *On the Origin of the Species by Means of Natural Selection*.[51] The spatial contours of whiteness are shaped by property and the law, but whiteness is also about sex, bodies, and preserving ideas about a fictive racial purity that never existed. Racialized cartoons represented unsettled fissures – the transformation of Aboriginal and non-Aboriginal subjects and mixed-racedness – in narratives of whiteness, and they inflected narratives about colonial society and the streetscape. The absence of the civilizing presence of the well-to-do white woman is a key element. Through these cartoons the fragile boundaries of whiteness and, indeed, of class were tested in the colonial polity. Although Harriet's cartoons were rendered in his own personal diary and were not published, we see that these themes were on his mind and in popular circulation.

In Philippa Levine's comparative study of prostitution and the intersection of colonialism, race, and gender in four colonies of the British Empire, she notes that "Britain's racial consciousness by the late nineteenth-century was considerable." But what constituted its white identity? Levine argues that "British identity was deeply bound to colonial success." Whiteness, Levine asserts, was "closely tied to sex – via the body, via reproduction, via deep fears about racial dilution and racial mixing, about racial uncertainties that might destabilise the fictions of racial purity and incompatibility."[52] Throughout the Empire there were fears that the Anglo-Saxon race would be compromised by rampant venereal disease and mixedness. Ports and port cities were especially feared because of their

Figure 18   "Nature and Art." *Melbourne Punch*, 1860.

"putative role as centres for the dispersal of disease, alongside their reputations in the West as havens for the promiscuous, accelerated fears of contamination and racial mixing."[53] In these ways the racial coordinates and social adjudications of empire were defined.

In the streetscape of the port city of Melbourne, the bodies of Aboriginal women not only became sites of anxiety regarding intimacy, prostitution, and disease, their children also elicited unsettled and dubious feelings among recently arrived settlers. Urban drawing-room satires such as Harriet's became more common as anxieties grew. This is evident in a cartoon, "Nature and Art," that appeared in *Melbourne Punch* on 5 January 1860. In it, ideas about civilized white womanhood in the street and in the home are played off against perceptions of Aboriginal barbarity and curiosity (see Figure 18). S.T. Gill's "Native Dignity" (1866), which depicts Aboriginal dandies and their mimicry of British bourgeois manners in the Melbourne streetscape, likewise mocks the transforming Aboriginal subject, revealing deep anxieties about the boundaries of civility and whiteness (see Figure 19).[54] Yet the urban frontier was largely a psychic one by the 1860s – there were few Aboriginal people left in Melbourne.

In 1868 the drawing-room cartoon "England – Black Fellows at Home," which appeared in *Sydney Punch* 15 August, garnered currency from the perceived dissonance of "uncivilized" Aborigines, swathed nobly in government-issue blankets, inhabiting the elegant, civilized drawing rooms of London's high

Figure 19   "Native Dignity," 1866 (artist, S.T Gill). State Library of Victoria.

society (see Figure 20). The cartoon was prompted by the now famous Aboriginal cricket team tour of England in 1868. [55] The cricket team performed that strange pageant of Englishness – cricket – in fifteen English counties of the "homeland," including at Lord's Cricket Ground. With the subtitle "They are kindly received in fashionable circles – ladies play the piano to them, etc.," *Sydney Punch* registered its indignation at the apparent dislocation of Aborigines being welcomed

ENGLAND.—BLACKFELLOWS AT HOME.

"They are kindly received in fashionable circles—ladies play the piano to them, etc."—*See London Press.*

Figure 20 "England – Black Fellows at home: 'They are kindly received in fashionable circles – ladies play the piano to them, etc.'" *Sydney Punch*, 15 August 1868.

in the heart of empire, and it no doubt played on prevalent debates about evolution and Social Darwinism.[56] The counterpart to this cartoon depicted Aborigines "at home" in the Australian bush engaged in drunkenness and brawling. Again, popular ideas turned on notions of a feigned civilization and an interminable savagery.

Thomas Harriet's cartoon was also about the transformation from savagery to civility of the Aboriginal woman. Playing on ideas about empire, home, and gender, cartoons that depicted such transformations unsettled the most intimate point of empire, the venerated domestic sphere, a realm traditionally guarded by white women. Ideas about transformation, mimicry, and miscegenation go hand in hand, for the joke is also the threat, one that hinged crucially on the stability of the domestic sphere. Ironically, within a decade of Harriet's drawings, Aboriginal women on missions and reserves in Victoria, who were being schooled by missionaries in the European domestic arts in an effort to transform and civilize them, would be forced to live in houses and enact a wifely, Christian, yeoman domesticity. While Aboriginal women largely lost their traditional lands and homes, European immigrant women, who were overwhelmingly from the British Isles and who were complicit in Aboriginal women's displacement, were intent on making settled homes in the southeastern colonies.[57]

Narratives of civilization and savagery and, importantly, of mixedness were heightened more then ever as racial attitudes hardened and as frontier towns became nodes in the network of empire. Growing towns became destinations for a range of new immigrants, including white women, who brought more rigid ideas about race, civility, and gender with them. By the 1870s many Aboriginal people from Coranderrk Station, the distant mission northeast of the city, were fearful of venturing into Melbourne.[58]

Race on Show: The 1866-67 Intercolonial Exhibition

Colonial and metropolitan cities were theatrical spaces in which narratives of race could be performed. Intercolonial exhibitions held in Britain's outlying colonial hubs were celebrations of empire that could be viewed by locals and other British subjects from around the globe. They were spaces in which ideas about Aboriginal people and culture were exhibited and managed discursively through public and international exhibitionary apparatuses. These nineteenth-century public and civic performances provide insight into the commodification and appropriation of Indigenous culture and reveal how knowledge about colonized Indigenous peoples was constructed and promulgated on the global stage.

While many authors have concentrated on standard missionary records and newspapers to trace ideas about Aboriginality in the 1860s, the 1866-67 Intercolonial Exhibition and responses to it by several writers provide a fascinating optic through which to examine the transformations of a colonizing bourgeois metropolis, ideas about Anglo-Saxon exceptionalism, and the co-fashioning of (white) Anglo-Saxon subjects and Aboriginal subjects.

Redeeming an Obligation to the Humble Race

Following London's Intercolonial Exhibition of 1862, Melbourne's Intercolonial Exhibition of 1866-67 was billed as an "event in colonial history" that would embrace "all the Australian colonies" and proudly display all their products and industries.[59] In the months leading up to the exhibition, newspapers discussed the progress of the Exhibition Commission and its intention to demonstrate the achievements of Australian colonial production. The Great Hall would feature all of the products of manufacture and attending exhibitioners would volunteer a variety of products, ranging from minerals, cereals, tobacco, soap, and salt to photolithography, ferns, mosses, wines, flowers, plants, and envelope-making machines. Yet the intercolonial exhibitions of the nineteenth century were so much more than grand trade fairs for Britain's colonies. They were celebrations of empire and an opportunity for sister settler colonies to flaunt their splendid achievements, to one another and to the metropole.

This celebration of empire in Victoria would also constitute a political and scientific forum in which the thorny issues of settler colonialism and the fate of Australian Indigenous peoples would be played out. In an article titled "The Condition of the Aborigines," *The Australasian* reflected on the "steady onward march to create the great Australasian nation" in light of the forthcoming exhibition. On the Aborigines, it opined that missionary efforts had failed and that it was impossible to "make a silk purse out of a sow's ear." The article continued: "We cannot whitewash the Ethiop, but we are not therefore to murder him, and in many, nay most cases, the treatment of the aborigines by the whites is civilised murder. To cause some hundreds of thousands of our fellow creatures to disappear – a powerful word, if understood – may be treated for the time being as a casualty, but is likely in the long run to prove a catastrophe."[60] The author of this compelling article offered a severe appraisal of colonialism around the globe. Columbus' encounter with the Americas had led to "overwork, contagious disease, starvation and despair" for the "proprietors of the soil." The fate of Native tribes in North America was tragic: "Once numbering twenty million," the author noted, they now represented "scarcely as many hundred thousands" and had "evaporated before the improvements of the Yankees." Furthermore, "the extinction of the native tribes entailed the African slave trade," a "cancer at the heart of America" that preyed on all "Anglo-Saxon masters alike." In the Antipodes, however, things were different. The Colony of Victoria did not exist in the fifteenth century but in the nineteenth, and humanity and good feeling surely played a part. Was it inevitable that the "native races" in Australia would die out, as they were in North America and Tahiti? Could these peoples be civilized? could they survive? or were the best efforts of missionaries and others a hopeless and financially wasteful task? Were the "aboriginal Australasians and Polynesians ... actually capable of coexistence by the side of the Europeans and their descendents or not?" he asked. The final urgent question was this: "Is this substitution of one race for another the consequence of inevitable law, or of European mismanagement and crime?" The article suggested that these questions, "now ripe for solution," could be addressed by a "species of scientific congress" to run alongside the Intercolonial Exhibition in Melbourne. The article's last injunction appealed to the public and political potential of the impending exhibition: "We think that *this subject of the native races should be thoroughly gone into* at the forthcoming Exhibition, and not left to the irregular and generally ignorant, though most well-intentioned efforts of ecclesiastical adventurers."[61]

A specific congress on these issues was never held; however, issues relating to the civilization or extinction of the "native races," colonial violence, and race in southeastern Australia in the 1860s were, nonetheless, apparent at the exhibition.

Although the subject of Aboriginal peoples was not explored as *The Australasian* would have wished, the editorial piece revealed a firm belief in the power of public exhibitionary formats to broker ideas about settler colonialism and racial violence. Aboriginal people may have been largely out of sight in Melbourne, but their treatment by settlers throughout the Australian colonies and the pressing tensions of race were not out of mind for some. Jane Lydon has observed that during times of turmoil exhibitions, "like other quickly established cultural institutions, stood as symbols of civilization in a dangerously volatile world."[62] Just as colonies were considered by some to be Europe's laboratories to test out new societies, so too official colonial and intercolonial exhibitions orchestrated in and by the colonies were civic forums in which issues that were specific and urgent to the colonies, such as the treatment and management of colonized Indigenous peoples, could be worked through.[63] This idea is apparent in the letters of the president of the Exhibition Commission, Judge Redmond Barry.

Judge Barry believed that the social and intellectual improvement of Aboriginal peoples could best be furthered by scientific study.[64] In March 1866 he sent a circular letter to a number of individuals who were associated, both closely and loosely, with the study of Aboriginal peoples. The Intercolonial Exhibition, he wrote, offered "a favourable opportunity for collecting materials relating to the history, traditions, customs, and language of the Aboriginal natives of Australia." The value of such an undertaking was clear to Barry: It was one in which "the combined operations of the European inhabitants of Australasia may be well engaged ... Moreover, it may form the groundwork of future more extended inquiries of a like nature, in the progress of which the intercourse with the Aborigines may lead to improvements in their intellectual and social as well as their physical condition. While *all employed may have the satisfaction of redeeming, in some degrees, the obligation they owe to the humble race – the primitive possessors of the soil.*" The collection of phenomena and ephemera relating to Aboriginal life and culture was rationalized by Barry as an endeavor that was scientific, preservationist, improving, and, importantly, redemptive. Barry conceptualized the joint European effort to collect and display Aboriginal culture as a form of collective, public redemption, as payment for a debt owed by the "European inhabitants of Australasia" to the "primitive possessors of the soil."[65]

Race on Show
At the exhibition, the colonies of Tasmania, South Australia, New South Wales, Victoria, Western Australia, New Zealand, French New Caledonia, and Dutch Batavia were on show. The exhibition was divided, by colony, into courts or pavilions and then subdivided into a range of categories.[66] In the courts of the

colonies of Victoria and Tasmania, Aboriginal cultural items and objects, as well as displays by Europeans that concerned Aboriginal peoples, were generally found in Class 4, "Manufactures and the Useful Arts," Section 14, "Articles of Clothing, Lace, Embroidery, Specimens of Native Workmanship."[67] These categories are strange to our twenty-first-century eye, yet they reveal much about systems of categorization in mid- to late nineteenth-century modernity. They were based largely on the standard divisions of London's Great Exhibition of 1851.

Our present understanding of these colonial displays is shaped predominantly by secondary texts. To study these exhibitions without considering the specific placement of Indigenous and non-Indigenous objects as revealed in the catalogue is to miss the narrative point and visual arc, which were designed by the exhibition's creators to instruct exhibition viewers in certain ways. To consider the viewer's experience of the exhibition, we need to read through the itemized catalogue, which traces the sequence of objects on display, and take an imaginary walk through the exhibition spaces. Although we cannot know with certainty how the nineteenth-century visitor received such exhibitions, we can make informed speculations based on knowledge of the historical context and public debates at the time. I therefore read the placement of objects with a postcolonial eye that is alert to the visual narratives of race on show.

The catalogue reveals that items made by women were plentiful in Section 14 of the Victoria Court. The largest display of Aboriginal objects was in this section of the Melbourne Division of the Victoria Court. The placement of artifacts made by Aboriginal people alongside the products of European women, such as lacework and embroidery, suggests some alignment between the handiwork of women and the material culture of Aboriginal people. The display was quite different from those in the Great Hall of European Fine Art and the Hall of Machinery, exhibits of progress that spoke to a universalized European masculinity. An imagined, universalized (white) masculinity was often contrasted to femininity and Aboriginality in many ethnologically inflected displays. This is apparent in Section 14's title.

In photographs of these displays, things seem to be all a jumble, like items in a Victorian curiosity shop, which at first appear to the uninitiated as an undifferentiated clutter. However, I propose that certain narratives were told through these displays. Sitting strangely next to lace needlework, hats, caps, and a knitted lace curtain made by the colony's white women, was a small box of "miniature Native weapons and implements used by the Natives of Australia before the advent of Europeans," which was made by Albert and Caroline Le Souëf, of Parliament House.[68] Nearby were 134 Aboriginal weapons and implements, collected from Aboriginal missions and stations, exhibited by the Central Board Appointed to Watch over the Interests of the Aborigines. Many spears, waddies, shields, throwing sticks, and other items were on display, and it is apparent from the catalogue that the makers were sometimes named. For example, traditional items such as "grass bags made by Maria," "grass nets made by Old King Tom," and "nets made by Old Mary" sat alongside examples of agriculture from Coranderrk Station. "The potatoes and oats were grown on the station, the ground being tilled by the Aborigines," notes the catalogue.[69] Next to this large display were articles of clothing and hats made by the inmates of Pentridge Prison. Adjacencies are powerful: it is perhaps not coincidental that the products of inmates of Pentridge Prison were on display alongside weapons and implements made by Aboriginal people at Coranderrk Station, who were not as physically confined as criminals but were, by 1866, largely under the control of the state. As Tony Bennett maintains, museums in the late nineteenth century were commonly viewed as machineries used in the "shaping of civic capacities." Exhibitions, in which "contrived and staged encounters between people and objects are arranged for the purpose of study," generated social messages for both civic and epistemological ends.[70] What civic messages were constructed for viewers at the Intercolonial Exhibition? In my reading, themes of improvement, transformation, and state correction implicitly linked several groups that were by this time wards of the state. We cannot be certain that visitors saw these linkages in 1866-67. Other readings are also possible.

Coranderrk Station, near Healesville, was considered a success story. As the 1866 report of the Central Board Appointed to Watch over the Interests of the Aborigines notes, it was deemed a showcase mission: "It is the most prosperous Aboriginal station in Victoria, or perhaps in Australia ... and it is not indebted for its success to any extraneous assistance."[71] With the assistance of Superintendent John Green, the Coranderrk residents established a township with some self-government, sought self-sufficiency based on the sale of hops and Aboriginal artifacts, and were proud of their achievements.[72] The agency of the people at Coranderrk needs to be marked. In April 1866 *The Argus* reported that "a number of the aborigines in the district of Coranderrk, Healesville, have expressed their intention of competing at the forthcoming Exhibition, opossum skin rugs, baskets, etc. being the articles in which they intend to exhibit their emulative skill to the test of public verdict."[73] It seems that Aboriginal people contributed these items willingly, although they did not receive any prizes for them. To the viewing public, the items made by Coranderrk's industrious residents and samples of oats and potatoes grown by them probably highlighted ideas about education and the improvement and civilization of the Aboriginal subject who had successfully learned to till the land through missionary instruction. Also on display were photographs of the Aboriginal stations at Coranderrk and Framlingham, which had been submitted by Brough Smyth of Melbourne, perhaps to promote the benefits of mission life.

The same court also featured items from Ebenezer Mission Station at Lake Hindmarsh that had been submitted by the Reverend F.W. Spieseke, a Moravian missionary. Included were European items of clothing made by Aboriginal women, such as "a pinafore made by Ruth," "a net for the hair by Rebecca," "one pin cushion, frock, collar and cuff" made by Margaret Elliot, a "chemise by Topsy," and a "pinafore by Lilley." These were juxtaposed with "Roman point-lace needlework" by Mrs. Claridge of Barry St. Carlton and a university gown by another non-Aboriginal woman. The intent to compare European and Aboriginal women's handiwork and comment on the education and improvement of Aboriginal women in the European domestic arts can be read here. Apparently, objects produced by these two different groups of women were not segregated. Strangely, the next section (which was still under the banner "Manufactures and the Useful Arts") displayed an array of objects – "spears, boomerangs, clubs, two Aboriginal skulls, one white kangaroo skin" – collected by C.M. Officer of Mount Talbot (for which he received an honourable mention) next to "ladies underclothing by Mrs Robinson of Brunswick street Fitzroy."[74]

Within the broad category of manufactures and the useful arts it was possible to read multiple, perhaps contradictory, themes. The items were seemingly placed at random, and many were indeed examples of "the useful arts." Nevertheless, we must account for objects like the "two Aboriginal skulls," which were not craft items, and the photographs. The arrangement of items both traditional and new by Aboriginal women, as well as the products of Aboriginal agricultural endeavours on missions, is also noteworthy. Furthermore, the placement of the products of Aboriginal people alongside those of prison inmates as described earlier cannot be overlooked. It may, of course, be overly deterministic to read a strategic colonizing intent into every exhibit and every object's placement, and the possibility that there could be a democratic juxtaposition of material, one that contrasted with the social realities of Victorian society outside the exhibition, should not be dismissed. It seems implausible, however, that these exhibitions were entirely devoid of political intent, that their only rationale was to create an appreciation for or sense of equivalence between European handiwork and that of Aboriginal peoples on missions. Despite the existence of a category for manufactures and the useful arts, Barry's overriding concerns when he called for Aboriginal items were scientific and preservationist, and he sought to demonstrate Aboriginal improvement. Yet we also cannot presume that the curatorial vision was singular; the displays were arranged by the exhibition commissioners who may have had divergent intentions. We cannot presume, therefore, that Barry's vision for the exhibition was always implemented in the displays.

It may be that these displays merely represented the random juxtaposition of craft items. This argument, however, suggests an easy pluralism that was not the case in 1866. The collective descriptors *craft items* and *handiwork* tend to obfuscate not only the specificity and type of objects selected by the commissioners but also from where and whom they came. Furthermore, the specular commerce of objects should not be underestimated. Objects, both individual and placed in sequence, operate beyond their formal boundaries by activating narratives in viewers that may well have been anticipated by the organizers. I suggest that the Melbourne display reveals the multivalency and fluidity of racial narratives in the 1860s. There is constant movement in these narrative sequences between incarceration and state protection and between Aboriginal subjects who had successfully taken on European ways and traditional items made by Aboriginal people such as "Old King Tom" and "Old Mary" who were deemed to be passing away. These items were also placed next to trophy and array-style displays of Aboriginal weaponry and randomly placed skulls of unnamed Aboriginal people. Array-style displays were an emulation of typological and ethnographic styles found increasingly in museums in Europe and the colonies. These displays were so much more than the comparison of craftwork. Appreciating their multiple themes as well as their ambiguities is key.

The inclusion of the Aboriginal skulls may have been for the sake of mere curiosity. Such placements, however, were often gestures to popular phrenology and growing concerns with racial science and taxonomic racial schema throughout the Empire. To whom did these Aboriginal skulls belong, and how did C.M. Officer of Mount Talbot obtain them? Tom Griffiths has documented the trend for collecting and sometimes nefariously exhuming Aboriginal skulls in the name of an emergent scientific racism that emerged in the Colony of Victoria during the 1860s and 1870s.[75] Barry himself had called for as many Aboriginal "skeletons and skulls ... as possible."[76] Objects such as skulls resonated or found purchase in the public imagination at this time because of the wide appeal of phrenology. We cannot ignore the broader social context and the confluence of powerful narratives of transformation, race, and science in the settler imagination that informed these displays.

The question of the "native races" was certainly being considered at the exhibition, although perhaps not in the ways that the editors of the *The Australasian* had hoped. And the issue of settler violence was not considered. Barry preferred a scientific approach, and his written instructions ran in accordance with scientific thought of the day. The Aboriginal people of Coranderrk Station may have possessed a certain amount of agency in the display of their own cultural materials, but they were also subject to much moral and scientific scrutiny at Barry's behest. In line with the practices of nineteenth-century ethnographers and reflecting a general interest in racial typologies, the residents of Coranderrk Station, many of whom were from the Melbourne area, were photographed systematically by Charles Walter. Walter had been commissioned by Barry to take the photographs.[77] A large panel of 104 portraits was titled "Portraits of ABORIGINAL NATIVES Settled at Coranderrk, near Healesville, about 42 miles from Melbourne. ALSO VIEWS Of the Station & LUBRAS BASKET-MAKING" and displayed in the fine arts section of the Intercolonial Exhibition. As Lydon has observed, the selection and arrangement of the portraits was important. People were divided by age, sex, and tribe, and the front view portraits revealed a "contemporary ethnographic interest in individuals as racial types." Furthermore, the older males at the top were denoted as "full blood," while those at the centre and bottom were described as "half caste," revealing an interest in blood quanta and issues of miscegenation. These were classic "type" portraits that were commonly associated with the emerging discipline of anthropology and used for purposes of systematic comparison.[78] Lydon writes that in a "final reductive moment this single object abridged 104 people, making them stand for the Aboriginal 'race.'"

In the court for the Colony of Tasmania, baskets made by Aboriginal women were placed beside a series of black-and-white photographic portraits of Aboriginal people – mainly older men and women such as "'Patty' or Cooneara ... nearly 70 years old," "'Wapperty' or Wanoteah Cootamena (Thunder and Lightening) ... nearly 70 years old," and "'Lalla Rook' or Truganini (Seaweed) ... nearly 60 years old" – who apparently represented the "last of" a dying race. One young man, William Lanney, who was about twenty-six years old, was also photographed and described as the "last of the Aborigines."[79] These photographic images had also been commissioned for the exhibition, and they were taken by photographer Charles Woolley. The Tasmanian photographs were of great contemporary significance; they were portrayed as tragic symbols of the last Aborigines of Tasmania and, therefore, made their own global journeys in books and museum displays.[80]

Whereas the transformation and civilization of Aboriginal peoples was a major theme in the Victoria Court, narratives of extinction were central in the Tasmanian Court. Also on display was a series of photographic plates of the "public buildings of Hobart town," with "statistics of the city and Corporation of Hobart" proudly displayed alongside "copies of the old and present seals of the colonies."[81] The narrative purchase of these adjacencies should not be underestimated. Aboriginal peoples disappear in the wake of progress, which is expressed effectively through images of the New World settler-colonial city on Indigenous land. The placement of progressive stadial themes – "last of" photographs juxtaposed with images of the progress of cities and white commerce, the regalia of the town councils, and the corporation of Hobart – is heavy with symbolism. In the colonial imaginary the settler-colonial city built on Aboriginal land was deemed to be the consummation of empire. Tony Bennett has shown the role that museums played as they mapped out both social space and time to create new entities such as "art, community, prehistory, or national pasts." Nineteenth-century museums, Bennett argues, organized the "socio-temporal coordinates of colonialism."[82] Just as they created new entities, however, they also replicated enduring themes popular in the collective imagination. In the Tasmanian display, the Western, historicizing narrative was apparent, and instructive linkages between the city, the state, city building, and the governance of Aboriginal peoples were on show for exhibition viewers.

Although the abundance of objects in the Tasmanian exhibition made it appear crowded and disorderly, the catalogue prepared by the exhibition organizers led the viewer through a clear sequence of objects. For example, photographs of two Aboriginal women by Mrs. Davidson of Hobart were next to a "sketch in oils of the baptism of Christ," which was followed by "life-size portraits of their Royal Highnesses the Prince and Princess of Wales." These were followed immediately by busts from the life of "Woureddy and Trugernina, Natives of Tasmania," who often figured in popular discourse as the "last" Tasmanian Aborigines. Also on display in this court was a tinted lithograph with the misnomer "Governor Davey's Proclamation to the Aborigines, 1816."[83] Illustrated with compelling images of friendship and equality before the law, including mutual punishment for Aborigines and Europeans alike, the lithograph reproduced images that had been issued by Governor George Arthur on boards and fastened to trees in Van Diemen's Land in 1829 and 1830 as a humanitarian call for friendship between Aboriginal peoples and newcomers and the cessation of frontier violence.[84] The lithograph was prepared specifically for the 1866 exhibition and was sent, along with other material relating to the Aboriginal peoples of Tasmania, to the Paris International Exhibition in 1867. The decision of the Tasmanian organizing committee to display this lithograph in Paris reveals the conscious discursive management of debates about Australian settler society, conciliation, and violence at the international level in the nineteenth century.

The juxtaposition of images of the "last" Tasmanian Aborigines, Christ, royalty, and the British rule of law side by side in the Tasmania Court of the Melbourne Intercolonial Exhibition proffered highly symbolic visual narratives of the British Empire, Christianity, and ideas about civilization. These displays contained very few captions and little that approximated the text panels of today's exhibitions. Low or partial literacy among some of the visitors also needs to be kept in mind. Learning through looking was a feature of nineteenth-century culture. Visual instruction and object-based pedagogy were central devices for Britain's museum curators and directors. At Melbourne's International Exhibition in 1880, the trustees promoted the exhibition's capacity as "a national educator, to teach by the eye."[85] Furthermore, as Annie Coombes reminds us, during the late 1860s "the middle-class viewer was too thoroughly steeped in evolutionary doctrines in relation to such material to avoid their association with an interpretation of the displays."[86] Although not all viewers may have been persuaded, ideas about ranking, the superiority of Europeans over Aboriginal peoples, and the benefits of Christianity for the improvement of Aboriginal peoples were, nevertheless, common. Objects and images may have elicited in viewers narratives that were already becoming regularized. It was precisely because the nineteenth-century public learned about much of its world by observation, rather than by reading, that visual instruction steeped in doctrines of progress was effective.

When colonial viewers looked at representations of Indigenous peoples, they were also being schooled in their position in imperial hierarchies and, consequently, racialized. How did exhibitions shore up ideas about white and Anglo-Saxon communities stretching throughout the colonies? Exhibition visitors who looked at imperial narratives were transformed into progressive, Anglo-Saxon subjects of empire. In this reflexive way, the race of the exhibition viewers was also explored. The medal struck for the exhibition, designed by Charles Summers, represented the allegorical figure of Victoria receiving her six colonial sisters, each of whom brings a contribution. The Latin quotation on the medal reads *Facies non omnibus una nec diversa tamen / Qualem decet esse sororum* (They all look different and yet alike, as sisters would). Visitors from the colonies were invited to imagine themselves as part of a family, as Anglo-Saxon subjects who, notwithstanding their differences, were racial kin connected through a transimperial network.

Anglo-Saxon Exceptionalism and the Racial Vigour of Colonists Compared
One visitor to the Intercolonial Exhibition did voice his opinion. According to Charles Wentworth Dilke, Melbourne was "exceptionally gay" and was receiving fifty thousand people a week – "a great number for the colonies." Dilke was a

fervent Anglo-Saxonist, and according to his book *Greater Britain: A Record of Travel in English-Speaking Countries during 1866 and 1867,* the Colony of Victoria was the "wealthiest of all the Australian nations, and India alone excepted, has the largest trade of any of the dependencies." He judged that "the progress of Melbourne is that of San Francisco."[87]

In Dilke's mind this economic success was entirely due to the "strong vitality of Melbourne men."[88] He attributed imperial success to the "unsurpassing vigour of the Victorians" and the fact that they were "far more thoroughly British" than the citizens of Sydney, the rival capital. Inviting a racialized environmentalism between Australia's colonies, he stated that people from Sydney were mere cornstalks "reared in semi-tropical climates," whereas the Victorians were "*full-blooded English immigrants,* bred in the more rugged climes of Tasmania, Canada, or Great Britain."[89] Victoria was, Dilke proclaimed, a "model colony," and he judged "her statistics" to be the most "perfect in the world." Evoking ideas about contiguous imperial spaces, he observed that "in many senses Melbourne is the London, and Sydney is the Paris of Australia."[90]

In his "sketches of Saxondom" around the globe, Dilke announced that "the Englishmen founds everywhere a New England – new in thought and soil."[91] And he concluded that he had "*followed England round the world* ... If I remarked that climate, soil, manners of life, that mixture with other peoples had modified the blood, I saw, too, *that in essentials the race was always one.*"[92] Above all, Dilke believed in the primacy and vigour of the Anglo-Saxon race and its ability to overcome moments of mixedness and miscegenation. Largely eschewing the dislocations and displacements of empire, Dilke was convinced that the Anglo-Saxon race would prevail; he believed in its "grandeur ... girdling the earth, which it is destined, perhaps, to overspread." He predicted that the dearer race would destroy the cheaper races and "Saxondom would rise triumphant from the struggle."[93]

If Victoria was the model colony, then the Canadas did not fit the mould, and British Columbia was nothing but stagnant. Commenting on the habits of the French, Dilke wrote, "In Canada and Tahiti the French intermingle with Native races, the Hurons are French in everything but name."[94] This was not the case in the United States: "In Kansas, Colorado, New Mexico, *miscegenation will never be brought about*" because of the English pride of race. The primacy of Anglo-Saxonism would be ensured in the United States and Australia, he believed, because of an "absolute bar to intermarriage" and even to "lasting connexions to Aborigines." The demise of Indigenous peoples in Tasmania and Victoria, he argued, would also occur in New Zealand and on the Plains of America. He recounted the views of a settler on the "Indian question" in America:

the Indigenous population in colonial outposts was dying out anyway because of war and whisky.[95] Indeed, evidence of racial vigour was apparent in that the "very scum and outcasts" of British society had moved out around the globe and "founded empires in every portion" of it.[96] Dilke's views did represent the extreme end of a rampant Anglo-Saxon exceptionalism, but they reflected discourses that were growing in the 1850s and 1860s and harnessed in the colonies. These discourses were offset by the many entreaties of humanitarians and others who held more tempered views.

Whiteness, especially in nineteenth-century British settler colonies, is best understood if it is historicized around the organizing and self-conscious "national and racial identity" of Anglo-Saxonism.[97] Accelerating ideas about racial uniqueness and an "Anglo-Saxon race" had crystallized for Britons by the mid-nineteenth century. British superiority, Robert Huttenback observes, was deemed to be, "not the result of anything as easily definable as education, climate, or the imperatives of economics or geography, it was due rather to the unique attributes of the British race."[98] With roots in at least the 1840s, ideas about Anglo-Saxon domination and a global brotherhood of English-speaking races and prophesies such as Dilke's about a great racial conflict from which "Saxondom will rise triumphant" began to develop and circulate.[99] Allen Frantzen and John Niles argue that Anglo-Saxonism became an identity that transformed into an origin myth of "vigorous emotive power."[100] In the British settler-colonial cities of the mid-nineteenth century, myths of Anglo-Saxon exceptionalism were mobilized in tandem with bourgeois metropolitanism in powerful ways.

In Dilke's mind British Columbia was indeed an inferior colony of the fur trade. The chief problem with Canada, he wrote, was that "our race is split in twain." On the Pacific side, it was settled mainly by Americans: "Situated for purposes of reinforcement, immigration, and supply at a distance of not less than twenty thousand miles from home, the British Pacific colonies can hardly be considered strong in their allegiance to the Crown; we have here the *reductio ad absurdum* of home government."[101] Government was reduced to the level of absurdity, he continued, and "if we take up the *British Columbian* we find the citizens of the mainland portion of the province proposing to sell the islands for twenty million dollars to the States." Lamenting lost wealth and missed opportunities, Dilke continued his disparaging commentary on the British colonies in Canada by noting that trade was hindered by "the presence of two sets of custom houses and two sets of coins between Halifax and Lake Superior." And he bemoaned the role of fur traders: "We have left a country the size of civilised Europe, and nearly as large as the United States – lying too, upon the track of commerce and the high road to China – to be despotically governed by a company of traders in skins and peltries, and to remain as long as it so pleases them in the dead stillness and desertion needed to ensure the presence of fur-bearing beasts."[102]

Dilke did not overtly mention mixed-race relations in British Columbia, but he did remark obliquely that the "fur-buying companies" had "enough to answer for."[103] The fur trade was linked implicitly with the stigma of mixed-race relations in many European minds, and a number of writers in British Columbia attributed the region's economic stagnation to the spectre of mixed-race relations. There were clear expressions of the belief that white men who cohabited with First Nations women lost their Anglo-Saxon industry and dedication to agriculture.[104] As Adele Perry observes, "colonial backwardness, class, and rurality were encapsulated in the mixed-race relationships." And for some scientists of the 1860s, observes Perry, mixed-race relationships were both "symbol and substance" of British Columbia's poor economic development.[105]

Imperialism is, above all else, a "zone of occult instability."[106] For Britons seeking a mirror of their own identity, the colonies caused confusion and anxiety. Despite the ruptures and anxieties of the colonial encounter in southeastern Australia, writers such as Dilke believed they could recognize with confidence the face of the Anglo-Saxon empire in Melbourne, and they easily dismissed miscegenation and the endurance of Aboriginal peoples in the face of expropriation and violence. Melbourne was the London of the Australian colonies. The high proportion of immigrants from the British Isles made this hope for cultural replications unsurprising. Yet uncertainty reigned in other locations of empire. In places such as British Columbia, the prevalence of mixed-race relationships and mixed-race peoples stretched and confounded metropolitan and middle-class ideas about Englishness. Rather than places of triumph, confidence, and sameness, these "territories of British imperialism [were] spaces of bewilderment and loss which continued to trouble and confound England's subjects."[107]

Outraged at the threat of a totalizing American ownership, Dilke called for an independent Canada: "Red River should be a second Minnesota, Halifax a second Liverpool, Esquimalt second San Francisco; but double government had done its work ... the Californians are expecting the proclamation of an American territorial government in the capital of Vancouver Island."[108]

The Colony of Victoria was celebrated as a model colony, the most successful of the British Empire. Potent ideas about Anglo-Saxon exceptionalism helped to construct overt linkages between the success of the Colony of Victoria, its supposed racial vigour and the purity of Victorians, and notions about masculinity in Melbourne. In comparison, fervent Anglo-Saxonists attributed British

Columbia's economic backwardness materially and symbolically to mixed-racedness. In British Columbia, imperialism had "gone awry."[109] If Esquimalt – the naval port near the Harbour of Victoria – should have been a second San Francisco, it was not to be. It is to this disappointing child of empire – Victoria, Vancouver Island – and its racialized urban spaces in the late 1850s and 1860s that I now turn.

From Bedlam to Incorporation: First Nations, Public Space, and the Emerging City
[Victoria, Vancouver Island, 1858-60s]

Who could doubt the reality of the great British empire of the North ... with free institutions, high civilisation, and entire freedom of speech and thought?

> – ALEXANDER MORRIS, LECTURE TO VICTORIA'S MERCANTILE LIBRARY ASSOCIATION, 1859[1]

[Victoria is the] fag end of the earth ... a chronic state of rocks, pine trees and natives ... a population with a Yankee cut and a Hebrew phiz, and a restless mass of miners.

> – ROBERT BURNABY, LETTER TO HIS SISTER, 1860[2]

THE GOLD RUSHES of southeastern Australia and the Pacific Northwest Coast radically altered Melbourne and Victoria. Both became gateways to the gold-fields, through which thousands of hopeful miners, men, women, and children from diverse places passed. The fur trade town of Victoria was transformed by the mania of the 1858 Fraser River Gold Rush into a city of immigrants who reorganized space and culture. In early 1858, when rumours of gold on the Thompson and Fraser rivers began to circulate in California, hopeful gold seekers began to leave their places of employment for the goldfields. But they first had to obtain a gold licence at Victoria. Seeking "El Dorado," fur traders likewise left their forts (it was feared that Fort Langley would be deserted) and crews abandoned their vessels. Many boats headed north from California. Vessels were often packed to overflowing when they arrived in Victoria. Other prospectors travelled by sea or overland from Oregon or Washington territories.[3] At the peak of the gold rush, the non-Indigenous population of Victoria rose to around six thousand.[4] As in Melbourne, a tent city sprang up. Chinese miners, African Americans seeking freedom from the constraints of the United States, Métis and Pacific Islander people working for the Hudson's Bay Company, and miners from California, Mexico, Australia, Italy, France, Russia, Ireland, and England made up the mix in Victoria's busy, but only partly formed, streets.

Within four months of the discovery of gold, Victoria's journalists, excited at the chance of finally drawing capital and labour to the struggling colony's shores, were promoting the town's prospects. In late 1858 Alfred Waddington, in classic bourgeois metropolitan style, waxed enthusiastic about the civic virtues of Victoria in the *British Colonist*. Ever conscious of the great republic to the south, he believed the city to be superior to any town in the United States:

> We shall say nothing of its climate, its unrivalled position and other natural advantages. But where, in spite of the stifling influences of monopoly, shall we find so much progress? Where in so short a time have there been so many streets laid out, built up and some of them graded, macadamised, planked and even lighted up as in Victoria? Eight substantial wharves carried out into the harbour, two brisk hotels ... twenty or thirty restaurants, and coffee houses, steamboats built and launched, in short all the beginnings of a large city. Where a more orderly population or law abiding? Where in the United States a city without taxes, lawyers, or public debt?[5]

Mining rights, expropriation of Indigenous lands, and settlement went hand in hand. Waddington called for greater freedom for miners ("Let miners make their own bye-laws and regulations") and for access to Indigenous lands ("Let the country be entirely thrown open"). He also called for "everyone [to] be allowed to buy land at American prices and not at five dollars an acre; and instead of throwing obstacles in the way of the colonist, give the poor bone fide [sic] settler a right of pre-emption and a premium of land, taken from the wild waste."[6]

Expropriation of Indigenous land, the use of the "wild waste," and the replacement of Indigenous peoples with "English-speaking men" would shape a familiar trajectory of dispossession in the gold-bearing colony. In the same year, 1858, the *Vancouver Island Gazette* organized its destiny around the growing discourses of transimperial Anglo-Saxonism and city building by announcing: "The destiny of England is to colonise and lay the foundations of Empire in distant lands, to raise up the flourishing cities under the shadow of primeval forests, and enrich the earth with settlements of English-speaking men."[7] Counterposing the primeval stage with ideas about the flourishing city as the highest stage in the narrative of progress, Waddington outlined a familiar transglobal story about destiny, white men, and the new land. In town, promoters and speculators wanted to replicate British civic space and imagined a New World city of wealth, civilization, and settlement. At the height of the Fraser River Gold Rush, in 1859, Alexander Morris delivered a lecture to an enthusiastic crowd at Victoria's Mercantile Library Association:

> In the rapid planning of the Anglo-Saxon civilisation, the finger of providence was manifest ... The discoveries of gold had singularly been the precursors of the

mixed races, which for want of a better name were the Anglo-Saxon race. Thus the discovery of gold in California, next Australia was more densely peopled, and now the discovery of gold in Columbia *had planted a new centre of light and civilisation on the Pacific* ... surely a time had come when all of it that was fit for settlement should be thrown open for the immigrant ... one cannot pass through this fair valley without feeling that it is destined sooner or later to become the happy home of civilised men, with their bleating flocks and lowing herds – with their schools and churches ... Vancouver's Island ... [is] a sort of England attached to America ... who could doubt the reality of the great British empire of the North ... with free institutions, high civilisation, and entire freedom of speech and thought ... it would yet be realised if the people of British North America were only true to themselves and their manifest destiny.[8]

The California, Australia, and Fraser River gold rushes were imagined as a gift of Providence, as material proof of the imperial destiny of the Anglo-Saxon race. Evoking ideas about England's cultural and geographic replication in the Pacific, Morris imagined that Vancouver Island would be "a sort of England attached to America." Racialized narratives of expropriation, settlement, and manifest destiny linked the British white settler colonies, and gesturing between them was common. In 1862, no doubt in a similar mood of gold rush optimism, R.C. Mayne wrote: "The least experienced eye could see the capabilities of the site of Victoria for a town, and that it was capable, should the occasion ever arise, of springing into importance as Melbourne or San Francisco had done."[9] Victoria's promoters imagined their city as a future hub of the British Empire in the Pacific that would dominate trade with Asia. Importantly, the "Anglo-Saxon" gold rushes were to plant new centres of "light and civilisation on the Pacific." These Anglo-Saxon enthusiasts also viewed themselves as "culture bringers," as people with superior knowledge of agriculture, cities, language, law, and religion. They would bring civilization and asserted that their presence on the Northwest Coast was preordained.[10]

Hierarchies of Empire: Progress and Transimperial Networks

In 1858 the *British Colonist*, in a gold rush mood, mentioned the "thrilling possibility" of the intercolonial railway being "built from Quebec to Halifax."[11] News items about technology's effect on travel and its potential to bring colonial subjects closer together excited readers, who interpolated ideas about progress, expansionism, and empire in the accounts. Technology, however, not only caused spatial collapse, so to speak, but also produced new spaces and ways of seeing them. Bruce Braun, who explores the relationship between landscape, power,

and colonialism on the Northwest Coast, discusses the way that new transportation technologies such as rail and steam of the mid- to late nineteenth century
helped to reconfigure vision and landscape in the city and its environs. Increased
mobility permitted the bourgeoisie to "experience the city and country as distinct
domains," to evoke stadial differentiations; thus, it was "constitutive of emerging
bourgeois subjectivities."[12] Building upon Cole Harris' ideas about an assembling
geography of power on the Northwest Coast, Braun notes that systems of
transportation and communication in the region were spatial extensions of
colonial power. Braun compellingly sums up Harris' findings:

> His point is simple yet critical: technological and spatial transformations at the
> time were not culturally or politically innocent; they *repositioned* people and
> things. For instance, the time-space compression that came with these networks
> allowed for capital to colonize space in British Columbia in new ways. From
> wagon roads to railroads, postal services to telegraphs, paths opening for people,
> capital and commodities that were not previously available enabled new social,
> economic and cultural transformations, reterritorialized the coast and ushered
> in new spaces of identity, culture and politics.[13]

By the late nineteenth century, tourism and increased connections to centres
of culture and commerce on the eastern coast, which were augmented by the
rise of steam travel, would help to produce the West Coast as a distinct Canadian
region in material and imaginative terms.[14]

Yet I argue that the imaginative production of the Colony of British Columbia
occurred simultaneously through its *relation* to other colonies and its position
in the hierarchical network of British-speaking domains. The interconnected-
ness of the British white settler colonies was also conceived through powerful
ideas about progress and industrial capital and notions about a universalized,
transglobal space of commerce, which was demonstrated by new forms of travel
and technology. Public speakers, newspapers, and global performances such as
intercolonial exhibitions allowed colonies to insert themselves into globalized
colonial discourses of development and progress. The *British Colonist,* for example, looking again to a colony that was one model for success, announced
that the "electronic telegraph between Sydney and Melbourne is nearly complete.
It is already in operation through Victoria, between Melbourne and Albury;
and through NSW from Sydney, as far as Gundagai."[15] Later, amid promising
announcements of more gold finds in the Colony of New South Wales, it noted
that the "intercolonial line of telegraphs between Tasmania and the mainland
has been opened. The first message was despatched from Hobart town, at twenty

minutes past four on Wednesday evening, and reached Sydney on Thursday morning."[16] Such notices welcomed the infrastructural development of the colonies and the collapse and reordering of space as measures of colonial success.

Highlighting the imbrication of imperial space and subjectivities, Élisée Reclus wrote of the transimperial subject *civis Britannicus* and ideas about globalized British colonial networks. Reclus' civis Britannicus was a thoroughly bourgeois, male, Anglo-Saxon subject who toured the British colonies and whose vision and subjectivity were altered and constituted through travel. As we have seen, Charles Wentworth Dilke, who perhaps was civis Britannicus personified, "followed England round the world" and optimistically imagined Anglo-Saxon cognate space wherever he went. Assessing these transimperial networks, Dilke wrote grandly, "The Englishman founds everywhere a new England – new in thought and soil."[17] New forms of transportation moved travellers through geographical space, causing a shrinking of space, a certain detachment, and a new relation that was primarily visual.[18]

New forms of travel had implications for the way that Europeans perceived and understood First Nations. Braun argues further that new geographies and scopic regimes altered encounters between Europeans and Indigenous peoples. The confinement of First Nations to missions throughout the late nineteenth century and the rise of a modernizing, panoramic style of travel reduced direct encounters with Native peoples. Braun argues that Euro-Canadians were no longer reliant on Native labour or knowledge by the late nineteenth century: First Nations were no longer intermediaries. The "emerging space economies of the late nineteenth century on the coast often by-passed their villages." Travellers frequently described First Nations villages as run down or dilapidated; they linked the villages to the idea of the inevitable extinction of Aboriginal peoples by using words or phrases such as *vanishing* or *becoming obsolete*.[19] In their stead white settlements were nodes that provided trade, services, and information in an expanding settler network.[20] Here again we have the powerful discourse of the settler-colonial city or metropolitan centre as triumphal and progressive in commercial and stadial terms, while the Native village is represented as a backward, anachronistic site from another stage.

Gestures between British colonies across the Pacific Ocean in public forums such as newspapers, public lectures, and travelogues bolstered colonists' idea of themselves as global, imperial subjects and reinforced popular belief in European, imperial, bourgeois progressivism. It is amply apparent that this type of imperial, spatial commerce entailed the production of space *and* subjectivities at global and local levels. Globalized narratives of Anglo-Saxon exceptionalism and bourgeois metropolitanism sought to triumphantly link Victoria to other British settler-colonial cities such as Melbourne.

For some immigrants to Vancouver Island, however, empire was a mixed up, uncertain place, and they voiced their disappointment. Robert Burnaby journeyed from England to British Columbia on hearing news of the gold rush. The Pacific Northwest was to be his El Dorado, the place where he hoped to make his fortune. Writing home to his mother, he expressed the belief that the "Fraser River excitement was such a mania that [I] could not do otherwise than react."[21] Within a year of his arrival, however, he wrote home that Victoria was not a great Anglo-Saxon hub of enterprise, it was the "fag end of the earth ... a chronic state of rocks, pine trees and natives ... a population with a Yankee cut and a Hebrew phiz, and a restless mass of miners."[22] In this "land of promise," prospects were slow. "Everyone is quietly lying by, a few people investing money, but no real business."[23] Burnaby observed the miners coming off the boats in Victoria's harbour and noted "80 Australian miners" and "others on the road." And with a racist foreboding similar to that found among miners and settlers in Port Phillip, he warned darkly that "our chief immigrants ... have been crowds of Chinese, who are more likely to become a pest to the country than any advantage."[24] Many, like Burnaby, had doubts about the future success of this piece of the British Empire in the Pacific.

The transformative gold rush period marked the beginning of the loss of control of land for many First Nations in British Columbia. But it also entailed the formation of a new colony. The Fraser River Gold Rush of the summer of 1858 led the British government to end the Hudson's Bay Company's grant and to resume direct control of Vancouver Island. It also prompted the establishment of the Colony of British Columbia in the mainland region known as New Caledonia. The Colonial Office issued James Douglas jurisdiction as lieutenant-governor of both colonies in the Pacific Northwest.[25]

Eden to Bedlam: Tensions in the Growing City

If one were to believe today's travel brochures, Victoria, the capital of British Columbia, is more English than the English.[26] The city on the edge of the Pacific Northwest Coast now markets itself as the "quintessential seaside resort of yesteryear," where the tourist may experience the British charm of high tea at the Empress Hotel or take a horse-drawn carriage around the neat, gridded city with its Victorian buildings. One travel writer, referring to the Queen's impending Golden Jubilee visit in 2002 remarked, "The Queen will probably feel a touch of nostalgia when she arrives in Victoria ... The streets are safe and the climate is mild" (see Figure 21).[27]

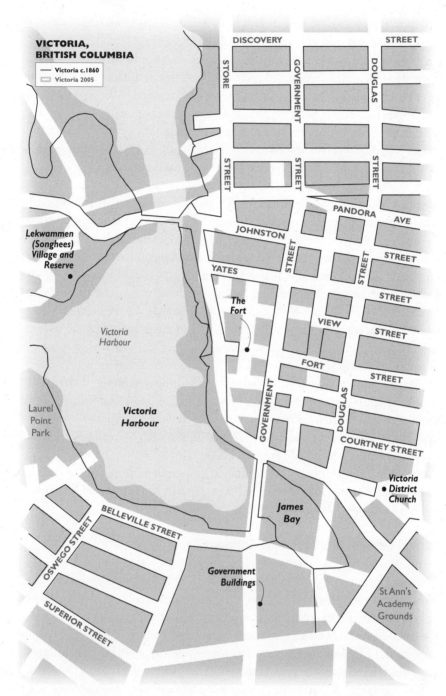

Figure 21 The city of Victoria, ca. 1860, compared with Victoria in 2005.
Cartography by Paul de Leur.

Yet the nineteenth-century British idyll that tourist brochures seek to evoke never existed. Similarly, the Anglo-Saxon hub of empire that gold rush promoters hoped to create was largely in the imagination. The *British Colonist* in 1859 decried the state of the colonial town, noting "the dark catalogue of Indian crime in our midst."[28] The place was a "slaughterhouse" marked by "aboriginal butcheries," vice, and intoxication.[29] "Place bolts on your doors at once," it warned.[30]

The population of this frontier gold rush town was plural and transient. First Nations, who far outnumbered Europeans and other immigrants, created anxiety for the settler population in town. Increasing numbers of First Nations groups, drawn by the new opportunities of the gold rush, flocked to town in canoes, often in the summer, to trade with one another and obtain work from Europeans. The *British Colonist* reported on 24 March 1860: "INDIANS – About 500 Fort Rupert Indians arrived by canoe last evening." Two weeks later it again reported: "MORE INDIANS – on Tuesday evening we counted, from Esquimalt Bridge fifty-four canoes filled with Hyder and Stickeen Indians just arrived from the North ... and yesterday crowded our principal streets offering furs and trinkets for sale."[31] No doubt this new European-style town in the heart of Lekwammen territory, with its multitude of new arrivals, was also a spectacle for First Nations. Drawn by curiosity and the promise of wealth, First Nations were quick to incorporate aspects of the European gold rush economy into their own economy of trade and culture of gift giving, as they had done so aptly with aspects of the mercantile fur trade economy since at least the eighteenth century.

In the summer of 1860, an alarmed Governor James Douglas wrote to the Colonial Office about Aboriginal peoples and described them as a "positive nuisance": "Fresh arrivals [are] constantly occurring, so that at the present moment there are nearly four thousand Indians in the outskirts of the town of Victoria ... with much apprehension felt by the inhabitants ... at the close contiguity of a body of Savages double to them in number."[32] As the fear and anxiety of settlers in the town approached its zenith, Aboriginal shanties and slum areas at the northern edge of town and the Aboriginal reserve were increasingly represented as bedlam, as a place of madness, degradation, and savagery. The sensationalism of the press can always be relied on. Highlighting the dislocations and displacements of empire and the imagined imperial city, the *British Colonist*, under the headline "Won't Go!" reported that police had been sent to summon "northern" Aboriginal people from the northern end of the town to leave, "but they refused to go." "They are a great nuisance," the article continued indignantly, "rendering *property in their quarter valueless*. Their camp is perfect Bedlam and one of the greatest dens of vice and crime ever permitted in a Christian community."[33] Figure 22 shows First Nations settlements or "shanties" in Victoria.

Figure 22   First Nations settlements or "shanties" in Victoria, 1867-68.
City of Vancouver Archives, A26498.

Nearly two decades earlier, James Douglas, surveying the southern tip of
Vancouver Island for the Hudson's Bay Company, had dubbed this New World
place a "perfect Eden," a place apparently "dropped from the clouds" by Providence.[34] If Eden functioned as a historical and spatial reference to the utopian
and the picturesque, as a harbinger of settlement, then the bedlam of the Native
camp evoked a disordered, chaotic space of madness that was weighted with
moral discrimination. In this sense, bedlam was a spoiled idyll. It was a countersite and a heterotopia to ideas about ordered urban space. In the settler imagination, Eden threatened to become bedlam.

Dispatches 19 and 33: Native Title, Land Sales, and Towns

In 1859 newspapers in British Columbia highlighted the violence of the streetscape, particularly violence visited upon First Nations women. "The body of
an Indian woman has been floating for some time in the water, near Finlayson's
saw mill," reported the *British Colonist*.[35] Although police had been notified, the

newspaper claimed that the woman had been floating for weeks, and police had "made no effort to bury the body, much to the disgust of all pedestrians who wander in that direction." The *Colonist* continued:

> In a community of professed Christians to treat "the image of God" like the carcass of a brute, neither speaks well of its humanity nor Christianity. On a government which asks to be exonerated for the abuse of power, on the ground of being best qualified to govern Indians, the instance we refer to is a melancholy commentary – showing how easily it is to preach but how difficult to practise. The spirit of "Despatch 19" forwarded from the Colonial Office to the Executive, originating with the Aborigines Protection Society in England, appears to have been forgotten.[36]

Dispatch 19 was issued by the secretary of state for the colonies, Edward Bulwer-Lytton, after the 1858 appointment of James Douglas as lieutenant-governor of Vancouver Island and the new Colony of British Columbia. It suggested not only that "Natives should ... be protected from wanton outrages on the part of the white population" but also that "Native title should be recognised in British Columbia." Noting that "the recognition of Native rights has latterly been a prominent feature in the aboriginal policy of both England and the United States," the dispatch emphasized that

> the English government should be prepared to deal with [Native] claims in a broad spirit of justice and liberality ... We would beg, therefore, most respectfully to suggest that the Native title should be recognised in British Columbia, and that some reasonable adjustment of their claims should be made by the British Government ... it would seem that a treaty should be promptly made between the delegates of British authority and the chiefs and their people, as loyal, just and pacific as that made between William Penn and the Indians of Pennsylvania, but that more stringent laws should be made to ensure its provision being maintained with better faith than was carried out on the part of the whites. *No nominal protector of the aborigines* – no annuity to a petted chief – no elevation of one chief above another, *will answer the purpose.*"[37]

Between 1850 and 1854 James Douglas had fashioned fourteen agreements or "treaties" with First Nations on Vancouver Island. Eleven were made near Victoria, one was made at Nanaimo, and two were made at Fort Rupert. Douglas was urged by Bulwer-Lytton to do the same in the new Colony of British Columbia. Unlike in Australia, where Native title was not acknowledged and treaties were not made, in British Columbia, the Colonial Office, which had been hesitant to intervene on title issues in the early 1850s, now suggested some recognition of Native title. However, despite Dispatch 19, the Colonial Office was ambivalent and, as Cole Harris has noted, put no real pressure on James Douglas to "face the issue of Native title on the mainland."[38]

Dispatch 19, it seemed, also referred to the failed protectorate system in Port Phillip when it noted that "*No nominal protector of the aborigines ... will answer the purpose.*" In the view of the Colonial Office, no protectorate system could stand in for treaties. And, indeed, although there were missionaries on Vancouver Island, no protectorate system was established. Furthermore, the dispatch suggested that "well-selected men, *more or less of Indian blood*" should be employed to promote the civilization of the "Indians." It suggested that mixed-race people, who came predominantly from Red River, were to be admitted into the administrative ranks of the colonial apparatus. Reminiscent of a style of indirect rule that was a growing feature of second-wave British colonialism, the Colonial Office suggested that a colonized elite should be given positions within the colonial system.

Although Dispatch 19 urged recognition of Native title, there was, in fact, a confusing assortment of Native land policies in the Empire in the mid-nineteenth century, and, as Harris observes, Colonial Office land policies respecting Vancouver Island and British Columbia were "fluid, parsimonious, and contradictory."[39] Native title issues were never confronted or resolved for these "two distant and relatively inconsequential colonies" on the Northwest Coast.[40]

Yet James Douglas' land policies had been liberal in intent. Legislation for the Aboriginal pre-emption of land was considered, but it would have been very difficult to achieve because the terms for Aboriginal pre-emption were heavy. First Nations could never hope to hold onto their land but could pre-empt it within the broad terms of colonial law. As Harris notes, however, most First Nations could never have afforded the labour costs of clearing, fencing, and building a house.[41] In addition, First Nations groups had been permitted to select their reserve sites on Vancouver Island and in the Fraser Valley on the Mainland, and, as Harris notes, the size of some reservations in British Columbia was generous. But by the time of Douglas' retirement in 1864, many reserves had been pegged out but not gazetted, and because they had never been enshrined in legislation, settlers could encroach upon them. Douglas' successors believed that this policy was "too open-handed."[42] Much has been written about Douglas' treaties and land polices, and in effect Douglas both extinguished and affirmed Native title through them.[43] My interest, however, lies in the Lekwammen Reserve in the city of Victoria and the particular spatial commerce that ensued in the streetscape.

It is no coincidence that dispatches regarding settlement were made in the same year as Dispatch 19. In October 1858, for example, Dispatch 33 stipulated that the "first object ... will be land sales" and that "you will not fail to regard with a military eye the best position for towns and cities, as well as for the engineering of roads and passes, [and] the laying the foundations of any public works."[44] Dispatch 33 also stated that although "policy will dictate every effort to conciliate" the "savage tribes" that surrounded the settlement, "some military strength and disciplined organisation are essential preservatives to the settlers."[45] The strategic, concomitant making of European colonial space and Indigenous space is apparent in this directive. A thoroughgoing reorganization and marking out of the landscape as property occurred. While towns and cities were gazetted with a military eye and auctions of allotted lands were promoted excitedly in newspapers, Indigenous spaces were reduced to small reserves that fit into the cadastral survey. In this way, the staged expropriation of First Nations land occurred.

The Lekwammen Reserve and Native Camps in Town

As the issues of Native title and the extinguishment of land were contested throughout the 1860s in the outlying frontier, authorities in the urbanizing frontier city increasingly reorganized and partitioned their residents along the axis of race. Native reserves and the terms of their creation became the subject of intense and long-standing legal and municipal debates, which have carried well into the present. In Victoria the Lekwammen actively negotiated for over fifty years to retain their reserve on the Inner Harbour across from the city.[46] The first reserve was a ten-acre site thought to have been established by Douglas in 1850. It is now the site of the Legislative Buildings, grand stone buildings with large domes built in the High Victorian style that represent the very force of the province. There is evidence that the Lekwammen offered to sell this reserve to the governor in 1854 and moved to the other side of the Inner Harbour.[47]

In 1852 the Hudson's Bay Company's surveyor, Joseph Despard Pemberton, laid out the second Native reserve, which was forty-seven acres, at nearby Esquimalt Harbour.[48] As Harris notes, it seems that neither Pemberton nor Douglas gave any thought to the placement of the rectangular reserves in respect to any pre-existing villages or to "cultivated" fields in the vicinity, as was stipulated in the language of the treaties.[49] Several other small reserves were established on the Inner Harbour. The one commonly recognized as the Lekwammen Village and Reserve, established around 1857, was between 90 and 112 acres (see Figure 23).[50] In 1858, with increased pressure on the town because of the gold rush, Governor Douglas gave instructions to Pemberton to lay out the extended town.[51]

Figure 23   The Lekwammen Reserve, looking towards the city of Victoria, ca. 1866-69. Admiral Hastings Album, BC Archives, F-09557.

Spectacle, Borders, and Margins: The Lekwammen Reserve

European perceptions of the Lekwammen Reserve were reminiscent of their apprehension of Indigenous people's camps around settler-colonial towns in southeastern Australia. Ideas about spectacle, slum life, dirt, and disease prevailed and gave rise to a colonial touristic experience, the thrill of European disloca-tion, which is now familiar to us. Indigenized spaces in the townscape such as shanties, slums, and reserves were places where Europeans feared property would be rendered valueless.

As in Port Phillip, the Lekwammen Reserve in Victoria was a site of spectacle for the imperial traveller. Robert Burnaby's letter to his sister in England took her on an imaginary, titillating tour of the reserve that evoked the voyeuristic accounts of journeys into dark London slums found in many newspapers. We can almost hear Burnaby's conspiratorial voice: "Let us now take a walk over the bridge to the other side of the harbour ... to which their houses are restricted. We can tell where their lodges are by the smoke that hangs over the spot, and now we are getting near for we see the skulking dogs ... and a few Klootchmen [Aboriginal women] scattered here and there in the bush; their gaudy blankets and showy silk handkerchiefs shewing gaily in the dark green foliage. Now for the smells! Horrible and filthy, and mind you pick your way. So we arrive at last amongst the huts. The rudest possible structures, uprights and lean-to's of

sticks."[52] Native camps at the edge of the town and in the reserve were represented as places of disorder, violence, and disease. They were bedlam compared to the ordered civil space of the growing city. Yet these were the homes of First Nations, and as Mary-Ellen Kelm argues, such living conditions were produced by colonization and were neither natural to First Nations nor indigenous to British Columbia.[53] Like so many cities, the developing spaces of Victoria had become inscribed in the European imagination with a moral topography of binaries and inversions. "The nature of the red man is savage and perverse," noted W.C. Grant to the Royal Geographical Society in London in 1859, "he prefers war to peace, noise to quiet, dirt to cleanliness."[54] We see in Burnaby's and Grant's accounts the idea that Aboriginal people had a "natural" tolerance for dirt and uncleanliness. But Native camps were not natural entities: they were constituted in relation to other spaces of colonization. In reference to the imaginary, moral, and material topographies in the urbanizing landscape, there were no places that existed outside of places produced through colonization and assimilation.

Inscribed with European medical ideas about racial hygiene that were circulating in the late 1850s and 1860s, Aboriginal spaces were viewed by European observers as dirty, disease-ridden places of vice and disorder, as the antithesis of the ordered, rational civil space of the gridded city. Aboriginal spaces were

Figure 24   Lekwammen housing, 1867-68. City of Vancouver Archives, A26499.

presented as uncivilized and savage, as madness materialized (see Figure 24). Above all, the reference to bedlam alerts us to ideas about borders and margins. As Mary Douglas has reminded us, just as dirt is matter out of place that defines and offends order, the notion of bedlam – crazy, chaotic, Aboriginal space – both defines and offends the boundaries and the terms of ordered, rational Christian civil space, of British cognate space.[55] The tension between ideas about civilization and savagery played itself out spatially in the townscape. In May 1860 an editorial in the *British Colonist* condemned the "aboriginal butcheries" in this "Christian town," and the disparity between Christianity and Aboriginality was likened to the "mythical gulf that divides Heaven and Hell." The writer complained of the "lesser evils of [Aboriginal people's] presence," including the "filling of our prisons and hospitals, the reduced *price of property* and the utter demoralisation that ever exists in their neighbourhood," and argued that they were "of themselves sufficient to cause their speedy removal."[56] The "madness" of Aboriginal spaces was conceived as an impediment to progress and, importantly, as a threat to property values. Europeans zealously protected the value of town property, which had only recently been converted from expropriated Indigenous land.

Native Title and Fights over the Lekwammen Reserve

Issues of Native title in settler colonies are frequently seen as being exclusive of cities, as if such issues were not equally pertinent to cities and the urban frontier as they were to the frontier. On the contrary, expropriation, Native title, the sequestering of Indigenous peoples, and the building of cities were thoroughly imbricated in policy and practice. In the same meeting at which Douglas proposed the creation of permanent Native villages on reserves, one of the first bills for "enfranchising the town of Victoria" was put forward.[57]

While speculators in town fought to protect their property, they also sought to expropriate any remaining Indigenous land in the town's vicinity. The Lekwammen Reserve quickly became an object of commercial desire for town speculators. An examination of the years 1859-63 through newspapers and the records of the Legislative Council and Corporation of Victoria minutes reveals the various methods that legislative and municipal authorities used to subvert Lekwammen control of the reserve. Certain members of the Legislative Council sought to purchase the reserve and allot its spaces. They were persistent in their efforts. In January 1859 Councillor James Yates moved that the "Indian reserve should be purchased from the Indians: the ground to be laid out in own lots. Sold to the highest bidder and that the proceeds or part of them shall be allotted for the purpose of removing obstructions and building bridges etc in Victoria Harbour."[58] The following week, Yates again questioned the Legislative Council: "Has the government ... the power to remove the Indians by purchase?[59] One year earlier when merchants were likewise pushing for the purchase of the Lekwammen Reserve on the other side of the harbour, James Douglas had stated in the House of Assembly that Native reserves had been "distinctly marked on the maps and surveys of the colony and ... the Government bound by the faith of a solemn agreement to protect them in their enjoyment of their agrarian rights." As Harris has noted, the title of reserve land was vested in the Crown, and First Nations could not sell or lease it.[60]

Douglas sought to walk a fine line between eager town developers and the rights of Lekwammen peoples, although he, as Crown representative, would eventually oversee the subdivision and lease of the reserve. Douglas sought to use the funds from the transaction for a school and a missionary teacher. "By such means," he argued, "a great benefit, worthy of the philanthropy of our country, will be conferred upon the Indians themselves, while at the same time, the improvement and the increase of the Town of Victoria will not be retarded by their *unprofitable occupation* of one of the most valuable portions."[61]

The extinguishment of title is implicit in any treaty. Treating with Indigenous peoples in the developing cityscape provisionally acknowledged Native title but also held the seeds of extinguishment through the efforts of colonial legislatures and municipal authorities. The existence of a reserve in the middle of Victoria's developing urban space affected the socio-spatial politics of the town in ways that differed from developments in Melbourne. In Melbourne, the peoples of the Kulin Nation were perennially displaced, and their camps, even the missionary camp, around the edge of the town grid were always viewed as illegitimate, other spaces. Ultimately, municipal authorities could eradicate these spaces merely by designating them as nuisances or unwholesome space that offended public order. In Victoria, however, things were different. The Lekwammen Reserve was at least nominally a legally enshrined space that could not be easily overturned. As James Douglas argued, "When the settlement of Victoria was formed certain reservations were made in favour of the Native Tribes ... *and the faith of the government is pledged, that their occupation shall not be disturbed*."[62] At the very least, the existence of treaties and reserves in British Columbia located the Lekwammen and other First Nations within a language or discourse of sovereignty. One exception, however, was the subversion of Lekwammen claims through alternative municipal manoeuvres. These manoeuvres were a means by which authorities could legitimately overturn Native title and exclude Aboriginal bodies through ideas about the rule of law enacted at the municipal level. As Renisa Mawani notes about Victoria and the segregation of First Nations, "authorities attempted to erase their own complicity in colonisation by creating their own subjectivities as virtuous, moral, and law-abiding." Mawani rightly notes that the "colonial authorities endeavoured to displace [the Lekwammen] with great care and trepidation, often debating the fairness and legality of the proposed displacement strategies."[63] While the colonial legislature enshrined white civic spaces by securing "public reserves for education and a public purposes," it also undermined the Lekwammen Reserve through the incremental process of allotment, which overturned Aboriginal communal ownership of land, commodified it, and prepared it for sale. In this formative transitional process, Indigenous land was gradually incorporated as private property. This was the distinct spatial commerce of Victoria as a settler-colonial city.

Councillor Yates continued to employ arguments about morality to call for the sale of the reserve. He declared that "the Indians [are] a nuisance often insulting to the modesty of females or families and ought to be removed ... His

Excellency the Governor's proposition was absurd, because while the Indians remained in a position where spirits could so easily be had nothing could be done in the way of civilising them; *besides the income derived from the sale of the reserve ... would bring an enormous income ...* and the Indians would have such an idea of the value of the land that thereafter their title could not be extinguished by this means."[64] One month later, surveyor J.D. Pemberton, who was also a councillor, made an address to the governor in which he disagreed with Yates on the issue of the Lekwammen Reserve, but for purely strategic and commercial reasons. He warned that the proposed plan to lease out allotments would be difficult to implement since the "Indians" would "diminish very greatly the value of land." Evoking ideas about imminent extinction, Pemberton was also concerned that "when the Indians who by right now occupy this Reserve become extinct, which will probably be the case in a very few years, this Reserve would once again become the property of the Crown instead of being the property of the Town of Victoria."[65]

It is abundantly clear that the extinguishment of Native title in outlying areas and the gradual subdivision and selling off of reserves in town was an interrelated process on Vancouver Island. Indeed, the reserve in the city was represented as a test case for the possibility of the quick extinguishment of lands in outlying areas. During the same meeting in which Pemberton made his address, Yates asked: "Would the Governor inform the House ... if the Indians who formerly owned the lands in the following Districts, viz. Nanaimo, Victoria, Esquimalt, Metchosin and Sooke have been paid in full; and if so do they fully understand that they have no further claims upon the Government for said lands, and may it please his excellency to state the cost of said lands per mile."[66] Yates also requested that a select committee be appointed to investigate the Lekwammen's title and how long they had inhabited the reserve land, which Councillor Helmcken considered a gross insult.[67] In addition to lobbying for the sale of the reserve and the extinguishment of Native title in outlying lands, Yates also prayed "for the immediate removal of the Northern Indians from the Towns of Victoria."[68] He, like many colonists, was deeply concerned about creating property through the expropriation of Aboriginal land and the segregation of the Lekwammen and other First Nations groups from the town and outlying areas. The removal of Indigenous bodies and the transformation of Indigenous space were clearly connected in Yates's mind.

Another means of partitioning and spatially controlling First Nations was through the Harbour Development Committee. Mawani has described the bridge between the town and the Lekwámmen Reserve as a liminal space, a border between civilization and savagery.[69] The Harbour Development Committee petitioned for its removal, and in March 1859 Pemberton addressed the Legislative Assembly and urged its members to consider moving the Lekwammen to Belle Vue Island, with the "interest of the sale of their land to be paid to them." If this did not happen, then they should remove the bridge and "thus at once isolate the Indians."[70]

The entire town of Victoria was a liminal space, but the bridge was a site of heightened anxiety. As Mawani notes, the bridge became a racial marker, and it "enabled authorities to divide society." Authorities attempted to push First Nations to the other side of the bridge through curfews and police surveillance. In April 1861, for instance, police were given powers to drive all Aboriginal people across the bridge away from the town. They decreed that an Aboriginal person found on the wrong side of the bridge after 10 p.m. could, at the discretion of police, be searched and detained.[71] Authorities ultimately used reserves as a kind of statute of limitations: Indigenous peoples were pushed out of the city back into the reserve, which became a space of confinement within the cityscape.

Just as the gold rush rhetoric of expropriation and settlement was racialized, so too were spaces in the developing settler-colonial townscape. The minutes of the colonial legislature and the city of Victoria reveal that the bureaucratization of city space took place along racial lines. As David Goldberg writes, "colonial administration required the bureaucratic rationalization of city space. This entailed that, as urbanization of the colonised accelerated ... the more urgently were those thus racialized forced to occupy a space apart from their European(ized) masters."[72] Rather than racial segregation being enacted through an unspoken convention, which is elusive and therefore difficult to analyze, it is clear that in Victoria, as in Melbourne, partitions in the urbanizing colonial landscape were consistently and strategically enacted though a variety of official instruments at the municipal level.

Few historians have studied the mutual operation of the extinguishment of Native title to lands in *outlying areas* and the regulation, segregation, and harassment of Indigenous peoples *within* settler-colonial towns. These manoeuvres were deeply interrelated. Dispossession was a spatial and ideological practice that operated in both urbanizing spaces and the hinterlands. The settler-colonial project sought to remove Indigenous peoples from the land and, concomitantly, to regulate and partition them in the streets. Thus, we must rethink notions about the "frontier." Dispossession was a dynamic that only increased over time as the exigencies of racialized space hardened and as the new settler-colonial geography was shored up internally and externally. As in Melbourne, in Victoria the frontier between emerging urban space and the lands beyond was a continuum of dispossession that was as permeable, anxious, and psychic as it was forcefully material.

Incorporation

Within several years of the gold rush boom, calls were made to incorporate Victoria as a city. After much lobbying by the Victoria Town Council, the colonial legislature assented to the incorporation of Victoria, which became the Corporation of the City of Victoria on 2 August 1862.[73] Run like a company, Victoria's rate-paying residents and property owners were its shareholders, the key constituents who petitioned the Corporation (as I shall call it) to improve infrastructure and, increasingly, to regulate city space through bylaws. Each officer employed by the Corporation solemnly swore the following oath: "I am a British Subject ... I will faithfully perform all the duties pertaining to my office as under the Corporation of the City of Victoria ... so help me God."[74]

The Corporation sought to broker public space by wrestling control from both the Hudson's Bay Company, the body that continued to own much property in the townscape, and the colonial legislature, whose ambit encompassed the entire Colony of Vancouver Island. The accelerated incorporation of town space profoundly affected attitudes towards Aboriginal peoples, who were increasingly viewed as impediments to progress. Few Aboriginal individuals held property, they did not have the franchise, and Aboriginal testimony was generally not accepted in court. First Nations women who married European men lost their legal status as Indians and gained the right to own property, although this tended to occur more in principle than in practice.[75] First Nations, therefore, had little control over the rapid commodification of the urban landscape. On the other hand, new British and European immigrants, property owners, and speculators with the franchise were concerned about the value of their property and its possible devaluation if land came to be coded as a "savage" space. The Corporation upheld the rights of these men, while First Nations were increasingly configured as nuisances and inconveniences in the streetscape. Importantly, the land that First Nations inhabited was constructed as valueless land or as devalued property; in Governor Douglas' words, it was an "unprofitable occupation." If there were perceptions that whiteness invested property with increased value, then its association with racialized others devalued it.

In 1863 the colonial legislature and the Corporation wrangled for control of the Lekwammen Reserve. In response to speculators' eager inquiries about the possible allotment and sale of the land, the Corporation demanded to know which body controlled the reserve, the colonial legislature or the Corporation? Writing to the colonial secretary, Lord Newcastle, the Corporation requested the "transfer of the Indian reserve to the Corporation." The colonial secretary responded that the governor of the colony had no power to transfer the reserve to the Corporation.[76] The Corporation insisted, as it would many times later, that "advertisements have been inserted in the public newspapers by parties who are leasing the Indian reserve and requesting to be informed from whom such parties obtained their authority to deal with these lands and that this council consider in as much as these lands are within the city limits the Council ought to have the control of them."[77] The push for regulation of First Nations in civic space was once again coupled with attempts to undermine the reserve across the harbour. The Corporations minutes for May 1863 record "a motion that the Indian reserve be handed over to the city of Victoria it being within the city limits" and that "His Excellency be petitioned to hand over the management of the Indian reserve to the city." The motion was carried and followed by another to introduce a bylaw to regulate the "sale of gunpowder to the Indians."[78] Although the treaty with the Lekwammen would be honoured in name, the colonial legislature and the Corporation constantly sought its circumvention through legislation that would allow for the lease of reserve land to farmers, the allotment of reserve land for its "improvement," and the creation of missions and schools.[79]

The litigation of First Nations identity at the federal or provincial levels has received considerable scholarly attention in British Columbia (and to a lesser extent in Australia), but scholars have tended to overlook the process of racialization at the level of municipal governance. A close examination of the minutes of the Corporation reveals that formative racializations were brokered spatially in the streetscape. On 10 June 1863 the Corporation dealt with a petition from some of the "property holders of Government Street in the neighbourhood of St. Nicholas Hotel requesting that a wooden sewer" be built. It dealt with another petition from "various property holders on Nagley Street calling attention to its condition and requesting the same be graded and macadamised." On the same day, the minutes recorded a resolution that the government's appointment of commissioners to manage the reserve was contrary to law. Furthermore, it was resolved that "as the [Lekwammen] reserve was within the City limits [it] ought by law and usage to be vested in the hands of the Corporation."[80] Alongside seemingly banal calls for the building of infrastructure, the minutes include references to the prohibition of the sale of liquor and gunpowder to First Nations, their surveillance, and the management of First Nations space.[81]

After the gold rush, the Lekwammen were much more resistant to attempts to remove their reserve. They were well aware of the economic advantages of being in the city, and their active role forced the government to take their position into consideration when negotiating a settlement.[82] The Lekwammen had initially been amenable to certain land deals, but they later vigorously resisted attempts to remove them from the city reserve. The Lekwammen continued to actively fight into the early twentieth century for their right to land within the sovereignty discourse created by the treaties, but their rights were always to be limited.[83]

The Corporation sought to take control of and manage the reserve as a corporate asset. Unlike the minutes of the colonial legislature, the minutes of the Corporation could not, of course, address Indigenous rights to land because this was not strictly within its jurisdiction. A check and balance existed, however, between the Corporation and the colonial legislature, and, coupled with the weight of the Colonial Office, this balance at the very least kept the Lekwammen Reserve in place, though tenuously, for the remainder of the century. In 1911, when the reserve was transferred to the Province of British Columbia, a select number of families were each paid ten thousand dollars and forced to relocate.[84]

Nervous Hybridity: Bodies, Spaces, and the Displacements of Empire
[Victoria, British Columbia, 1858-71]

We will not amalgamate with them. Our race sweeps on, our civilisation knows no halt; and as fast as we cut down the trees the red man disappears."
— BRITISH COLONIST, 1860[1]

Empire ... is less a place where England asserts control than the place where England loses command of its own narrative identity.
— IAN BAUCOM, OUT OF PLACE[2]

AS THE CONTEST OVER the Lekwammen Reserve continued throughout the late 1850s and 1860s, the control and bureaucratization of First Nations in the street-scape only increased. Just as settler space was closely managed, so too was the production of bodies in those spaces. This was an implicit part of colonial modernity's urbanizing process, and its racialized contours were striking. The colonial legislature and the Corporation of the City of Victoria attempted to control Indigenous peoples and Europeans, especially First Nations women, to bolster ideas about a fictive racial purity and white space. First Nations, however, asserted their presence in the town, and at times greatly intimidated the authorities that sought to control them. As is the case for Melbourne, records of crime and spatial infringements in Victoria reveal a great deal about everyday litigations in the streetscape. Empire struggled for control in the urbanizing frontier and applied increasingly modern strategies to regulate First Nations and mixed-race relations.

"These Rebellious Indians": Managing Aboriginal Peoples
As calls for the extinguishment of Native title to lands outside Victoria accelerated in the 1860s, hostility increasingly turned to First Nations residents and others who made seasonal journeys to trade and camp in the northern sections of Victoria. The Lekwammen and other First Nations far outnumbered European immigrants in the town.

In 1859 Governor James Douglas described the Lekwammen Reserve, which was in such close proximity to the town, as a public inconvenience.[3] If the reserve was an inconvenience, then so, too, the authorities believed, were First Nations. Members of the colonial legislature pushed Douglas to "remove the Northern tribes from the position which they now occupy near the Public road to a point where their inconvenience would not be felt." In the chambers of the legislature, Douglas conceded that First Nations in Victoria's streets were a public inconvenience, but he argued that their violent removal would be neither "just nor politic."[4]

Despite this, Aboriginal people who travelled to Victoria from northern regions, especially in the summer, were cleared from the streets by policemen to abate settler fears that the town had become "a human slaughter house, through the criminal neglect of the authorities."[5] "The savages," complained the *British Colonist* in March 1860, were "accorded privileges in this community which are denied to civilised whites. In broad noonday our streets are thronged with Indians carrying knives, pistols, and guns with a recklessness that is perfectly terrifying." It warned that Aboriginal people had a "large number of keys in their possession which will fit the locks of many of the houses about town."[6]

In the view of the *British Colonist*, "Indians" were insubordinate and police were regularly intimidated by them. Presenting a constant refrain of threat and loss of control, the paper reported in March 1860 that two policemen had gone to the northern encampment to arrest an Aboriginal man who had been accused of stealing a watch. When the police attempted to take the prisoner, they were "set upon by about one hundred men and women armed with pistols, knives and clubs who demanded his release." Although the police "used their batons freely," continued the reporter, Aboriginal people rescued the prisoner and "compelled the officers to return to town."[7] One month later, the *Colonist* relayed another incident that involved Indigenous retaliation when it reported that a policeman had been beaten in the camp. The police had tried to arrest an "Indian boy" for stealing "sundry articles of children's clothing" and pursued him to the camp. The "Indians," the article continued, "rallied in full strength" and "knocked the policemen down with clubs and kicked and beat them so severely that [they] were fast to beat a retreat into town." The *Colonist* concluded: "If these rebellious Indians do not behave themselves they should be compelled to return to their homes in the far north." In April 1860 it reported that the "young Indian thief" was recaptured and sentenced to "three months work in the chain gang." A few days later, another Aboriginal man stole a cap from a store on Yates Street, and the *Colonist* noted that he was also "sent to the chain gang for one month."[8] Under the title "More Indian Outrages! What's to Be Done?," also published in April, the *Colonist* reported that on the edge of town a group of First Nations had "held up a wagon with eleven passengers and pelted passengers with bottles and stones. Police too fearful to go to the camp."[9]

Although the gold rush had increased the size of its European population, Victoria sat on the edge of vast territories occupied by Aboriginal peoples.

European immigrants were outnumbered by First Nations, who were clearly not afraid to assert their presence and retaliate. Yet the penalties for such retaliation were harsh. Newspaper reports about attacks on whites and the arrival of many First Nations in canoes were reminders, if highly sensationalized ones, of the acute feelings of vulnerability that the small newcomer enclave in Victoria held. Authorities sought to keep "Northern Indians" at bay and to partition them on the other side of the harbour from town. In April 1860, the *British Colonist* reported that the police had pulled down shanties at the edge of the town: "A posse of Policemen under Chief of Police Bailey, proceeded to the Indian tents and shanties at the rear of Youngs warf and pulled them down ... yesterday morning ... his posse tore down the remaining shanties this side of the Bay, and the Indians were busy transporting their goods to the other side. *There is not now an Indian camp on the Northern section of the city.*"[10] "Indian shanties" around town were deemed illegitimate spaces. Unlike the Lekwammen Reserve, which police could not legitimately regulate, shanties and camps were "other" unlawful spaces that could be treated as nuisances and destroyed at a will. Authorities turned their attention to the clearing of public space and the active surveillance and removal of First Nations. One month later, under the headline "Clearing the Streets," the *British Colonist* reported: "About seven o'clock every evening the policemen begin the arduous task of driving the Indians and squaws to their encampments. Starting from the centre of Government Street, one walks in a northerly direction to Johnson. Every squaw and buck is turned 'face about' and compelled to precede the policemen; and if found in the streets after dark is immediately marched off."[11]

The spectacle of violence between First Nations groups was a topic of frequent newspaper reports. No doubt, there were tensions between the many recently arrived groups who had come to the city either out of interest or to trade and find work and who clustered around the city's perimeter and competed for resources. The *British Colonist,* passing judgment on the morality of the spectacle in the streetscape in the summer of 1860, contrasted the "crowds who gather in the churches" with those who "line the wharves and shore, and crowd the bridges, to witness the bloody strife of tribe against tribe." It noted further, "Another Indian war has broken out across the bay," where the "Stickeens and Tongahs ... allied against the Hydahs." These feuds, the reporter argued, were a serious evil, and the road to Esquimalt "bristles with armed savages."[12]

Increased numbers of First Nations in Victoria prompted Douglas to attempt to institute other spatial measures of regulation. In July 1860 he reported to the Colonial Office in London that "large numbers of Indians, from almost every Tribe inhabiting the northern coasts of British Columbia have been gradually collecting around this place."[13] In August Douglas stated that "there are nearly four thousand Indians in the outskirts of the town of Victoria," and there is "much apprehension felt by the inhabitants."[14] His solution was as follows: "The only really effective means of remedying the evil ... is to improve the social condition of the Indian: at the same time maintaining every proof of physical superiority ... I have already allotted a portion of ground, and ... we are laying it in streets running in straight lines – the different Tribes will be located separately, and each Tribe will have a native constable."[15] The grid plan of the settler-colonial city has been described as a "matrix of colonization," as a method of imposing order on chaos. It appears that Douglas believed in the discipline of the grid and equated it with physical superiority. His intention, which he signalled to the Colonial Office, was the implementation of this distinct feature of colonial modernity. Rather than using overt forms of violence, Douglas would manage First Nations through the civilizing power of the grid. The grid plan, with the help of police surveillance on every corner, he hoped, would both organize and discipline First Nations subjects and reshape their subjectivities.

Foucauldian interpretations of the control of bodies are illuminating, for they shed light on how spatial arrangements were employed to discipline Aboriginal bodies in the nineteenth century. Foucault detailed a shift throughout the late eighteenth and early nineteenth century from the spectacle of punishment of the body to the adoption of modern techniques of power, which through surveillance would both discipline and produce subjects.[16] Disciplinary technologies, Foucault contended, create, transform, improve, and regulate docile bodies through the control of space, and disciplinary power was one of the primary inventions of bourgeois society.[17] However, the following caveat by Derek Gregory should be kept in mind: in the creation of colonial modernities, spaces of exclusion were also made largely through the "appropriation of land and territory backed by the exceptional violence of sovereign (not disciplinary) power."[18] Physical force and coercion worked in tandem. The refashioning of Indigenous subjects through the grid plan may have been attempted, but Douglas also resorted to the spectacle of intimidating, physical force when required, as in 1856 when fears of "Northern Indians" prompted him to call in a naval frigate to defend Vancouver Island.

In 1861 First Nations men, and later First Nations women, were ordered to leave the town precinct at night. A form of a pass system, another strategy of containment, was put in place. First Nations found in town at night were detained and prevented from returning home across the bridge until morning, unless they could show documentation from a white employer that legitimated their presence in town. European residents later complained that the system was not being enforced.[19] Merchants, however, protested the removal of First Nations and declared to the editor of the *British Colonist:*

> We, the undersigned storekeepers on Johnson street, wish to inform you that our principal trade is with the Indian population, from whom we derive our subsist-ence, and that when you incite the government to drive the Indians away, you seek to deprive us of our livelihood, and of the means to pay our rent and taxes ... We feel unable to discuss the usefulness or faults of their race, but we call your notice to the fact that it would be far more worthy to organize some better means for christianizing and improving them, than to drive them away merely to get rid of them; and that when you accuse them, for instance, of stealing, if you were to send away all those who are suspected of improbity, you would compel a great many others besides Indians to leave the country ... Signed – Levy & Co., Salna, John Silver, W. Cohn, T. Fleury.[20]

First Nations peoples were good customers, and local merchants depended on their presence in the city for their livelihood. In Victoria, as in Melbourne, the negotiation of public space and the social order is apparent in the tensions between European residents, police, and merchants. Although authorities saw First Nations in town as nuisances, others viewed them as valuable labourers and customers.

Anti-Chinese and -African American sentiments were also fostered and de-bated in the newspapers of this gold rush town. The *British Colonist* reported that during a public meeting to discuss the possibility of a Chinese land and poll tax, some who attended objected to taxes being collected "from Chinamen any more than from any other foreigners." Yet, noted the newspaper, others believed the Chinese were nothing more than a "nuisance – a moral scourge – a curse" who should pay a tax of $100 per head."[21] It is unlikely that First Nations or Chinese settlers could write to newspapers to put forward their case, but African Americans facing prejudice in the streetscape wrote urgently to the *British Colonist* to protest their treatment. In a letter to the editor, an African American known only as "F.S." asked, "Mr Editor, have the coloured people realized their fond anticipations in coming to Vancouver Island? I answer *no.* And if not what is the position they occupy in this colony? I answer certainly a degrading one and certainly not one to be borne by men of spirit."[22] Com-menting on the injustices suffered by "coloured people," F.S. drew attention to the "mildew like feeling that lurks in the hearts of our enemies, i.e. prejudice." Upon hearing news of the gold rush, he stated, African Americans had wanted to come to Vancouver Island since they "cherished a friendly feeling for the

British government" because of its "liberal policy toward coloured people generally." Like whites, African Americans had hoped to

> occupy this virgin soil ... to enjoy all the rights and privileges enjoyed by others,
> but how sadly many of us have been disappointed. All the hotels, inns, whisky
> shops, are closed against us, and a coloured gentleman was ordered out of the
> steamer ... they shut us out from their concerts, and a member of the church says
> give us $500 and he will build a gallery in the English church, in which to huddle
> us together ... so I am informed there is in town a secret association of wicked
> white men... whose ostensible purpose is to keep coloured men out of the jury
> box, and from serving on the Grand jury."[23]

Considering the experiences of the several hundred African Americans who
came to Victoria gives added dimension to our understanding of the racialized
streetscape. As Kirsty Sim argues, in the negotiation of social order in nineteenth-
century Victoria, the spheres of religion, politics, and leisure were sites for the
negotiation of race.[24] There were heated debates about the issue of segregation
in public places such as churches, theatres, transportation systems, and other
civic amenities to which many First Nations could never hope to have access.
African Americans desired participation in jury service and the franchise, and
they wanted to be able to stand for Parliament, rights normally accorded to
male British citizens with property. African Americans could purchase tickets
in theatres for segregated seating, but this "privilege" was not offered to First
Nations. African Americans could not be as easily dismissed as First Nations,
and they protested their partition from civil society. Indeed, some combatted
segregation and asserted their rights by sitting in theatre seats reserved for
whites. They were physically abused for such resistance. The author known as
F.S. concluded that the "obnoxious seeds of prejudice [are] deeply rooted in the
white man's heart ... I believe it utterly impossible for the African and the Anglo-
Saxon races ever to live together on terms of equality."[25]

Race, Space, and the Law

As in colonial Melbourne, First Nations in Victoria – who were referred to in-
cessantly as "nuisances" or "inconveniences" – were constructed in powerful
ways in the streetscape. For instance, a photograph of First Nations sitting on
the road in Victoria in 1862, which originally had the provocative title "From
the Gaol to the Gin House," constructed them as criminal, drunken, displaced,
and anomalous in the streetscape (see Figure 25). In fact, First Nations often
waited outside the court house for friends and relatives.

Figure 25 "Gaol in Bastion Square, Victoria," Victoria, View Street, 1862.
BC Archives, H-03766.

Vagrancy, however, was a more complex category than that of nuisance or inconvenience. It may have been implied, but compared to colonial Melbourne the term *vagrant* was invoked much less frequently in Victoria's newspapers, records of the colonial legislature, and criminal records. In a sample search of these records, there were few instances of a First Nations individual being charged by police officers for vagrancy. Not one clear vagrancy charge was found in a survey of crimes committed in the Victoria streetscape in 1858-59 or in a survey of crimes involving First Nations women as perpetrators or victims between 1866 and 1868.[26] The Esquimalt precinct stood over the bridge from Victoria near the Lekwammen Reserve, and the Esquimalt road was, apparently, a notorious route of vice and prostitution. Yet the charge book for the Esquimalt Police from 1862 to 1865 lists no First Nations charged with vagrancy, but First Nations individuals were charged with many other offences, including being drunk and disorderly.[27]

In Victoria the rhetoric of the "vagrant Indian" was occasionally evoked in newspapers, reflecting highly conflicted European stereotypes of Indigenous peoples as, by turns, either indolent or hard-working and eager to participate in colonial labour. Yet it seems that vagrancy laws were not actually applied to First Nations in Victoria. As in Melbourne, Europeans, not First Nations, were apprehended in Victoria for the spatial crime of vagrancy, particularly for loitering or cohabiting with First Nations or being found at the Lekwammen Reserve. Officials, it seems, disliked Europeans living in or around indigenizing, or First Nations, spaces. For example, in July 1860 the *British Columbian* reported, "Vagrancy – eight young men were arrested on Sunday, charged with having no means of visible support. They are suspected of making a living by supplying Indians with whisky, and occupied cabins on the vicinity of the Bella-Bella encampment. Three of the number were discharged by the Police magistrate, and the remaining five held until they can produce testimonials as to their means of gaining a livelihood."[28] In May 1864 Silvester Keene, "having no visible means of support," was arrested, charged with being a vagrant, and "ordered to be examined by a doctor." No punishment was recorded.[29] Later, "Tim David (a Kanaka) arrested ... with being a rogue and a vagabond. Property none. Sentence, three months imprisonment with hard labour."[30] The arrest of "Tim David (a Kanaka)" shows that Pacific Islanders or Hawaiians were also arrested for vagrancy and punished severely. Although punishments varied, European men suffered less harsh penalties than racialized others.

An examination of Indigenous "crime" and other spatial infringements in the streetscape reveals how the colonial order and the boundaries of whiteness were policed. The same sources show further instances of the spatial crime of infringement.[31] The road from Victoria to Esquimalt was particularly rough, and the Esquimalt police charge books show that in fact much crime was committed by European men. Many were apprehended for "breaking leave" from ships in the British navy, and many were charged with assault, property theft, or being drunk and disorderly. Some charges such as being suspicious, a rogue, a vagabond, or of suspicious character appear to be highly subjective and value laden, and they were applied at the discretion of the individual police officer.

Victoria and Esquimalt police charge books reveal instances of the uneven application of the law and of racialized crime in the Victoria streetscape and on the Esquimalt road. The following drunk and disorderly charges were recorded, for example, throughout 1858 to 1862. On 21 July 1858, "an Indian" was arrested for being drunk and discharged. Two days later William Meyer was "arrested ... for being drunk, was brought to gaol in a handcart. Fined $1.25 and $3.25 costs." On 23 July, an Indian was arrested "for being drunk and disorderly.

Sentence: usual punishment 1 doz. lashes." And on 24 July, Abraham Doran was arrested for theft and drunkenness. He was "fined $5 and costs $3.25 or 7 days in prison." The Esquimalt police charge book noted that on 13 July 1862, "Kitty, a Simpsean Indian woman" was charged with being "drunk and disorderly. Fined $5 in default of payment 6 hours in prison." Europeans and First Nations with money usually paid fines, but some First Nations, especially males, were punished physically, a practice that reflected the Hudson's Bay Company's early military-style governance of Vancouver Island.

The outcome of arrests for alcohol-related "crimes" also show that severe punishment was meted out to Aboriginal people. On 23 July 1859, Patrick Laennard, a European, was "apprehended by order of the Sheriff for obtaining money from Indians to purchase liquor." No penalty was recorded. But a week later, on 30 July, an Aboriginal man was arrested for "having in his possession a bottle of whiskey. Discharged with 1 doz lashes."[32] Physical punishment may have been applied in lieu of a fine, but in the charge books examined, there are no instances of a European being lashed.

Theft and property damage, as shown in the Victoria police charge books, were treated seriously. Charge books reveal that First Nations usually stole food and provisions. On 6 December 1858, an Aboriginal man was arrested for "stealing shingles. Property 25 cents. Sentence two days imprisonment." On 3 July 1859, an Aboriginal man was arrested for "stealing chickens. Remanded and discharged." On 16 December of the same year, an Aboriginal man was arrested for "stealing from another person's tent. Sentence: prison one week." On 5 July an Aboriginal man was arrested for stealing blankets from Aboriginal people; he was "remanded till tomorrow. Discharged 7th July." On the same day, an Aboriginal man was arrested for "breaking into a house. Pleaded guilty, two months imprisonment with hard labour." In Esquimalt, on 7 February 1864, a European, Thomas Hogan was "charged with stealing a pair of brass row locks ... Pleads guilty and sentenced to three months imprisonment with hard labour." On 29 May 1865, Charlie, identified as a "Fort Rupert Indian," was arrested ... for "stealing two shirts valued at $5.00 the property of Samuel William ... Sentenced to three months imprisonment with hard labour." The police treated *inter se* (First Nations to First Nations) charges less seriously than charges that involved a First Nations person stealing from a European. Yet Europeans such as Thomas Hogan also suffered imprisonment and hard labour for stealing. Punishment for stealing was applied equally, it seems, to Europeans and First Nations. If First Nations individuals had money, they could pay a fine.

First Nations assaults on Europeans were often used by newspapers as evidence of Aboriginal people's unpredictability and savagery. However, European attacks on First Nations in the streetscape also occurred; more importantly, they were far more common in police charge books. Sometimes police responded; Europeans were usually fined, sometimes in lieu of prison. On 30 July 1858, Charles Dickenson was arrested for stealing from a "Chinaman" and assault. He was remanded "till Monday [and] fined $10.00 and costs or a months imprisonment." On 18 December 1858, "Charley an Indian [was] arrested for drawing a knife and threatening ... Discharged. Knife taken from the Indian until he leaves for his own country." On 4 July 1859, James Gordon was "arrested for assaulting an Indian. Fined $1.25 with $2.00 costs in default of payment 7 days in prison." On 9 July A.L. Crane was "arrested ... by virtue of a warrant, charged with abducting a white squaw belonging to the bella bella tribe, with a view of carrying her off to California. The woman retained as evidence. Property $43.75 Discharged." On 28 April 1860, Benjamin Allen, reported the *Colonist,* was fined for beating an Aboriginal man and "bruising him pretty badly around the face and the head." He "paid 20s ... to the Police Judge for his exercise."[33] On 13 July 1862, Charles O'Malley was arrested for "creating a disturbance in the street with an Indian women. Admitted to bail $25." In Esquimalt, on 2 July 1863, Elijah Kemp was arrested for robbing a "chinee man of $25 on the Esquimalt Road and cutting his tail." No punishment was recorded. And on 6 June 1864, Henry Carter was "arrested [for] assaulting Leha-nach an Indian with intent to do him the said Leha-nach grievous bodily harm. Sentence committed for trial."[34] If crime marks out the boundaries of whiteness and the colonial order, then Europeans held sway, and violence towards First Nations was clearly a common part of the colonial order.

The police charge books for Victoria from 1866 to 1868 reveal that a great deal of violence took place in the streetscape. Significantly, the violence was gendered.[35] On 15 January 1866, Kitty, identified as an "Indian woman," assaulted Otto Charles. She was fined ten dollars in lieu of one month's imprisonment. This is one of the few incidences recorded in which a First Nations woman assaulted a man. Police charge books reveal that as a matter of course brutal assault was unfailingly in the reverse. The record books also include several instances of First Nations or Métis men assaulting their wives or other Aboriginal women and instances of Aboriginal women assaulting one another. On 23 March 1866, both Jim, described as a "Skidgate Indian," and Kato-gat, a "Hydah Indian," violently assaulted Walla, a "Tsimpean woman." They were each fined five dollars in lieu one month in prison.[36]

In general, however, violence by European men against Aboriginal women was frequent and stunningly brutal. The entries in the police charge books are often abrupt, but they do give a sense of an archive that reveals a catalogue of violence directed towards Aboriginal women. On 1 November 1866, Thomas Moore assaulted Kitty, a "Stickeen women ... with a fist in the face." He was fined twenty dollars in lieu of fourteen days in prison. On 30 November Joseph Taylor assaulted Annie Porteous with an umbrella and received the same sentence. On 17 December of the same year, Edwin Kitson threw Kitty, a "Tongas woman," down and kicked her. He, too, met with the same punishment. On 17 May 1867, George Selmes kicked Mary, "a Cowichan," in the face, and Angelo Keifer kicked and slapped Lucy a "Tongas woman." Both men were fined, but the amounts are unclear. On 5 August 1867, William Bonner was arrested for striking and kicking Kitty, a "Tsimpsean," and received twenty-five dollars bail. And on 23 August Henry Miller assaulted May "of Fort Rupert" and received the same penalty. Kitty, a "Stickeen woman," was assaulted by Charles Fisher on 29 September, but the charge was dismissed. Fisher assaulted Kitty again four days later and was fined ten dollars.[37]

If caught, European men who beat Aboriginal women were usually fined. They were rarely imprisoned. Recounted here are the instances in which an arrest was made; no doubt many other violent incidents went unrecorded. The records do, however, provide a snapshot of the ongoing frequency of gendered, racialized violence against First Nations women in the urbanizing frontier. Few First Nations were charged with assaulting Europeans in Victoria in 1858-59, and the Esquimalt police charge book suggests that the "savage" Indian attacks recorded in the *British Colonist* were made out to be far more common than they were. Furthermore, the charge book for 1866-68 shows an increase in violence against First Nations women in Victoria. Markedly, European men, many of whom had arrived with the gold rush, perpetrated violence against First Nations women. The survey shows clearly that when Europeans assaulted First Nations they were often fined or discharged. While First Nations were sometimes punished brutally – with hard labour and, earlier, a lashing – for theft, property damage, or possession of alcohol, European men who assaulted First Nations women received a fine. In no instances did the charge books record the lashing of a European.

Some historians argue that the Victoria and Esquimalt police charge books do not reveal inequities in the streetscape, that the law was applied equally to settlers and First Nations, depending on the whim of the individual police officer and the offender's ability to pay a fine. At some moments, penalties seem random and fines were paid in lieu of prison in cases involving both Europeans and First Nations. However, I argue that in many instances First Nations were imprisoned for longer periods and were given hard labour or physical punishment for petty offences, whereas European men did not attract such penalties. In addition, European male violence against First Nations women was particularly severe and typically went unpunished. Records of "crime" and other infringements therefore amply reveal the unequal application of the law and the boundaries of the emerging colonial order.

In his study of First Nations people and the law, Sydney Harring surmises that the large number of executions of First Nations in mid-nineteenth-century British Columbia belies the myth of a peaceful Canadian frontier. Highlighting the disproportionate number of First Nations executions, Harring notes that Judge Matthew Baillie Begbie executed more First Nations than were killed in some wars. His observation underscores Begbie's role, which was to "assert British control of the unstable gold rush frontier."[38] Begbie hanged twenty-six men in total: twenty-two were First Nations, one was white, and three were Chinese. Indeed, Harring states that there is no equivalent to these executions anywhere in the many colonies that Britain founded, even in the penal colony of New South Wales. Recounting the public hangings of First Nations, which were "symbolic displays of state power," Harring describes the founding of British Columbia as a "bloody colonial enterprise."[39] Likewise, in the streets of Victoria, First Nations, especially women, suffered greatly at the hands of Europeans. The outlying frontier and the urban frontier were interrelated sites, each revealing various aspects of a continuum of colonial violence towards Indigenous peoples.

The structural and discursive differences between southeastern Australia and the Pacific Northwest Coast have been outlined. These differences are marked, yet certain common themes repeated themselves with an uncanny durability in these urbanizing colonial spaces. As has been shown, in the early streets of Victoria and Melbourne, Indigenous peoples were routinely described as "inconvenient," "immoral," "nuisances," "vagrants," or "prostitutes," but to varying degrees. These categories, I propose, take us to the heart of the socio-spatial relations that are distinctive to settler colonialism and reveal how law and property served to racialize the streetscape. Racializations were not only amplified in these colonial contexts, they were also particular to the urbanizing settler landscape. In Melbourne and Victoria, Aboriginal people's camps were not natural entities but spaces produced through colonial relations; likewise, colonized Indigenous bodies or subjects were materially produced as abject, unnatural, and inconvenient entities. These productions, I argue, were directly related to the settlement phase, when the taking of First Nations land became a key objective. In this process bodies and spaces were mutually imbricated, and as Councillor Joseph Despard Pemberton put it succinctly in the colonial legislature in 1859, "It was only now that these lands had become valuable that the Indians were found to be a nuisance ... if the Indians inquired how we had acquired their lands, we should stand in much worse light than they would with their reserve."[40]

The Intimate Urban Frontier: First Nations Women and Prostitution

The number of First Nations women in the Victoria streetscape was frequently higher that that of First Nations men.[41] This situation differed from that of Melbourne, where far fewer Aboriginal people remained in the townscape and few of those who survived were women. Many of the Aboriginal women in Victoria were married to European men, and others worked as traders in the streets, where they sold goods such a clothes and oysters. Some were interpreters or house servants. The *British Colonist* reported that First Nations women were making "four and five dollars a day ... bringing in oysters from Victoria Arm, Sooke or Cowichan, and peddling them around town ... indeed, they monopolize the whole [trade]."[42]

Nevertheless, many Europeans depicted First Nations women as being synonymous with prostitution and vice in the streetscape. Similar to constructions of Aboriginal women in the Australian colonies, colonial discourse in British Columbia constructed First Nations women as lustful and threatening "squaws" who were sexually available and ready to prostitute themselves. Ideas about the "easy squaw" who was less than a lady legitimated violence against First Nations.[43] Representations of First Nations women as perennial prostitutes who were inherently tradeable were powerful. In 1860 Robert Burnaby wrote to his sister in England and described Aboriginal men and their "klootchmen (women) whom they used formerly to kill as unprofitable, and sell them out and out, or traffic with them as they would with a lot of sheep."[44] Burnaby echoed the sentiments of many settlers who arrived with the gold rush. They were British immigrants who brought with them a harsh racism that derided the mixed society that emerged out of the Hudson's Bay Company's mercantilism. They voiced their moral and racial abhorrence of intermarriage between Europeans and First Nations. Miscegenation was increasingly held to be highly undesirable, and men with Aboriginal wives were often derided.[45] While some Englishmen found the prospect of marrying a woman of First Nations descent unattractive, others such as Dr. John Sebastian Helmcken and Thomas Bushby entered into such marriages. As Adele Perry recounts, Bushby was "deeply enamoured by his future wife, Governor Douglas' mixed–blood teenage daughter, Agnes, especially with what he saw as her darkness."[46] He was also, no doubt, motivated by her status as Douglas' daughter, for colonial class relations also play a role here. Robert Burnaby, however, was not possessed of the same attitude as his friend. He described the Work daughters as "half breeds" and commented that he could not approve of Bushby's marriage to Douglas' daughter because one "can never get rid of the taint of Indian blood." Commenting on the balls and dancehalls of Victoria, Burnaby wrote dryly of the "belles sauvages," "You can detect in their black eyes, high cheekbones, and flattened heads whence they came." He later wrote to his family in England that "there are no eligible ladies of the right sort here."[47]

In the view of Edmund Hope Verney, an officer in the Royal Navy, the Hudson's Bay Company had given an immoral caste to the town. He criticized the non-English background of James Douglas and lamented that a "refined English gentlemen is sadly wanted at the head of affairs." Although Verney wrote that Douglas was a "very good, kind hearted man," he noted that the less said about Douglas' wife and daughters the better: "I do not conceive that I can do any good by recounting instances of their ignorance and barbarism."[48]

Intermarriage in the face of increasing segregation between Europeans and First Nations called into question the very identity of the town's inhabitants. What was the currency of whiteness, Englishness, and Indianness in the streetscape?[49] The boundaries of identity were indeed precarious, changeable, and, for some, tense. If mixed-race marriages unsettled some members of Victoria's society, then First Nations women in the street, who may or may not have been soliciting, were perceived by moral reformers as an even greater threat. Bishop George Hills wrote, "The Road to Esquimalt on Sunday is lined with the poor Indian women offering to sell themselves to the white men passing by – and instances are to be seen of open bargaining."[50] The *British Colonist* often reported with an offhand authority that made First Nations women, especially women from the north, appear to be synonymous with prostitution. For instance, it noted that the "women have rendered the whole outskirts of the town a perfect brothel" and "prostitution was so common with Northern [Indian] women."[51]

Jean Barman has observed that in the Victorian cultural climate, Aboriginal women's sexuality was not openly discussed; however, prostitution and all that it implied was to be publicly condemned.[52] Barman is correct when she argues that notions of gender among First Nations were very different and suggests that we cannot begin to reconstruct them.[53] However, by the 1860s Victoria had grown because of the gold rush and Esquimalt was a naval port. In this context, some First Nations women likely traded on sexual terms out of necessity. This does not brand them as fundamentally amoral: it is a testament to colonial relations, which materially produced new relations and certain gendered, colonial bodies, just as it did spaces, with all their attendant violations. Why did the Aboriginal prostitute became so menacing a figure and prostitution such an amplified narrative of morality in the Victoria streetscape at this point in time?

Barman has noted that Aboriginal women were sexualized as prostitutes.[54] The corollary is that prostitution was also racialized. Prostitution flagrantly threatened the boundaries of a fictive Victorian society that existed only tenuously on the Coast. "The prostitute," writes Miles Ogborn, "disordered the state and threatened empire."[55] Ports were especially feared by colonial authorities as putative sites of contamination, racial mixing, and the dispersal of venereal disease. Indigenous women and prostitution were particular sites of anxiety for colonial officials and missionaries.

Although few imperial texts explicitly discuss the control of contagious sexual diseases, Philippa Levine writes that in the mid-nineteenth century almost every British colonial possession was subject to contagious diseases regulations that identified female prostitutes as the main source of contagion.[56] The requirement for colonial authorities to "bring to heel sexual disorder among colonised peoples" was strong. It was feared that venereal disease would weaken the Anglo-Saxon race; health, thus, became a moral and national problem. Such diseases were material realities of the time, not mere constructions. But since the majority of the British population in the colonies was male, the spread of disease was deemed "potentially ruinous to Britain's empire" and a threat to the superiority of the Anglo-Saxon race. Venereal diseases were "presented as racial poison."[57] Although it was in fact the diseased bodies of British men in the colonies that were at stake, anxieties focused on colonized Indigenous women. Throughout the British colonies, issues of racial hygiene became prominent.

It was not only venereal disease that was viewed as a threat but also the bodies of First Nations women, which were marked as such in Victoria's streetscape. As Tony Ballantyne and Antoinette Burton argue, the body can be "read by us as evidence of how ... gender assumptions undergird empires in all their complexity."[58] As I have maintained, the particular spatial commerce of the settler-colonial city produced Indigenous peoples as inconveniences or nuisances, and some settlers attempted to construct them as redundant. Colonial hierarchies of race and gender likewise both produced and proscribed the body of the First Nations woman as prostitute. It is timely to recall Judith Butler's ideas about the materiality of the produced, gendered body and the way "bodies tend to indicate a world beyond themselves" by revealing the constitutive nature of gender and space.[59] What was the world beyond these Indigenous women? To Europeans, especially moral reformers and new arrivals, the body of the Aboriginal woman came to signify prostitution and mixed-racedness. But ideas about Aboriginal women's bodies also coalesced with new ideas and anxieties about sanitation, disease, and the medicalization of raced bodies, which were so fundamentally threatening to empire. The First Nations woman was, thus, subject to multiple disciplines and violations. The management of First Nations women was vital to maintain fictive ideas about white racial purity in the domestic and intimate domains, along with fictive ideas about contiguous imperial public space. Gendered constructs of Indigeneity and whiteness were made through both discursive and bodily markers. We must bear in mind Lefebvre's key proposition on the cultural and procedural aspects of space – that space is the "outcome of a sequence and set of operations, and thus cannot be reduced to the rank of a simple object."[60] In this sense the nineteenth-century settler-colonial city was less a site than a process of transformation. In her examination of prostitution in nineteenth-century British Columbia, Renisa Mawani argues that "discussions of prostitution emerged at a moment when the state's interests changed from exploiting the land and resources to permanently acquiring them."[61] In other words, white settlement required the maintenance of fictive ideas about bodily racial purity and the maintenance of white space; mercantilism, by contrast, did not.

In Victoria, although many settlers, including clergy and moral reformers, condemned First Nations women as prostitutes, prostitution per se was not a crime, and charge books indicate that the police were well aware of this. There is no clear record in these sources of First Nations women being picked up for soliciting or prostitution. Perry, for example, has noted that First Nations were removed from the city limits of Victoria from 1859, when curfews for men were expanded to include women, and that women were specifically targeted. As evidence, she cites the an article from *British Colonist* titled "Arrest of Street-walkers."[62] Perry explains, however, that the expanded curfew led the press to presume that the removal of First Nations was "directed against First Nations women specifically" and that, although of dubious legality, it was "enforced by local police officers."[63] In Victoria, as in colonial Melbourne, police discretion and prejudice was in operation. Individual policemen forcibly moved Indigenous people, and their actions were based on the assumption that Indigenous people were inherently prostitutes or vagrants. The categories of vagrancy and prostitution were moral and spatial infringements that were elastic in their applicability. Jarrod White has examined this phenomenon in the policing of colonial Australian towns and has linked it to present policing practices.[64] White argues that police decision making has had an internally consistent nature based on knowledge of a constructed Aboriginal subject within a specific rural town context. White writes that "policing necessarily involves the exercise of discretion" at many levels of the police organization. "On the street ... choices are made about the use of particular charges, who should be charged, and more broadly, which location/person should be policed more or less intensively."[65]

As settlement proceeded in the nineteenth century, mixed-racedness was deemed to be increasingly threatening, as were the physical bodies that most represented this threat – those of Indigenous women. As in Melbourne, Victoria's urbanizing frontier was fragile and anxious, and satires played upon the uneasy transformation of Indigenous women and the prospect of mixed-race children.

In response a constant discursive and physical management was required for the success of the colonial project. Putting on a brave face in the midst of a highly mixed-race society, an editorial in the *British Colonist* declared, "We will not amalgamate with them. Our race sweeps on, our civilisation knows no halt; and as fast as we cut down the trees the red man disappears."[66] Ideas about the imminent extinction of First Nations were used to assuage fears about ongoing interracial mixing. As Perry and other scholars have noted, many believed that only white women could redeem the colony. Between 1849 and 1871, four assisted immigration schemes for white women were implemented to obviate the need for mixed relations, and the presence of white women was portrayed in both moral and economic terms as necessary for the maturation and success of the colony.[67]

Medical Modernity: Disease, Sanitation, and the Intimacies of Empire

In 1862 the *British Columbian* stated that First Nations in the city were an "evil on two grounds – moral and sanitary."[68] Sanitation drives were another key signature of urban modernity in the 1860s, and they were a distinct element of the formation of urban space in many of Britain's colonies. The Corporation of Victoria (hereafter the Corporation) sought to control First Nations bodies in public space, and the weight of public opprobrium from officials and missionaries, under the modernizing guise of improvement and sanitation, came down heavily on the body of the First Nations woman. The great Victorian sanitary idea – an urbanizing trend regarding public health, disease, and cities – had by the mid-nineteenth century moved under the guise of racial hygiene efforts from Britain to the colonial cities of its empire. In the name of public health, First Nations spaces in Victoria were represented as being synonymous with dirt, disease, and vice, and First Nations women were viewed as their embodiment.

Several scholars have written about sanitation as a feature of urbanizing bourgeois modernity in the colonies, particularly how it was harnessed to manage colonized peoples and regulate both urban bodies and spaces.[69] The sanitation movement was nascent in Melbourne during the 1840s and 1850s, when the Melbourne Town Council attempted to clean up urban space by removing nuisances and unwholesome places. This urbanizing trend was far more thoroughgoing in Victoria by the 1860s. Victoria's incorporation in 1862 was accompanied by an attempt to evict all Aboriginal people from the city, a development that underlines the link between the commodification of Aboriginal land and their control. Although First Nations had been pushed out of the city limits since 1859, this trend intensified when sanitation as an apparatus of control and modernity dovetailed with fears about the presumed site of degradation in public space – the body of the First Nations woman. In June 1862 the colonial legislature "read for the first time an Act for the appointment of a Sanitary Commission for the town of Victoria, and to define the powers thereof."[70] On 22 December 1862, amid tenders for the "grading and macadamising of Yates and Johnson streets," the Corporation specifically targeted First Nations women through a motion for a bylaw "declaring it to be unlawful for any person to harbour Indian women within the city limits."[71] The Corporation argued that it was "expedient to take measures for *improving the sanitary conditions of the city* of Victoria ... as follows: it shall be unlawful for any person to harbour Indian Women within the precinct of the city."[72] The only exceptions would be married women and women employed as servants.

"Squaw dancing houses," dance halls in which First Nations women worked, were also targeted as places of mixed-race licentiousness. The Corporation proposed a further resolution that "squaw dancing houses within the city limits are a nuisance and the parties keeping such are amenable to the penalties as are competent to be levied in the case of any other nuisance under the ordinance on nuisances passed by this Council."[73] First Nations women and the places they frequented were regulated through the categories "nuisance" and "sanitation." As Perry notes, reformers tried to close dance halls by denying them licences or, failing that, by locating "them outside of the white settlement."[74] Yet because these dance halls were often owned by merchants or influential members of the colonial elite, their complete eradication was not desirable. Furthermore, the councillor who made these propositions sought to achieve them through the rationale that the "squaws might all be considered as prostitutes and that was sufficient grounds for ejection." The mayor and the police magistrate advised that this was "beyond the limits of legal justification."[75]

Given that ideas about colonial violence worked in tandem with coercion and surveillance, it is apparent that by the 1860s the bureaucratization and racialization of the Victoria streetscape was well underway. Not only were the hierarchies of race and gender central to colonial rule, they were also increasingly imbricated in Western medical ideas about sanitation and racial hygiene, phenomena that would become only stronger by the close of the century. As Frederick Cooper and Ann Laura Stoler have observed, during the embourgeoisement of imperialism, racialized violence and exclusions were increasingly linked to some kind of progressive reform.[76]

Renisa Mawani has argued in her study of mid- to late nineteenth-century British Columbia that there was an apparent "legal ambivalence" regarding prostitution. This ambivalence, in practice, enabled certain spaces to be marked as degenerate and others to be marked as white and respectable. This legal ambivalence was also related to the discretionary power inherent in policing.

Figure 26   A Lekwammen group in 1867-68 (photographer, J.C. Eastcott).
City of Vancouver Archives, A26502.

First Nations women were increasingly pushed out of cities and towns, but the continued existence of certain immoral spaces in which they maintained a presence served a purpose – it secured the "respectability of white urban cities" and maintained white men's access to First Nations women.[77] We see this in Victoria's streetscape. The sexualized exigencies of colonialism required "immoral" spaces, just as racial purity required "moral" spaces. The settler-colonial project in both British Columbia and southeastern Australia was indeed one of "gendered territorialism."[78] And it was ever so in the urban frontier.

Mixed-race relationships in Victoria ultimately confounded attempts at segregation. Perry has noted that First Nations women who lived in town with their partners and children resisted such partitions. One newspaper noted that they refused to leave the city or to be separated from their children (see Figure 26). When the segregation rules were transformed into a pass system in 1862, by which men with Aboriginal servants and wives had to formalize their arrangements with the police office, struggles to control the streetscape were subverted by the lived experience of its inhabitants.[79]

The smallpox epidemic of 1862-63 spurred the Corporation and the colonial legislature to enforce segregation in the city with increased zeal.[80] The equation of Aboriginal shanties, camps at the northern end of town, and the Lekwammen Reserve with the outbreak of disease peaked during the epidemic. Moral environmentalism, which was based on fear of First Nations and the spaces they inhabited, caused many First Nations to be evicted from Victoria through nuisance and sanitation laws. As Perry observes: "Smallpox precipitated radical responses because it crystallized white fears of sexual and social contact with the Aboriginal community and fuelled and legitimated existing visions of racial segregation ... Across the imperial world, colonial administrators conflated disease with local bodies, and control over space became control over native social and sexual relations."[81] The focus therefore became limiting contact between whites and First Nations. But this was impossible because of the legacy of the fur trade's mixed marriages and the presence – as labourers, servants, and purveyors and consumers of food and goods – of First Nations in town. A neat partitioning of the urban frontier was not possible. The *British Colonist* complained: "They line our streets, fill the pit in our theatre, are found at nearly every open door during the day, and evening of the town; and are even employed as servants in our dwellings, and in the culinary department of our restaurants and hotels."[82] Despite attempts to segregate it, the urban frontier was as fluid, intimate, mixed, and psychic as it was material. Nevertheless, the smallpox epidemic legitimated a series of forced removals.[83] In May 1862 "Northern Indians," deemed to be the seat of disease, were forced out of the harbour by gunboat. This act led to the spread of smallpox and the deaths of many First Nations farther up the Coast, an event that was devastating in its effect on the Indigenous population. In 1866, after the colonies of Vancouver Island and British Columbia united, city governments passed laws for the wholesale removal of Aboriginal people.

By 1869 First Nations and Chinese were conflated as nuisances, and the northern streets of Victoria, where First Nations and Chinese lived, once again became a moral and racialized topography. An article in the *British Columbian* titled "The Seat of Disease" stated:

There is a section of this city lying north of Johnson and between Government and Store streets, which bids fair to prove a prolific source of disease during the approaching summer. It is inhabited chiefly by Indians and Chinese, who dwell in low and filthy cabins, and display the most profound disregard for all recognized codes of cleanliness ... These people, as they now conduct themselves, are a nuisance and a plague-spot upon this fair city, and they should be made either to live as become the civilized beings, and keep their premises in proper condition, or take themselves beyond the limits of the city.[84]

When the *Columbian* called for the application of the new health bill, the increased medicalization of race was ensured. In 1869 Victoria's civic government passed laws to "remove Indians from the City of Victoria."[85] It is clear that before the emergence of provincial or federal laws, First Nations identity was litigated at the municipal level through bylaws, and racializations were constructed in this way through the legal ambit of urban space. In sum, the increased medicalization of Indigenous bodies and spaces and their regulation through sanitation were key features of bourgeois, urbanizing modernity.

Although the criminal category of vagrancy was not applied to First Nations throughout much of the 1860s, in 1869 Augustus F. Pemberton, the police magistrate, attempted to apply it to First Nations to effect their removal. He aspired to a community in which "such Indians as have no visible means of support and are the associates of thieves, or prostitutes who are disorderly be *treated as vagrants,* are to be given the option either to remove to the Indian reserve, or be dealt with under 5 Geo. 4. C. 83, and be sent to prison."[86] Vagrancy – which was, according to Zygmunt Barman, a state of extraterritorialization – was finally legally applied to First Nations in the Victoria streetscape, although, of course, they had been forcibly moved by the police for years.[87]

Victoria was never a white town. The project to make Victoria white largely failed, at least for the better part of the nineteenth century and despite increasingly harsh racializations borne of bylaws and other attempts to segregate settlers from First Nations and other non-European peoples (see Figure 27).[88] Notwithstanding the power of public discourse and an array of strategies to partition and regulate space by municipal and colonial governance bodies, mixed-race marriages and peoples had created a heterogeneous society. In addition, First Nations were increasingly required as labourers; those who were deemed inconvenient nuisances or prostitutes were in fact crucial to the wider industrial economy of forestry and fisheries. Indeed, as John Lutz has rightly noted, "Aboriginal people were not made redundant by settlement. In fact they were the main labour force of the early settlement era, essential to the capitalist development of British Columbia."[89]

Figure 27 Lekwammen people with a northern-style canoe at the head of James Bay, Victoria, 1875. BC Archives, I-30804.

Twenty-Three Crosses in the England of the Pacific

In 1865 Matthew MacFie published a survey of the "varieties of race represented in Victoria" that applied an elaborate system of taxonomy to the streetscape. MacFie determined that one could "certainly calculate upon twenty-three crosses, in different degrees, resulting from the blending of the Caucasian, the aboriginal American, and the Negro." MacFie marvelled that there could be found in Victoria "almost every tribe and nationality under heaven," a result of "remarkable matrimonial alliances" and "illicit commerce between the various races." But his prognosis was fearful. It is evident, he warned, "that our population cannot escape the infusion of a considerable hybrid offspring."[90] In addition, although MacFie found the Chinese to be an "industrious and law abiding class," he nevertheless warned that if they were not checked, "Canton will be in Victoria."[91]

Applying the emerging Victorian science of hybridity, MacFie had arrived at his "twenty-three crosses" by utilizing Johann Jakob von Tschudi's classification of human hybrids, which had been adopted by Josiah Clark Nott and George R. Glidden in their "able work" *Types of Mankind.*[92] Nott and Glidden, prominent

American ethnologists, had popularized polygenesis, and their book's object was to refute the theory of the universality of the human race by showing that the African race was wholly separate from and inferior to the Caucasian race. It thereby endorsed the enslavement of Africans. The year of the book's publication, 1854, was the same year that the anti-slavery Republican Party was formed in the United States. The book aimed to validate slavery by providing scientific proof of a hierarchical racial schema. Slavery sympathizers, unsurprisingly, embraced the book as scientific proof of the subordinate status of African Americans.[93] Clearly opposed to interracial mixing, Nott argued that Africans and whites should not intermarry and that their progeny were aberrant.

MacFie likewise believed that the proliferation of "human varieties" was detrimental to "that type which we wish to preponderate."[94] This type, of course, was Anglo-Saxon. After all, argued MacFie, Vancouver Island held the proud appellation "England of the Pacific." Yet MacFie was dismayed: "The peculiar elements composing the nucleus of the population render it physically impossible for that exact form of national character we have been accustomed to ascribe to Great Britain to be perpetuated in the island of the far West." Presenting racial purity as synonymous with and, indeed, as prerequisite for nation, MacFie looked at the streetscape of colonial Victoria and argued that inferior races were contaminating and "tainting the young nation's blood" by creating debased hybrids. These illicit liaisons, he surmised, were a threat to the "advancement of the nation."[95] If mixed-raced colonies were increasingly associated with economic backwardness, as many had suggested in reference to the Northwest Coast's fur trade stagnation, then preparedness for nationhood (modernity) required an illusory racial purity. In MacFie's view, the city was indeed a representation of the state.

According to Patrick Wolfe, "Race is endemic to [Western] modernity."[96] In the gradual transformation from mercantilism to an industrialized and settled nation-state, MacFie's taxonomy reflected colonial modernity's requirement to create and manage racial schema. In MacFie's mind, miscegenation threatened modernity's transformative project from colony to nation-state, and Victoria's cityscape was its barometer. Records reveal the increased bureaucratization and medicalization of race in the streetscape, but MacFie projected onto the lived space of the streetscape a complex taxonomy – a stratified, organizing grammar and systematicity. According to stadial ideas and a driving Western, historicizing narrative, the settler-colonial city was the consummation of empire. By the late 1860s, the consummation of such an empire was deemed to be the nation, a racially coherent polity. For MacFie, the settler-colonial streetscape of Victoria was, thus, the mirror of an anxious, transformative modernity.

In 1871, when British Columbia joined the Dominion of Canada as a province, a census of its constituents was called. The census of Victoria showed the lived, mixed streetscape – the object of MacFie's taxonomic concerns.[97] People were categorized as white, Native, Chinese, or coloured. Perhaps these four equally illusory categories were all that the foot police who collected such "information" could handle. Victoria was a site that anxious taxonomies could not master. Where was empire? Rather than a place of confidence, empire was implicitly a place of dislocation; rather than a place where England could exert hegemony, empire was a place where England struggled for control of its own identity.

Conclusion

It is illuminating to consider the processes, both internal and external, that occurred in colonies on each side of the Pacific in the 1870s and 1880s. By the late nineteenth and early twentieth centuries, the reorganization and regulation of bodies and spaces in the desired formation of white settler-colonial polities was thoroughgoing. An overt and vigorous transnational discourse of whiteness, white man's land, and white labour had formed throughout the British settler colonies.[1] Indeed, British Columbia was known as the white man's province by the early twentieth century. And by 1908 Australia's *Bulletin* magazine had on its masthead the now infamous declaration: "Australia for the White Man." By this time *white* and *white man* pertained to an overt, transnational identity that was forming within and between British settler sites.[2] At the transcolonial level, white spaces were organized and shored up outwardly through the sharing of restrictive immigration policies among (former) British colonies. Internally, "at home," Aboriginality was increasingly regulated and litigated discursively and physically, and reserve policies in both Canada and Australia became more restrictive and diminished Aboriginal entitlements. Simultaneously, various immigration schemes brought more white settlers to these Pacific shores.

The influence of anti-Asian policies on both colonies reveals the circuits of empire in the Pacific. In the 1850s Vancouver Island's gold rush boosters had looked enthusiastically towards San Francisco and Melbourne as models for success. Victoria, they hoped, would be another hub of British civilization in the Pacific Ocean. In the 1870s and 1880s British Columbians again looked to their colonial counterparts in the Pacific Rim for answers to various "problems." How, for instance, should they manage Chinese immigrants? As racial tensions grew in the province, British Columbians expressed their severe antipathy towards Chinese people. Such feelings were shared by white settlers in other former British colonies, particularly those in Australia and the western United States, especially California.[3] During his tenure as governor of the Colony of Vancouver Island, James Douglas had upheld the rule of law and sought to protect Chinese immigrants from discrimination in Victoria and on the Mainland; however, general hostility towards Chinese immigrants began to increase in the mid-1860s.[4]

The colonies of Victoria and New South Wales in Australia had introduced a head tax on Chinese immigrants in the mid-1850s and 1860s. There were calls for a similar tax in British Columbia, but, as John McLaren has noted, the tax failed to gain majority support. However, in 1878 the Legislative Assembly of British Columbia, emulating the Colony of Queensland's actions of 1877, "enacted a discriminatory quarterly tax against Chinese residents in the province."[5] The legislation was challenged by Ottawa. In 1884 a group of bills, based on Australian legal precedents, was again passed in British Columbia. The Chinese Immigration Act and the Chinese Regulation Act were both contested, in the first instance by the governor general and in the second by Parliament. In 1885 the Dominion Chinese Immigration Act, which proposed a fifty-dollar head tax, was passed. It was based on the 1881 Act to Restrict the Influx of Chinese into New South Wales.[6]

Legal models were shared among the white colonies of the British Empire within a political climate in which white supremacist thinking would only grow by the close of the nineteenth century. Australia, Canada, and New Zealand had by 1885 a dual immigration policy comprising the Immigration Act, which had "a low fees and tonnage ratio designed to encourage immigration from European countries," and its counterpart, the Chinese Immigration Act, which had "a differential and high tonnage ratio calculated to reduce Chinese immigration."[7] And powerful sentiments regarding white labour and trade, travel, and communication between white dominions, especially in the Pacific, fostered feelings of white exclusivity and ideas about a shared common cause against "Asian intruders."[8]

Internally, as thinking about race became bureaucratized and systematized, definitions of Aboriginality became increasingly narrow and regulated in both Pacific sites. In British Columbia, Indian affairs became in theory a federal affair when the province joined Confederation in 1871; in reality, many issues were mediated with the new provincial authorities. The Indian Act of 1876, which was enacted by Parliament under the provisions of section 91(24) of the Constitution Act, 1867, provided Canada's federal government exclusive authority to legislate in relation to "Indians and Lands Reserved for Indians." The partition of powers between the provinces and the federal government was, however, at times unclear. The Act both centralized power over Aboriginal peoples and instituted a change in the definition of Aboriginality. "Indian" status was conferred only by paternal descent.[9]

Following this legislation, the most pressing issues were Aboriginal title and the management of Aboriginal land. First Nations were placed under increased pressure to use reserve lands in ways deemed to be civilized and in line with dominant society's expectations; when this did not happen, it was argued that they did not deserve their land. These ideas and arguments had a long history, as the lengthy debates between the colonial legislature and the Victoria Town Council discussed in Chapter 7 show. Indeed, as Cole Harris has noted, the 1870s were "pivotal to the Native land question in British Columbia." There was a determination that the weakening of the Douglas land policies would continue, and the "men who reversed the policies in the late 1860s," writes Harris, "watched in the 1870s to ensure that nothing like them returned."[10]

At the turn of the century, the thorny issue of reversionary rights came to the fore when premier Richard McBride, in office from 1903 to 1915, asserted that the province had a reversionary right to both Crown and First Nations lands.[11] Based on this declaration, British Columbia's two main city reserves, in Victoria and Vancouver, were targeted for expropriation. In 1911 the Indian Act was amended so that the residents of any Indian reserve that "adjoins or is situated wholly or partly within an incorporated town or city having a population of not less than eight thousand" could be removed legally without the First Nation's permission, if the removal was in the "interests of the public and of the Indians in the band."[12]

In 1911 the province purchased the Lekwammen Reserve on Victoria's Inner Harbour (see Figure 28). As Jean Barman has noted, Prime Minister Wilfrid Laurier rationalized the action by noting the "large sum of money" paid out – ten thousand dollars per family.[13] The Lekwammen were relocated to a new reserve known as Maplebank in Esquimalt. Reporting on the "Historic Event on Reserve," the *Victoria Daily Colonist* concluded that the "leave taken by the Songhees of their home and that of their fathers was marked by dignity, good feeling and restraint." The Lekwammen had on their "best apparel and entered quietly and cordially into the ceremonies."[14] Onlookers later reported with some indignation that the Lekwammen had been seen "driving about in the city with their own autos!"[15]

Two years later, in 1913, the Aboriginal peoples of Vancouver, the Squamish and Musqueam, who lived mainly in the False Creek Reserve near today's Burrard Street Bridge, lost their land in a similar manner. As they rowed away on the appointed day, with their payments ensured by bank books given out to them, their shacks were burned to the ground.[16]

As in British Columbia, the Colony of Victoria maintained control over all issues pertaining to Aboriginal peoples until it joined in federation with the other Australian colonies in 1901. As Chapter 6 shows, Aborigines on the small missions that remained in Victoria, although not criminals, had, by the 1870s and

Figure 28 Members of the Lekwammen Nation at the ceremony to transfer the title of their reserve to the province, 4 April 1911. BC Archives, E-00251.

1880s, been effectively incarcerated and subjected to an array of disciplinary measures and spatial regimes. Key to the administration's conception of these missions was their goal to reorder notions of gender and class among Aboriginal peoples to align them with modern settler society. Coranderrk Station near Healesville had once been a place of agency for Aboriginal people, but by the 1870s overseer John Green, popular with Aboriginal residents, had been forced to resign and increased restrictions were placed on residents. Legislation such as the 1869 Act for the Protection and Management of the Aboriginal Natives of Victoria gave greater powers to the Board for the Protection of Aborigines. The Act, for instance, gave the board extensive control over many aspects of Aboriginal people's lives, including marriage, employment, place of residence, and social life. In 1886 the residents of Coranderrk Station petitioned the board to protest against the new Aborigines Protection Act, which gave the board in cases of insubordination the power to remove people from stations or suspend rations. Aboriginal people continued to actively fight for their freedom, as evinced in a petition by prominent men of Coranderrk that was published in the Melbourne *Herald:* "Could we get our freedom to go away shearing and harvesting, and to come home when we wish, and also to go for the good of our health when we need it; and we aboriginals all wish and hope to have freedom, not to be bound down by the protection of the board, as it says in the Bill (Clause 5), but we should be free like the white population."[17] The Coranderrk reserve lands, originally 4,850 acres, also became a site of struggle. In the same year, 1886, half of the land was taken away – only 2,300 acres remained. Within less than sixty years, the remainder of the land would be sold, mainly for soldier settlements.[18]

The 1886 Act initiated a policy to remove Aboriginal people of mixed descent from stations or reserves in an apparent effort to merge them into white society. Also known as the Half-Caste Act, it had a profound effect on Aboriginal people in Victoria. Any Aboriginal person of mixed descent under the age of thirty-four was ordered to leave the reserve. The initiative further, and systematically, dislocated Aboriginal families and culture. One of the most devastating polices for Aboriginal peoples in the Colony of Victoria was passed in the same year that Franz Boas walked the streets of Victoria, Vancouver Island, and commented on the large number of First Nations labourers. The Half-Caste Act sought to deny that Aboriginal communities had changed following contact with Europeans, and, in the face of the hybrid frontier culture created by colonialism, it reinforced impossible notions about racial purity. The effects of the Act were devastating. It broke up families and forced many Aboriginal people out of missions, where they eked out a difficult existence on the outskirts of towns among a white population that generally did not accept them.

Two years later, at the Centennial Exhibition in Melbourne, Thomas Avoca; his wife, Rose; and two children not related to them were placed on display in an ethnographic-style tableau vivant. Avoca had actively protested infringements of his rights at Coranderrk Station and had been a signatory, along with other senior Aboriginal men such as William Barak, to several petitions, including the petition published in the *Herald* in 1886. In the heart of Melbourne, however, he and Rose were presented performatively for local and overseas tourists as part of a living diorama of savage authenticity that included carefully arranged traditional objects and a *mia mia* or bark dwelling (a shelter not usually permitted on missions at this time) (see Figure 1). The director of the Zoological Gardens, Albert Le Souëf, a long-term member of the Board for the Protection of Aborigines, initiated the display.[19] Melbourne was dubbed "Marvellous Melbourne" and was said to rival industrialized cities in Britain such as Birmingham. By contrast, colonized Indigenous peoples on display in various cities throughout the world came to be known as *zoos humains* or *Völkerschauen*. Aspiring Melbourne followed these cities' lead by seeking a vision of its past through the celebration of its modernity.

When it joined Federation in 1901, the census of the State of Victoria counted only 36 Aboriginal people in Melbourne. It is likely that they were domestic

Figure 29   Bunjil, the creator spirit, stands, looking out over the cityscape and Wurundjeri Way, in Melbourne (photographer, P. Edmonds).

servants. As Richard Broome notes, only 652 Aboriginal people were counted in the entire state – a pernicious system based on blood quanta deemed 271 "pure" and 381 "half caste."[20] Internally and externally, these former British colonies in the Pacific Rim, in the pursuit of a transcolonial polity of Anglo-Saxon colonies, had reordered bodies and spaces and, by doing so, systematically made new spaces of modernity.

Today, the striking sculpture of Bunjil the Eagle, the creator spirit of the Wurundjeri, sits on the site of the former Batman's Hill and looks out over Melbourne and beyond to Port Phillip Bay (See Figure 29). The Melbourne City Council over the last decade has worked hard to rename and re-inscribe the urban landscape with Aboriginal place names. The recently named Wurundjeri Way is nearby, and Aboriginal walking trails have been marked and marketed throughout the cityscape and surrounding areas. Scarred trees have been designated heritage sites, and the redeveloped riverside parklands are called Birrarung Marr, which means "the side of the river of mists." Many efforts have been made to re-inscribe Indigeneity into the postcolonial cityscape of Melbourne, to acknowledge the presence of Kulin people. But features such as sculptures, scarred trees, and trails tend to celebrate pre-contact artifacts and moments, which do not threaten, and in fact reinforce, the epic trajectory of settler-colonial history.

The presence of living Aboriginal people in the cityscape and their protests have been treated very differently. In early March 2006, the Black GST group (stop genocide, recognize sovereignty, and make treaty) set up a protest camp in a public park in the heart of Melbourne. Camp Sovereignty, as it was called, was situated in the King's Domain to protest the "Stolenwealth Games." Seeking to bring international attention to the plight of Aboriginal peoples, Black GST, in the words of its spokesman, sought to "expose the racist nature of Australian society that continues ... to deny us our basic human rights! Let's Stop the Genocide, Assert Aboriginal Sovereignty and negotiate a Treaty!"[21] Thousands of people visited the site to offer support to the protesters. However, the protest was described by *The Age* as being "on a collision course with police and the Queen."[22] The Melbourne City Council served an eviction notice and over several months sought to use municipal legislation to remove Aboriginal protesters from camping on Crown land in the central business district. "Melbourne City Council is poised to remove Aboriginal activists from their camp in the King's Domain, near Melbourne's Botanic Gardens," reported *The Age*.[23]

The King's Domain is not only Wurundjeri land, it is also close to the site of the first Aboriginal mission in Melbourne. As we have seen, 160 years ago the same council used municipal measures and police to push Aboriginal people from the cityscape. Victoria's Premier Steve Bracks argued that it "was the council's duty to manage the land under planning laws and community services committee" and stated that the camp would soon be disbanded. In a manner evocative of colonial attempts in the 1840s to get rid of Native camps, the premier continued, "We're talking to them and letting them know that they can't stay on permanently and the tents and the caravan and the fire have to go." He added that the council would help the campers to relocate.[24]

Although the protest was highly controversial, even among local Aboriginal communities, it drew attention to local and international issues at the heart of the Aboriginal protest movement, which continues to highlight the lack of recognition, land rights, and a treaty process in Australia. As Wayne Atkinson has pointed out in *The Age:* "The Victorian Government has a shameful legacy in regard to indigenous land claims, and it still lacks the political will to deal with the matter in a fair and just manner. But the indigenous solidarity protest in King's Domain that has continued since the Commonwealth Games has returned the issue of land justice to the public agenda."[25]

Notwithstanding a recent successful land claim by the Gunditjmara in western Victoria – which was a shared land use agreement rather than an agreement for the full return of land – the Victoria state government does indeed have a poor record in relation to Native title issues. It has delivered very little land back to Aboriginal claimants. Unlike the situation in Victoria, British Columbia, there are no acknowledged or legitimate historical treaties in the inner-city area around which to base a land claim, and financial compensation has not been made. Postcolonial cities such as Melbourne remain sites of negotiation and contest. While Native title debates are commonly associated with pastoral leases and places somewhere out in the countryside, it has been forgotten that Melbourne was also a frontier, an often violent contact zone in which Kulin people were dispossessed of their lands.

Indigeneity has also been re-inscribed into the streetscape of Victoria, British Columbia. On a city walking tour, visitors may see Songhees Point, which has a totem pole named the Spirit of Lekwammen that was presented to the city to commemorate the 1994 Commonwealth Games. First Nations have continued to assert their claims and to seek effective legal redress. As Cole Harris has noted, the increase in First Nations voices on the land question is "more to the fore than ever" and perhaps "more volatile than at anytime since the 1870s."[26]

In November 2006 the Lekwammen and Esquimalt First Nations and the Canadian government settled a land claim for Victoria's inner city. The claim, which had been filed in 2001, asserted that Canada and British Columbia had breached certain duties owed to First Nations and that the land in question had been set aside as a four-hectare reserve in 1854 by Governor James Douglas. Government authorities had taken the land back for the construction of the province's legislature buildings without obtaining a surrender of the reserve from First Nations. As part of the litigation, the two First Nations called for "a declaration that the First Nations have existing Douglas treaty rights to the James Bay Reserve," and they called for damages for trespass and for breaches of Douglas treaty rights and fiduciary duty. On 19 November 2006, a settlement was made.[27] A spokesperson for the Turtle Island Native Network commented: "Chief Robert Sam of the Songhees First Nation called it historic. The description of the event was not a superlative. In fact, witnessed by Natives and non-Natives at the BC legislature Saturday, the ceremony to initial legal documents was historic – for BC, Canada and two southern Vancouver Island urban First Nations, Songhees and Esquimalt."[28] Jim Prentice, minister of Indian affairs and northern development and federal interlocutor for Métis and Non-Status Indians, stated that the settlement would "underline a commitment by Canada's New Government to resolve claims through negotiation rather than litigation

... This is a cause for celebration, and another step forward in strengthening positive relationships." Nevertheless, the process began with litigation, and the settlement released Canada and British Columbia from all further Esquimalt and Songhees claims to the land.[29] Described as a settlement that provided "full and final resolution of this litigation without any admissions of fact or liability," the agreement requires Canada and British Columbia to pay a settlement of $31.5 million to be shared between the Songhees and the Esquimalt First Nations.[30] In addition, a Replacement Lands Committee was established as part of a process to identify replacement lands to be purchased with the funds. Chief Andy Thomas of the Esquimalt Nation stated: "Today I am humbled by my grandfathers, whose strength and wisdom has protected and preserved these lands for the past 150 years. They have left us a precious gift, which will become the medicine for our children and our future generations."[31] Despite ongoing tensions over Native title issues in British Columbia, the Douglas treaties and the creation of reserves in British Columbia at least located First Nations within a language or discourse of sovereignty.

The present is created by the past. Our present-day cities are sites shaped by settler colonialism, its violence and vicissitudes, its shared spaces and cross-cultural moments. We cannot exclude cities when we think of the settler-colonial project. And Aboriginal histories are necessarily urban histories. In this book I have reimagined the frontier, re-Indigenized the history of the colonial city, and examined the antecedent structures of racialized spaces to understand key events in the present such as the Black GST protests in the King's Domain and the Lekwammen and Esquimalt First Nations land claim. To see the colonial structures of segregation, dispossession, and reclamation that continue to mark the postcolonial landscape, we must reject any suggestion of a break between the past and present. The removal of Aboriginal people from the King's Domain and other associated urban cleanups in and out of settler cities show that processes of exclusion are far from isolated events – they are part of a sustained historical pattern, the process of internal colonialism. Our cities are syncretic entities. The Lekwammen and Esquimalt First Nations land claim settlement owed its existence to a claim from the past – a reserve set out for First Nations over which the legislative buildings of an entire province were built.

Frontiers do not exist solely in the bush or the borderlands; nor do they reside solely in the historical imagination: they exist in our urban spaces today. Our cities have been and continue to be shifting, transactional frontier sites, vital aspects of the settler-colonial process. Despite a pervasive collective amnesia among settler populations – in fact, a politically and structurally condoned tendency to forget Indigenous peoples' sovereignty and the legacy of segregation and violation in our early colonial cities – this book began with the contention that the racialized landscapes of today's cities have pasts that can be understood only through an examination of the extended genealogies of segregation. With an overarching interest in imperial spatiality and the formation of colonial modernities, I set out to compare the operations of race and segregation in Melbourne and Victoria. By focusing on the localized historical conditions and generative moments that fashioned these racialized urban spaces in the nineteenth century, I opened a window on the broad macrohistorical processes of British colonialism in the Pacific Rim and the intimate micro-geographies of peoples' everyday lives. These settler-colonial cities are complex historical and political entities, each of which must be taken on its own terms. Nevertheless, the common urbanizing spatial commerce of these two settler cities is apparent, and by tracing similarities as well as differences, *Urbanizing Frontiers* reveals some of the broader transformative structures of settler-colonialism's urbanizing frontier.

Significantly, the settler-colonial city should be viewed as a *process* rather than as a site of colonial modernity. Close study of Melbourne and Victoria reveals a key process of settler colonialism: the crucial and rapid transformation of communally owned Indigenous land into private property, which underpinned the colonial order. Inherent in this transformation was the violent and coercive reorganization and production of bodies and spaces to shape white, British, imperial urban landscapes. Inherently racialized processes increasingly sought to regulate and remove Indigenous people from the urban frontier and were bolstered by stadial theory; a driving Western, historicizing narrative of Anglo-Saxon expansionism; and bourgeois metropolitanism. In the idealized narrative of historical development, the settler city represented the highest and most progressive stage of empire, and its precondition was the absence of Indigenous peoples. By the mid- to late nineteenth century, attempts to shape a white or Anglo-Saxon colonial polity and associated struggles over bodies and spaces in the urbanizing frontier were paramount to the success of the settler-colonial enterprise and to each colony's imagined self. That the city was viewed as a reflection of the state and as a metaphor for the territory and how to govern reveals just how deeply ideas about the city as the consummation of empire were entrenched in the imperial imagination.

The management of race in the city therefore had great symbolic and economic significance within the increasingly globalized network of nineteenth-century English-speaking colonies. Each colony was interpolated into a powerful discourse of Anglo-Saxon expansionism and progress that located it within the global British colonial hierarchy. This transcolonial British network produced new subjectivities and spaces at both the global and local level. These subjectivities and spaces were exemplified at one level by geographer Élisée Reclus' stereotypically male *civis Britannicus* (who was configured by his imperial, transcolonial, and spatial entitlements and who exemplified imperial success and unity) and at the other by the colonized Indigenous woman (who was constructed as the abject prostitute, an identity that threatened settler colonialism's requirement for racial coherence). In the increasingly industrialized city of Melbourne and the growing town of Victoria, colonial success demanded that bodies and spaces be managed closely. By the late 1860s, the creation of specific colonial polities was seen as crucial for the eventual transformation to nationhood. But metropolitan narratives of Anglo-Saxon exceptionalism and city building foundered on the shores of these Pacific colonies, for they were also Indigenous or newly indigenized spaces, at least in the early settlement years.

In the transformation to plural but different colonial modernities, Melbourne and Victoria became anxious sites, nervous terrains, and increasingly stratified and bureaucratized ideas about race were marked out recursively on bodies and spaces alike. Common colonial structures with distinct but related sequences of change became apparent. In this context applying the concept of plural modernities is appropriate. In the nineteenth century, Indigenous encounters with Western modernity throughout the Pacific Rim were unremittingly dialectical – that is, Indigenous and Western practices shaped each other and produced alternative, plural modernities.[32] The importance of adopting a nuanced approach to the study of colonial modernities and their histories cannot be underestimated. Attending to the general and the particular, Dilip Parameshwar Goankar describes colonial modernities as sites of "double negotiation ... alternative modernities produce combinations and recombinations which are endlessly surprising."[33] Thus, as two sites of study, Melbourne and Victoria are as instructive in their differences as they are in their similarities.

Population ratios between Indigenous groups and immigrants, especially at the time of the gold rushes, were very different on each side of the Pacific. Several hundred thousand Aboriginal people inhabited the Pacific Northwest Coast, and a relatively small number of European immigrants arrived in the early years of the nineteenth century. In the Port Phillip District, by contrast, relatively few Aboriginal people, perhaps fifteen thousand, were confronted with thousands of settlers seeking pastoral lands and then several hundreds of thousands of immigrants seeking gold.

Varying forms of the nineteenth-century industrial economy likewise shaped each "edge of empire" in different ways. Pastoralism in southeastern Australia required few labourers and the wholesale removal of Aboriginal peoples from the land. By contrast, British Columbia's extractive economy, based on forestry and the fisheries, did require First Nations workers during the mid-nineteenth century, although the colonial project also deemed that they be sequestered in reserves. Mixed-race relationships, a legacy of the fur trade, were far more prevalent in British Columbia and were accepted more widely there than in southeastern Australia, at least in the earlier part of the nineteenth century. In southeastern Australia, mixed marriages may not have been common, or accepted in "good" society, but sexual abuse of Aboriginal women certainly was.

Despite these differences, both regions began with mercantilist economies that shifted to ones that were industrialized and settler-based. In both places Indigenous peoples were affected deeply by European diseases, pushed off their land, and sequestered in reserves and missions. And the gold rushes radically altered socio-spatial relations in the colonies' major cities. Finally, both places were used to underwrite ideas about Anglo-Saxon destiny and Britain's entitlement to the Pacific. The gold rushes were viewed as gift from Providence to the Anglo-Saxon race. Powerful transcolonial narratives of Anglo-Saxon expansionism, settlement, and manifest destiny linked the white, British settler colonies, and gestures between them were common, if at times one-sided.

The outcomes of colonialism were different on each side of the Pacific. Diverse Indigenous cultures, distinct economic conditions, varying immigrant populations, and different approaches to treaty making and Aboriginal policy made each edge of empire unique. In Victoria contestations over the Lekwammen Reserve were linked to arguments about Native title in the outlying frontier. In Melbourne there were no legally enshrined reserves in town, just as there were no, until the mid- to late nineteenth century, legally enshrined (however nominal) reserves made through treaty in the outlying frontier. In Victoria, just as in Melbourne, control of the urban landscape was concerned with property, but, crucially, it also hinged on control of the Lekwammen Reserve and debates about Native title within the cityscape and its implication for lands beyond the city. What was common to both sites is that partitions between the urban frontier and the frontier were largely imaginary. The urbanizing frontier and the outer frontier were linked by Indigenous dispossession across various settler-colonial spaces. Violence, especially in Australia, often characterized land dispossession, and its existence belies traditional notions of a civil city space offset by an unruly outer prairie or pastoral frontier.

Both Melbourne and Victoria were initially fluid, plural sites, and three interlinked processes made and unmade the settler-colonial landscape. The forces of colonization, immigration, and Indigenization, although uneven, fashioned new spaces and subjectivities, with all their countervailing currents. These processes were not sequential, but for a time, until advanced settlement and a more thoroughgoing Indigenous dispossession and displacement occurred, they were simultaneously complicit and conflictual.[34] Early Melbourne and Victoria were transactional contact zones, where urbanizing spaces were both shared and contested. They were new, mixed, unprecedented spaces in the urban project of settler colonialism.

On the Northwest Coast, notions of whiteness were highly expansive and fugitive. In the city of Victoria, Indigenous peoples and families of mixed descent, the legacy of the fur trade, represented an indigenized polity. As settlement increased, however, in line with hardening metropolitan mores on race, these families sought to Anglicize themselves.[35] In early Melbourne, where mixed relations had always been viewed as marginal to middle-class European mores and denigrated as belonging only to the realm of the lower orders, European men sought to disavow or hide their relations with Aboriginal women and their connection to children of mixed descent. These relations were at first mentioned euphemistically, but by the 1850s and 1860s, when there were few Aboriginal people living in Melbourne, satires of miscegenation were prevalent and revealed the great anxiety that existed regarding an inverted order that threatened notions of white settled society. The Melbourne Town Council sought various means to remove nuisances, unwholesome spaces, and the inconvenience of Aborigines from the town in the 1840s, and its actions predated the sanitation movement and other urbanizing trends associated with colonial modernity. Bylaws, police surveillance, and relentless settler violence conspired to partition the peoples of the Kulin Nation from the streetscape, until they came to (discursively) signify displacement. By the 1860s writers such as Charles Wentworth Dilke lauded the Colony of Victoria as a model colony, one of racial purity and Anglo-Saxon vigour. Anglicization, which was most pronounced in British Columbia but also apparent in the Colony of Victoria, shaped the face of the streetscape. And following the almost total banishment of Kulin peoples from Melbourne, proclamations about robust and full-blooded English immigrants in this apparently white colony were persuasive.[36] Similarly, as the century moved on in Victoria, British Columbia, despite the presence of Indigenous labourers and consumers in the city, a shift occurred from fluid and cross-cultural moments to the harder exigencies of racialized violence and segregation, which were made through increasingly modern instruments and bureaucratized systems of governance and categorization. Town bylaws, curfews, and legislation based on the underlying goal of sanitation were designed to regulate contact between Europeans and First Nations.

Some have argued that racial segregation operated largely through unspoken conventions, particularly in the Australian urban frontier. But the idea of segregation by convention is elusive, and these processes are too easily naturalized and, therefore, difficult to trace. Instead, processes that appear to be conventional can be unpacked to reveal their strategic operations. In colonial cities, convention can be exposed to reveal a range of deliberate racialized manoeuvres, everyday adjudications of the streetscape, that were clearly enacted by municipal authorities and other official instruments to create geographies of exclusion. These manoeuvres were naturalized and became invisible as they were rendered as everyday and normal occurrences. At the same time, as police logbooks and other archival sources indicate, other means of segregation, created by a continuum of unofficial (yet structurally condoned) violent acts, were also used.

Victoria developed later than Melbourne, and its small, white population, especially after the gold rush, used direct bylaws, organized sanitation drives, and sheer violence to regulate the thousands of Aboriginal people who appeared to threaten it. By the 1860s and 1870s, increasingly modern systems of surveillance and coercion operated in tandem with instances of harsh disciplinary violence. Victoria sat within a network of imperial discourses on the management of urban spaces along rational lines, and the increased surveillance and medicalization of colonized peoples increasingly came to be enmeshed in ideas about racial hygiene and embourgeoisement. While complex taxonomies of race were projected onto the lived space of the streetscape and employed as an organizing grammar with a scientific guise, segregations and violence in the streetscape were harnessed to progressive reform. By the late 1860s, the consummation of empire was deemed to be the nation-state, and the city was its metaphor. For Matthew MacFie, with his anxious calculation of "twenty-three crosses, in different degrees," the settler-colonial streetscape of Victoria was the mirror of an uneasy, transformative modernity, and its management along racial lines was imperative.[37]

Settler-colonial cities involve the accelerated and often violent reorganization of bodies and spaces in the rapid transformation of Indigenous lands to private property. Spaces of purity and other "unwholesome" spaces were relational sites that were both produced and required by the colonial structure. In the nineteenth-century European imagination, as is well documented in Victoria's and Melbourne's municipal proceedings, expropriated Indigenous peoples were more than an anomaly in city space: they were constructed and materially produced, to varying degrees, as inconvenient and immoral vagrants, nuisances, or prostitutes through the particular spatial commerce of the emergent settler-colonial formation and its city. Indeed, racializations were amplified or writ large in the streetscape. And these categories take us to the heart of settler-colonial relations and to the racialized shaping of the streetscape through law and property. In the urbanizing frontier, bodies and spaces were truly mutually defining entities whose relations were regulated and mediated by the state.[38]

That Indigenous peoples were represented in similar ways in both cities tells us many things. Rather than being merely local or superficial formations, the urban categories "vagrant" and "prostitute" as applied to Indigenous peoples in fact reveal the twin goals of the settler-colonial project as manifested by an urbanizing colonial modernity – that is, the removal of Indigenous peoples from the land (dispossession) and their replacement through immigration (settlement): in other words, a coterminal extraterritorialization and a gendered territorialization.[39] These processes and their associated streetscape categories were effected in the urbanizing settler-colonial frontier with an astoundingly violent rapidity.

In Melbourne and Victoria, the bodies of Aboriginal women and mixed-raced peoples became particular sites of anxiety, and tensions in the cityscape tended to cleave along the intimate aspects of empire. The Indigenous woman as prostitute was powerfully and materially produced by settler-colonialism's gendered project of territorialism, a phenomenon that increased as settlement proceeded. Anxieties about miscegenation required the regulation of Indigenous womens' bodies in the streetscape. Whiteness was concerned with property, but whiteness was also about bodies, sex, and gender and colonial efforts to shore up ideas about a fictive racial purity. Depictions of First Nations women as prostitutes resonated with settlers as the sanitation movement gained strength in the city and as fears of disease, which signified racial disorder and threatened the loss of colonial and moral control, endangering the Empire's success. Colonial fears and mores produced the spectre of the Indigenous prostitute in the city space, but moral reformers and colonial officials also tried to correct and erase such an identity. Tracing this struggle reveals the countervailing tensions of an emergent colonial modernity. The gendered contours of developing frontier cities and the lives of Indigenous and white women in them are vital sites of inquiry, for their discursive positioning reveals the racial imperatives and coordinates of empire. Vagrancy and prostitution were categories that garnered increased currency within the streetscape, and they were produced through complex colonial relations that were symptomatic of a shift from mercantilism to a settled industrialism that required an idealized geography of (white) racial purity.

The growing and organizing "logic" of Anglo-Saxon exceptionalism from the 1840s onward and its coupling with strong currents of bourgeois metropolitanism shaped and mobilized ideas about expansionism and the superiority of Anglo-Saxon governance at both the local and global or transimperial levels. But powerful imaginings of Anglo-Saxon exceptionalism and city building were unmoored at the edges of Britain's empire. In Victoria, British Columbia, despite increasingly harsh racializations, mixed-race relationships had reorganized social space by the 1860s and subverted attempts to create and partition social space as an exclusively white realm. Here were the dislocations of empire. The mixed texture of the cityscape prevailed for much of the nineteenth century. Melbourne was a different case. Although it had a larger British population than Victoria, anxieties about the precariousness of whiteness and the issue of miscegenation were great. And newspaper reports and cartoons reveal that the boundaries of whiteness were anxiously patrolled. Neither Victoria nor Melbourne was "London reproduced": they were, instead, unprecedented, mixed New World spaces.

Indigenous peoples resisted and refuted the new spatial hegemony, and in the cityscape they subverted the colonial order through "crime" and spatial infringements, instances of anti-cadastral activity, and direct violence. They tested the precarious boundaries of whiteness and Anglo-Saxon or British cognate space. Kulin peoples in and around Melbourne may have lived increasingly in the gaps of the spreading cadastral grid, but they were also determined to stay on their land and resist the colonial spatial order. In Victoria, First Nations far outnumbered immigrants, and they moved in and out of town, asserting their presence in their own territory. Attempts to establish white cities and colonial order were refuted and challenged by the lived relations of the city and the lives of Indigenous and non-Indigenous peoples who would not conform. A constant European refrain of threat and loss of control was apparent in Victoria. First Nations, who were clearly not afraid to assert their presence and retaliate, unsettled European immigrants. In both colonial cities, Aboriginal or Indigenized cross-cultural spaces such as reserves, shanties, or camps were conceived as other spaces, as countersites of vice, dirt, madness, and chaos to the imaginary gridded, civil, and ordered city. Yet no such spaces were produced outside the relations of colonization. These sites were the homes of Indigenous peoples transformed by empire.

Indigenous peoples and peoples of mixed-descent had markedly different experiences of emplacement and power than European men and women in urbanizing colonial landscapes. New Indigenized social spaces and landscapes were forming as a corollary to the complicit processes of colonization. Furthermore, intimate empire's mixed relationships and mixed-race peoples created a new spatial politics, one that often subverted official attempts to segregate the streetscape. If we look closely at our postcolonial cities, we can see the continuance and lineage of these operations.

Where was the location of empire? And, recalling Lefebvre's question, what or whom does the settler-colonial city signify? In Victoria and Melbourne, empire was mutable, fragile, and complex; it at once created diversity and demanded its erasure. By the end of the nineteenth century, this erasure was complete. The dislocations of empire in these colonial cities reveal the everyday lives of Indigenous and non-Indigenous peoples. If, as Dilke grandly hoped, Englishmen were to found a new England everywhere "in thought and soil," he and others like him were to be sorely disappointed. For many of empire's urbanizing spaces were places of anxiety and bewilderment. Melbourne was not London reproduced, nor was Victoria the England of the Pacific. Rather, these new spaces were places of dislocation and rapid transculturation for newcomers and Indigenous peoples alike. Upon reimagining the nineteenth-century urbanizing frontier, it is clear that these cities were not as white as many hoped or imagined but were, instead, new mixed sites in which Britain's narrative identity was confounded and subverted. These Pacific settler-colonial cities were an integral part of a dynamic process by which colonial modernity emerged; they were vital to settler colonialism's ongoing project of reterritorialization and the formation of modern settler-colonial states.

Notes

Abbreviations Used in Notes
BCA British Columbia Archives
HBC Hudson's Bay Company
NLA National Library Australia
PROV Public Record Office Victoria
SLNSW State Library of New South Wales
SLV State Library of Victoria
UBCL University of British Columbia Library

Introduction

1 Quoted in John Lutz, "After the Fur Trade: The Aboriginal Labouring Class of British Columbia, 1849-1890," *Journal of the Canadian Historical Association* 3, 1 (1992): 82.
2 The Kulin Nation comprises five related cultural-linguistic groups of southeastern Australian Aboriginal people who are the traditional owners of the area now referred to as the Port Phillip region. These are the Wurundjeri (Woiwurrung-speaking), who own the land upon which Melbourne metropolis now sits, stretching north to Mount William near Lancefield; the Wathawurrung, who own land on the western side of Port Phillip Bay and the Bellarine Peninsula and into the Otway ranges; and the Boonwurrung, who live on what is now the Mornington Peninsula, around Western Port Bay, and possibly as far east as Wilson's Promontory and as far north as the southern-most reaches of the Dandenongs. The Daungwurrung own the territory, including the Goulburn River valley, as far north as Euroa and as far east as Mount Buller; Djadjawarrung peoples own the region of the Loddon and Avoca rivers, as far west as St. Arnaud. The Wurundjeri-willam were the clan that lived along Melbourne's Yarra River and its tributaries and were often referred to by early Europeans as the Yarra Yarra tribe. Other Woiwurrung clans include the Marin-Bulluk, Kurung-Jang-Bulluk, Wurundjeri-Balluk, and Balluk-willam. *Wurundjeri* is now the common term for descendants of all the Woiwurrung clans. See Richard Broome, *Aboriginal Victorians: A History since 1800* (Crows Nest, NSW: Allen and Unwin, 2005), xxi. Throughout this book I have used spellings as per Broome. See also Gary Presland, *Aboriginal Melbourne: The Lost Land of the Kulin* (Melbourne: McPhee Gribble, 1994), 36. On the Pacific Northwest Coast, First Nations people in the area around the southeastern tip of Vancouver Island are known as the Lekwammen and are part of the Coast Salish family. Europeans referred to them as Songhees.
3 Melbourne City Council, Indexes, vol. 1, PROV, VPRS 8947/P0001.
4 Johann and Carl Graf, quoted in Thomas Darragh and Robert N. Wuchatsch, eds., *Hamburg to Hobson's Bay: German Emigration to Port Phillip (Australia Felix), 1848-51* (Melbourne: Wendish Heritage Society, 1999), 222.
5 *The Age*, 3 August 1888. Penelope Edmonds, "The Le Souëf Box: Reflections on Imperial Nostalgia, Material Culture, and Exhibitionary Practice in Colonial Victoria," *Australian Historical Studies* 127 (April 2006): 134, 135. See also Jane Lydon, *Eye Contact: Photographing Indigenous Australians* (Durham: Duke University Press, 2005), 203. Thanks to Jane Lydon,

who tentatively identified Thomas Avoca and his wife Rose (formerly Rose Philips), married in 1882, as the people in this photograph.

6 Tony Bennett, *The Birth of the Museum: History, Theory, Politics* (London: Routledge, 1995), 188.

7 James Ballantyne, quoted in David Hamer, *New Towns in the New World: Images and Perceptions of the Nineteenth-Century Urban Frontier* (New York: Columbia University Press, 1990), 81.

8 See, for example, Lynette Russell, "Introduction," in *Colonial Frontiers: Indigenous-European Encounters in Settler Societies*, ed. Russell (Manchester: Manchester University Press, 2001), 1-16.

9 Faye Gale, *Urban Aborigines* (Canberra: Australian National University Press, 1972).

10 Gary Foley, personal communication with author, 12 June 2004.

11 Jordan Stanger-Ross, "Municipal Colonialism in Vancouver: City Planning and the Conflict over Indian Reserves, 1928-1950s," *Canadian Historical Review* 89, 4 (2008): 541-80.

12 Evelyn J. Peters, "Conceptually Unclad: Feminist Geography and Aboriginal Peoples," *Canadian Geographer* 48, 3 (2004): 255.

13 Nicholas Blomley, *Unsettling the City: Urban Land and the Politics of Property* (New York: Routledge, 2005), 114.

14 Data is collected differently in each county. In Australia, *Indigenous* refers to people who identify as Aboriginal or Torres Strait Islanders. Indigenous Australians represent 2.3 percent of the total Australian population. The Australian Bureau of Statistics divides Australia by state and into regions of relative remoteness, a system developed in response to a demand for a statistical geography that allowed quantitative comparisons between "city" and "country" Australia, where the defining difference between city and country is physical remoteness from goods and services. In greater metropolitan Sydney, 1.2 percent of people identify as Indigenous, whereas 2.1 percent of people in the state of New South Wales do so. In the Northern Territory, 28 percent of people are Indigenous, and 9.7 percent of the population in its capital city, Darwin, is Indigenous. See Australian Bureau of Statistics website. In Canada government census data revealed in 2001 that "almost half (494,095) of the 976,305 people identifying themselves as members of at least one of Canada's Aboriginal groups (North American Indian, Métis or Inuit) resided in urban areas. Of this urban Canadian Aboriginal population, almost 20% (175,760) lived in five cities: Winnipeg, Edmonton, Vancouver, Calgary and Toronto": Canada, Indian and Northern Affairs Canada, "Canada's Urban Aboriginal Population Fact Sheet," Indian and Northern Affairs Canada, http://www.ainc-inac.gc.ca/ai/ofi/uas/fs/uasfs-eng.asp.

15 Blomley, *Unsettling the City*, xiv.

16 I use the term *Native title* to refer to a common law attempt to encapsulate Indigenous title.

17 Robert Freestone, review of *Of Planning and Planting: The Making of British Colonial Cities*, by Robert Home, *Journal of Historical Geography* 24, 3 (1998): 381.

18 Thanks to Tracey Banivanua Mar for our discussions.

19 For work on settler postcolonial cities, see, for example, the insightful work of Blomley, *Unsettling the City*; Jane Jacobs, *Edge of Empire: Postcolonialism and the City* (London: Routledge, 1996); Kay Anderson and Jane Jacobs, "Urban Aborigines to Aboriginality and the City: One Path through the History of Australian Cultural Geography," *Australian Geographical Studies* 35, 1 (1997): 12-22; Kay Anderson, "Sites of Difference: Beyond a Cultural Politics of Race Polarity," in *Cities of Difference*, eds., Ruth Fincher and Jane Jacobs (New York: Guilford Press, 1998), 201-25; Evelyn J. Peters, "Subversive Spaces: First Nations Women and the City," *Environment and Planning D: Society and Space* 16, 6 (1998): 665-85; Coll Thrush, *Native Seattle: Histories from the Crossing-Over Place* (Seattle: University of Washington Press, 2008).

20 See, for example, the following noteworthy works relating to Australia and North America: Paul Carter, *The Road to Botany Bay: An Essay in Spatial History* (London: Faber and Faber, 1987); Daniel Clayton, *Island of Truth: The Imperial Fashioning of Vancouver Island* (Vancouver: UBC Press, 2000); Richard White and John M. Findley, eds., *Power and Place in the North American West* (Seattle: University of Washington Press, 1999); Cole Harris, *Making Native Space: Colonialism, Resistance, and Reserves in British Columbia* (Vancouver: UBC Press, 2002); Neil Smith and Ann Godlewska, eds., *Geography and Empire* (Oxford: Blackwell, 1994); and Lindsay J. Proudfoot, ed., *(Dis)placing Empire: Renegotiating British Colonial Geographies* (Hampshire: Ashgate, 2005). These historical works are either inspired by cultural geography or are historical endeavours by cultural geographers. As Derek Gregory has observed, throughout the 1990s a "mutual interpolation of geography and social theory" occurred: Derek Gregory, *Geographical Imaginations* (Cambridge: Blackwell, 1994), 4. Gregory's wide-ranging study traces multiple discourses that have led to developments in geography, the social sciences, and the humanities. Gregory lists (he admits it is an incomplete list) the following scholars who have shaped thinking: Henri Lefebvre, Michel Foucault, Fredric Jameson, Donna Haraway, bell hooks, Edward Said, and Guyatri Chakravorty Spivak.

21 I thank Patrick Wolfe for our discussions, which have assisted my thinking in this area.

22 Sherene Razack, ed., *Race, Space, and the Law: Unmapping a White Settler Society* (Toronto: Between the Lines, 2003).

23 See Henri Lefebvre, *The Production of Space*, trans. Donald Nicholson-Smith (Cambridge: Basil Blackwell, 1991), 73. See also, Andy Merrifield, "Henri Lefebvre: A Socialist in Space," *Thinking Space*, ed. Mike Crang and N.J. Thrift (London: Routledge, 2000), 168.

24 Lefebvre, *Production of Space*, 73, 113.

25 Ibid., 17-18.

26 Jacobs, *Edge of Empire*, 104.

27 Michael Cross and Michael Keith, eds., *Racism, the City and the State* (London: Routledge, 1993), 3.

28 Razack, *Race, Space, and the Law*, passim.

29 Lefebvre, *Production of Space*, 113.

30 Robert Dixon, *The Course of Empire: Neoclassical Culture in New South Wales, 1788-1860* (Melbourne: Oxford University Press, 1986), 61.

31 Elizabeth Grosz, *Space, Time, and Perversion: Essays on the Politics of Bodies* (New York: Routledge, 1995), 107-8.

32 Penelope Edmonds, "From Bedlam to Incorporation: Whiteness and the Racialisation of Settler-Colonial Urban Space in Victoria, British Columbia, 1840s-1880s," in *Exploring the British World: Identity – Cultural Production – Institutions*, ed. Kate Darian-Smith et al. (Melbourne: RMIT Publishing, 2004), 62.

33 Patricia Nelson Limerick, "Going West and Ending Up Global," *Western Historical Quarterly* 32, 1 (2001): 5-23.

34 Frederick Cooper and Ann Laura Stoler, "Between Metropole and Colony: Rethinking a Research Agenda," in *Tensions of Empire: Colonial Cultures in a Bourgeois World*, ed. Cooper and Stoler (Los Angeles: University of California Press, 1997), vii-x.

35 Phillip D. Morgan, "Encounters between British and 'Indigenous' Peoples, c. 1500–c. 1800," in *Empire and Others: British Encounters with Indigenous Peoples, 1600-1850*, ed. Martin Daunton and Rick Halpern (Philadelphia: University of Pennsylvania Press, 1999), 68.

36 Marc Bloch, "Pour une histoire comparée des sociétées européenes," *Revue de synthèse historique* 46 (1925): 15-50. See also Julie Evans et al., *Equal Subjects, Unequal Rights: Indigenous Peoples and Political Rights in British Settlements, 1830-1910* (Manchester: Manchester University Press: 2003).

37   Mary Louise Pratt, *Imperial Eyes: Travel Writing and Transculturation* (New York: Routledge, 1993), 4.
38   Jonathan Raban, *Soft City* (London: Hamilton, 1974).
39   Cooper and Stoler, "Between Metropole and Colony."
40   See Adele Perry, *On the Edge of Empire: Gender, Race, and the Making of British Columbia, 1849-1871* (Toronto: University of Toronto Press, 2001); Katie Pickles and Myra Rutherdale, eds., Introduction, *Contact Zones: Aboriginal and Settler Women in Canada's Colonial Past* (Vancouver: UBC Press, 2005), 1.
41   See Perry, *On the Edge of Empire;* Tony Ballantyne and Antoinette Burton, eds., *Bodies in Contact: Rethinking Colonial Encounters in World History* (Durham: Duke University Press, 2005).
42   Judith Butler, *Bodies That Matter: On the Discursive Limits of "Sex"* (New York: Routledge, 1993), ix, 33.
43   Ballantyne and Burton, "Introduction: Bodies, Empires, and World Histories," in *Bodies in Contact,* 5.
44   Ann Laura Stoler, "Tense and Tender Ties: The Politics of Comparison in North American History and (Post) Colonial Studies," *Journal of American History* 88, 3 (2001): 830.
45   Homi Bhabha, "The White Stuff," *Artforum International,* May 1998, 21.
46   Cheryl Harris, "Whiteness as Property," *Harvard Law Review* 106 (1993): 1709-91.
47   James Ballantyne, quoted in Hamer, *New Towns in the New World,* 81.
48   See Gayatri Chakravorty Spivak, "Can the Subaltern Speak?" in *Marxism and the Interpretation of Culture,* ed. C. Nelson and L. Grossburg (Chicago: University of Illinois Press, 1988), 271-313.
49   Nihal Perera, "Indigenizing the Colonial City: Late Nineteenth-Century Colombo and Its Landscape," *Urban Studies* 39, 9 (2002): 1703–21.

Chapter 1: Extremities of Empire

1   Alexander Morris, lecture delivered at the Mercantile Library Association, *British Colonist,* 13 July 1859.
2   On the anticipatory geography of colonialism, see Daniel Clayton, *Island of Truth: The Imperial Fashioning of Vancouver Island* (Vancouver: UBC Press, 2000).
3   "Emigration and Colonisation", *Illustrated London News,* 22 July 1848, 33.
4   Adele Perry, *On the Edge of Empire: Gender, Race, and the Making of British Columbia, 1849-1871* (Toronto: University of Toronto Press, 2001), 3.
5   Quoted in A.G.L. Shaw, *The History of the Port Phillip District: Victoria before Separation* (Melbourne: Miegunyah Melbourne, Melbourne University Press, 1996), 45; E.M. Curr, *Recollections of Squatting in Victoria, Then Called the Port Phillip District (from 1841 to 1851) Melbourne* (Sydney: George Robertson, 1883), 40.
6   For example, Bishop Hall's *Mundus Alter Et Idem* (1605) depicted terra australis incognita as an inversion or mirror of English Renaissance society – degenerate, upside down, and yet the same. Derrick Moors, "Imaginary Voyages," in *The Great South Lands,* ed. Des Cowley (Melbourne: Library Council of Victoria, 1988), 8. Simon Ryan, *The Cartographic Eye: How Explorers Saw Australia* (Cambridge: Cambridge University Press, 1996), 104.
7   The phrase *the West beyond the West* is discussed in Jean Barman's book *The West beyond the West: A History of British Columbia,* rev. ed. (Toronto: University of Toronto Press, 1996). Adele Perry, "On Not Going on a Field Trip: Presence, Absence, and the Writing of BC History," *BC Studies* 123 (Winter 2001): 57-63.
8   K.M. Dallas, "Commercial Influences on the First Settlements in Australia," *Tasmanian Historical Association* 16, 2 (1968): 36; Ann Laura Stoler, "Tense and Tender Ties: The Politics

of Comparison in North American History and (Post) Colonial Studies," *Journal of American History* 88, 3 (2001): 840.

9 Stuart Banner, *Possessing the Pacific: Land, Settlers and Indigenous Peoples from Alaska to Australia* (Cambridge, MA: Harvard University Press, 2007), 7.

10 Derek Pethick, *Victoria: The Fort* (Vancouver: Mitchell Press, 1968), 26.

11 Jeremy Whiteman, *Reform, Revolution and French Global Policy, 1787-1791* (Farnham: Ashgate, 2003), 115.

12 Ibid., 121.

13 Dallas, "Commercial Influences on the First Settlements in Australia," 39. La Pérouse and his ships were lost in a storm in the Pacific Ocean close to the Solomon Islands in 1788.

14 Pethick, *Victoria*, 27.

15 Ibid., 29.

16 On 8 April 1802 the British *Investigator*, sailing west from Cape Leewin (Western Australia), sighted the French ship *Le Geograph*, commanded by Nicholas Baudin. Baudin's goal was also to chart the circumference of Australia. Paul Brunton, *Matthew Flinders: The Ultimate Voyage* (Sydney: State Library of New South Wales, 2001), 17, 4.

17 Michael Cannon, ed., *Historical Records of Victoria* (Melbourne: Victoria Government Printing Office, 1982), 1:xiii (hereafter cited as *HRV*).

18 Matthew Flinders (1774-1814) was imprisoned by the French in Mauritius in December 1803 for six and a half years. It was there that he drew his famous map of Australia. Brunton, *Matthew Flinders*, 19. The settlement at Sorrento was a precursor to the eventual settlement of Melbourne.

19 Dallas, "Commercial Influences on the First Settlements," 48.

20 On disease, see Cole Harris, "Voices of Smallpox around the Strait of Georgia," *The Resettlement of British Columbia: Essays On Colonialism and Geographical Change* (Vancouver: UBC Press, 1997), 3-30.

21 John Sutton Lutz, "Work, Wages and Welfare in Aboriginal-Non-Aboriginal Relations, British Columbia, 1849-1970" (PhD diss., University of Ottawa, 1994), 197. See also John Sutton Lutz, *Makúk: A New History of Aboriginal-White Relations* (Vancouver: UBC Press, 2009).

22 In *Contact and Conflict: Indian-European Relations in British Columbia, 1774-1890*, 2nd ed. (Vancouver: UBC Press, 1992), Robin Fisher notes that specific evidence describing population losses in detail is scant. James Douglas, chief factor of the Hudson's Bay Company and later governor of British Columbia, wrote in 1838 that smallpox had killed one third of the population on the northern Coast. On population estimates, see Harris, "Voices of Smallpox," 281.

23 Lutz, "Work, Wages and Welfare," 197. Lutz notes that George Vancouver observed the pockmarks on the faces of the Lekwammen's Georgia Strait neighbours in 1792.

24 Ibid., 198.

25 Cole Harris, "Social Power and Cultural Change in Pre-Colonial British Columbia," *BC Studies* 115/116 (Autumn/Winter 1997/98): 68.

26 Richard Broome, "Victoria," in *Contested Ground: Australian Aborigines under the British Crown*, ed. Ann McGrath (Sydney: Allen and Unwin, 1995), 124. See also, N.G. Butlin, *Our Original Aggression: Aboriginal Populations of Southeastern Australia, 1788-1850* (Sydney: Allen and Unwin, 1983); J. Campbell, "Smallpox in Aboriginal Australia, 1829-31," *Historical Studies* 20, 81 (1983): 536-56, and "Smallpox in Aboriginal Australia: The Early 1830s," *Historical Studies* 21, 84 (1985): 336-58; N.G. Butlin, "Macasssans and Aboriginal Smallpox: The '1789' and the '1829' Epidemics," *Historical Studies* 21, 84 (1985): 315-35.

27 Shaw, *The History of the Port Phillip District*, 11. See Shaw for a survey argument of popula-
    tion estimates. See also Michael Christie, *Aborigines in Colonial Victoria, 1835-86* (Sydney:
    Sydney University Press, 1979), 7.
28 On assimilation programs in Canada, see Susanne Fournier, *Stolen from Our Embrace:
    The Abduction of First Nations Children and the Restoration of Aboriginal Communities*
    (Vancouver: Douglas and McIntyre, 1997). First Nations children taken into care in British
    Columbia are also referred to as the lost generation, 9. See also Australian Human Rights
    Commission, *Bringing Them Home: Report of the National Inquiry into the Separation of
    Aboriginal and Torres Strait Islander Children from their Families* (Sydney: Human Rights
    and Equal Opportunity Commission, 1997). For a comparison of missionary endeavours
    in British Columbia and Australia, see Peggy Brock, "Mission Encounters in the Colonial
    World: British Columbia and South West Australia," *Journal of Religious History* 24, 2 (June
    2000): 159-79.
29 Robert A.J. McDonald, *Making Vancouver, 1863-1913* (Vancouver: UBC Press, 1996), xiv;
    John Lutz, "After the Fur Trade: The Aboriginal Labouring Class of British Columbia,
    1849-1890," *Journal of the Canadian Historical Association* 3, 1 (1992): 70. See also Rolf
    Knight, *Indians at Work: An Informal History of Native Labour in British Columbia* (Van-
    couver: New Star Books, 1996).
30 For broader structural explorations on this topic, see Patrick Wolfe, "Land, Labour, and
    Difference: Elementary Structures of Race," *American Historical Review* 106, 3 (2001):
    866-905. Throughout the late nineteenth and twentieth centuries, the cattle industry of
    Northern Australia depended on the underpaid labour of Aboriginal workers. Likewise,
    many middle-class homes in Australia during this later period used the unpaid labour of
    female Aboriginal domestic servants. See Anne McGrath, *Born in the Cattle: Aborigines
    in Cattle Country* (Sydney: Allen and Unwin, 1987), and Victoria Haskins, *One Bright Spot*
    (Basingstoke: Palrave McMillan, 2005).
31 Victoria Freeman, "Attitudes towards 'Miscegenation' in Canada, United States, New
    Zealand, and Australia, 1860-1914," *Native Studies Review* 16, 1 (2005): 41-69.
32 Barman, *West beyond the West*, 32.
33 Fisher, *Contact and Conflict*, 3.
34 Ibid., 2.
35 Barman, *West beyond the West*, 36; Fisher, *Contact and Conflict*, 21.
36 In 1806 Fraser established Fort St. James at Stuart Lake, and he established Fort George
    at the confluence of the Fraser and Nechako rivers the following year. Other companies
    were in operation, such as the Pacific Fur Trading Company, which built Fort Astoria at
    the mouth of the Columbia River, where it had all-important sea access. Fisher, *Contact
    and Conflict*, 25.
37 Ibid., 24. New Caledonia was located between the fifty-first and fifty-seventh parallels.
38 Barman, *West beyond the West*, 33.
39 Harris, "Social Power and Cultural Change," 55.
40 Fisher, *Contact and Conflict*, xi.
41 Ibid., xxviii, xi.
42 See, for example, Harris, "Social Power and Cultural Change," 45-82, and Sydney L. Har-
    ring, *White Man's Law: Native People in Nineteenth-Century Canadian Jurisprudence*
    (Toronto: University of Toronto Press, 1998).
43 Ibid., 47.
44 Clayton, *Island of Truth*; Harring, *White Man's Law*; Cole Harris, *The Resettlement of British
    Columbia: Essays on Colonialism and Geographical Change* (Vancouver: UBC Press, 1997),
    and Making Native Space: Colonialism, Resistance, and Reserves in British Columbia (Van-
    couver: UBC Press, 2002); and Tina Loo, *Making Law, Order, and Authority in British*

Columbia, 1821-71 (Toronto: University of Toronto Press, 1994), to cite a few, have constructed their analyses using contemporary theories on colonialism, cultural geography, race, law, and imperial commerce to further understandings of colonial endeavours in British Columbia.

45 Harris, "Social Power and Cultural Change," 45-82.

46 Fisher, *Contact and Conflict*, 24.

47 See, for example, Barry M. Gough, *Gunboat Frontier: British Maritime Authority and Northwest Coast Indians, 1846-1890* (Vancouver: UBC Press, 1984).

48 Fisher, *Contact and Conflict*, 39, 40; Harris, "Social Power and Cultural Change," 45-82.

49 Harris mentions "other stratagems of control," and work preceding Foucault, particularly that of Antonio Gramsci, may be fruitful to help us to appreciate the continuum of colonial hegemony that encompassed European violence, coercion, and First Nations' consent on the Northwest Coast. Gramsci's social distinction between political hegemony (e.g., the army, the police, and the central bureaucracy) and civil hegemony (e.g., schools, families, and unions) shows that domination may be achieved through a combination of power *and* consent. This is of interest to the study of colonial situations, because recent scholarship has suggested that "harsh coercion worked in tandem with a 'consent' that was part voluntary or part contrived": see Anai Loomba, *Colonialism/Postcolonialism* (London: Routledge, 1998), 31. Loomba notes that Gramsci's work has enabled a rethinking of the relation between the realm of culture or ideology and that of economics or material reality (24). Furthermore, Gramscian notions of hegemony stress the incorporation and transformation of ideas and practices belonging to those who are dominated, rather than a simple imposition from above. These transformations are seen increasingly as being central to colonial rule. Thus, theories of articulation (in which one mode is subordinate to and facilitates another) can amplify Gramsci's ideas on hegemony in which an incorporation or harnessing of subaltern practices – for example, the traditional Native economy to the colonial economy – furthers colonial capitalist goals. Gramsci's views are scattered in his various prison diaries and *Prison Notebooks*, written between 1929 and 1931. See David Forgacs, ed., *An Antonio Gramsci Reader: Selected Writings, 1916-1935* (New York: Schoken Books, 1988).

50 Fisher, *Contact and Conflict*, 40; Lutz, "Work, Wages and Welfare," 172, 173.

51 Fisher, *Contact and Conflict*, 40.

52 In the 1970s and '80s, Louis Althusser's work influenced Marxist anthropologists and economic historians by challenging the Marxist teleology that each mode of production emerged as a predetermined stage of unilinear development. Instead, he suggested that actual social formations conjoined (articulated) in unique ways a number of modes of production. One mode of production, or society, was dominant, and it subordinated the others to the requirements of its own historical production. In the colonies these occurred in different and unpredictable ways. See Patrick Wolfe, "History and Imperialism: A Century of Theory, from Marx to Postcolonialism," *American Historical Review* 102, 2 (1997): 397.

53 Fisher, *Contact and Conflict*, 26.

54 Ibid., 31, 29; Lutz, "Work, Wages and Welfare," 173.

55 Lutz, "Work, Wages and Welfare," 18, 19. Knight, *Indians at Work*.

56 Harris, "Social Power and Cultural Change," 56.

57 Marnie Bassett, "Governor Arthur and the Opposite Coast," *Tasmanian Historical Association* 2, 5 (1953): 83.

58 See *HRV*, 2a:xvi-xvii, for an overview of British humanitarian sentiment, the abolition of slavery, and the Select Committee of 1837.

59 Preface, United Kingdom, House of Commons, *British House of Commons Report of the Parliamentary Select Committee on the Aboriginal Tribes (British Settlements), Reprinted with Comments by the Aborigines Protection Society* (London: William Ball, 1837).

60 Elizabeth Elbourne, "The Sins of the Settler: The 1835-36 Select Committee on Aborigines and Debates over Virtue and Conquest in the Early Nineteenth-Century British White Settler Empire," *Journal of Colonialism and Colonial History* 4, 3 (2003): 1-39.
61 United Kingdom, *Report of the Parliamentary Select Committee*, 1.
62 Ibid., viii.
63 Elbourne, "The Sins of the Settler," 4.
64 Ibid.
65 *HRV*, 2a, xvii.
66 Governor Darling's 1827 limits of location statute stipulated that settlement could not occur outside a certain coastal penumbra that stretched from the northern New South Wales coast to the southern coastal town of Moruya.
67 Harring, *White Man's Law*, 25.
68 Ibid., 26.
69 Christie, *Aborigines in Colonial Victoria*, 87, 89; M. Lakic and R. Wrench, eds., *Through Their Eyes: An Historical Record of the Aboriginal People of Victoria as Documented by the Officials of the Port Phillip Protectorate, 1839-1841* (Melbourne: Museum Victoria, 1994), 13.
70 "Correspondence and Other Papers Relating to the Hudson's Bay Company, the Exploration of the Territories ... and Other Affairs in Canada," dispatch no. 19, August 1858, in *Irish University Series of British Parliamentary Papers – Colonies: Canada, vol. 22* (Shannon: Irish University Press, 1969), 59, 60.
71 Pethick, *Victoria*, 31.
72 Michael Cannon, *Old Melbourne Town Before the Gold Rush* (Victoria: Loch Haven Books, 1991), 8.
73 W.C. Grant, "Remarks on Vancouver Island, Principally concerning Town Sites and Native Population," *Journal of the Royal Geographical Society* 31 (1861): 208-13.
74 Alexander Morris, lecture at the Mercantile Library Association in Victoria, *British Colonist*, 13 July 1859.
75 Barman, *West beyond the West*, 65; Fisher, *Contact and Conflict*, 58.
76 See Peter McDonald, "Demography," *Encyclopedia of Melbourne*, ed. Andrew Brown-May and Shurlee Swain (Melbourne: Cambridge University Press, 2005). McDonald cites the statistician of the Colony of New South Wales, Timothy Coghlan, whose estimation of the population of Melbourne in 1851 was twenty-three thousand; however, this estimate excluded various outlying suburbs. John McCarty, economic historian, has taken these areas into account and has estimated the population of Melbourne at this time to be twenty-nine thousand: J.W. McCarty and C.B. Schedvin, eds., *Australian Capital Cities: Historical Essays* (Sydney: Sydney University Press, 1978).
77 Barman, *West beyond the West*, 74.
78 Ravi de Costa, "The Treaty Process in British Columbia: Some Thoughts for Australian Treaties" (paper presented at "Treaty – Advancing Reconciliation," Murdoch University, Perth, 27 June 2002).
79 Banner, *Possessing the Pacific*, 195.
80 Ibid., 2, 3, 13-46, 195-230.
81 Kenneth Nguyen, "Tears of Joy as Land Struggle Comes to an End," *The Age*, 31 March 2007, 7. The Gunditjmara are the second group to have Native title rights recognized after a Native title determination in 2005 in the Wimmera region of Victoria.
82 *HRV*, 1:5-10; Christie, *Aborigines in Colonial Victoria*, 25.
83 Christie, *Aborigines in Colonial Victoria*, 25, 26.
84 Bassett, "Governor Arthur and the Opposite Coast," 90. George Arthur to Secretary Hay, September 1832.

85 Sir John Franklin, who succeeded Arthur in Van Diemen's Land, was also his successor in the governance of Upper Canada.
86 Port Phillip Association's application to the British government: "The object of the association is to obtain a recognition and confirmation of the treaties ... or should HM Minister see any objection to this ... a royal grant of territories." Frederick Watson, ed., *Historical Records of Australia* (W.G. Murray, Government Printer: Commonwealth of Australia, 1971), series 1, 18:381-82 (hereafter cited as *HRA*).
87 *HRV*, 1:3.
88 Bain Attwood, *Possession: Batman's Treaty and the Matter of History* (Melbourne: Miegunyah Press, 2009), 72, 296-98.
89 From 1816 to 1822, Francis Forbes was the chief justice of the Supreme Court of Newfoundland. See letter dated 26 July 1835 to Sir Richard Bourke, governor of New South Wales, in which Forbes advises Bourke to take measures to prevent settlers from purchasing land from Aborigines. Francis Forbes to Governor Sir Richard Bourke, 26 July 1835, NLA, MS 1293.
90 Banner, *Possessing the Pacific*, 26.
91 Francis Forbes (1784-1841), letter to Governor Sir Richard Bourke, 26 July 1835, NLA, MS 1293.
92 Governor Bourke's proclamation, dated 26 August 1835, *HRV*, 1:14.
93 *HRV*, 1:xiii.
94 Hamar Foster, "Letting Go the Bone: The Idea of Indian Title in British Columbia, 1849-1927," in *Essays in the History of Canadian Law: British Columbia and the Yukon*, ed. Hamar Foster and John McLaren (Toronto: University of Toronto Press, 1995), 40. A confidential memorandum noted that "in parting with the land of the Island, Her Majesty parts only with her own right therein, and that whatever measures she was bound to take in order to extinguish the Indian title are equally obligatory on the [Hudson's Bay] Company." Confidential Memorandum, Colonial Office 305, no. 1 at 342-48, cited in Foster, 75n67.
95 Ibid., 40, 44.
96 Harring, *Whiteman's Law*, 191; Foster, "Letting Go the Bone," 43.
97 Foster, "Letting Go the Bone," 41. See also Harris, *Making Native Space*, 19. The New Zealand Company was founded in 1839 in London to promote the systematic colonization of New Zealand in accordance with the principles of Edward Gibbon Wakefield, whose emigration system professed higher, more noble aims than mere financial profit.
98 United Kingdom, House of Commons, Report of the Select Committee on New Zealand, together with the Minutes of the Evidence, Appendix, and Index, 1844, in Irish University Series of British Parliamentary Papers (Shannon: Irish University Press, 1968). See also Emer de Vattel, The Law of Nations, Or, Principles of the Law of Nature Applied to the Conduct of Nations and Sovereigns (Newberry: London, 1760 [1758]), Book 1, 91.
99 Foster, "Letting Go the Bone", 41, 43; see also Harris, *Making Native Space*, 17, 19.
100 Harris, *Making Native Space*, 19, 21.
101 Harring, *Whiteman's Law*, 191.
102 Harris, *Making Native Space*, 26.
103 Ibid., 25.
104 Foster, "Letting Go the Bone," 41.
105 Ibid., 42.
106 Harris, *Making Native Space*, 20.
107 Banner, *Possessing the Pacific*, 216-18.
108 Foster, "Letting Go the Bone," 45.
109 Banner, *Possessing the Pacific*, 26.

110   Stoler notes the work of de Alva in "Tense and Tender Ties," 830, 840.

111   Ibid., 838.

112   Perry, *On the Edge of Empire*, 19. See Sylvia Van Kirk, *"Many Tender Ties": Women in Fur-Trade Society, 1670-1870*, 2nd ed. (Norman: University of Oklahoma Press, 1983).

113   There are few studies in this area of Australian history, which is a major gap in scholarship. See Katherine Ellinghaus, "Margins of Acceptability: Class, Education and Interracial Marriage in Australia and America," *Frontiers* 23 (2002): 55-75. Ellinghaus, however, is concerned largely with the late nineteenth century.

114   Nancy E. Wright and Brooke Marie Collins-Gearing, "Comparative Study of the Status of Women in Canada and Australia," *Australian Canadian Studies* 22, 1 (2004): 1-7.

115   Lisa Chilton, *Agents of Empire: British Female Migration to Canada and Australia, 1860s-1930* (Toronto: University of Toronto Press, 2007).

116   Marilyn Lake and Henry Reynolds, *Drawing the Global Colour Line* (Carlton: Melbourne University Press, 2008).

Chapter 2: Settler-Colonial Cities

1   William Adeney departed Portsmouth for Hobart Town on 19 August 1842 on the ship *Jane Frances*. Adeney was a middle-class and somewhat religious man in his twenties whose writing offers an eyewitness account of the development of the Port Phillip Colony and a travelogue of his round trip through the Western District in 1842-43. William Adeney, diary, SLV, MS 8520A, 296-7, 27 January 1843.

2   Johannes Fabian, *Time and Other: How Anthropology Makes Its Object* (New York: Columbia University Press, 1983); Patrick Wolfe, "On Being Woken Up: The Dreamtime in Anthropology and in Australian Settler Culture," *Comparative Studies in Society and History* 33, 2 (1991): 197-224.

3   Anthony D. King, *Colonial Urban Development* (London: Routledge and Kegan Paul, 1973), xiii.

4   Anthony D. King, "Colonial Cities: Global Pivots of Change," in *Colonial Cities: Essays on Urbanism in a Colonial Context*, ed. Ronald Ross and Gerard Telkamp (Boston: Martinus Nijhoff Publishers/Leiden University Press, 1985), 7-18.

5   Ibid., 7.

6   Ronald Ross and Gerard Telkamp, eds., *Colonial Cities: Essays on Urbanism in a Colonial Context* (Boston: Martinus Nijhoff Publishers/Leiden University Press, 1985).

7   King, "Colonial Cities," 9.

8   Robert Freestone, review of *Of Planning and Planting*, by Robert Home, *Journal of Historical Geography* 24, 3 (1998): 381; Felix Driver and David Gilbert, eds., *Imperial Cities: Landscape, Display, and Identity* (Manchester: Manchester University Press, 2003); Robert Home, *Of Planning and Planting: The Making of British Colonial Cities* (New York: Routledge, 1997).

9   Lorenzo Veracini, "The Imagined Geographies of Settler Colonialism," in *Making Settler Colonial Space: Perspectives on Land, Race and Identity*, ed. Tracey Banivanua Mar and Penelope Edmonds (Basingstoke: Palgrave, 2010).

10   David Hamer, *New Towns in the New World: Images and Perceptions of the Nineteenth-Century Urban Frontier* (New York: Columbia University Press, 1990).

11   Lionel Frost, "Anglo-Saxon Cities on the Pacific Rim," in *Megalopolis: The Giant City in History*, ed. T.C. Barker and A. Sutcliffe (Basingstoke: Macmillan, 1993).

12   B.M. Stave, "A Conversation with Gilbert A. Stelter: Urban History in Canada," *Journal of Urban History* 6, 2 (1980): 177-209.

13   Lionel Frost, "The Urban History Literature of Australia and New Zealand," *Journal of Urban History* 22, 1 (1995): 141, 142.

14 Kay Anderson and Jane Jacobs, "Urban Aborigines to Aboriginality and the City: One Path through the History of Australian Cultural Geography," *Australian Geographical Studies* 35, 1 (1997): 12-22; Kay Anderson, "Sites of Difference: Beyond a Cultural Politics of Race Polarity," in *Cities of Difference,* ed. Ruth Fincher and Jane Jacobs (New York: Guilford Press, 1998), 201-25.

15 Kay Anderson, *Vancouver's Chinatown: Racial Discourse in Canada, 1875-1980* (Montreal and Kingston: McGill-Queen's University Press, 1991); Adele Perry, *On the Edge of Empire: Gender, Race, and the Making of British Columbia, 1849-1871* (Toronto: University of Toronto Press, 2001); Jean Barman, "Taming Aboriginal Sexuality: Gender, Power, and Race in British Columbia, 1850-1900," *BC Studies* 115/116 (Autumn/Winter 1997/98): 237-66, and "Aboriginal Women on the Streets of Victoria: Rethinking Transgressive Sexuality during the Colonial Encounter," in *Contact Zones: Aboriginal and Settler Women in Canada's Past,* ed. Katie Pickles and Myra Rutherdale (Vancouver: UBC Press, 2005), 205-27; Renisa Mawani, "'The Iniquitous Practice of Women': Prostitution and the Making of White Spaces in British Columbia, 1898-1905," in *Working through Whiteness: International Perspectives,* ed. Cynthia Leine-Rasky (New York: SUNY Press, 2002), 43-68.

16 Marcia Langton, "Urbanising Aborigines: The Social Scientists' Great Deception," *Social Alternatives* 2 (1981): 16-22.

17 Ibid., 18, 19.

18 Ibid., 20.

19 Tim Rowse, "Transforming the Notion of the Urban Aborigine," *Urban Policy and Research* 18, 2 (2000): 171-90.

20 Faye Gale, *Urban Aborigines* (Canberra: Australian National University Press, 1972), 27; Rowse, "Transforming the Notion of the Urban Aborigine," 173.

21 Rowse, "Transforming the Notion of the Urban Aborigine," 174. Rowse argues that these urban immigrants, as Gale calls them, were often involuntary migrants: one third of those who moved to the city of Adelaide, for example, were actually moved because of government decisions to improve access to medical services or place children in government foster homes or children's homes. Some of the children were removed or stolen from their families.

22 Rowse, "Transforming the Notion of the Urban Aborigine," 184.

23 Evelyn J. Peters, "Subversive Spaces: First Nations Women and the City," *Environment and Planning D: Society and Space* 16 (1998): 665.

24 Evelyn J. Peters, "Conceptually Unclad: Feminist Geography and Aboriginal Peoples," *Canadian Geographer* 48, 3 (2004): 252.

25 Ibid.

26 Nihal Perera, "Indigenizing the Colonial City: Late Nineteenth-Century Colombo and Its Landscape," *Urban Studies* 39, 9 (2002): 1707, 1706.

27 Jay T. Johnson et al., "Creating Indigenous Geographies: Embracing Indigenous Peoples' Knowledges and Rights," *Geographical Research* 45, 2 (2007): 117, 118.

28 Michel Foucault and Paul Rabinow, "Space, Knowledge, and Power," interview in *The Foucault Reader,* ed. Paul Rabinow (New York: Pantheon Books, 1984), 242.

29 Anonymous, *Melbourne As It Is and Ought To Be, by Anon (1850), with Remarks on Street Architecture Generally* (Melbourne: J. Pullar; J. Harrison, 1850), 4-10, reprinted and revised from the first issue of *The Australasian.*

30 R.L. Meek, *Social Sciences and the Ignoble Savage* (Cambridge: Cambridge University Press, 1976); R.L. Meek, "Smith, Turgot and the 'Four Stages' Theory," *Smith, Marx and After* (London: Chapman and Hall, 1977), 18-32.

31 John Locke, *Two Treatises of Government, 1690* (Cambridge: Cambridge University Press, 1988).

32 David Macey, *The Penguin Dictionary of Critical Theory* (London: Penguin Books, 2000), 111. Quote from John Gascoigne, *The Enlightenment and the Origins of European Australia* (Cambridge: Cambridge University Press, 2002), 2.

33 Meek, *Social Sciences and the Ignoble Savage*, 230.

34 Meek, "Smith, Turgot and the 'Four Stages' Theory," 3.

35 Ibid.

36 Meek argues that these ideas were, in fact, a joint Scottish-French phenomenon. One of the greatest influences on Smith was the works of Montesquieu, particularly his *Spirit of Laws* (1748), Book 18, in which Montesquieu developed his ideas on the notion that "difference, manner and social institutions are related to differences in the mode of subsistence." Meek, "Smith, Turgot and the 'Four Stages' Theory," 23, 29.

37 Johannes Fabian, *Time and the Other: How Anthropology Makes Its Object* (New York: Columbia University Press, 1983), 26.

38 Georg Wilhelm Friedrich Hegel, *Lectures on the Philosophy of History,* delivered in 1822-23, quoted in Derek Gregory, "Power, Knowledge, and Geography," *Explorations in Critical Human Geography* (Heidelberg: Department of Geography, University of Heidelberg, 1998), 16.

39 Patrick Wolfe, *Settler Colonialism and the Transformation of Anthropology* (London: Cassell, 1999), 44.

40 Anne McClintock, *Imperial Leather: Race, Gender, and Sexuality in the Colonial Contest* (New York: Routledge, 1995), 40-42.

41 Nicholas Blomley, *Unsettling the City: Urban Land and the Politics of Property* (New York: Routledge, 2005), 116.

42 Barbara Arneil, *John Locke and America: The Defence of English Colonialism* (London: Oxford University Press, 1996), 182.

43 Rod Macneil, "Time after Time: Temporal Frontiers and Boundaries in Colonial Images of the Australian landscape," in *Colonial Frontiers: Indigenous-European Encounters in Settler Societies,* ed. Lynette Russell (Manchester: Manchester University Press, 2001), 61.

44 James Wallis, *An Historical Account of the Colony of New South Wales,* 1821, quoted in Tim Bonyhady, *The Colonial Earth* (Melbourne: Miegunyah Press, 2000), 83.

45 George Mackaness, ed., *The Correspondence of John Cotton, Victorian Pioneer, 1842-1849,* Part 3, *1847-1849* (Dubbo, NSW: Review Publications, 1978), 9 (original manuscript held in the Plymouth Municipal Library).

46 Alexander Morris, lecture at the Mercantile Library Association, *British Colonist,* 13 July 1859.

47 Blomley, *Unsettling the City,* 115, 116. See also William Cronin, *Changes in the Land: Indians, Colonists, and the Ecology of New England* (New York: Hill and Wang, 1983).

48 See Maria Tippett, *From Desolation to Splendor: Changing Perceptions of the British Columbia Landscape* (Toronto: Clarke, Irwin, and Company, 1977); Bruce Braun, "Colonialism's Afterlife: Vision and Visuality on the Northwest Coast," *Cultural Geographies* 9 (2002): 202-47.

49 Ian Baucom, *Out of Place: Englishness, Empire, and the Locations of Identity* (Princeton: Princeton University Press, 1999), 80.

50 Foucault and Rabinow, "Space, Knowledge, and Power," 239, 240.

51 Ibid., 241, 242.

52 James S. Buckingham, *National Evils and Practical Remedies, with the Plan of a Model Town* (London: Peter Jackson, Late Fisher, Son and Co., 1849), 183-96.

53 James C. Scott, *Seeing Like a State: How Certain Schemes To Improve the Human Condition Have Failed* (New Haven: Yale University Press, 1998).

54 Élisée Reclus, *The Earth and Its Inhabitants: Oceania* (New York: D. Appleton and Company, 1898), 5 (my emphasis).
55 Marie Flemming, *The Geography of Freedom* (Montreal: Black Rose Press, 1988), 115.
56 See Dipesh Chakrabarty, *Provincializing Europe: Postcolonial Thought and Historical Difference* (Princeton: Princeton University Press, 2001).
57 Reclus, *The Earth and Its Inhabitants*, 353.
58 Wolfe, *Settler Colonialism*, 44.
59 Reclus, *The Earth and Its Inhabitants*, 39. Theories of race and the apprehension of difference come up repeatedly in the work of geographers of the mid- to late nineteenth century. Reclus was perhaps ahead of his time because he eschewed a hard taxonomy of race as expressed, for example, by writers such as Gobinea.
60 Ibid., 353.
61 See, for example, Gwendolyn Wright, "Tradition in the Service of Modernity: Architecture and Urbanism in French Colonial Policy, 1900-1930," in *Tensions of Empire: Colonial Cultures in a Bourgeois World*, ed. Frederick Cooper and Ann Laura Stoler (Berkeley: University of California Press, 1997),322-45.
62 Edwin Lloyd, *A Visit to the Antipodes: With Some Reminiscences of a Sojourn in Australia by a Squatter* (London: Smith Elder and Co., 1846), 83, 82.
63 Ibid., 83.
64 Ibid., 84.
65 John Martineau, *Letters from Australia*, 1869, quoted in Hamer, *New Towns in the New World*, 69.
66 Hamer, *New Towns in the New World*, 178.
67 Ibid., 65.
68 Quoted in ibid., 81.
69 See John Norman, *Edward Gibbon Wakefield: A Political Reappraisal* (Fairfield: Fairfield University, 1963). See the chapter "The Durham Report: Wakefield in Canada" in Graeme Anderson, *Edward Gibbon Wakefield and the Colonial Dream: A Reconsideration* (Wellington: The Friend of the Turnbull Library, GP Publications, 1997).
70 John Stuart Mill, *Principles of Political Economy, with Some of Their Applications to Social Philosophy*, ed. Stephen Nathanson (Indianapolis: Hackett Publishing, 2004), 49; Edward Gibbon Wakefield, *A Letter from Sydney, the Principal Town of Australasia, Together with the Outline of a System of Colonization* (London: Joseph Cross, 1829).
71 See "Wakefield Towns" and "The Durham Report: Wakefield in Canada," 12, in Anderson, *Edward Gibbon Wakefield and the Colonial Dream*. Wakefield's ideas influenced John Stuart Mill and Jeremy Bentham, for whom Wakefield had much admiration. Wakefield owed much to the works of Robert Gourley, who, in *A Statistical Account of Upper Canada* (1817), argued that wasteland in colonies should be sold, not given away, and the proceeds devoted to foster immigration. He also put forth the idea that a tax on the sale of land should be used for the promotion of immigration; thus, the cycle of colonization based on the proportion of land and labour continued.
72 Robert Rotenburg, "Metropolitanism and the Transformation of Urban Space in Nineteenth-Century Metropoles," *American Anthropologist* 103, 1 (2001): 14.
73 Jane Jacobs, *Edge of Empire: Postcolonialism and the City* (New York: Routledge, 1996), 3.
74 Rotenburg, "Metropolitanism and the Transformation of Urban Space," 7, 9.
75 Hamer, *New Towns in the New World*, 43.
76 Lloyd, *A Visit to the Antipodes*, 182.
77 Alan Lester, "British Settler Discourse and the Circuits of Empire," *History Workshop Journal* 54 (2002): 25-48.

Chapter 3: "This Grand Object"

1 John Pascoe Fawkner, "Reminiscences of the Settlement at Sorrento under David Collins and the Settlement at Port Phillip," 1862, John Pascoe Fawkner papers, SLV, MS 8528, Box 993/1, Folders 3a and b.

2 Ibid.

3 For example, the Keilor river terraces near the site of Melbourne show archaeological evidence of continuous occupation for forty thousand years. P.J.F. Coutts and R.M. Cochrane, *The Keilor Archaeological Area* (Melbourne: Victoria Archaeological Survey, 1977). See also Richard Broome, *Arriving* (Sydney: Fairfax, Syme, and Weldon Associates, 1984), 3-7, on early archaeological evidence.

4 Richard Broome, "Victoria," in *Contested Ground: Australian Aborigines under the British Crown,* ed. Ann McGrath (Sydney: Allen and Unwin, 1995), 125.

5 A.G.L. Shaw, *The History of the Port Phillip District: Victoria before Separation* (Melbourne: Miegunyah Melbourne, Melbourne University Press, 2005), 11, 12.

6 Jane Lydon, *Eye Contact: Photographing Indigenous Australians* (Durham: Duke University Press, 2005), xiv; Ian D. Clark, *Aboriginal Languages and Clans: An Historical Atlas of Central and Western Australia, 1800-1900* (Melbourne: Department of Geography and Environmental Science, Monash University, 1990), 20.

7 Fawkner, "Reminiscences," 30, 31.

8 Lynette Russell and Ian McNiven, "The Wurundjeri of Melbourne, Australia," in *Endangered Peoples of Oceania: Struggles to Survive and Thrive,* ed. Judith M. Fitzpatrick (Westport, CT: Greenwood Press, 2001), 234.

9 William Thomas, Victoria, Legislative Assembly, Select Committee on Aborigines, *Votes and Proceedings,* 1858-59, 61.

10 Broome, *Arriving,* 8.

11 Ibid.; Richard Broome, *Aboriginal Victorians: A History since 1800* (Crows Nest, NSW: Allen and Unwin, 1995), xx.

12 Russell and McNiven, "The Wurundjeri of Melbourne," 233.

13 As Russell and McNiven note, "archaeological research since the 1980s has revealed hundreds of old campsites in the form of scatters of stone tools along creek banks and piles of shells (middens) along the shores of Port Phillip Bay." Ibid., 239.

14 Ibid.

15 William Thomas, Assistant Protector, Journal, April 1840, Mitchell Library, SLNSW, MSS 214/2, item 1, microfilm CY2605, frame 86.

16 Gary Presland, *Aboriginal Melbourne: The Lost Land of the Kulin People* (Melbourne: McPhee Gribble, 1994), 19. Bearbrass was one of the names by which early Melbourne was known. Other variations included Bareheep, Barehurp, and Bareberp. See Robyn Annear, *Bearbrass: Imagining Early Melbourne* (Port Melbourne: Mandarin Press, 1995), 2.

17 Thomas Mitchell, *Three Expeditions into the Interior of Eastern Australia, with Descriptions of the Recently Explored Australia Felix, and of the Present Colony of New South Wales,* vol. 2 (London: T. and W. Boone, 1839), 171.

18 Edward Said, "Representing the Colonized: Anthropology's Interlocutors," *Critical Inquiry* 15, 2 (1989) 218; Derek Gregory, *Geographical Imaginations* (London: Blackwell, 1994), 168.

19 Paul Carter, *The Road to Botany Bay: An Essay in Spatial History* (London: Faber and Faber, 1987), xxii, xxiv.

20 Tim Bonyhady, *The Colonial Earth* (Melbourne: Miegunyah Press, 2000), 77.

21 For a detailed account of this history and of the Port Phillip Association, see Alistair H. Campbell, *John Batman and the Aborigines* (Victoria: Kibble Books, 1987).

22   Miles Lewis, *Melbourne: The City's History and Development* (Melbourne: City of Melbourne, 1995), 16.

23   Patricia Seed, *Ceremonies of Possession in Europe's Conquest of the New World, 1492-1640* (Cambridge: Cambridge University Press, 1995), 18.

24   John Batman, Journal, SLV, MS 13181. Penelope Edmonds, "Founding Myths," *Encyclopedia of Melbourne*, ed. Andrew Brown-May and Shurlee Swain (Cambridge: Cambridge University Press, 2005), 288, 289.

25   Some historians, however, now believe that the large river Batman referred to may have been the Maribyrnong River. Lewis, *Melbourne,* 16.

26   Jan Kociumbus, *The Oxford History of Australia*, vol. 2, *1770-1860: Possessions* (Melbourne: Oxford University Press, 1995), 190.

27   23 September 1835, transcription of J.P. Fawkner's journal, in possession of William Oliver, South Yarra, 27 June 1932, John Pascoe Fawkner papers, SLV, MS 13273, Box 3661, Folder 9a and b. Fawkner, "Reminiscences," 22. Fawkner is described as an "ex-convict inn keeper and newspaper editor": Kociumbus, *Oxford History of Australia*, vol. 2, 191.

28   See A.G.L. Shaw, *The History of the Port Phillip District: Victoria before Separation* (Melbourne: Miegunyah Melbourne, Melbourne University Press, 1996), 56.

29   Margaret Weidenhofer, ed., *Garryowen's Melbourne: A Selection from the Chronicles of Early Melbourne, 1835 to 1852, by Garryowen* (Melbourne: Nelson, 1967).

30   The convict William Buckley had absconded from the failed Sorrento penal settlement in 1803 and lived with the Wathawurrung for over thirty-two years. Although this is not his story, he was a key transitional figure in negotiations between Europeans and Indigenous peoples, and he looked on as Europeans created a new settler space on Aboriginal land. Buckley was pardoned by Governor Arthur on 25 August 1835 because of the intercession of Batman and Wedge. James Bonwick, *Discovery and Settlement of Port Phillip,* ed. Hugh Anderson (Melbourne: Red Rooster Press, 1999), 57 (first published in 1856 by George Robertson, Melbourne).

31   A.G.L. Shaw, The History of the Port Phillip District, 42.

32   See Michael Christie, *Aborigines in Colonial Victoria, 1835-86* (Sydney: Sydney University Press, 1979) for a survey of first contact in the bay area.

33   Ibid., 27.

34   Fawkner, "Reminiscences," 30.

35   Seed, *Ceremonies of Possession,* 16-18.

36   Ibid.

37   John Helder Wedge, field book, 1835, SLV, MS 10768, Box 23, Folder 30.

38   Ibid.

39   Ibid.

40   Ibid.

41   Wedge to Simpson, 9 August 1835 and 3 September 1835, Port Phillip Association, unpublished manuscript, SLV, quoted in Christie, *Aborigines in Colonial Victoria,* 27; Campbell, *John Batman and the Aborigines,* 133.

42   Wedge, field book, 53.

43   Joseph Tice Gellibrand, "January 26, 1836: Memorandum of a Trip to Port Phillip," in *Letters from Victorian Pioneers, Being a Series of Papers on the Early Occupation of the Colony,* ed. Lloyd O'Neil (Melbourne: Heinemann, 1969), 11.

44   Ibid.

45   Annear, *Bearbrass,* 17.

46   Governor Bourke's proclamation, dated 26 August 1835, in Michael Cannon, ed., *Historical Records of Victoria* (Melbourne: Victoria Government Printing Office, 1982), 1:14 (hereafter *HRV*).

47 Kociumbus, *The Oxford History of Australia,* vol. 2, 180.
48 Ibid.
49 Fawkner, "Reminiscences," 32.
50 The sealing and whaling industry, which stretched along the southeastern coast of Australia to Tasmania, produced many mixed relationships between Aboriginal women and sealers and whalers, often in violent circumstances. Some Kulin people today can trace their heritage to the Aboriginal Tasmanians through these early trading relationships.
51 Fawkner, "Reminiscences," 33.
52 Ibid.
53 Ibid., 34, 36.
54 Ibid., 38.
55 *HRV,* 1:89.
56 George Langhorne, "Statement of Mr George Langhorne and Reminiscences of William Buckley," 85, SLNSW, microfilm CY907.
57 As a transitional figure, Buckley was not only caught between two worlds, Indigenous and European, but also between the Wathawurrung and the Wurundjeri groups. Langhorne wrote of Buckley's difficult position between these two groups in "Statement of Mr George Langhorne," 85.
58 *HRV,* 1:89.
59 George Langhorne, "Statement of Mr George Langhorne and Reminiscences of William Buckley."
60 Ibid.
61 W.R.H. Reece, *Aborigines and Colonists: Aborigines and Colonial Society in New South Wales in the 1830s and 1840s* (Sydney: Sydney University Press, 1974), 24.
62 *Sydney Gazette,* 12 August 1824, quoted in ibid., 110.
63 Lauren Benton, *Law and Colonial Cultures: Legal Regimes in World History, 1400-1900* (Cambridge: Cambridge University Press, 2002), 202.
64 Anna Haebich, *Broken Circles: Fragmenting Indigenous Families, 1800-2000* (Freemantle: Freemantle Arts Centre Press, 2000), 70.
65 David Hamer, *New Towns in the New World: Images and Perceptions of the Nineteenth-Century Urban Frontier* (New York: Columbia University Press, 1990), 48, 49. See also Elizabeth Ferrier, "Mapping Power: Cartography and Contemporary Cultural Theory," *Antithesis* 4, 1 (1990): 35-49.
66 Hamer, *New Towns in the New World,* 48, 49.
67 Ibid.
68 *Cadastral,* a common technical term in surveying (and tax collecting), means "of or showing the extent, value, and ownership of land for taxation." The term came into English by way of French and Italian from the Greek *katastikhon* (list or register) from *kata stikhon* (line by line). It comes from the French *cadastre* (register of property): *Oxford Dictionary and Thesaurus,* 1993.
69 As D.N. Jeans notes, "Until that time around half a dozen towns had been established in the Cumberland country area, such as Sydney, Parramatta, Wilberforce, Pitt Town, Windsor, Richmond, Castlereagh, Newcastle, Campbelltown and Balgowlah." Between 1829 and 1842, as many as fifty-three new government towns were planned as settlers moved out to take new land. Although Melbourne, Geelong, and Portland were outside the limits of location, settlement continued unabated and, as Jeans notes, "many small villages had been privately established during his time along the Sydney to Port Phillip road, and around Twofold Bay, Brisbane, and Moreton Bay." D.N. Jeans, "Town Planning in New South Wales, 1829-1842," *Australian Planning Institute Journal* (October 1965): 191.

70 Lewis notes that several sites, such as St. Francis' Church, the Tavistock Hotel (383-387 Flinders Lane), Fawkner's first cultivated site, and Batman's outbuildings on the southern slopes of Batman's Hill, have survived. Lewis, *Melbourne,* 15.

71 Ibid., 26.

72 Ibid., 27.

73 Robert Hoddle (1791-1881), "Account of First Land Sales," 1 June 1837–18 June 1840, J.K. Moir Collection, SLV, MS 6471.

74 P.L. Brown, ed., *The Narrative of George Russell of Golf Hill* (London: Oxford University Press, 1935), 130.

75 Ibid. (emphasis mine).

76 "Extract from a Letter from the Hon. Mr Justice Burton to His Excellency Major General Richard Bourke," 31, Sydney, 22 November 1835, SLNSW, microfilm CY907.

77 Ibid., 43.

78 Shaw, *History of the Port Phillip District,* 68.

79 Alexander McCleay, "Memorandum to Mr Langhorne, Colonial Secretary, NSW, 26 Nov, 1836," SLNSW, microfilm CY907.

80 Alexander McCleay, "Memorandum to Serve as Instruction for Mr Langhorne, Colonial Secretary, NSW, 9th December, 1836," SLNSW, microfilm CY907.

81 Langhorne to Major General Richard Bourke, 26 November 1836, George Langhorne, correspondence, PROV 1837/29, VPRS 4729, Box 1.

82 Quoted in Thomas Darragh and Robert N. Wuchatsch, eds., *Hamburg to Hobson's Bay: German Emigration to Port Phillip (Australia Felix), 1848-51* (Melbourne: Wendish Heritage Society, 1999), 203.

83 Langhorne, "Statement of Mr George Langhorne," 66.

84 Ibid.

85 Colonial secretary's draft memorandum to George Langhorne, 9 December 1836 and G.K. Holden to G.M. Langhorne, 25 March 1836, *HRV,* 2:163, 171.

86 Ibid.

87 Ibid., 2a:206.

88 Ibid., 2a:214, Langhorne to Colonial Secretary, Mission Report, 30 April 1838.

89 Ibid., 2a:233, Mission Report, 30 November 1838.

90 Ibid., 2a:235, 236, Mission Report, 28 February 1839.

91 Ibid., Mission Report, 31 January 1839.

92 Ibid., 2a:236, Mission Report, 31 March 1839.

93 Langhorne, "Statement of Mr George Langhorne," 94.

Chapter 4: First Nations Space, Protocolonial Space

1 *British Colonist,* 23 November 1859.

2 *Vancouver Sun,* 15 October 2003.

3 *British Colonist,* 4 July 1859.

4 Keith Thor Karlson, ed., *A Stó:lō–Coast Salish Historical Atlas* (Vancouver: Stó:lō Heritage Trust/Douglas and McIntyre, 2001), 20.

5 Ibid., 20; R.L. Carlson, "The First British Columbians," in *The Pacific Province: A History of British Columbia,* ed. Hugh M. Johnson (Vancouver: Douglas and McIntyre, 1996), 13.

6 Karlson, *A Stó:lō–Coast Salish Historical Atlas,* 20. See Paul Tennant, *Aboriginal Peoples and Politics: The Indian Land Question in British Columbia, 1849-1989* (Vancouver: UBC Press, 1990), 3.

7 R.L. Carlson, "The First British Columbians," 32; Sydney L. Harring, *White Man's Law: Native People in Nineteenth-Century Canadian Jurisprudence* (Toronto: University of

Toronto Press, 1998), 190; Fisher, "Contact and Trade, 1774-1849," in *The Pacific Province: A History of British Columbia,* ed. Hugh M. Johnson (Vancouver: Douglas and McIntyre, 1966), 48.

8 Jean Barman, *The West beyond the West: A History of British Columbia,* rev. ed. (Toronto: University of Toronto Press, 1996), 38; Carlson, "The First British Columbians," 32.

9 Carlson, "The First British Columbians," 18.

10 Terry Glavin, "Kwak'waka'wakw People Practised Extensive Mariculture," *Georgia Straight,* 23 October 2003.

11 Carlson, "The First British Columbians," 31.

12 One village was at Swhaymalthelth (Esquimalt Harbour), and the other main village was at Sungayka (Cadboro Bay), even though this was itself a change, as each Lekwammen family group had previously occupied its own winter village. See Derek Pethick *Victoria: The Fort* (Vancouver: Mitchell Press, 1986), 53-55. The Central Coast Salish are composed of five linguistically related groups: Squamish, Halkomelem, Nootsack, Northern Straits, and Clallam. According to Wayne Suttles, this group possessed the southern end of the Strait of Georgia, most of the Strait of Juan de Fuca, the Lower Fraser Valley, and it had expanded over what would become British Columbia and Washington State prior to the European incursion. Suttles notes that although the Squamish, Nootsack, and Clallam can be referred to as tribes in a non-political sense, Halkomelem and Northern Straits are primarily languages, although they have also become identifiable as tribes. Wayne Suttles, ed., *Handbook of North American Indians,* vol. 7, *Northwest Coast* (Washington: Smithsonian Institution, 1990), 256, 453.

13 John Lutz, "Work, Wages and Welfare in Aboriginal-Non-Aboriginal Relations, British Columbia, 1849-1970" (PhD diss., University of Ottawa, 1994), 144.

14 See, for example, Susan Roy, "Litigating Aboriginal Identity" (paper presented at BC Studies conference, "Rethinking Ourselves," Vancouver, May 2003); Cole Harris, *Making Native Space: Colonialism, Resistance, and Reserves in British Columbia* (Vancouver: UBC Press, 2002).

15 Lutz, "Work, Wages and Welfare," 159.

16 Harris, *Making Native Space,* xi.

17 John Lutz, "Preparing Eden: Aboriginal Land Use and European Settlement" (paper presented to the annual meeting of the Canadian Historical Association, Montreal, 1995), 3.

18 Sir John H. Pelly to Benjamin Hawes, Esq., Colonial Office, 24 October 1846, Colonial Office Records, CO 305/1.

19 Pethick, *Victoria: The Fort,* 47.

20 Quoted in ibid., 48.

21 Jean-B.Z. Bolduc, *Mission of the Columbia,* trans. Edward J. Kowirch (1843; repr., Fairfield, WA: Ye Galleon Press, 1979). Quoted in Lutz, "Preparing Eden," 9; John Lutz, "Work, Wages and Welfare," 193.

22 James Douglas to James Hargrave, 5 February 1843, in G.P. de T. Glazebrook, ed., *Hargrave Correspondence* (Toronto: Champlain Society, 1938) (hereafter *Hargrave Correspondence*), 420 (emphasis mine).

23 Anne Burnaby McLeod and Pixie McGeachie, eds., *Land of Promise: Robert Burnaby's Letters from Colonial British Columbia, 1858-1863* (Vancouver: City of Burnaby, 2002).

24 John Pascoe Fawkner, "Reminiscences of the Settlement at Sorrento under David Collins and the Settlement at Port Phillip," 1862, John Pascoe Fawkner papers, SLV, MS 8528 and MS 13273.

25 James Douglas to John McLoughlin, 12 July 1842, printed in *The Beaver,* Outfit 273 (March 1943): 4-6.

26 Quoted in Lutz, "Preparing Eden," 6.

27 Berthold Seeman, *Narrative of the Voyages of HMS Herald,* 2 vols. (London: Reeve and Co., 1853), 101-4.

28 Paul Carter, *The Road to Botany Bay: An Essay in Spatial History* (London: Faber and Faber, 1987), 101.

29 For an excellent, detailed account of two constructed spaces, one that juxtaposes colonial space with Indigenous land practices, which also constructed a landscape on the Northwest Coast, see Lutz, "Preparing Eden," 9.

30 Carter, *The Road to Botany Bay,* 253, 254.

31 Lutz, "Preparing Eden," 7, 16; see also Nancy Turner and Marcus Bell, "The Ethnobotany of the Coast Salish Indians of Vancouver Island," *Economic Botany* 25, 1 (1971): 63-104.

32 James Douglas to James Hargrave, 5 February 1843, *Hargrave Correspondence,* 420-21, quoted in Lutz, "Work, Wages and Welfare," 169.

33 Bolduc, *Mission of the Columbia,* 107.

34 Harris, *Making Native Space,* xvi.

35 Ibid., xxiv.

36 Dorothy Blakey Smith, ed., *Reminiscences of Dr. Helmcken* (Vancouver: UBC Press, 1975), 81, 83.

37 "Colonisation of Vancouver Island," *Illustrated London News,* 26 August 1848.

38 Lutz, "Work, Wages, Welfare," 173.

39 Ibid., 169.

40 Ibid., 169, 170.

41 Ibid., 171.

42 Robin Fisher, *Contact and Conflict: Indian-European Relations in British Columbia, 1774-.1890,* 2nd ed. (Vancouver: UBC Press, 1992). Fisher writes, "Isolated in their little outposts, fur traders were highly vulnerable. The Indians probably had the power to destroy them, and yet they refrained, not because they feared the white traders, but because they valued their presence" (37).

43 Lutz, "Preparing Eden," 19.

44 Pethick, *Victoria,* 56.

45 Roderick Finlayson, *Biography* (Victoria: n.p., 1891), 13, quoted in ibid.

46 Ibid., 58.

47 Lutz, "Work, Wages and Welfare," 175.

48 Blakey Smith, ed., *Reminiscences of Dr. Helmcken,* 134.

49 Lutz, "Work, Wages and Welfare," 177.

50 Douglas to Barclay, 16 April 1851, in Lutz, "Work, Wages and Welfare," 177; James Douglas, Correspondence: Vancouver Island, Douglas to Newcastle, 28 July 1853, CO 305/4, 9499.

51 William Miller to Addington, Esq., Colonial Office, 23 October 1848, CO 305/1.

52 "Colonisation of Vancouver Island."

53 Harris, *Making Native Space,* 15.

54 "Colonisation of Vancouver Island."

55 James E. Hendrickson, ed., *Journals of the Colonial Legislatures of the Colonies of Vancouver Island and British Columbia, 1851-1871,* vol. 1, *Journals of the Council, Executive Council, and Legislative Council of Vancouver Island, 1851-1855* (Victoria: British Columbia Provincial Archives, 1980), xxvi.

56 "Colonisation of Vancouver Island."

57 Ibid.

58 Hendrickson, *Journal of the Colonial Legislatures,* 1:xxvi.

59 Vancouver Island was not established as a Crown colony, which would lack representative institutions. Crown colonies were ruled by a governor and a council appointed by the

Crown and were known as ceded or occupied colonies. The Colony of Vancouver Island was a proprietary colony, modelled on those of the British West Indies. The charter of the Virginia House of Burgesses of 1616, the first representative assembly of British peoples outside of Britain, had established the concept that "Englishmen were entitled to representative institutions." Hence the governments of colonies that were subsequently settled by Britain, the so-called settled colonies, consisted of a governor, nominated by the Crown, and a bicameral legislature. Although no specific, organic act was made to create the government of the Colony of Vancouver, its constitution was formed through a royal commission and instructions given to Blanshard. An act of Parliament provided for the administration of justice by the colonial legislature. See Hendrickson, *Journals of the Colonial Legislatures*, 1:xxvii.

60 Charter of Grant to Vancouver's Island to Hudson's Bay Company, in ibid., Appendix A, 376, 375, 378.
61 Ibid., 377.
62 Harris, *Making Native Space*, 16.
63 "Commission and Instructions to Richard Blanshard, Governor of Vancouver Island," in Hendrickson, ed., *Journals of the Colonial Legislatures*, Appendix B, 1:382.
64 Fisher, *Contact and Conflict*, 58.
65 James Douglas to Archibald Barclay, 10 October 1853, quoted in J.K. Lamb, "The Census of Vancouver Island, 1855," *British Columbia Historical Quarterly* 4, 1 (1940): 52.
66 Adele Perry, "The State of Empire: Reproducing Colonialism in British Columbia, 1849-1871," *Journal of Colonialism and Colonial History* 2, 21 (2001).
67 Blakey Smith, ed., *Reminiscences of Dr. Helmcken*, 81, 83. In the Australian colonies, the term *Kanakas* often referred to peoples of the Southwest Pacific; by contrast, on the Pacific Northwest Coast, they were often Hawaiian employees of the Hudson's Bay Company.
68 Cole Harris, "The Making of the Lower Mainland," *The Resettlement of British Columbia: Essays On Colonialism and Geographical Change* (Vancouver: UBC Press, 1997), 76.
69 Pethick, *Victoria*, 44.
70 Lutz, "Preparing Eden," 1.
71 Ibid., 21.
72 Lutz, "Work, Wages and Welfare," 35, 41. See also Terry Goldie, *Fear and Temptation: The Image of the Indigene in Canadian, Australian, and New Zealand Literatures* (Montreal and Kingston: McGill-Queen's University Press, 1989).
73 Lutz, "Work, Wages and Welfare," 40.
74 Fisher, *Contact and Conflict*, 74.
75 Ibid., 74.
76 Ibid., 74-76; see also Margaret Jolly, "'Natured Comparisons': Racism and Relativism in European Representations of ni-Vanuatu from Cook's Second Voyage," *History and Anthropology* 5, 3-4 (1992): 331-63.
77 Fisher, *Contact and Conflict*, 74-76.
78 Ibid., 81.
79 Ibid.
80 Ibid., 83.
81 Several authors have thoughtfully explored this theme and the intersection of gender, race, and empire, and I draw on much thinking from this scholarship. See, for example, Sylvia Van Kirk, *"Many Tender Ties": Women in Fur-Trade Society, 1670-1870*, 2nd ed. (Norman: University of Oklahoma Press, 1983); Sylvia Van Kirk "Tracing the Fortunes of Five Founding Families of Victoria," *BC Studies* 115/116 (Autumn/Winter 1997/98): 149-77;

Adele Perry, *On the Edge of Empire: Gender, Race, and the Making of British Columbia, 1849-1871* (Toronto: University of Toronto Press, 2001); Jean Barman, "Taming Aboriginal Sexuality: Gender, Power, and Race in British Columbia, 1850-1900," *BC Studies* 115/116 (Autumn/Winter 1997/98): 237-66.

82 The census was prepared by James Douglas. Lamb, "The Census of Vancouver Island, 1855," 51-58.

83 Van Kirk, *"Many Tender Ties,"* 75.

84 Ibid.

85 Ibid., 77.

86 Nancy E. Wright, "Comparative Study of the Status of Women in Canada and Australia," *Australian Canadian Studies* 22, 1 (2004): 1-7.

87 Perry, *On the Edge of Empire,* 61.

88 Ibid., 62.

89 Ibid.

90 Van Kirk, "Tracing the Fortunes," 149-77.

91 Ibid., 151.

92 Ibid., 167.

93 Discussion with staff of the City of Victoria Archives. Also, historian John Adams, personal communication with author, Victoria, 19 October 2003.

94 Anglican burial records, Christ Church Cathedral, City of Victoria Archives.

95 In the transcribed records that I was able to access at the City of Victoria Archives, abodes are not usually listed.

96 St. Andrew's Catholic Church, death register, Victoria, BCA, BCARS, microfilm, drawer 1A-1B (4). Translated from the French and Latin for the Old Cemeteries Society by C. Pallister and S. Daly.

97 According to John Adams, early records show that English-speaking fur traders were generally Scottish Presbyterian, while French-speaking settlers and fur traders tended to be Catholic. Hawaiians or Kanakas tended to be Congregationalists.

98 Many Chinese remains were interred for about seven years, after which time they were exhumed and sent home to China. Japanese remains are also present, although many Japanese people converted to Christianity.

99 Marjorie Morgan, *The Old Melbourne Cemetery* (Victoria: Australian Institute of Genealogical Studies), 1982.

100 Celestina Sagazio, ed., *Cemeteries: Our Heritage* (Melbourne: National Trust of Australia, 1992), 51.

101 Perry, *On the Edge of Empire.*

102 Ibid., 58.

103 Ibid., 61.

104 Lutz, "Work, Wages and Welfare," 62.

105 Douglas to Newcastle, 24 October 1853, CO 305/4, 12345, quoted in Lutz, Work, Wages and Welfare," 63.

106 Lutz, "Work, Wages and Welfare," 63.

107 Lutz, "After the Fur Trade: The Aboriginal Labouring Class of British Columbia, 1849-1890," *Journal of the Canadian Historical Association* 3, 1 (1992): 71.

108 Ibid.

109 Minutes of the Council of Vancouver Island, 27 February 1856, in Hendrickson, *Journals of the Colonial Legislatures,* 1:17.

110 Minutes of the First House of Assembly of Vancouver Island, 12 August 1856, ibid., 2:5-6.

Chapter 5: The Imagined City and Its Dislocations

1 Robert Rotenburg, "Metropolitanism and the Transformation of Urban Space in Nineteenth-Century Metropoles," *American Anthropologist* 103, 1 (2001): 9.
2 David Munro, draft of a letter describing New South Wales, 17 August 1842, SLNSW, A 6936, p. 12. The letter includes an account of Port Phillip.
3 George Arden, *Recent Information Respecting Port Phillip, and the Promising Province of Australia Felix, in the Great Territory of New South Wales; Including Their History, Geography and Important Natural Resources, with Interesting Sketch of the Aboriginal Inhabitants, and Valuable Advice to Emigrants by the Editor of the Port Phillip Gazette, Melbourne* (London: Smith, Elder and Co., 1841), 72.
4 Ibid., 70, 73.
5 William Kyle, 2 October 1841, quoted in Meyer Eidelson, *The Melbourne Dreaming: A Guide to the Aboriginal Places of Melbourne* (Canberra: Aboriginal Studies Press, 1997), 14.
6 George Frederick Belcher, quoted in ibid.
7 W.R.H. Reece, *Aborigines and Colonists: Aborigines and Colonial Society in New South Wales in the 1830s and 1840s* (Sydney: Sydney University Press, 1974), 8.
8 George Frederick Belcher, Diary, 1839, SLV, MS 6219, Box 234/3.
9 William Thomas, Journal, April 1839, Mitchell Library, SLNSW microfilm CY2604. To "conciliate" Aboriginal Tasmanians, George Augustus Robinson took them to remote Flinders Island, where many perished of disease.
10 Ibid.
11 Ibid.
12 Sally (Sarah Suzanna) Bunbury, letter to Robert C. Sconce, Esquire, 3 July 1843, Bunbury Family Letters, SLV, SPA 98/14, Letter 101.
13 Ibid. (my emphasis).
14 P.L. Brown, ed., *The Narrative of George Russell of Golf Hill* (London: Oxford University Press, 1935), 130. See also John Mackenzie, ed., *Imperialism and Popular Culture* (Manchester: Manchester University Press, 1986).
15 Timothy Mitchell, *Colonising Egypt* (New York: Cambridge University Press, 1988), 6, 7.
16 See Isobel Crombie, "The Sorcerer's Machine: A Photographic Portrait by Douglas Kilburn, 1847," *Art Bulletin of Victoria*, 41 (2000): 7-12.
17 Ian D. Clarke, ed., *The Journals of George Augustus Robinson, Chief Protector, Port Phillip Aboriginal Protectorate* (1840; repr., Melbourne: Heritage Matters, 1998), 18 March 1840, 342.
18 Edmund Finn, *The Chronicles of Early Melbourne, 1835-1852*, 2 vols. (Melbourne: Heritage Publications, 1976), 1:110.
19 Louisa Anne Meredith, *Notes and Sketches of New South Wales during a Residence in that Colony from 1839 to 1844 by Mrs. Charles Meredith* (London: John Murray, 1846), 37.
20 Ibid., 36, 92.
21 See, for example, I. Hannaford, *Race: The History of an Idea in the West* (Baltimore: Johns Hopkins University Press, 1996); K. Mahlik, *The Meaning of Race: Race, History and Culture in Western Society* (London: Macmillan, 1996).
22 Margaret Jolly, "'Ill-Natured Comparisons': Racism and Relativism in European Representations of ni-Vanuatu from Cook's Second Voyage," *History and Anthropology* 5, 3-4 (1992): 333; Charles Darwin, *On the Origin of the Species by Means of Natural Selection* (London: John Murray, 1859).
23 Jolly, "Ill-Natured Comparisons," 333. See also Nicholas Thomas, *Colonialism's Culture: Anthropology, Travel and Government* (Cambridge: Polity Press, 1994), 101.
24 John Dunmore Lang to T.F. Buxton, 10 June 1834, SLNSW, microfilm CY2604.
25 Arden, *Recent Information Regarding Port Phillip*, 98, 9.

26 John Schouler, quoted in Stuart Banner, *Possessing the Pacific: Land, Settlers and Indigenous Peoples from Alaska to Australia* (Cambridge, MA: Harvard University Press, 2007), 200.

27 Ibid.

28 William Thomas, Journal, June 1839, Mitchell Library, SLNSW, MS MLMSS214, microfilm CY2604.

29 See, for example, Warren Montag, "The Universalisation of Whiteness: Racism and the Enlightenment," in *Whiteness: A Critical Reader,* ed., Mike Hill (New York: New York University Press, 1997), 281-93.

30 See Penelope Edmonds, "'I Followed England Round the World': The Rise of Trans-Imperial Anglo-Saxon Exceptionalism and the Spatial Narratives of Nineteenth-Century British Settler Colonies of the Pacific Rim," in *Re-Orienting Whiteness: Transnational Perspectives on the History of an Identity,* ed. Leigh Boucher, Jane Carey, and Katherine Ellinghaus (New York: Palgrave, 2009), 99-115.

31 John Cotton, 9 and 1 August 1843, in George Mackaness, ed., *The Correspondence of John Cotton, Victorian Pioneer, 1842-1849* (Dubbo, NSW: Review Publications, 1978), 22.

32 Ibid.

33 William Adeney, Diary, 27 January 1843, SLV, MS 8520A, 296-97.

34 *The Australian,* 27 December 1838.

35 Zygmunt Bauman, quoted in Nigel Dodd, *Social Theory and Modernity* (Cambridge: Polity Press, 1999), 172.

36 Clarke, ed., *Journals of George Augustus Robinson,* 1 January 1839, 30 September 1840, and 27 March 1839.

37 "I have the honour to lay before you a census of the Aborigines in my district who have as yet come under my notice. The Bonurungs [sic] mentioned contain near the whole of the tribe – there may be 20 more Warurungs [sic], but by what I can glean not more, so that the whole of the two tribes when united probably would not exceed two hundred and thirty – among the Warurongs are nine aged." William Thomas to George A. Robinson, 20 November 1839, Protector's records, PROV 4467.

38 *Port Phillip Herald,* 7 January 1840.

39 Ibid.

40 Michael Christie, *Aborigines in Colonial Victoria, 1835-86* (Sydney: Sydney University Press, 1979), 64.

41 Ibid., 63.

42 William Thomas, Journal, April 1839, Mitchell Library, SLNSW, MS MLMSS214, microfilm CY2604, frame 44-46.

43 New South Wales, *Votes and Proceedings of the Legislative Council,* 1, F4120 (1844): 718-19.

44 New South Wales, "Report of the Committee on Police and Gaols," *Votes and Proceedings of the Legislative Council,* 2, F2815 (1839): 75, quoted in Reece, *Aborigines and Colonists,* 24.

45 Christie suggests that "if we accept that there were at least 11,500 Aborigines in Victoria when the white man arrived, then the loss of Aboriginal life during the frontier period numbered 8,000 or more. Introduced diseases, alcohol, changes to diet, and inter-tribal strife accounted for a large proportion of deaths, but it is realistic to accept E.M. Curr's assessment that between fifteen and twenty-five percent or 2,000 Aborigines, if we take the higher percentage, died 'by the rifle,'" *Aborigines in Colonial Victoria,* 78.

46 Adeney, Diary, 3 January 1843.

47 Reece, *Aborigines and Colonists,* 28.

48 Jessie Mitchell, "'A City on a Hill': Aboriginal Missions and British Civilisation, 1830-1850," in *Exploring the British World: Identity – Cultural Production – Institutions*, ed. Kate Darian-Smith et al. (Melbourne: RMIT Publishing, 2004), 3.

49 *Sydney Morning Herald*, 12 and 14 November 1838, 10 December 1838.

50 Arden, *Recent Information Respecting Port Phillip*, 102.

51 Mitchell, "A City on a Hill," 1.

52 Mackaness, ed., *Correspondence of John Cotton Victorian Pioneer*, 1 August 1843.

53 See the PROV series on the Aboriginal Protectorate, Board for the Protection of Aborigines, Correspondence Files, PROV, VPRS 1694.

54 William Thomas to Sir George Gipps, 20 December 1839, VPRS 4467.

55 Clarke, ed., *Journals of George Augustus Robinson*, 25 December 1839, 1:115.

56 Ibid., 1:39.

57 Ibid., 5 May 1839, 1:40.

58 Ibid., 1:73.

59 William Westgarth, *Personal Recollections of Early Melbourne and Victoria* (Melbourne: George Robertson and Co., 1888), 14.

60 Robinson to La Trobe, 22 October 1839, in Michael Cannon, ed., *Historical Records of Victoria* (Melbourne: Victoria Government Printing Office, 1982), 2b:596 (hereafter cited as *HRV*). See also Beverly Nance, "The Level of Violence: Europeans and Aborigines in Port Phillip," *Australian Historical Studies* 19 (October 1981): 532-49.

61 Thomas to Robinson, 19 October 1839, *HRV*, 2b:596.

62 La Trobe to Robinson, 28 October 1839, *HRV*, 2b:598.

63 Clarke, ed., *Journals of George Augustus Robinson*, 19 May 1839, 1:45.

64 Ibid., 24 April 1839, 1:34.

65 Ibid., 26 September 1839, 1:85.

66 William Thomas, Journal, 17 and 19 October 1839, Mitchell Library, SLNSW, MS MLMSS214, microfilm CY2604, frames 36 and 37.

67 William Thomas to G.A. Robinson, 17 July 1840, PROV 11/4467.

68 *Port Phillip Herald*, 14 and 17 January 1840.

69 William Thomas, Journal, 4 December 1841, 25, Mitchell Library SLNSW, MS MLMSS214, microfilm CY2604, frame 89.

70 James Dredge, Diaries, October 1839, SLV, MS 5244.

71 *Port Phillip Herald*, 20 March 1840.

72 William Thomas, Journal, 30 April 1840, January-May 1840, Mitchell Library, SLNSW, MS MLMSS214, microfilm CY2604, frame 95.

73 Ibid.

74 La Trobe to Robinson, 12 September 1840, PROV 11/4467.

75 Ibid.

76 Christie, *Aborigines in Colonial Victoria*, 111.

77 Ibid., 110-12.

78 Ibid., 111.

79 Ibid.

80 Ibid., 112. At the trial, Thomas was not permitted to translate for the Aborigines.

81 *Port Phillip Gazette*, 17 October 1840.

82 Hanmer Bunbury to Henry Bunbury, 27 April 1841, Bunbury Family Letters, SLV, SPA 96/126, Letter 8.

83 William Thomas, Journal, vol. 1, 13 September 1840, Mitchell Library, SLNSW, MS MLMSS214, microfilm CY2604.

84 Sally Bunbury to R.C. Sconce, 26 April 1841, Bunbury Family Letters, SLV, SPA 96/126, Letter 7.

85 Patricia Grimshaw and Julie Evans, "Colonial Women on Intercultural Frontiers: Rosa Campbell Praed, Mary Bundock, and Katie Langloh Parker," *Australian Historical Studies* 106 (1996): 79-95.
86 Later, while living on the Mornington Peninsula, McCrae drew portraits of Aboriginal people. See Brenda Niall, *Georgiana: A Biography of Georgiana McCrae, Painter, Diarist, Pioneer* (Carlton South: Melbourne University Press, at the Meigunyah Press, 1994), 135, 155.
87 Denis Byrne, "Nervous Landscapes," *Journal of Social Archaeology* 3, 2 (2003): 177, 179.
88 William Thomas, Journal, 6 July 1841, Mitchell Library, SLNSW, MS MLMSS214, microfilm CY2604, frame 307.
89 Ibid.
90 *Port Phillip Gazette*, 12 February 1840.
91 Ibid.
92 Hanmer Bunbury to Henry Bunbury, 18 December 1841, Bunbury Family Letters, SLV, SPA 96/126, Letter 12.
93 The town councils of Melbourne and Sydney were made by order of an act of the Legislative Council of New South Wales in 1842. A search of the records of the Sydney Town Council for the years 1842-44 revealed no mention of Aboriginal peoples. Sydney had been settled since 1788 and, therefore, had partitioned Aboriginal people through other various mechanisms for over fifty years. Melbourne and Adelaide, by comparison, were still "frontier" towns in 1842, and the Melbourne Town Council minutes include references to Aboriginal peoples.
94 Melbourne Town Council, Minutes, 1843, PROV, VPRS 8910/P0001.
95 Ibid., 12 September 1843, 236.
96 G.A. Robinson, 28 November 1844, PROV, VPRS 3622, cited in Andrew Brown-May, *Melbourne Street Life* (Melbourne: Australian Scholarly Publishing/Museum Victoria, 1998), 68, 69.
97 Melbourne Town Council, Minutes, 12 September 1843, 237.
98 Ibid. See also Brown-May, *Melbourne Street Life*, 64-88.
99 Melbourne Town Council, Minutes, 28 November 1843.
100 Rotenburg, "Metropolitanism and the Transformation of Urban Space," 12.
101 Ibid., 9.
102 Ibid., 14.
103 Melbourne Town Council, Index to the Minutes, vol. 1, Item 1093, PROV, VPRS 0894/2.
104 Melbourne Town Council, Minutes, 9 and 30 May 1845, 560, 566.
105 Melbourne Town Council, Index, vol. 1.
106 William Thomas, Journal, 31 October 1844, Mitchell Library, SLNSW, MS MLMSS214, microfilm CY2604.
107 *Port Phillip Gazette*, 15 February 1843.
108 Ibid., 9 November 1843.
109 Ibid., 28 October 1843.
110 William Thomas, Journal, 16-21 May 1845, Mitchell Library, SLNSW, MS MLMSS214, microfilm CY260.
111 Karl Marx, "Bloody Legislation against the Expropriated," *Capital: A Critique of Political Economy*, vol. 1 (Moscow: Progress Publishers, 1954), 734 (emphasis mine). In this fascinating chapter, Marx draws attention to England's bloody and brutal prohibitions against vagrancy (735-36).
112 Judith Butler, *Bodies That Matter: On the Discursive Limits of "Sex"* (New York: Routledge, 1993), ix, 33.
113 United Kingdom, House of Commons, *British House of Commons Report of the Parliamentary Select Committee on the Aboriginal Tribes (British Settlements), Reprinted with*

Comments by the Aborigines Protection Society (London: William Ball, 1837), 118. In the Cape Colony, where Indigenous Khoi had become a landless labouring class, there were intense debates about vagrancy laws throughout the 1830s and 1840s. As Timothy Keegan notes, in the Cape Colony, vagrancy laws and other means to control Indigenous populations were promoted endlessly by settlers, especially at this time. These issues were related to the question of labour supply and control since coerced labour was increasingly thought to promote indolence and indifference. Vagrancy laws were also used to control an apparent criminal underclass, which was of course racialized. John Phillip, superintendent of the London Missionary Society, was opposed to vagrancy laws, "the most demoralizing, the most degrading, the most cruel and pitiless of all systems of slavery." Philip lobbied metropolitan humanitarians on this issue. In the Cape there was much agitation against the 1834 vagrancy law, and Khois asserted that they were being returned to a state of slavery. See Timothy Keegan, *South Africa and the Origins of the Racial Order* (London: Leicester University Press, 1996), 73, 104, 112, 120.

114 An Act for the prevention of Vagrancy and for the punishment of idle and disorderly persons, rogues and vagabonds and incorrigible rogues in the colony of New South Wales, 25th August, 1835, *Public General Statues of New South Wales*, 6 Wm. IV, No. 6. It seems that by the end of the nineteenth century the punishment became more harsh. Suzanne Davies has noted that from 1880 to 1907 a non-Aboriginal person "lodging with or wandering with" an Aboriginal person could be convicted as an "idle and disorderly person" and would face one year in jail. Susanne Davies, "Vagrancy and the Victorians: The Social Construction of the Vagrant in Melbourne, 1880-1907" (PhD diss., University of Melbourne, 1990), 623.

115 *Port Phillip Herald*, 3 January 1840.

116 House of Commons Select Committee Report, *HRV*, 2a:63.

117 Clarke, ed., *Journals of George Augustus Robinson*, vol. 1, 11 June 1839.

118 Ibid.

119 Melbourne Town Council, Minutes, 26 September 1843, 566.

120 Tony Birch, "Erasing Koori Culture from Landscapes," in *Text, Theory, Space: Land, Literature and History in South Africa and Australia*, ed. Kate Darian-Smith, Liz Gunner, and Sarah Nuttal (London: Routledge, 1996), 173-88.

121 William Thomas, Journal, 1-9 May 1845, Mitchell Library, SLNSW, MS MLMSS214, microfilm CY2604.

122 Ibid., January 1849.

123 Ibid., December 1846.

124 Ibid.

125 Richard Broome, *Aboriginal Victorians: A History since 1800* (Crows Nest: Allen and Unwin, 2005), 104. By 1849 the protectorate system had been dismantled on the advice of a select committee. Thomas was the only protector to be kept on and was given the title guardian of the Aborigines. In practice, his role, at the behest of Governor La Trobe, was to keep Aboriginal peoples out of Melbourne through the provision of free rations. Christie, *Aborigines in Colonial Victoria*, 138.

126 David Hamer, *New Towns in The New World: Images and Perceptions of the Nineteenth-Century Urban Frontier* (New York: Columbia University Press, 1990), 59.

127 William Thomas, Journal, 8 December 1844, Mitchell Library, SLNSW, MS MLMSS214, microfilm CY2604.

128 Michel Foucault, "Of Other Spaces," quoted in Benjamin Genocchio, "Discourse, Discontinuity, Difference: The Question of 'Other Spaces,'" in *Postmodern Cities and Spaces*, ed. Sophie Watson and Katherine Gibson (Oxford: Blackwell, 1995), 36.

129 Ibid., 24.
130 Rodney James Giblett, "Where Land and Water Meet," *Postmodern Wetlands: Culture, History, Ecology* (Edinburgh: Edinburgh University Press, 1996), 4.
131 Ibid., 3, 4.
132 Clark, ed., *Journals of George Augustus Robinson,* 29 October 1839, 1:95.
133 Ernst Bernhardt Heyne, letter from Melbourne, 8 March 1849, in Thomas Darragh and Robert N. Wuchatsch, eds., *Hamburg to Hobson's Bay: German Emigration to Port Phillip (Australia Felix), 1848-51* (Melbourne: Wendish Heritage Society, 1999), 155.
134 See, for instance, Jan Critchett, *A Distant Field of Murder: Western District Frontiers, 1834-1848* (Carlton: Melbourne University Press, 1990); A. Bunt and G. Rose, eds., *Writing Women and Space: Colonial and Postcolonial Geographies* (New York: Guildford Press, 1994); Sara Mills, *Gender and Colonial Space* (Manchester: Manchester University Press, 2005).
135 Nance, "The Level of Violence," 544.
136 See Lynette Russell, "Introduction," in *Colonial Frontiers: Indigenous-European Encounters in Settler Societies,* ed. Russell (Manchester: Manchester University Press, 2001), 8, and Patricia Nelson Limerick, *The Legacy of Conquest: The Unbroken Past of the American West* (New York: W.W. Norton and Co., 1987), 49.
137 Adele Perry, *On the Edge of Empire: Gender, Race, and the Making of British Columbia, 1849-1871* (Toronto: University of Toronto Press, 2001), 49.
138 Ann Laura Stoler, "Tense and Tender Ties: The Politics of Comparison in North American History and (Post) Colonial Studies," *Journal of American History* 88, 3 (2001): 832.
139 Larissa Behrendt traces cases of extreme sexualized violence against Aboriginal women in colonial Australia and discusses these patriarchal operations as antecedents to the contemporary violence visited upon Aboriginal women. See "Consent in a (Neo) Colonial Society: Aboriginal Women as Sexual and Legal 'Other,'" *Australian Feminist Studies* 15, 33 (2000): 353-67; Patricia Grimshaw and Andrew May, "Inducements to the Strong To Be Cruel to the Weak: Authoritative White Colonial Male Voices and the Construction of Gender in Koori Society," in *Australian Women: Contemporary Feminist Thought,* ed. Norma Grieve and Ailsa Burns (Carlton: Melbourne University Press, 1994); Nicki Henningham, "Picking Up Colonial Experience: White Men, Sexuality and Marriage in North Queensland, 1890-1910" in *Raiding Clio's Closet: Postgraduate Presentations in History,* ed. Martin Crotty and Doug Scobie (Melbourne: Department of History, University of Melbourne, 1997), 89-104.
140 Behrendt, "Consent in a (Neo) Colonial Society," 364.
141 Ibid.
142 Ibid.
143 Henningham, "Picking Up Colonial Experience," 92.
144 William Thomas, Journal, 6 November 1839, quoted in *HRV,* 2b:556.
145 Clarke, ed., *Journals of George Augustus Robinson,* 17 May 1839, 1:44.
146 William Thomas, Journal, 13 November 1839, quoted in *HRV,* 2b:560.
147 Behrendt, "Consent in a (Neo) Colonial Society," 355.
148 Grimshaw and May, "Inducements to the Strong To Be Cruel to the Weak," 100.
149 William Thomas, Journal, 9 November 1839, quoted in *HRV,* 2b:559.
150 Ibid.
151 William Thomas, Journal, 16 November 1839, quoted in *HRV,* 2b:562.
152 William Thomas, Journal, 14 May 1839, Mitchell Library, SLNSW, MS MLMSS214, microfilm CY2604, frame 84.
153 Ibid., March 1841, frame 24.

154 Ibid., 26 August 1840, frame 72, and 15-17 November 1839. Thomas gives a detailed account of a search for Ninggollobin's (Captain Turnbull's) wife in the settlement. Police Magistrate William Lonsdale again refused Thomas police aid on the Aborigines' behalf.

155 *Gendered territorialism* is the phrase used by Patrick Wolfe in "Nation and MicegeNation: Discursive Continuity in the Post-Mabo Era," *Social Analysis* 36 (October 1994): 95. Furthermore, Adele Perry suggest that dispossession and resettlement were deeply inter-twined and that "gender is where the abiding bonds between dispossession and coloniza-tion become most clear": *On the Edge of Empire*, 19.

156 William Thomas, Journal, 9-11 July 1844, Mitchell Library, SLNSW, MS MLMSS214, microfilm CY2604, frame 205.

157 William Westgarth, *A Report on the Condition, Capabilities, and Prospects of the Australian Aborigines* (Melbourne: William Clarke, 1846), 12 (emphasis mine).

158 Melbourne Town Council, Minutes, 17 December 1846, 754 (emphasis mine).

159 Ibid.

160 Ibid., 967, 968.

161 Byrne, "Nervous Landscapes," 180.

162 Ibid.

163 Ibid., 177.

164 Ibid.

165 Ibid.

166 William Thomas, Journal, 24-26 July 1844, Mitchell Library, SLNSW, MS MLMSS214, microfilm CY2604, frame 210; fence burning, 9 April 1845, frame 271, and 15-20 April 1845, frame 272; C.J. La Trobe, 9 February and 23-26 December 1846.

167 Gillian Cowlishaw, "Policing the Races," *Social Analysis* 36 (1994): 71.

168 Understandings of the whiteness of the law underpin these assumptions. See, for example, Janet Ransely and Alena Marchetti, "The Hidden Whiteness of the Australian Law," *Griffith Law Review* 1, 1 (2001): 139-52.

169 Records come largely from colonial newspapers, missionary records, and European ac-counts because early crime records are incomplete.

170 *Port Phillip Gazette*, 17 April 1839.

171 "The Blacks," *Melbourne Intelligencer*, 12 October 1842.

172 Clarke, ed., *Journals of George Augustus Robinson*, 21 November 1839, 1:107.

173 Alexander Southerland, *Victoria and Its Metropolis*, 2 vols. (Melbourne: McCarron Bird, 1888), 1:241.

174 *Port Phillip Gazette*, 8 and 18 November 1843.

175 Ibid., 30 September 1840.

176 William Thomas, Journal, Letter 165, 23 September, 1839, Mitchell Library, SLNSW, MS MLMSS214, microfilm CY2604, frame 12.

177 *HRV,* 2a:199

178 *HRV,* 2a:201.

179 Ibid.

180 Chris Cunneen, "Racialisation, Criminalisation and Punishment in the Context of Austral-ian Nationhood and Citizenship," paper presented to the Institute of Criminology, Sydney University Law School, Sydney, 24 May 2001, 1. See also Chris Cunneen, *Conflict, Politics and Crime: Aboriginal People and the Police* (Crows Nest, NSW: Allen and Unwin, 2001).

181 John McGuire, "Judicial Violence and the 'Civilising Process': Race and the Transition from Public to Private Executions in Australia," *Australian Historical Studies* 29, 111 (1988): 187-209.

182 Ibid., 209.

183 Christie, *Aborigines in Colonial Victoria*, 57-60.
184 See *Port Philip Gazette*, 22 December 1841; Christie, *Aborigines in Colonial Victoria*, 112-14.
185 See Susanne Davies, "Aborigines, Murder and the Criminal Law in Early Port Phillip," *Australian Historical Studies* 22, 88 (1987): 313-35; I. MacFarlane, "Pevay: A Casualty of War," *Papers and Proceedings: Tasmanian Historical Research Association* 48, 4 (2001): 280-305.
186 P.L. Brown, ed., *The Narrative of George Russell of Golf Hill*, 130.

Chapter 6: Narratives of Race in the Streetscape

1 The protectorate system was deemed a failure by some. The secretary of state for the colonies, Earl Grey, advised that "in addition to protectorate stations small reserves should be set aside for Aborigines." The select committee, by contrast, argued that this was financially untenable. Michael Christie, *Aborigines in Colonial Victoria, 1835-86* (Sydney: Sydney University Press, 1979), 137, 138.
2 Ibid., 136.
3 Geoffrey Serle, *The Golden Age: A History of the Colony of Victoria, 1851-1861* (Melbourne: Melbourne University Press, 1963), 11, 126.
4 William Howitt, *Land, Labour and Gold, Or Two Years in Victoria with Visits to Sydney and Van Diemen's Land, 1855* (1855; repr., Kilmore: London Publishing, 1972), 158.
5 Andrew Markus, *Fear and Hatred: Purifying Australia and California, 1850-1901* (Sydney: Hale and Ironmonger, 1979), 14.
6 David Goodman, *Gold Seeking: Victoria and California in the 1850s* (Stanford: Stanford University Press, 1994), ix.
7 Serle, *The Golden Age*, 369.
8 George Arden, *Recent Information Respecting Port Phillip, and the Promising Province of Australia Felix, in the Great Territory of New South Wales; Including Their History, Geography and Important Natural Resources, with Interesting Sketch of the Aboriginal Inhabitants, and Valuable Advice to Emigrants by the Editor of the Port Phillip Gazette, Melbourne* (London: Smith, Elder and Co., 1841), 72; Peter McDonald, "Demography," *Encyclopedia of Melbourne*, ed. Andrew Brown-May and Shurlee Swaine (Melbourne: Cambridge University Press, 2005). McDonald – citing the statistician of the Colony of New South Wales, Timothy Coghlan – estimates the population of Melbourne in 1851 at twenty-three thousand; however, Coghlan's estimate excluded various outlying suburbs. John McCarty, economic historian, who has taken into account these areas, estimates the population at this time to be twenty-nine thousand. See J.W. McCarty and C.B. Schedvin, eds., *Australian Capital Cities: Historical Essays* (Sydney: Sydney University Press, 1978), and Markus, *Fear and Hatred*, 14.
9 Jean Barman, *The West beyond the West: A History of British Columbia*, rev. ed. (Toronto: University of Toronto Press, 1996), 65.
10 Alexander Morris, lecture delivered at the Mercantile Library Association, *British Colonist*, 13 July 1859.
11 W.C. Grant, "Remarks on Vancouver Island, Principally concerning Town Sites and Native Population," *Journal of the Royal Geographical Society* 31 (1861): 210.
12 Richard Broome, *Aboriginal Victorians: A History since 1800* (Crows Nest, NSW: Allen and Unwin, 2005), 107; Christie, *Aborigines in Colonial Victoria*, 138. For an overview of Aboriginal policy by neglect and also various missionary efforts to assist Aborigines in the 1850s, see Christie's chapter, "Rags and Riches: Aborigines and the Colonist in the 1850s," 136-56.

13   David Goodman, "Gold," *Encyclopedia of Melbourne,* http://www.emelbourne.net.au/biogs/EM00652b.htm.

14   Carl Traugott Hoehne, *Carl Traugott Hoehne's Emigration to Australia and Return to the Fatherland Related by Himself and Combined with Further Authentic Information about Australia,* (Bautzen: C.G. Hiecke, 1853), extract in Thomas Darragh and Robert N. Wuchatsch, eds., *From Hamburg to Hobson's Bay: German Emigration to Port Phillip (Australia Felix), 1848-51* (Melbourne: Wendish Heritage Society, 1999), 176-217.

15   Ibid.

16   Goodman, "Gold."

17   Howitt, *Land, Labour and Gold,* 141-44.

18   Edward Stone Parker, *The Aborigines of Australia: A Lecture Delivered in the Mechanics Hall, Melbourne, before the John Knox Young Men's Association, May 10* (Melbourne: Hugh McColl, 1854), 26, 28.

19   See Christie, *Aborigines in Colonial Victoria,* 146; Broome, *Aboriginal Victorians,* 111; and, for further elaborations on Indigenous labour, see Fred Cahir, "Dallong-Possum Skin Rugs: A Study of an Inter-Cultural Trade Item in Victoria," *Provenance: Journal of Public Record Office Victoria* 4 (September 2005): 1-6.

20   William Thomas to Colonial Secretary, 15 January 1853, quoted in Nathan Wolski, "All's Not Quiet on the Western Front: Rethinking Resistance and Frontiers in Aboriginal Historiography," in *Colonial Frontiers: Indigenous-European Encounters in Settler Societies,* ed. Lynette Russell (Manchester: Manchester University Press, 2001), 216.

21   Christie, *Aborigines in Colonial Victoria,* 136.

22   James Ballantyne, quoted in David Hamer, *New Towns in the New World: Images and Perceptions of the Nineteenth-Century Urban Frontier* (New York: Columbia University Press, 1990), 81.

23   *The Argus,* 14 March 1856, quoted in Christie, *Aborigines in Colonial Victoria,* 152.

24   Markus, *Fear and Hatred,* 14. Markus notes that "as a proportion of the total population in 1861, the Chinese comprised 4.56 percent in Victoria and 3.63 percent in New South Wales" (14).

25   Kay Anderson, "Sites of Difference: Beyond a Cultural Politics of Race Polarity," in *Cities of Difference,* ed., Ruth Fincher and Jane M. Jacobs (New York: Guilford Press, 1998), 203.

26   Christie, *Aborigines in Colonial Victoria,* 154.

27   Ibid. Christie quotes from *The Argus,* 2 April 1856.

28   Charles A. Price, *The Great White Walls Are Built: Restrictive Immigration to North America and Australasia, 1836-1888* (Canberra: Australian University Press, 1974), 70.

29   Quoted in ibid., 72.

30   "Imaginings of 'Celestial' Melbourne 2000 AD," *Melbourne Punch,* 19 June 1856.

31   Ibid.

32   Anonymous, *Melbourne As It Is and Ought to Be, by Anon (1850), with Remarks on Street Architecture Generally* (Melbourne: J. Pullar; J. Harrison, 1850), 4-10.

33   *The Argus,* 3 April 1903, quoted in Andrew Brown-May, *Melbourne Street Life* (Melbourne: Australian Scholarly Publishing/Museum Victoria, 1998), 28.

34   "A Letter to Send to Friends," *Newsletter of Australasia,* 9 (March 1857): 1-2.

35   William Henry Archer, *Statistical Notes on the Progress of Victoria* (Melbourne: John Ferres, Govt. Printer, [1860?]), 37.

36   Broome, *Aboriginal Victorians,* 123, 124. See also Lynette Russell and Ian McNiven, "The Wurundjeri of Melbourne, Australia," in *Endangered Peoples of Oceania: Struggles to Survive and Thrive,* ed. Judith M. Fitzpatrick (Westport, CT: Greenwood Press, 2001), 240.

37   Broome, *Aboriginal Victorians,* 123, 124.

38 Ibid., 124.

39 Ibid.

40 "In 1877, five Aboriginal people remained in the Melbourne district": Russell and McNiven, "Wurundjeri of Melbourne," 237.

41 Broome, *Aboriginal Victorians*, 126.

42 Ibid., 146.

43 Thomas Warre Harriet, "Sketches on Board the Barque Mary Harrison and Ashore in Australia, 1852-54," SLNSW, PXB341.

44 A.J. Hammerton, *Emigrant Gentlewomen: Genteel Poverty and Female Emigration, 1830-1914* (Vancouver: UBC Press, 1979); Lisa Chilton, *Agents of Empire: British Female Migration to Canada and Australia, 1860s-1930s* (Toronto: University of Toronto Press, 2007), 69.

45 Dianne Barwick, quoted in Broome, *Aboriginal Victorians*, 108.

46 Katherine Ellinghaus, "Regulating Koori Marriages: The 1886 Victorian Aborigines Protection Act," in "Fresh Cuts: New Talents 2001," ed. Elizabeth Ruinard and Elspeth Tilley, special issue, *Journal of Australian Studies* 67 (2001): 22-29. See also Katherine Ellinghaus, "Taking Assimilation to Heart: Marriages of White Women and Indigenous Men in Australia and North America, 1870s to 1930s (PhD diss., University of Melbourne, 2001).

47 Nicki Henningham, "Picking Up Colonial Experience: White Men, Sexuality and Marriage in North Queensland, 1890-1910," in *Raiding Clio's Closet: Postgraduate Presentations in History*, ed. Martin Crotty and Doug Scobie (Melbourne: Department of History, University of Melbourne, 1997), 92, 99.

48 Adele Perry, *On the Edge of Empire: Gender, Race, and the Making of British Columbia, 1849-1871* (Toronto: University of Toronto Press, 2001), 70-71.

49 See, for example, Gretchen Gerzina, *Black England* (London: John Murray, Albemarle Street, 1995).

50 Catherine Hall, *Civilising Subjects: Metropole and Colony in the English Imagination, 1830-186* (Cambridge: Polity, 2002), 8.

51 Charles Darwin, *On the Origin of the Species by Means of Natural Selection* (London: John Murray, 1859).

52 Philippa Levine, *Prostitution, Race and Politics: Policing Venereal Disease in the British Empire* (London: Routledge, 2003), 6.

53 Ibid., 5.

54 This image is highly reminiscent of a cartoon published in 1829 by Edward Williams Clay titled "Life in Philadelphia," which mocks an African American bourgeoisie.

55 Many of the cricket players came from Coranderrk Aboriginal Station near Melbourne.

56 "England – Black Fellows at Home," *Sydney Punch*, 15 August 1868. Regarding the famous tour, Richard Broome notes, "they were received with great interest, their race, their blackness and physical features attracting press attention at a time when race was becoming a key concept in defining and explaining humanity ... They were seen positively ... and generally feted in luncheon tents ... gazed upon as being exotic": *Aboriginal Victorians*, 152-53.

57 See Patricia Grimshaw and Ann Standish, "Making Tasmania Home: Louisa Meredith's Colonizing Prose," *Frontiers* 28, 1-2 (2007): 1-17.

58 Broome, *Aboriginal Victorians*, 144.

59 *The Australasian*, 3 March 1866 and 25 August 1866.

60 Ibid., 11 August 1866.

61 Ibid. (emphasis mine).

62 Jane Lydon, *Eye Contact: Photographing Indigenous Australians* (Durham: Duke University Press, 2005), 91.

63   Authors such as Alexis de Tocqueville (1835-40) were crucially concerned with new societies and the democratic process.
64   Judge Redmond Barry was involved with every Melbourne exhibition from 1854 to 1875. Redmond Barry, letter regarding the Intercolonial Exhibition, Melbourne, 5 March 1866, Miscellaneous Papers Relating to the Aborigines, 1839-71, SLNSW, MSSA610, CY979. See also David Dunstan, *Victorian Icon: The Royal Exhibition Building Melbourne* (Kew, Victoria: Exhibition Trustees, 1996), 23.
65   Redmond, Letter Regarding the Intercolonial Exhibition (emphasis mine).
66   Intercolonial Exhibition 1866-67, official catalogue, SLV, MS 12392, Box 3194/5.
67   Ibid.
68   Ibid. See also Penelope Edmonds, "The Le Souëf Box: Reflections on Imperial Nostalgia, Material Culture, and Exhibitionary Practice in Colonial Victoria," *Australian Historical Studies* 127 (April 2006): 117-39.
69   Intercolonial Exhibition 1866-67, official catalogue, 27, 28.
70   Tony Bennett, "Civic Laboratories: Museums, Cultural Objecthood and the Governance of the Social," *Cultural Studies* 19, 5 (2005): 522, 525.
71   Central Board Appointed to Watch over the Interests of the Aborigines, *Sixth Report of the Central Board Appointed to Watch over the Interests of the Aborigines in the Colony of Victoria* (Melbourne: John Ferres, Government Printer, 1866), 4.
72   Diane Barwick, *Rebellion at Coranderrk* (Canberra: Aboriginal History, Inc., 1998).
73   *The Argus,* 24 April 1866.
74   Intercolonial Exhibition 1866-67, official catalogue, 28, 29.
75   Tom Griffiths, *Hunters and Collector: The Antiquarian Imagination in Australia* (Cambridge: Cambridge University Press, 1996), 28-54.
76   Redmond, Letter Regarding the Intercolonial Exhibition.
77   Lydon, *Eye Contact,* 73-121.
78   Ibid., 82.
79   Intercolonial Exhibition 1866-67, official catalogue, 82.
80   In addition to the exhibition in Paris, they later appeared as engravings in James Bonwick's *The Last of the Tasmanians* (1870) and in the Italian ethnologist Enrico H. Gigioli's *I Tasmaniani* (1874).
81   Intercolonial Exhibition 1866-67, official catalogue, 82.
82   Bennett, "Civic Laboratories," 525-28.
83   Intercolonial Exhibition 1866-67, official catalogue and related papers.
84   Thomas Davey (1758-1823), lieutenant-governor of Van Diemen's Land, made no such visual proclamation during his short term in office from 1813 to 1816.
85   Tony Bennett, *Pasts beyond Memory: Evolution, Museums, and Colonialism* (London: Routledge, 2004), 160.
86   Annie Coombes, "Temples of Empire: The Museum and Its Publics," in *Reinventing Africa: Material Culture and Popular Imagination in Late Victorian and Edwardian England,* ed. Annie Coombs (New Haven: Yale University Press, 1994), 119.
87   Charles Wentworth Dilke, *Greater Britain: A Record of Travel in English-Speaking Countries during 1866 and 1867,* 2 vols. (London: Macmillan and Co., 1869), 2:106, 2:21.
88   Ibid., 2:23.
89   Ibid. (emphasis mine).
90   Ibid., 2:25, 2:23.
91   Ibid., 1:68.
92   Ibid., Preface (emphasis mine).
93   Ibid., Preface.
94   Ibid., 1:125.

95 Ibid.
96 Ibid., 1:406.
97 Allen J. Frantzen and John D. Niles, "Anglo-Saxonism and Medievalism," in *Anglo-Saxonism and the Construction of Social Identity*, ed. Frantzen and Niles (Miami: University of Florida, 1997), 1. See also Reginald Horsman, *Race and Manifest Destiny: The Origins of American Racial Anglo-Saxonism* (Cambridge, MA: Harvard University Press, 1981).
98 Robert A. Huttenback, *Racism and Empire: White Settlers and Coloured Immigrants in the British Self-Governing Colonies* (Ithaca, NY: Cornell University Press, 1976), 15. Huttenback writes that "historians of the period, no doubt influenced by the precepts of Social Darwinism and the continental racial theorists, 'discovered' the roots of Anglo-Saxon genius as far back as the fifth century." Furthermore, there was the conviction that the Anglo-Saxon race "possessed a special capacity for governing itself (and others) through a constitutional system which combined justice and efficiency" (15).
99 On the circulation of these ideas, see Hall, *Civilising Subjects*, 368.
100 Frantzen and Niles, "Anglo-Saxonism and Medievalism," 2.
101 Dilke, *Greater Britain*, 1:77, 1:73.
102 Ibid., 1:73.
103 Ibid., 1:71.
104 Perry, *On The Edge of Empire*, 70.
105 Ibid., 71.
106 Ian Baucom, *Out of Place: Englishness, Empire, and the Locations of Identity* (Princeton: Princeton University Press, 1999), 3. Baucom quotes Frantz Fanon.
107 Ibid., 4.
108 Ibid., 74.
109 Ibid., 73.

Chapter 7: From Bedlam to Incorporation

1 Alexander Morris, lecture to Victoria's Mercantile Library Association, 1859, *British Colonist*, 11 December 1858.
2 Letter from Robert Burnaby to Harriet, 28 February 1860, Anne Burnaby McLeod and Pixie McGeachie, eds., *Land of Promise: Robert Burnaby's Letters from Colonial British Columbia, 1858-1863* (Burnaby: City of Burnaby, 2002), 134.
3 Jean Barman, *The West beyond the West: A History of British Columbia*, rev. ed. (Toronto: University of Toronto Press, 1996), 68.
4 Ibid., 66. See Robin Fisher, "Gold Miners and Settlers," *Contact and Conflict: Indian-European Relations in British Columbia, 1774-1890*, 2nd ed. (Vancouver: UBC Press, 1992), 95-117.
5 Alfred Waddington, *British Colonist*, 11 December 1858.
6 Ibid.
7 *Vancouver Island Gazette*, 1858, quoted in Irene G.M. Zaffaroni, "The Great Chain of Being: Racism and Imperialism in Colonial Victoria, 1858-1871" (master's thesis, Department of History, University of Victoria, 1987), 33.
8 Alexander Morris, lecture, reported in *British Colonist*, 13 July 1859 (emphasis mine).
9 R.C. Mayne, *Four Years in British Columbia and Vancouver Island: An Account of Their Forests, Rivers, Coasts, Gold Fields, and Resources for Colonisation* (London: John Murray, 1862), 31.
10 On culture bringers, see "The Origins of Violence," *Perspective*, with guest historian John Docker, aired 12 November 2008, ABC, transcript, http://www.abc.net.au/rn/perspective/stories/2008/2415450.htm.
11 *British Colonist*, 11 December 1858.

12 Bruce Braun, "Colonialism's Afterlife: Vision and Visuality on the Northwest Coast," *Cultural Geographies* 9 (2002): 202-47. Braun asserts that "seeing itself has a material history" and takes the view that there is not "one history of 'space,' another of society, and a third of technology": these must be "thought together." Braun cites as influential Nicholas Green's study of nineteenth-century Paris, which highlights the crucial role of new transportation technologies in the fashioning of bourgeois subjects. See Nicholas Green, *The Spectacle of Nature: Landscape and Bourgeois Culture in Nineteenth-Century France* (Manchester: Manchester University Press, 1990).

13 Braun, "Colonialism's Afterlife," 218. Braun quotes Cole Harris' *The Resettlement of British Columbia.*

14 Ibid., 219.

15 *British Colonist,* 11 December 1858.

16 *British Colonist,* 12 January 1860.

17 Charles Wentworth Dilke, *Greater Britain: A Record of Travel in English-Speaking Countries during 1866 and 1867,* 2 vols. (London: Macmillan and Co., 1869), 1:68.

18 Braun cites Wolfgang Schivelbusch's formative work on panoramic travel. See *The Railway Journey: The Industrialization of Time and Space in the Nineteenth Century* (Berkeley: University of California Press, 1986). See also Lieven de Cauter, "The Panoramic Ecstasy: On World Exhibitions and the Disintegration of Experience," *Theory, Culture, and Society* 10, 4 (1993): 1-23.

19 Braun, "Colonialism's Afterlife," 220, 242.

20 Ibid., 242.

21 Robert Burnaby, Letter 4, 15 November 1858; Letter 7, 19 December 1858, in McLeod and McGeachie, eds., *Land of Promise,* 49, 57.

22 Ibid., 134, Letter 29, 28 February 1860.

23 Ibid., 63, Letter 10, 22 February 1859.

24 Ibid., 63, 149, Letter, 22 January 1859; Letter 35, 6 August 1860.

25 James E. Hendrickson, ed., *Journals of the Colonial Legislatures of the Colonies of Vancouver Island and British Columbia, 1851-1871,* vol. 1, *Journals of the Council, Executive Council, and Legislative Council of Vancouver Island, 1851-1855* (Victoria: British Columbia Provincial Archives, 1980), xxxii, xxxviii.

26 See, for example, Terry Reksten, *More English Than the English: A Very Social History of Victoria* (Victoria: Orca, 1986).

27 Mike Currie, "True Brit," *Weekend Australian,* 28-29 September 2002. Jubilee visit of 4 October 2002.

28 *British Colonist,* 5 September 1859.

29 Ibid., 12 September 1859 and 29 May 1860.

30 Ibid., 10 March 1860.

31 Ibid., 24 March and 15 April 1860.

32 Douglas to Newcastle, 7 July and 8 August 1860, regarding Indian affairs, James Douglas, Correspondence: Vancouver Island, University of British Columbia Library, Colonial Office, CO 305/14.

33 "Won't Go!" *British Colonist,* 12 September 1859 (emphasis mine).

34 James Douglas to James Hargrave, 5 February 1843, in G.P. de T. Glazebrook, ed., *Hargrave Correspondence* (Toronto: Champlain Society, 1938), 420.

35 *British Colonist,* 5 September 1859.

36 Ibid.

37 United Kingdom, House of Commons, "Correspondence and Other Papers Relating to the Hudson's Bay Company, the Exploration of the Territories ... and Other Affairs in

Canada," dispatch no. 19, August 1858, in *Irish University Series of British Parliamentary Papers – Colonies: Canada, vol.* 22 (Shannon: Irish University Press Series, 1969), 59, 60 (emphasis mine).

38 Cole Harris, *Making Native Space: Colonialism, Resistance, and Reserves in British Columbia* (Vancouver: UBC Press, 2002), 32.

39 Ibid., 15, 24.

40 Ibid., 15.

41 Indigenous pre-emptors were to live continuously on their farms for two years and build a house. In the first year, they were to clear, fence, and cultivate the surrounding five acres; in the second to sixth years, they were to clear three acres of forest or six acres of prairie. Ibid., 36.

42 Wilson Duff, *The Indian History of British Columbia: The Impact of the White Man* (Victoria: Royal British Columbia Museum, 1997), 86.

43 For a detailed discussion of Douglas' land policies, see Harris, *Making Native Space*, Chapter 2, "The Douglas Years, 1850-64."

44 United Kingdom, House of Commons, "Correspondence and Other Papers," dispatch 33, 29 October 1858, 73, 74.

45 Ibid.

46 Jeannie L. Kanakos, "The Negotiations to Relocate the Songhees Indians, 1843-1911" (master's thesis, Simon Fraser University, 1982).

47 Harris, *Making Native Space*, 28, quotes Douglas to Barclay, Fort Victoria, 26 August 1854, BCA, Fort Victoria Correspondence, Outward to the Hudson's Bay Company, 220-22. Kanakos also notes that the Lekwammen sold the reserve site. See "The Negotiations to Relocate the Songhees Indians," 16.

48 Harris, *Making Native Space*, 27.

49 Ibid.

50 Ibid., Appendix, 325. See also Kanakos, "The Negotiations to Relocate the Songhees Indians," 15, 16, for various theories on the claims of different First Nations and their movements around the Inner Harbour at this time.

51 Hendrickson, ed., *Journals of the Colonial Legislatures*, 9 November 1858, 1:60.

52 Robert Burnaby, Letter 33, 8 June 1860, in McLeod and McGeachie, eds., *Land of Promise*, 143.

53 Mary-Ellen Kelm, *Colonizing Bodies: Aboriginal Health and Healing in British Columbia, 1900-50* (Vancouver: UBC Press, 1998), 39.

54 W.C. Grant, "Remarks on Vancouver Island, Principally concerning Town Sites and Native Population," *Journal of the Royal Geographical Society* 31 (1861): 210.

55 Mary Douglas, *Purity and Danger: An Analysis of the Concepts of Pollution and Taboo* (London: Routledge, Kegan and Paul, 1966), 2.

56 *British Colonist*, 29 May 1860.

57 Hendrickson, *Journals of the Colonial Legislatures*, 25 March 1859, 1:25.

58 Minutes of the First Houses of Assembly of Vancouver Island, 18 January 1859, in James E. Hendrickson, *Journals of the Colonial Legislatures of the Colonies of Vancouver Island and British Columbia, 1851-1871*, vol. 2, *Journals of the House of Assembly, Vancouver Island, 1856-1863* (Victoria: British Columbia Provincial Archives, 1980), 67.

59 Ibid., 25 January 1859.

60 James Douglas to the Speaker and Gentlemen of the House of Assembly, Victoria, 5 February 1859, James Douglas, Correspondence: Vancouver Island, Colonial Office, CO 305/10, 454-47, quoted in Harris, *Making Native Space*, 28.

61 Harris, *Making Native Space*, 29 (emphasis mine).

62 Governor James Douglas to the Speaker and Gentlemen of the House of Assembly, 1859, minutes of the First House of Assembly of Vancouver Island, in Hendrickson, *Journals of the Colonial Legislatures,* 2:71-72 (emphasis mine).

63 See Renisa Mawani, "Legal Geographies of Aboriginal Segregation in British Columbia, 1850-1911," in *Isolation: Places and Practices of Exclusion,* ed. Carolyn Strange and Alison Bashford, (New York: Routledge, 2003), 187.

64 Minutes of the First Houses of Assembly of Vancouver Island, 15 February 1859, in Hendrickson, *Journals of the Colonial Legislatures,* 2:75.

65 Ibid., 3 March 1859, 2:74.

66 Ibid.

67 Ibid., 2:75.

68 Ibid., 2:77.

69 Mawani, "Legal Geographies of Aboriginal Segregation," 180.

70 Minutes of the First House of Assembly of Vancouver Island, 3 March 1859, in Hendrickson, *Journals of the Colonial Legislatures,* 2:81.

71 Adele Perry, *On the Edge of Empire: Gender, Race, and the Making of British Columbia, 1849-1871* (Toronto: University of Toronto Press, 2001), 113. Perry cites, "A Much Needed Regulation" *British Colonist,* 20 April 1861.

72 David T. Goldberg, *Racist Culture: Philosophy and the Politics of Meaning* (Oxford: Blackwell Publishing, 1993), 187.

73 Corporation of the City of Victoria, Minutes, 2 August 1862, City of Victoria Archives.

74 Ibid.

75 Jean Barman, professor emerita, University of British Columbia, personal communication with author, 3 November 2004.

76 Corporation of the City of Victoria, Minutes, 26 May 1863.

77 Ibid.

78 Ibid., 11 May 1863.

79 Irene Zaffaroni, "The Great Chain of Being: Racism and Imperialism in Colonial Victoria, 1858-1871" (master's thesis, Department of History, University of Victoria, 1987), 87.

80 Corporation of the City of Victoria, Minutes, 15 June 1863.

81 Ibid., 20 October 1862.

82 Kanakos, "Negotiations to Relocate the Songhees Indians," xii.

83 Ibid., 114.

84 Mawani, "Legal Geographies of Aboriginal Segregation," 185.

Chapter 8: Nervous Hybridity

1 *British Colonist,* 22 August 1860.

2 Ian Baucom, *Out of Place: Englishness, Empire, and the Locations of Identity* (Princeton: Princeton University Press, 1999), 3.

3 Cole Harris, *Making Native Space: Colonialism, Resistance, and Reserve in British Columbia* (Vancouver: UBC Press, 2002), 28.

4 Minutes of the First House of Assembly of Vancouver Island, 8 February 1859, in James E. Hendrickson, ed., *Journals of the Colonial Legislatures of Vancouver Island and British Columbia, 1851-1871,* vol. 2, *Journals of the House of Assembly, Vancouver Island, 1856-1863* (Victoria: British Columbia Provincial Archives, 1980), 72.

5 *British Colonist,* 4 July 1859.

6 Ibid., 13 and 15 March 1860.

7 Ibid., 13 March 1860.

8 Ibid., 19 and 28 April 1860.

9 "More Indian Outrages! What's to Be Done?" *British Colonist,* 24 April 1860.

10 *British Colonist,* 28 April 1860 (emphasis mine).

11 "Clearing the Streets," *British Colonist,* 10 May 1860.

12 *British Colonist,* 29 May 1860.

13 Douglas to Newcastle, 7 July 1860, James Douglas, Correspondence: Vancouver Island, University of British Columbia Library, Colonial Office, CO 305/14.

14 Ibid., 8 August 1860.

15 Ibid., Douglas, Victoria, to Admiral Baynes, Esquimalt, 3 August 1860.

16 Alec McHoul and Wendy Grace, *A Foucault Primer: Discourse, Power, and the Subject* (Melbourne: Melbourne University Press, 1993), 69, 70.

17 Paul Rabinow, introduction to *The Foucault Reader,* ed. Paul Rabinow (New York: Pantheon Books, 1984), 17; McHoul and Grace, *A Foucault Primer,* 71.

18 Derek Gregory, "Power, Knowledge, and Geography," *Explorations in Critical Human Geography* (Heidelberg: Department of Geography, Heidelberg University, 1998), 9-40.

19 "A Much Needed Regulation," *British Colonist,* 20 April 1861, and "Indians," *Victoria Press,* 18 August 1861, cited in Adele Perry, *On the Edge of Empire: Gender, Race, and the Making of British Columbia, 1849-1871* (Toronto: University of Toronto Press, 2001), 113.

20 *British Colonist,* 6 September 1861.

21 *British Colonist,* 6 March 1860.

22 Letter to the editor, *British Colonist,* 13 June 1859.

23 Ibid.

24 Kirsty Clare Sim, "Negotiating Victoria: The African-American Challenge to Public Space in Colonial British Columbia" (honours thesis, University of British Columbia, 2001), 62.

25 Letter to the editor, *British Colonist,* 13 June 1859.

26 See Vancouver Island, Police and Prisons Department, Victoria, Charge Books, 11 July 1858 to 26 January 1859, BCA, GR 0848. The second survey from 1866 to 1868 was conducted by the historian Chris Hannah, 9 May 1999.

27 Vancouver Island, Police and Prisons Department, Esquimalt, Charge Book, 1862-1865, BCA, GR 0428.

28 *British Columbian,* 10 July 1860.

29 Esquimalt, Charge Book, 21 May 1864.

30 Ibid., 5 May 1865.

31 As examples, I have selected crimes and their sentences by offenders who appear to be European, and I have matched these against offenders who appear to be non-European or First Nations to assess the possible unequal application of the law. Charge books usually identify First Nations individuals as "Indian" and state their origin.

32 Victoria, Charge Books, 11 July 1858 to 26 January 1859.

33 *British Colonist,* 28 April 1860.

34 Esquimalt, Charge Book, 1862-65, Vancouver Island, Police and Prisons Department, BCA, GR 0428.

35 I thank historian Chris Hanna for providing this data. Hanna collected this data while searching for incidents in which First Nations women were the perpetrators or victims of violence. The interpretations are my own.

36 Victoria, Charge Books, 1858-1868, Police and Prisons Department, BCA, GR 0848.

37 Ibid., 1858-68.

38 Sydney L. Harring, *White Man's Law: Native People in Nineteenth-Century Canadian Jurisprudence* (Toronto: University of Toronto Press, 1998), 206.

39 Ibid.

40 Minutes of the First House of Assembly of Vancouver Island, 8 February 1859, in Hendrickson, *Journals of the Colonial Legislatures,* 2:75.

41   Of the First Nations population of Vancouver Island, W.C. Grant wrote in 1859 that the "number of males is 12000 to 17000 females," "Remarks on Vancouver Island, Principally concerning Town Sites and Native Population," *Journal of the Royal Geographical Society* 31 (1861): 210.

42   *British Colonist,* 21 October 1862.

43   See Perry, *On the Edge of Empire,* 49-58, for an extended discussion of constructions of First Nations women.

44   Anne Burnaby McLeod and Pixie McGeachie, eds., *Land of Promise: Robert Burnaby's Letters from Colonial British Columbia, 1858-1863* (Burnaby: City of Burnaby, 2002), Letter 33, 8 June 1860, 143.

45   Sylvia Van Kirk, "Tracing the Fortunes of Five Founding Families of Victoria," *BC Studies* 115/116 (Autumn/Winter 1997/98): 150, 176.

46   Perry, *On the Edge of Empire,* 51. See Van Kirk, "Tracing the Fortunes." Van Kirk shows the mutual relations of race, class, and gender as she traces the mixed-race children of founding families in Victoria.

47   McLeod and McGeachie, eds., *Land of Promise,* Letter 30, 14 March 1860, 137; Letter 10, 22 February 1859, 65; Letter 4, 23 June 1859, 95.

48   Allen Pritchard, ed., *The Letters of Edmund Hope Verney, 1862-1865* (Vancouver: UBC Press, 1996), 20 August 1862, 84.

49   As Van Kirk has shown, while daughters who married white men were "passing" in Victoria's society, the sons were doing less well. In other words, daughters of First Nations descent were marrying up; their gender allowed them to transgress class boundaries because women were in demand in gold rush society. Van Kirk, "Tracing the Fortunes," 149-79.

50   Bishop George Hills, Diary, 24 September 1860, BCA, MS 1526.

51   *British Colonist,* 18 April 1861 and 7 September 1861. Jean Barman, "Aboriginal Women on the Streets of Victoria: Rethinking Transgressive Sexuality during the Colonial Encounter," in *Contact Zones: Aboriginal and Settler Women in Canada's Past,* ed. Katie Pickles and Myra Rutherdale (Vancouver: UBC Press, 2005), 205.

52   Jean Barman, "Taming Aboriginal Sexuality: Gender, Power, and Race in British Columbia, 1850-1900," *BC Studies* 115/116 Autumn/Winter 1997/98): 242.

53   Ibid., 243.

54   Ibid., 245.

55   Miles Ogborn, *Spaces of Modernity: London's Geographies, 1680-1880* (New York: Guilford Press, 1998), 47.

56   Philippa Levine, *Prostitution, Race and Politics: Policing Venereal Disease in the British Empire* (London: Routledge, 2003), 1.

57   Ibid., 2, 4.

58   Tony Ballantyne and Antoinette Burton, "Introduction: Bodies, Empires, and World Histories," in *Bodies in Contact: Rethinking Colonial Encounters in World History,* ed. Ballantyne and Burton (Durham: Duke University Press, 2005), 5.

59   Judith Butler, *Bodies That Matter: On the Discursive Limits of "Sex"* (New York: Routledge, 1993), 33.

60   Henri Lefebvre, *The Production of Space,* trans. Donald Nicholson-Smith (Cambridge: Basil Blackwell, 1991), 73.

61   Renisa Mawani, "'The Iniquitous Practice of Women': Prostitution and the Making of White Spaces in British Columbia, 1898-1905," in *Working through Whiteness: International Perspectives,* ed., Cynthia Leine-Rasky (New York: SUNY Press, 2002), 63.

62   Perry, *On the Edge of Empire,* 113, 229; "Arrest of Streetwalkers," *British Colonist,* 8 May 1860.

63 Perry, *On the Edge of Empire*, 113.
64 Jarrod White, "Power/Knowledge and Public Space: Policing the 'Aboriginal Towns,'" *Australian and New Zealand Journal of Criminology* 30, (1997): 275-91.
65 Ibid., 276.
66 *British Colonist*, 22 August 1860.
67 Adele Perry, "'Fair Ones of a Purer Cast': White Women and Colonialism in Late Nineteenth-Century British Columbia," *Feminist Studies* 23 (1997): 504; Lisa Chilton, *Agents of Empire: British Female Migration to Canada and Australia, 1860s-1930* (Toronto: University of Toronto Press, 2007).
68 "The Indian Question," *British Colonist*, 3 May 1862.
69 See, for example, Harriet Deacon, "Racial Segregation and Medical Discourse in Nineteenth-Century Cape Town," *Journal Of Southern African Studies* 22, 2 (1996): 287-308; Vivienne Bickford-Smith, *Ethnic and Racial Prejudice in Victorian Cape Town: Group Identity and Social Practice* (Cambridge: Cambridge University Press, 1995); Timothy Mitchell, *Colonising Egypt* (New York: Cambridge University Press, 1988).
70 Minutes of the Second House of Assembly of Vancouver Island, 27 June 1862, in Hendrickson, *Journals of the Legislative Council*, 2:286.
71 Corporation of the City of Victoria, Minutes, 22 December 1862.
72 Ibid.
73 Ibid.
74 Perry, *On the Edge of Empire*, 110.
75 Ibid., 119.
76 Frederick Cooper and Ann Laura Stoler, "Between Metropole and Colony: Rethinking a Research Agenda," in *Tensions of Empire: Colonial Cultures in a Bourgeois World*, ed. Cooper and Stoler (Berkeley: University of California Press, 1997), 31.
77 Mawani, "The Iniquitous Practice of Women," 63.
78 Patrick Wolfe, "Nation and MicegeNation: Discursive Continuity in the Post-Mabo Era," *Social Analysis* 36 (October 1994): 95.
79 Perry, *On the Edge of Empire*, 118. Perry quotes "Compulsory Departure of the Indians," *Victoria Press*, 28 May 1862.
80 Perry, *On the Edge of Empire*, 111. As Perry notes, this is not to suggest that smallpox was an imperial ruse to move Indigenous people; it was a material reality. In 1862-63 alone at least twenty thousand First Nations died of this disease.
81 Ibid.
82 Ibid., 114, quotes "The Smallpox among the Indians," *British Colonist*, 28 April 1862.
83 Ibid.
84 "The Seat of Disease," *British Columbian*, 25 March 1869.
85 Perry, *On the Edge of Empire*, 122.
86 Ibid., 119, quotes A.F. Pemberton to Acting Colonial Secretary, 27 July 1869; A.F. Pemberton to Colonial Secretary, 2 March 1870, BCA, Colonial Correspondence, GR 1372, Reel B-1357 (emphasis mine).
87 Attributed to Zygmunt Bauman in Nigel Dodd, *Social Theory and Modernity* (Cambridge: Polity Press, 1999), 172.
88 Perry, *On the Edge of Empire*, 113. Perry has also observed that the project to make Victoria white failed.
89 John Lutz, "After the Fur Trade: The Aboriginal Labouring Class of British Columbia, 1849-1890," *Journal of the Canadian Historical Association* 3, 1 (1992): 70.
90 Matthew McFie, *Vancouver Island and British Columbia: Their History, Resources and Prospects* (London: Longman, Roberts and Green, 1865), 33, 97.
91 Ibid.

92 Ibid.

93 Josiah Clark Nott and George R. Gliddon, eds., *Types of Mankind: Or, Ethnological Researches, Based upon the Ancient Monuments, Paintings, Sculptures, and Crania of Races, and upon Their Natural, Geographical, Philological and Biblical History Illustrated by Selections from the Unedited Papers of Samuel George Morton* (Philadelphia: J.B. Lippincott, 1857).

94 Ibid., 380.

95 Ibid., 380, 381.

96 Patrick Wolfe, "Race and Racialisation: Some Thoughts," *Postcolonial Studies* 5, 1 (2002): 55.

97 Esquimalt, Charge Book, 1871 census.

Conclusion

1 Marilyn Lake and Henry Reynolds, *Drawing the Global Colour Line* (Carlton: Melbourne University Press, 2008).

2 This masthead was removed only in 1961. See also Marilyn Lake, "White Man's Country: The Trans-National History of a National Project," *Australian Historical Studies* 34, 122 (October 2003): 346-63.

3 John P.S. McLaren, "The Burdens of Empire and the Legalisation of White Supremacy in Canada, 1860-1910," in *Legal History in the Making: Proceedings of the Ninth British Legal History Conference, Glasgow,* ed. W.M. Gordon and T.D. Fergus (London: Hambledon Press, 1989), 187.

4 Ibid., 188. See also Patricia E. Roy, *A White Man's Province: British Columbia Politicians and Chinese and Japanese Immigrants, 1858-1914* (Vancouver: UBC Press, 1989), 4-5.

5 McLaren, "The Burdens of Empire," 188.

6 Act to Restrict the Influx of Chinese into New South Wales, Stat. N.S.W. 1881, no. 11.

7 McLaren, "The Burdens of Empire," 191.

8 Ibid., 197. See also Charles A. Price, *The Great White Walls Are Built: Restrictive Immigration to North America and Australia, 1836-88* (Canberra: Australian Institute of International Affairs/Australian National University Press, 1974).

9 Cole Harris, *Making Native Space: Colonialism, Resistance, and Reserves in British Columbia* (Vancouver: UBC Press, 2002), 70.

10 Ibid., 70, 71.

11 Quoted in Jean Barman, "Erasing Indigenous Indigeneity in Vancouver," *BC Studies* 155 (Autumn 2007): 5, 6. See Canada, *House of Commons Debates* (24 April 1913), 86, 77.

12 Ibid.

13 Ibid., 6.

14 "Historic Event on Reserve," *Victoria Daily Colonist,* 5 April 1911.

15 Quoted in Barman, "Erasing Indigenous Indigeneity," 6. See C.F. Galloway, *The Call of the West: Letters from British Columbia* (London: T. Fisher Unwin, 1916), 82.

16 Barman, "Erasing Indigenous Indigeneity," 18.

17 "*Herald* (Melbourne), 21 September 1886. The Protection Bill and the Coranderrk Blacks," in Bain Attwood and Andrew Markus, eds., *The Struggle for Aboriginal Rights: A Documentary History* (Crows Nest, NSW: Allen and Unwin, 1999), 50.

18 Diane Barwick, *Rebellion at Coranderrk* (Canberra: Aboriginal History, Inc., 1998).

19 Penelope Edmonds, "The Le Souëf Box: Reflections on Imperial Nostalgia, Material Culture, and Exhibitionary Practice in Colonial Victoria," *Australian Historical Studies* 127 (April 2006): 117-39.

20 Richard Broome, *Aboriginal Victorians: A History since 1800* (Crows Nest, NSW: Allen and Unwin, 2005), 194.

21 "Black GST Campaign Launched on Invasion Day in Melbourne," 26 January 2005, Black GST News Centre, http://www.kooriweb.org/gst/news.html.
22 Peter Ker, "Protestors to Site Camp in No-Go Zone," *The Age,* 26 February 2006.
23 "Aboriginal Camp 'Will Be Disbanded,'" *The Age,* 6 April 2006.
24 Ibid.
25 Wayne Atkinson, "Fine Words But Few Deeds," *The Age,* 10 April 2006.
26 Harris, *Making Native Space,* 293.
27 Ministry of Aboriginal Relations and Reconciliation, Indian and Northern Affairs Canada, "Proposed Settlement Resolves Victoria Land Claim," News Release, 18 November 2006, and "Thomas Litigation: Proposed Settlement Agreement," News Release, 18 November 2006; Richard Reynolds, "Canadian Indian Group Settles Land Claim for $28M," in ABC News online, 19 November 2006, http://www.abc.net.au/news/stories/2006/11/19/1792128.htm.
28 "One Man's Opinion: News and Comment by Tehaliwaskenhas – Bob Kennedy, Oneida," *Turtle Island Native Network,* News, http://www.turtleisland.org.
29 Ministry of Aboriginal Relations and Reconciliation, Indian and Northern Affairs Canada, "Proposed Settlement Resolves Victoria Land Claim."
30 Ibid.
31 Ibid. The settlement agreement was concluded outside the context of the British Columbia Treaty Commission process, which was designed to conclude treaties that will clarify the rights and title of Aboriginal groups.
32 Edward LiPuma, *Encompassing Others: The Magic of Modernity in Melanesia* (Ann Arbor: University of Michigan Press, 2001), 5.
33 Dilip Parameshwar Goankar, "On Alternative Modernities," *Public Culture* 11, 1 (1999): 18.
34 Nihal Perera, "Indigenizing the Colonial City: Late Nineteenth-Century Colombo and Its Landscape," *Urban Studies* 39, 9 (2002): 1707, 1706.
35 Sylvia Van Kirk, "Tracing the Fortunes of Five Founding Families of Victoria," *BC Studies* 115/116 (Autumn/Winter 1997/98): 149-77.
36 Charles Wentworth Dilke, *Greater Britain: A Record of Travel in English-Speaking Countries during 1866 and 1867* (London: Macmillan and Co., 1869), 2:21, 106.
37 Matthew McFie, *Vancouver Island and British Columbia: Their History, Resources and Prospects* (London: Longman, Roberts and Green, 1865), 379.
38 Elizabeth Grosz, *Space, Time, and Perversion: Essays on the Politics of Bodies* (New York: Routledge, 1995), 107-8. See also Judith Butler, *Bodies That Matter: On the Discursive Limits of "Sex"* (New York: Routledge, 1993), 33.
39 Adele Perry, in *On the Edge of Empire: Gender, Race, and the Making of British Columbia, 1849-1871* (Toronto: University of Toronto Press, 2001), elaborates on the twin forces of colonization and immigration.

Bibliography

Archival Sources

Adeney, William. Diary. SLV, MS 8520A, 296-7.

Anglican burial records, Christ Church Cathedral. City of Victoria Archives, Victoria, British Columbia.

Barry, Redmond. Letter Regarding the Intercolonial Exhibition, Melbourne, 5 March, 1866. Miscellaneous Papers Relating to the Aborigines, 1839-71. SLNSW, MSSA610, CY979.

Batman, John. Journal. SLV, MS 13181.

Belcher, George Frederick. Diary, 1887-89. SLV, MS 6219, Box 234/3.

Board for the Protection of Aborigines. Correspondence Files. PROV 4467, VPRS 1694.

Bunbury Family Letters. SLV.

Corporation of the City of Victoria. Minutes. City of Victoria Archives, Victoria, British Columbia.

Douglas, James. Correspondence: Vancouver Island. Colonial Office, CO 305/4, UBCL.

Dredge, James. Diaries. SLV, MS 5244.

"Extract from a Letter from the Hon. Mr Justice Burton to His Excellency Major General Richard Bourke." SLNSW, microfilm CY907.

Fawkner, John Pascoe. Papers. SLV, MS 8528 and MS 13273.

Forbes, Francis. Letter to Governor Sir Richard Bourke, 26 July 1835. NLA, MS 1293.

Harriet, Thomas Warre. "Sketches on Board the Barque Mary Harrison and Ashore in Australia, 1852-54." SLNSW, PXB341.

Hills, Bishop George. Diaries. BCA, MS 1526.

Hoddle, Robert, "Account of First Land Sales." J.K. Moir Collection. SLV, MS 6471.

Intercolonial Exhibition 1866. Official catalogue and related papers. SLV, MS 12392, Box 3194/5.

Lang, John Dunmore. Letter to T.F. Buxton, 10 June 1834. SLNSW, microfilm CY2604.

Langhorne, George. Correspondence. PROV 1837/29, VPRS 4729, Box 1.

–. "Statement of Mr George Langhorne and Reminiscences of William Buckley." SLNSW, microfilm CY907.

McCleay, Alexander. "Memorandum to Mr Langhorne, Colonial Secretary, NSW, 26 Nov, 1836." SLNSW, microfilm CY907.

–. "Memorandum To Serve as Instruction for Mr Langhorne, Colonial Secretary, NSW, 9th December, 1836." SLNSW, microfilm CY907.

Melbourne City Council. Indexes. Vol. 1. PROV, VPRS 8947/P0001.

Melbourne Town Council. Index to the Minutes. Vol. 1. PROV, VPRS 0894/2.

Melbourne Town Council. Minutes. PROV, VPRS 8910/P0001.

Miller, William. Letter to Addington, Esq., Colonial Office, 23 October 1848, CO 305/1, UBCL.

Munro, David. Draft of a letter describing New South Wales. SLNSW, A 6936.

Pelly, Sir John H. Letter to Benjamin Hawes, Esq., Colonial Office, 24 October 1846. Colonial Office Records CO 305/1, UBCL.

St. Andrew's Catholic Church. Death register, Victoria. BCA, BCARS, microfilm, drawer 1A-1B (4).
Thomas, William. Journal. William Thomas Papers. Mitchell Library, SLNSW, MLMSS214/1, microfilm CY2604.
Vancouver Island. Police and Prisons Department, Esquimalt. Charge Book, 1862–1865. BCA, GR 0428.
–. Police and Prisons Department, Victoria. Charge Books, 1858-1868. BCA, GR 0848.
Wedge, John Helder. Field book, 1835. SLV, MS 10768, Box 23, 36.

Newspapers
The Age
The Argus
The Australasian
British Colonist
British Columbian
Illustrated London News
Melbourne Intelligencer
Melbourne Punch
Port Phillip Gazette
Port Phillip Herald
Sydney Morning Herald
Sydney Punch
Victoria Daily Colonist

Published Sources
Anderson, Graeme. *Edward Gibbon Wakefield and the Colonial Dream: A Reconsideration.* Wellington: Friend of the Turnbull Library, GP Publications, 1997.
Anderson, Kay. "Sites of Difference: Beyond a Cultural Politics of Race Polarity." In *Cities of Difference*, eds., Ruth Fincher and Jane Jacobs, 201-25. New York: Guilford Press, 1998.
–. *Vancouver's Chinatown: Racial Discourse in Canada, 1875-1980.* Montreal and Kingston: McGill-Queen's University Press, 1991.
Anderson, Kay, and Jane Jacobs. "Urban Aborigines to Aboriginality and the City: One Path through the History of Australian Cultural Geography." *Australian Geographical Studies* 35, 1 (1997): 12-22.
Annear, Robyn. *Bearbrass: Imagining Early Melbourne.* Port Melbourne: Mandarin Press, 1995.
Anonymous. *Melbourne As It Is and Ought to Be, by Anon (1850), with Remarks on Street Architecture Generally.* Melbourne: J. Pullar; J. Harrison, 1850.
Arden, George. *Recent Information Respecting Port Phillip, and the Promising Province of Australia Felix, in the Great Territory of New South Wales; Including Their History, Geography and Important Natural Resources, with Interesting Sketch of the Aboriginal Inhabitants, and Valuable Advice to Emigrants by the Editor of the Port Phillip Gazette, Melbourne.* London: Smith, Elder and Co., 1841.
Arneil, Barbara. *John Locke and America: The Defence of English Colonialism.* London: Oxford University Press, 1996.
Archer, William Henry. *Statistical Notes on the Progress of Victoria.* Melbourne: John Ferres, Govt. Printer, [1860?].
Attwood, Bain. *Possession: Batman's Treaty and the Matter of History.* Melbourne: Miegunyah Press, 2009.

Attwood, Bain, and Andrew Markus, eds. *The Struggle for Aboriginal Rights: A Documentary History*. Crows Nest, NSW: Allen and Unwin, 1999.

Australian Human Rights Commission. *Bringing Them Home: Report of the National Inquiry into the Separation of Aboriginal and Torres Strait Islander Children from their Families.* Sydney: Human Rights and Equal Opportunity Commission, 1997.

Ballantyne, Tony, and Antoinette Burton. "Introduction: Bodies, Empires, and World Histories." In *Bodies in Contact: Rethinking Colonial Encounters in World History,* ed. Ballantyne and Burton, 1-18. Durham: Duke University Press, 2005.

Banner, Stuart. *Possessing the Pacific: Land, Settlers and Indigenous Peoples from Alaska to Australia.* Cambridge, MA: Harvard University Press, 2007)

Barman, Jean. "Aboriginal Women on the Streets of Victoria: Rethinking Transgressive Sexuality during the Colonial Encounter." In *Contact Zones: Aboriginal and Settler Women in Canada's Past,* ed. Katie Pickles and Myra Rutherdale, 205-27. Vancouver: UBC Press, 2005.

–. "Erasing Indigenous Indigeneity in Vancouver." *BC Studies* 155 (Autumn 2007): 3-31.

–. "Taming Aboriginal Sexuality: Gender, Power, and Race in British Columbia, 1850-1900." *BC Studies* 115/116 (Autumn/Winter 1997/98): 237-66.

–. *The West beyond the West: A History of British Columbia.* Rev. ed. Toronto: University of Toronto Press, 1996.

Barwick, Diane. *Rebellion at Coranderrk.* Canberra: Aboriginal History, Inc., 1998.

Bassett, Marnie. "Governor Arthur and the Opposite Coast." *Tasmanian Historical Association* 2, 5 (1953): 82-85.

Baucom, Ian. *Out of Place: Englishness, Empire, and the Locations of Identity.* Princeton: Princeton University Press, 1999.

Behrendt, Larissa. "Consent in a (Neo) Colonial Society: Aboriginal Women as Sexual and Legal 'Other.'" *Australian Feminist Studies* 15, 33 (2000): 353-67.

Bennett, Tony. *The Birth of the Museum: History, Theory, Politics.* London: Routledge, 1995.

–. "Civic Laboratories: Museums, Cultural Objecthood and the Governance of the Social." *Cultural Studies* 19, 5 (2005): 521-47.

–. *Pasts beyond Memory: Evolution, Museums, and Colonialism.* London: Routledge, 2004.

Benton, Lauren. *Law and Colonial Cultures: Legal Regimes in World History, 1400-1900.* Cambridge: Cambridge University Press, 2002.

Bhabha, Homi. "The White Stuff." *Artforum International,* May 1998.

Bickford-Smith, Vivienne. *Ethnic and Racial Prejudice in Victorian Cape Town: Group Identity and Social Practice.* Cambridge: Cambridge University Press, 1995.

Birch, Tony. "Erasing Koori Culture from Landscapes." In *Text, Theory, Space: Land, Literature and History in South Africa and Australia,* ed. Kate Darian-Smith, Liz Gunner, and Sarah Nuttal. London: Routledge, 1996. 173-188.

Blakey Smith, Dorothy, ed. *Reminiscences of Dr. Helmcken.* Vancouver: UBC Press, 1975.

Bloch, Marc. "Pour une histoire comparée des sociétées européenes." *Revue de synthèse historique* 46 (1925): 15-50.

Blomley, Nicholas. *Unsettling the City: Urban Land and the Politics of Property.* New York: Routledge, 2005.

Bolduc, Jean-B.Z. *Mission of the Columbia.* Trans. Edward J. Kowirch. 1843. Reprint, Fairfield, WA: Ye Galleon Press, 1979.

Bonwick, James. *Discovery and Settlement of Port Phillip.* Ed. Hugh Anderson. 1856. Melbourne: Red Rooster Press, 1999.

Bonyhady, Tim. *The Colonial Earth.* Melbourne: Miegunyah Press, 2000.

Braun, Bruce. "Colonialism's Afterlife: Vision and Visuality on the Northwest Coast." *Cultural Geographies* 9 (2002): 202-47.

Brock, Peggy. "Mission Encounters in the Colonial World: British Columbia and South West Australia." *Journal of Religious History* 24, 2 (June 2000): 159-79.

Broome, Richard. *Arriving*. Sydney: Fairfax, Syme, and Weldon Associates, 1984.

–. *Aboriginal Victorians: A History since 1800*. Crows Nest, NSW: Allen and Unwin, 2005.

–. "Victoria." In *Contested Ground: Australian Aborigines under the British Crown*, ed. Ann McGrath, 121-67. Sydney: Allen and Unwin, 1995.

Brown, P.L., ed. *The Narrative of George Russell of Golf Hill*. London: Oxford University Press, 1935.

Brown-May, Andrew. *Melbourne Street Life*. Melbourne: Australian Scholarly Publishing/ Museum Victoria, 1998.

Brunton, Paul. *Matthew Flinders: The Ultimate Voyage*. Sydney: State Library of New South Wales, 2001.

Buckingham, James S. *National Evils and Practical Remedies, with the Plan of a Model Town*. London: Peter Jackson, Late Fisher, Son and Co., 1849.

Bunt, A., and G. Rose, eds. *Writing Women and Space: Colonial and Postcolonial Geographies*. New York: Guildford Press, 1994.

Butler, Judith. *Bodies That Matter: On the Discursive Limits of "Sex."* New York: Routledge, 1993.

Butlin, N.G. "Macasssans and Aboriginal Smallpox: The '1789' and the '1829' Epidemics." *Historical Studies* 21, 84 (1985): 315-35.

–. *Our Original Aggression: Aboriginal Populations of Southeastern Australia, 1788-1850*. Sydney: Allen and Unwin, 1983.

Byrne, Denis. "Nervous Landscapes." *Journal of Social Archaeology* 3, 2 (2003): 169-93.

Byrt, Pauline, ed. *Thomas Papers in the Mitchell Library: A Comprehensive Index*. Melbourne: Centre for Australian Indigenous Studies, Monash University, 2004.

Cahir, Fred. "Dallong-Possum Skin Rugs: A Study of an Inter-Cultural Trade Item in Victoria." *Provenance: Journal of Public Record Office Victoria* 4 (September 2005): 1-6.

Campbell, Alistair H. *John Batman and the Aborigines*. Victoria: Kibble Books, 1987.

Campbell, J. "Smallpox in Aboriginal Australia, 1829-31." *Historical Studies* 20, 81 (1983): 536-56.

–. "Smallpox in Aboriginal Australia: The Early 1830s." *Historical Studies* 21, 84 (1985): 336-58.

Canada. Indian and Northern Affairs Canada. "Canada's Urban Aboriginal Population Fact Sheet." Indian and Northern Affairs Canada. http://www.ainc-inac.gc.ca/ai/ofi/ uas/fs/uasfs-eng.asp.

Cannon, Michael, ed. *Historical Records of Victoria*. 3 vols. Melbourne: Victoria Government Printing Office, 1981-84.

–. *Old Melbourne Town before the Gold Rush*. Victoria: Loch Haven Books, 1991.

Carlson, R.L. "The First British Columbians." In *The Pacific Province: A History of British Columbia*, ed. Hugh M. Johnson, 12-46. Vancouver: Douglas and McIntyre, 1996.

Carter, Paul. *The Road to Botany Bay: An Essay in Spatial History*. London: Faber and Faber, 1987.

Central Board Appointed to Watch over the Interests of the Aborigines. *Sixth Report of the Central Board Appointed to Watch over the Interests of the Aborigines in the Colony of Victoria*. Melbourne: John Ferres, Government Printer, 1866.

Chakrabarty, Dipesh. *Provincializing Europe: Postcolonial Thought and Historical Difference*. Princeton: Princeton University Press, 2001.

Chilton, Lisa. *Agents of Empire: British Female Migration to Canada and Australia, 1860s-1930*. Toronto: University of Toronto Press, 2007.

Christie, Michael. *Aborigines in Colonial Victoria, 1835-86*. Sydney: Sydney University Press, 1979.

Clark, Ian D. *Aboriginal Languages and Clans: An Historical Atlas of Central and Western Australia, 1800-1900*. Melbourne: Department of Geography and Environmental Science, Monash University, 1990.

–, ed. *Journals of George Augustus Robinson, Chief Protector, Port Phillip Aboriginal Protectorate*. 1840. 6 vols. Reprint, Melbourne: Heritage Matters, 1998.

Clayton, Daniel. *Islands of Truth: The Imperial Fashioning of Vancouver Island*. Vancouver: UBC Press, 2000.

Coombes, Annie. "Temples of Empire: The Museum and Its Publics." In *Reinventing Africa: Material Culture and Popular Imagination in Late Victorian and Edwardian England*, ed. Annie Coombs, 109-28. New Haven: Yale University Press, 1994.

Cooper, Frederick, and Ann Laura Stoler. "Between Metropole and Colony: Rethinking a Research Agenda." In *Tensions of Empire: Colonial Cultures in a Bourgeois World*, ed. Cooper and Stoler, 1-58. Berkeley: University of California Press, 1997.

Coutts, P.J.F., and R.M. Cochrane. *The Keilor Archaeological Area*. Melbourne: Victoria Archaeological Survey, 1977.

Cowlishaw, Gillian. "Policing the Races." *Social Analysis* 36 (1994): 71-92.

Critchett, Jan. *A Distant Field of Murder: Western District Frontiers, 1834-1848*. Carlton: Melbourne University Press, 1990.

Crombie, Isobel. "The Sorcerer's Machine: A Photographic Portrait by Douglas Kilburn, 1847." *Art Bulletin of Victoria* 41 (2000): 7-12.

Cronin, William. *Changes in the Land: Indians, Colonists, and the Ecology of New England*. New York: Hill and Wang, 1983.

Cross, Michael, and Michael Keith, eds. *Racism, the City and the State*. London: Routledge, 1993.

Cunneen, Chris. *Conflict, Politics and Crime: Aboriginal People and the Police*. Crows Nest, NSW: Allen and Unwin, 2001.

–. "Racialisation, Criminalisation and Punishment in the Context of Australian Nationhood and Citizenship." Paper presented to the Institute of Criminology, Sydney University Law School, Sydney, 24 May 2001.

Curr, E.M. *Recollections of Squatting in Victoria, Then Called the Port Phillip District (from 1841 to 1851) Melbourne*. Sydney: George Robertson, 1883.

Dallas, K.M. "Commercial Influences on the First Settlements in Australia." *Tasmanian Historical Association* 16, 2 (1968): 36-48.

Darragh, Thomas, and Robert N. Wuchatsch, eds. *Hamburg to Hobson's Bay: German Emigration to Port Phillip (Australia Felix), 1848-51*. Melbourne: Wendish Heritage Society, 1999.

Darwin, Charles. *On the Origin of the Species by Means of Natural Selection*. London: John Murray, 1859.

Davies, Susanne. "Aborigines, Murder and the Criminal Law in Early Port Phillip." *Australian Historical Studies* 22, 88 (1987): 313-35.

–. "Vagrancy and the Victorians: The Social Construction of the Vagrant in Melbourne, 1880-1907." PhD diss., University of Melbourne, 1990.

Deacon, Harriet. "Racial Segregation and Medical Discourse in Nineteenth-Century Cape Town." *Journal of Southern African Studies* 22, 2 (1996): 287-308.

de Cauter, Lieven. "The Panoramic Ecstasy: On World Exhibitions and the Disintegration of Experience." *Theory, Culture, and Society* 10, 4 (1993): 1-23.

de Costa, Ravi. "The Treaty Process in British Columbia: Some Thoughts for Australian Treaties." Paper presented at "Treaty – Advancing Reconciliation," Murdoch University, Perth, 27 June 2002.

de Vattel, Emerich. *The Law of Nations, Or, Principles of the Law of Nature Applied to the Conduct of Nations and Sovereigns.* Newberry: London, 1760.

Dilke, Charles Wentworth. *Greater Britain: A Record of Travel in English-Speaking Countries during 1866 and 1867.* 2 vols. London: Macmillan and Co., 1869.

Dixon, Robert. *The Course of Empire: Neoclassical Culture in New South Wales, 1788-1860.* Melbourne: Oxford University Press, 1986.

Dodd, Nigel. *Social Theory and Modernity.* Cambridge: Polity Press, 1999.

Douglas, Mary. *Purity and Danger: An Analysis of the Concepts of Pollution and Taboo.* London: Routledge, Kegan and Paul, 1966.

Driver, Felix, and David Gilbert, eds. *Imperial Cities: Landscape, Display, and Identity.* Manchester: Manchester University Press, 2003.

Duff, Wilson. *The Indian History of British Columbia: The Impact of the White Man.* Victoria: Royal British Columbia Museum, 1997.

Dunstan, David. *Victorian Icon: The Royal Exhibition Building Melbourne.* Kew, Victoria: Exhibition Trustees, 1996.

Edmonds, Penelope. "From Bedlam to Incorporation: Whiteness and the Racialisation of Settler-Colonial Urban Space in Victoria, British Columbia, 1840s-1880s." In *Exploring the British World: Identity – Cultural Production – Institutions,* ed. Kate Darian-Smith, Patricia Grimshaw, Kiera Lindsey, and Stuart Macintyre, 60-90. Melbourne: RMIT Publishing, 2004.

–. "'I Followed England Round the World': The Rise of Trans-Imperial Anglo-Saxon Exceptionalism and the Spatial Narratives of Nineteenth-Century British Settler Colonies of the Pacific Rim." In *Re-Orienting Whiteness: Transnational Perspectives on the History of an Identity,* ed. Leigh Boucher, Jane Carey, and Katherine Ellinghaus, 99-115. New York: Palgrave, 2009), 99-115.

–. "The Le Souëf Box: Reflections on Imperial Nostalgia, Material Culture, and Exhibitionary Practice in Colonial Victoria." *Australian Historical Studies* 127 (April 2006): 117-39.

–. "Founding Myths." In *Encyclopedia of Melbourne,* ed. Andrew Brown-May and Shurlee Swain, 288-89. Cambridge: Cambridge University Press, 2005.

Eidelson, Meyer. *The Melbourne Dreaming: A Guide to the Aboriginal Places of Melbourne.* Canberra: Aboriginal Studies Press, 1997.

Elbourne, Elizabeth. "The Sins of the Settler: The 1835-36 Select Committee on Aborigines and Debates over Virtue and Conquest in the Early Nineteenth-Century British White Settler Empire." *Journal of Colonialism and Colonial History* 4, 3 (2003): 1-39.

Ellinghaus, Katherine. "Margins of Acceptability: Class, Education and Interracial Marriage in Australia and America." *Frontiers* 23 (2002): 55-75.

–. "Regulating Koori Marriages: The 1886 Victorian Aborigines Protection Act." In "Fresh Cuts: New Talents 2001," ed. Elizabeth Ruinard and Elspeth Tilley, special issue, *Journal of Australian Studies* 67 (2001): 22-29.

–. "Taking Assimilation to Heart: Marriages of White Women and Indigenous Men in Australia and North America, 1870s to 1930s." PhD diss., University of Melbourne, 2001.

Evans, Julie, Patricia Grimshaw, David Philips, and Shurlee Swain. *Equal Subjects, Unequal Rights: Indigenous Peoples and Political Rights in British Settlements, 1830-1910.* Manchester: Manchester University Press, 2003.

Fabian, Johannes. *Time and Other: How Anthropology Makes Its Object.* New York: Columbia University Press, 1983.

Ferrier, Elizabeth. "Mapping Power: Cartography and Contemporary Cultural Theory." *Antithesis* 4, 1 (1990): 35-49.

Fincher, Ruth, and Jane M. Jacobs, eds. *Cities of Difference*. New York: Guilford Press, 1998.

Finn, Edmund. *The Chronicles of Early Melbourne, 1835-1852.* 2 vols. Melbourne: Heritage Publications, 1976.

Fisher, Robin. *Contact and Conflict: Indian-European Relations in British Columbia, 1774-1890.* 2nd ed. Vancouver: UBC Press, 1992.

–. "Contact and Trade, 1774-1849." In *The Pacific Province: A History of British Columbia*, ed. Hugh M. Johnson, 48-67. Vancouver: Douglas and McIntyre, 1996.

Flemming, Marie. *The Geography of Freedom*. Montreal: Black Rose Press, 1988.

Forgacs, David, ed. *An Antonio Gramsci Reader: Selected Writings, 1916-1935.* New York: Schoken Books, 1988.

Foster, Hamar, "Letting Go the Bone: The Idea of Indian Title in British Columbia, 1849-1927." In *Essays in the History of Canadian Law: British Columbia and the Yukon*, ed. Hamar Foster and John McLaren, 28-86. Toronto: University of Toronto Press, 1995.

Fournier, Susanne. *Stolen from Our Embrace: The Abduction of First Nations Children and the Restoration of Aboriginal Communities.* Vancouver: Douglas and McIntyre, 1997.

Foucault, Michel, and Paul Rabinow. "Space, Knowledge, and Power." Interview in *The Foucault Reader*, ed. Paul Rabinow, 239-56. New York: Pantheon, 1984.

Frantzen, Allen J., and John D. Niles. "Anglo-Saxonism and Medievalism." In *Anglo-Saxonism and the Construction of Social Identity*, ed. Frantzen and Niles, 1-16. Miami: University of Florida, 1997.

Freeman, Victoria. "Attitudes towards 'Miscegenation' in Canada, United States, New Zealand, and Australia, 1860-1914." *Native Studies Review*, 16, 1 (2005): 41-69.

Freestone, Robert. Review of *Of Planning and Planting: The Making of British Colonial Cities*, by Robert Home. *Journal of Historical Geography* 24, 3 (1998): 381.

Frost, Lionel. "Anglo-Saxon Cities on the Pacific Rim." In *Megalopolis: The Giant City in History*, ed. T.C. Barker and A. Sutcliffe, Chapter 10. Basingstoke: Macmillan, 1993.

–. "The Urban History Literature of Australia and New Zealand." *Journal of Urban History* 22, 1 (1995): 141-53.

Gale, Faye. *Urban Aborigines*. Canberra: Australian National University Press, 1972.

Galloway, C.F. *The Call of the West: Letters from British Columbia*. London: T. Fisher Unwin, 1916.

Gascoigne, John. *The Enlightenment and the Origins of European Australia*. Cambridge: Cambridge University Press, 2002.

Gellibrand, Joseph Tice. "January 26, 1836: Memorandum of a Trip to Port Phillip." In *Letters from Victorian Pioneers, Being a Series of Papers on the Early Occupation of the Colony*, ed. Lloyd O'Neil. Melbourne: Heinemann, 1969.

Genocchio, Benjamin. "Discourse, Discontinuity, Difference: The Question of 'Other Spaces.'" In *Postmodern Cities and Spaces*, ed. Sophie Watson and Katherine Gibson, 35-46. Oxford: Blackwell, 1995.

Gerzina, Gretchen. *Black England*. London: John Murray, Albemarle Street, 1995.

Giblett, Rodney James. *Postmodern Wetlands: Culture, History, Ecology.* Edinburgh: Edinburgh University Press, 1996.

Glazebrook, G.P. de T., ed. *Hargrave Correspondence*. Toronto: Champlain Society, 1938.

Goankar, Dilip Parameshwar. "On Alternative Modernities." *Public Culture* 11, 1 (1999): 1-18.

Goldberg, David T. *Racist Culture: Philosophy and the Politics of Meaning.* Oxford: Blackwell Publishing, 1993.

Goldie, Terry. *Fear and Temptation: The Image of the Indigene in Canadian, Australian, and New Zealand Literatures*. Montreal and Kingston: McGill-Queen's University Press, 1989.

Goodman, David. "Gold." In *The Encyclopedia of Melbourne*. http://www.emelbourne.net.au/biogs/EM00652b.htm.

–. *Gold Seeking: Victoria and California in the 1850s*. Stanford: Stanford University Press, 1994.

Gough, Barry M. *Gunboat Frontier: British Maritime Authority and Northwest Coast Indians, 1846-1890*. Vancouver: UBC Press, 1984.

Grant, W.C. "Remarks on Vancouver Island, Principally concerning Town Sites and Native Population." *Journal of the Royal Geographical Society* 31 (1861): 208-13.

Green, Nicholas. *The Spectacle of Nature: Landscape and Bourgeois Culture in Nineteenth-Century France*. Manchester: Manchester University Press, 1990.

Gregory, Derek. *Geographical Imaginations*. Cambridge: Blackwell, 1994.

–. "Power, Knowledge, and Geography." *Explorations in Critical Human Geography*, 9-40. Heidelberg: Department of Geography, Heidelberg University, 1998.

Griffiths, Tom. *Hunters and Collector: The Antiquarian Imagination in Australia*. Cambridge: Cambridge University Press, 1996.

Grimshaw, Patricia, and Julie Evans. "Colonial Women on Intercultural Frontiers: Rosa Campbell Praed, Mary Bundock, and Katie Langloh Parker." *Australian Historical Studies* 106 (1996): 79-95.

Grimshaw, Patricia, and Andrew May. "Inducements to the Strong To Be Cruel to the Weak: Authoritative White Colonial Male Voices and the Construction of Gender in Koori Society." In *Australian Women: Contemporary Feminist Thought*, ed. Norma Grieve and Ailsa Burns, 92-106. Carlton: Melbourne University Press, 1994.

Grimshaw, Patricia, and Ann Standish. "Making Tasmania Home: Louisa Meredith's Colonizing Prose." *Frontiers* 28, 1-2 (2007): 1-17.

Grosz, Elizabeth. *Space, Time, and Perversion: Essays on the Politics of Bodies*. New York: Routledge, 1995.

Haebich, Anna. *Broken Circles: Fragmenting Indigenous Families, 1800-2000*. Freemantle: Freemantle Arts Centre Press, 2000.

Hall, Catherine. *Civilising Subjects: Metropole and Colony in the English Imagination, 1830-1867*. Cambridge: Polity, 2002.

Hamer, David. *New Towns in the New World: Images and Perceptions of the Nineteenth-Century Urban Frontier*. New York: Columbia University Press, 1990.

Hammerton, A.J. *Emigrant Gentlewomen: Genteel Poverty and Female Emigration, 1830-1914*. Vancouver: UBC Press, 1979.

Hannaford, I. *Race: The History of an Idea in the West*. Baltimore: Johns Hopkins University Press, 1996.

Harring, Sydney L. *White Man's Law: Native People in Nineteenth-Century Canadian Jurisprudence*. Toronto: University of Toronto Press, 1998.

Harris, Cheryl. "Whiteness as Property." *Harvard Law Review* 106 (1993): 1709-91.

Harris, Cole. *Making Native Space: Colonialism, Resistance, and Reserves in British Columbia*. Vancouver: UBC Press, 2002.

–. *The Resettlement of British Columbia: Essays on Colonialism and Geographical Change*. Vancouver: UBC Press, 1997.

–. "Social Power and Cultural Change in Pre-Colonial British Columbia." *BC Studies* 115/116 (Autumn/Winter 1997/98): 45-82.

–. "Voices of Smallpox around the Strait of Georgia." *The Resettlement of British Columbia: Essays On Colonialism and Geographical Change*, 3-30. Vancouver: UBC Press, 1997.

Haskins, Victoria. *One Bright Spot.* Basingstoke: Palrave McMillan, 2005.

Hendrickson, James E., ed. *Journals of the Colonial Legislatures of the Colonies of Vancouver Island and British Columbia, 1851-1871.* Vol. 1, *Journals of the Council, Executive Council, and Legislative Council of Vancouver Island, 1851-1855.* Victoria: British Columbia Provincial Archives, 1980.

–. *Journals of the Colonial Legislatures of the Colonies of Vancouver Island and British Columbia, 1851-1871.* Vol. 2, *Journals of the House of Assembly, Vancouver Island, 1856-1863.* Victoria: British Columbia Provincial Archives, 1980.

Henningham, Nicki. "Picking Up Colonial Experience: White Men, Sexuality and Marriage in North Queensland, 1890-1910." In *Raiding Clio's Closet: Postgraduate Presentations in History,* ed. Martin Crotty and Doug Scobie, 89-104. Melbourne: Department of History, University of Melbourne, 1997.

Hoehne, Carl Traugott. *Carl Traugott Hoehne's Emigration to Australia and Return to the Fatherland Related by Himself and Combined with Further Authentic Information about Australia.* In *From Hamburg to Hobson's Bay: German Emigration to Port Phillip (Australia Felix), 1848-51,* ed. Thomas Darragh and Robert N. Wuchatsch, 176-217. Melbourne: Wendish Heritage Society, 1999.

Home, Robert. *Of Planning and Planting: The Making of British Colonial Cities.* London: Routledge, 1997.

Horsman, Reginald. *Race and Manifest Destiny: The Origins of American Racial Anglo-Saxonism.* Cambridge, MA: Harvard University Press, 1981.

Howitt, William. *Land, Labour and Gold, Or Two Years in Victoria with Visits to Sydney and Van Diemen's Land, 1855.* 1855. Reprint, Kilmore: London Publishing, 1972.

Huttenback, Robert A. *Racism and Empire: White Settlers and Coloured Immigrants in the British Self-Governing Colonies.* Ithaca, NY: Cornell University Press, 1976.

Jacobs, Jane. *Edge of Empire: Postcolonialism and the City.* New York: Routledge, 1996.

Jeans, D.N. "Town Planning in New South Wales, 1829-1842." *Australian Planning Institute Journal* (October 1965): 191-96.

Johnson, Jay T., Garth Cant, Richard Howitt, and Evelyn Peters. "Creating Indigenous Geographies: Embracing Indigenous Peoples' Knowledges and Rights." *Geographical Research* 45, 2 (2007): 117-20.

Jolly, Margaret. "'Ill-Natured Comparisons': Racism and Relativism in European Representations of ni-Vanuatu from Cook's Second Voyage." *History and Anthropology* 5, 3-4 (1992): 331-63.

Kanakos, Jeannie L. "The Negotiations to Relocate the Songhees Indians, 1843-1911." Master's thesis, Simon Fraser University, 1982.

Karlson, Keith Thor, ed. *A Stó:lō–Coast Salish Historical Atlas.* Vancouver: Stó:lō Heritage Trust/Douglas and McIntyre, 2001.

Keegan, Timothy. *South Africa and the Origins of the Racial Order.* London: Leicester University Press, 1996.

Kelm, Mary-Ellen. *Colonizing Bodies: Aboriginal Health and Healing in British Columbia, 1900-50.* Vancouver: UBC Press, 1998.

King, Anthony D. "Colonial Cities: Global Pivots of Change." In *Colonial Cities: Essays on Urbanism in a Colonial Context,* ed. Ronald Ross and Gerard Telkamp, 7-18. Boston: Martinus Nijhoff Publishers/Leiden University Press, 1985.

–. *Colonial Urban Development.* London: Routledge and Kegan Paul, 1973.

Knight, Rolf. *Indians at Work: An Informal History of Native Labour in British Columbia.* Vancouver: New Star Books, 1996.

Kociumbus, Jan. *The Oxford History of Australia.* Vol. 2, *1770-1860: Possessions.* Melbourne: Oxford University Press, 1995.

Lake, Marilyn. "White Man's Country: The Trans-National History of a National Project." *Australian Historical Studies* 34, 122 (2003): 346-63.

Lake, Marilyn, and Henry Reynolds. *Drawing the Global Colour Line.* Carlton: Melbourne University Press, 2008.

Lakic, M., and R. Wrench, eds. *Through Their Eyes: An Historical Record of the Aboriginal People of Victoria as Documented by the Officials of the Port Phillip Protectorate, 1839-1841.* Melbourne: Museum Victoria, 1994.

Lamb, J.K. "The Census of Vancouver Island, 1855." *British Columbia Historical Quarterly* 4, 1 (1940): 51-58.

Langton, Marcia. "Urbanising Aborigines: The Social Scientists' Great Deception." *Social Alternatives* 2 (1981): 16-22.

Lefebvre, Henri. *The Production of Space.* Trans. Donald Nicholson-Smith. Cambridge: Basil Blackwell, 1991.

Lester, Alan. "British Settler Discourse and the Circuits of Empire." *History Workshop Journal* 54 (2002): 25-48.

Levine, Philippa. *Prostitution, Race and Politics: Policing Venereal Disease in the British Empire.* London: Routledge, 2003.

Lewis, Miles. *Melbourne: The City's History and Development.* Melbourne: City of Melbourne, 1995.

Limerick, Patricia Nelson. "Going West and Ending Up Global." *Western Historical Quarterly* 32, 1 (2001): 5-24.

–. *The Legacy of Conquest: The Unbroken Past of the American West.* New York: W.W. Norton and Co., 1987.

LiPuma, Edward. *Encompassing Others: The Magic of Modernity in Melanesia.* Ann Arbor: University of Michigan Press, 2001.

Lloyd, Edwin. *A Visit to the Antipodes: With Some Reminiscences of a Sojourn in Australia by a Squatter.* London: Smith Elder and Co., 1846.

Locke, John. *Two Treatises of Government.* 1690. Cambridge: Cambridge University Press, 1988.

Loo, Tina. *Making Law, Order, and Authority in British Columbia, 1821-71.* Toronto: University of Toronto Press, 1994.

Loomba, Anai. *Colonialism/Postcolonialism.* London: Routledge, 1998.

Lutz, John Sutton. "After the Fur Trade: The Aboriginal Labouring Class of British Columbia, 1849-1890." *Journal of the Canadian Historical Association* 3, 1 (1992): 69-93.

–. *Makúk: A New History of Aboriginal-White Relations* Vancouver: UBC Press, 2009.

–. "Preparing Eden: Aboriginal Land Use and European Settlement." Paper presented to the meeting of the Canadian Historical Association, Montreal, 1995.

–. "Work, Wages and Welfare in Aboriginal-non-Aboriginal Relations, British Columbia, 1849-1970." PhD diss., University of Ottawa, 1994

Lydon, Jane. *Eye Contact: Photographing Indigenous Australians.* Durham: Duke University Press, 2005.

Macey, David. *The Penguin Dictionary of Critical Theory.* London: Penguin Books, 2000.

MacFarlane, I. "Pevay: A Casualty of War." *Papers and Proceedings: Tasmanian Historical Research Association* 48, 4 (2001): 280-305.

Mackaness, George, ed. *The Correspondence of John Cotton, Victorian Pioneer, 1842-1849.* Part 3, *1847-1849.* Dubbo, NSW: Review Publications, 1978.

Mackenzie, John, ed. *Imperialism and Popular Culture.* Manchester: Manchester University Press, 1986.

Macneil, Rod. "Time after Time: Temporal Frontiers and Boundaries in Colonial Images of the Australian Landscape." In *Colonial Frontiers: Indigenous-European Encounters in*

Settler Societies, ed. Lynette Russell, 47-67. Manchester: Manchester University Press, 2001.

Mahlik, K. *The Meaning of Race: Race, History and Culture in Western Society.* London: Macmillan, 1996.

Markus, Andrew. *Fear and Hatred: Purifying Australia and California, 1850-1901.* Sydney: Hale and Ironmonger, 1979.

Marx, Karl. "Bloody Legislation against the Expropriated." *Capital: A Critique of Political Economy.* Vol. 1. Moscow: Progress Publishers, 1954.

Mawani, Renisa, "'The Iniquitous Practice of Women': Prostitution and the Making of White Spaces in British Columbia, 1898-1905." In *Working through Whiteness: International Perspectives,* ed. Cynthia Leine-Rasky, 43-68. New York: SUNY Press, 2002.

–. "Legal Geographies of Aboriginal Segregation in British Columbia, 1850-1911." In *Isolation: Places and Practices of Exclusion,* ed. Carolyn Strange and Alison Bashford, 173-90. New York: Routledge, 2003.

Mayne, R.C. *Four Years in British Columbia and Vancouver Island: An Account of Their Forests, Rivers, Coasts, Gold Fields, and Resources for Colonisation.* London: John Murray, 1862.

McCarty, J.W., and C.B. Schedvin, eds. *Australian Capital Cities: Historical Essays.* Sydney: Sydney University Press, 1978.

McClintock, Anne. *Imperial Leather: Race, Gender, and Sexuality in the Colonial Contest.* New York: Routledge, 1995.

McDonald, Peter. "Demography." In *Encyclopedia of Melbourne,* ed. Andrew Brown-May and Shurlee Swaine. Melbourne: Cambridge University Press, 2005.

McDonald, Robert A.J. *Making Vancouver, 1863-1913.* Vancouver: UBC Press, 1996.

McFie, Matthew. *Vancouver Island and British Columbia: Their History, Resources and Prospects.* London: Longman, Roberts and Green, 1865.

McGrath, Ann. *Born in the Cattle: Aborigines in Cattle Country.* Sydney: Allen and Unwin, 1987.

–, ed. *Contested Ground: Australian Aborigines under the British Crown.* Crows Nest, NSW: Allen and Unwin, 1995.

McGuire, John. "Judicial Violence and the 'Civilising Process': Race and the Transition from Public to Private Executions in Australia." *Australian Historical Studies* 29, 111 (1988): 187-209.

McHoul, Alec, and Wendy Grace. *A Foucault Primer: Discourse, Power, and the Subject.* Melbourne: Melbourne University Press, 1993.

McLaren, John P.S. "The Burdens of Empire and the Legalisation of White Supremacy in Canada, 1860-1910." In *Legal History in the Making: Proceedings of the Ninth British Legal History Conference, Glasgow,* ed. W.M. Gordon and T.D. Fergus, 187-200. London: Hambledon Press, 1989.

McLeod, Anne Burnaby, and Pixie McGeachie, eds. *Land of Promise: Robert Burnaby's Letters from Colonial British Columbia, 1858-1863.* Burnaby: City of Burnaby, 2002.

Meek, R.L. "Smith, Turgot and the 'Four Stages' Theory." *Smith, Marx and After: Ten Essays in the Development of Economic Thought.* London: Chapman and Hall, 1977.

–. *Social Sciences and the Ignoble Savage.* Cambridge: Cambridge University Press, 1976.

Meredith, Louisa Anne. *Notes and Sketches of New South Wales during a Residence in that Colony from 1839 to 1844 by Mrs. Charles Meredith.* London: John Murray, 1846.

Merrifield, Andy. "Henri Lefebvre: A Socialist in Space." *Thinking Space,* ed. Mike Crang and N.J. Thrift, 167-182. London: Routledge, 2000.

Mill, John Stuart. *Principles of Political Economy, with Some of Their Applications to Social Philosophy.* Ed. Stephen Nathanson. Indianapolis: Hackett Publishing, 2004.

Mills, Sara, *Gender and Colonial Space*. Manchester: Manchester University Press, 2005.

Mitchell, Jessie. "'A City on a Hill': Aboriginal Missions and British Civilisation, 1830-1850." In *Exploring the British World: Identity – Cultural Production – Institutions*, ed. Kate Darian-Smith, Patricia Grimshaw, Keira Lindsay, and Stuart Macintyre. Melbourne: RMIT Publishing, 2004.

Mitchell, Thomas. *Three Expeditions into the Interior of Eastern Australia, with Descriptions of the Recently Explored Australia Felix, and of the Present Colony of New South Wales*. Vol. 2. London: T. and W. Boone, 1839.

Mitchell, Timothy. *Colonising Egypt*. New York: Cambridge University Press, 1988.

Moors, Derrick. "Imaginary Voyages." In *The Great South Lands*, ed. Des Cowley, 8-14. Melbourne: Library Council of Victoria, 1988.

Montag, Warren. "The Universalisation of Whiteness: Racism and the Enlightenment." In *Whiteness: A Critical Reader*, ed., Mike Hill, 281-93. New York: New York University Press, 1997.

Morgan, Marjorie. *The Old Melbourne Cemetery*. Victoria: Australian Institute of Genealogical Studies, 1982.

Morgan, Phillip, D. "Encounters between British and 'Indigenous' Peoples, c. 1500–c. 1800." In *Empire and Others: British Encounters with Indigenous Peoples, 1600-1850*, ed. Martin Daunton and Rick Halpern. Philadelphia: University of Pennsylvania Press, 1999.

Nance, Beverly. "The Level of Violence: Europeans and Aborigines in Port Phillip." *Australian Historical Studies* 19 (October 1981): 532-49.

Newsletter of Australasia: A Narrative of Events, Or a Letter to Send Friends 9 (March 1857): 1-4.

Niall, Brenda. *Georgiana: A Biography of Georgiana McCrae, Painter, Diarist, Pioneer*. Carlton South: Melbourne University Press, at the Meigunyah Press, 1994.

Norman, John. *Edward Gibbon Wakefield: A Political Reappraisal*. Fairfield: Fairfield University, 1963.

Nott, Josiah Clark, and George R. Gliddon, eds. *Types of Mankind: Or, Ethnological Researches, Based upon the Ancient Monuments, Paintings, Sculptures, and Crania of Races, and upon Their Natural, Geographical, Philological and Biblical History, Illustrated by Selections from the Unedited Papers of Samuel George Morton*. Philadelphia: J.B. Lippincott, 1857.

Ogborn, Miles. *Spaces of Modernity: London's Geographies, 1680-1880*. New York: Guilford Press, 1998.

"The Origins of Violence." *Perspective*, with guest historian John Docker. Aired 12 November 2008, ABC, transcript. http://www.abc.net.au/rn/perspective/stories/2008/2415450.htm.

Parker, Edward Stone. *The Aborigines of Australia: A Lecture Delivered in the Mechanics Hall, Melbourne, before the John Knox Young Men's Association, May 10*. Melbourne: Hugh McColl, 1854.

Pethick, Derek. *Victoria: The Fort*. Vancouver: Mitchell Press, 1986.

Perry, Adele. "'Fair Ones of a Purer Cast': White Women and Colonialism in Late Nineteenth-Century British Columbia." *Feminist Studies* 23 (1997): 501-24.

–. *On the Edge of Empire: Gender, Race, and the Making of British Columbia, 1849-1871*. Toronto: University of Toronto Press, 2001.

–. "On Not Going on a Field Trip: Presence, Absence, and the Writing of BC History." *BC Studies* 123 (Winter 2001): 57-63.

–. "The State of Empire: Reproducing Colonialism in British Columbia, 1849-1871." *Journal of Colonialism and Colonial History* 2, 21 (2001).

Pickles, Katie, and Myra Rutherdale, eds. *Contact Zones: Aboriginal and Settler Women in Canada's Past.* Vancouver: UBC Press, 2005.

Pratt, Mary Louise. *Imperial Eyes: Travel Writing and Transculturation.* New York: Routledge, 1993.

Perera, Nihal. "Indigenizing the Colonial City: Late Nineteenth-Century Colombo and Its Landscape." *Urban Studies* 39, 9 (2002): 1703-21.

Peters, Evelyn J. "Conceptually Unclad: Feminist Geography and Aboriginal Peoples." *Canadian Geographer* 48, 3 (2004): 251-65.

–. "Subversive Spaces: First Nations Women and the City." *Environment and Planning D: Society and Space* 16 (1998): 665-85.

Presland, Gary. *Aboriginal Melbourne: The Lost Land of the Kulin People.* Melbourne: McPhee Gribble, 1994.

Price, Charles A. *The Great White Walls Are Built: Restrictive Immigration to North America and Australasia, 1836-88.* Canberra: Australian Institute of International Affairs/ Australian University Press, 1974.

Pritchard, Allen, ed. *The Letters of Edmund Hope Verney, 1862-1865.* Vancouver: UBC Press, 1996.

Proudfoot, Lindsay J., ed. *(Dis)placing Empire: Renegotiating British Colonial Geographies.* Hampshire: Ashgate, 2005.

Raban, Jonathan. *Soft City.* London: Hamilton, 1974.

Rabinow, Paul, "Introduction." *The Foucault Reader,* ed. Paul Rabinow, 3-30. New York: Pantheon books, 1984.

Ransely, Janet, and Alena Marchetti. "The Hidden Whiteness of the Australian Law." *Griffith Law Review* 1, 1 (2001): 139-52.

Razack, Sherene, ed. *Race, Space, and the Law: Unmapping a White Settler Society.* Toronto: Between the Lines, 2003.

Reclus, Élisée. *The Earth and Its Inhabitants: Oceania.* New York: D. Appleton and Company, 1898.

Reece, W.R.H. *Aborigines and Colonists: Aborigines and Colonial Society in New South Wales in the 1830s and 1840s.* Sydney: Sydney University Press, 1974.

Reksten, Terry. *More English Than the English: A Very Social History of Victoria.* Victoria: Orca, 1986.

Ross, Ronald, and Gerard Telkamp, eds. *Colonial Cities: Essays on Urbanism in a Colonial Context.* Boston: Martinus Nijhoff Publishers/Leiden University Press, 1985.

Rotenburg, Robert. "Metropolitanism and the Transformation of Urban Space in Nineteenth-Century Metropoles." *American Anthropologist* 103, 1 (2001): 7-15.

Rowse, Tim. "Transforming the Notion of the Urban Aborigine." *Urban Policy and Research* 18, 2 (2000): 171-90.

Roy, Patricia E. *A White Man's Province: British Columbia Politicians and Chinese and Japanese Immigrants, 1858-1914.* Vancouver: UBC Press, 1989.

Roy, Susan. "Litigating Aboriginal Identity." Paper presented at BC Studies conference, "Rethinking Ourselves," Vancouver, May, 2003.

Russell, Lynette, "Introduction." In *Colonial Frontiers: Indigenous-European Encounters in Settler Societies,* ed. Russell, 1-16. Manchester: Manchester University Press, 2001.

Russell, Lynette, and Ian McNiven. "The Wurundjeri of Melbourne, Australia." In *Endangered Peoples of Oceania: Struggles to Survive and Thrive,* ed. Judith M. Fitzpatrick, 233-38. Westport, CT: Greenwood Press, 2001.

Ryan, Simon. *The Cartographic Eye: How Explorers Saw Australia.* Cambridge: Cambridge University Press, 1996.

Sagazio, Celestina, ed. *Cemeteries: Our Heritage*. Melbourne: National Trust of Australia, 1992.

Said, Edward. "Representing the Colonized: Anthropology's Interlocutors." *Critical Inquiry* 15, 2 (1989): 205-25.

Scott, James C. *Seeing Like a State: How Certain Schemes to Improve the Human Condition Have Failed*. New Haven: Yale University Press, 1998.

Seed, Patricia. *Ceremonies of Possession in Europe's Conquest of the New World, 1492-1640*. Cambridge: Cambridge University Press, 1995.

Seeman, Berthold. *Narrative of the Voyages of HMS Herald*. 2 vols. London: Reeve and Co., 1853.

Serle, Geoffrey. *The Golden Age: A History of the Colony of Victoria, 1851-1861*. Melbourne: Melbourne University Press, 1963.

Shaw, A.G.L. *History of the Port Phillip District: Victoria before Separation*. Melbourne: Miegunyah Melbourne, Melbourne University Press, 1996.

Shivelbusch, Wolfgang. *The Railway Journey: The Industrialization of Time and Space in the Nineteenth Century*. Berkeley: University of California Press, 1986.

Sim, Kirsty Clare. "Negotiating Victoria: The African-American Challenge to Public Space in Colonial British Columbia." Honours thesis, University of British Columbia, 2001.

Smith, Neil, and Ann Godlewska, eds. *Geography and Empire*. Oxford: Blackwell, 1994.

Southerland, Alexander. *Victoria and Its Metropolis*. 2 vols. Melbourne: McCarron Bird, 1888.

Spivak, Gayatri Chakravorty. "Can the Subaltern Speak?" In *Marxism and the Interpretation of Culture*, ed. Cary Nelson and Lawrence Grossburg, 271-316. Chicago: University of Illinois Press, 1988.

Stanger-Ross, Jordan. "Municipal Colonialism in Vancouver: City Planning and the Conflict over Indian Reserves, 1928-1950s." *Canadian Historical Review* 89, 4 (2008): 541-80.

Stave, B.M. "A Conversation with Gilbert A. Stelter: Urban History in Canada." *Journal of Urban History* 6 (1980): 177-209.

Stoler, Ann Laura, "Tense and Tender Ties: The Politics of Comparison in North American History and (Post) Colonial Studies." *Journal of American History* 88, 3 (2001): 829-65.

Suttles, Wayne, ed. *Handbook of North American Indians*. Vol. 7, *Northwest Coast*. Washington: Smithsonian Institution, 1990.

Tennant, Paul. *Aboriginal Peoples and Politics: The Indian Land Question in British Columbia, 1849-1989*. Vancouver: UBC Press, 1990.

Thomas, Nicholas. *Colonialism's Culture: Anthropology, Travel and Government*. Cambridge: Polity Press, 1994.

Coll Thrush. *Native Seattle: Histories from the Crossing-Over Place*. Seattle: University of Washington Press, 2008.

Tippett, Maria. *From Desolation to Splendor: Changing Perceptions of the British Columbia Landscape*. Toronto: Clarke, Irwin, and Company, 1977.

Turner, Nancy, and Marcus Bell. "The Ethnobotany of the Coast Salish Indians of Vancouver Island." *Economic Botany* 25, 1 (1971): 63-104.

United Kingdom. House of Commons. *British House of Commons Report of the Parliamentary Select Committee on the Aboriginal Tribes (British Settlements), Reprinted with Comments by the Aborigines Protection Society*. London: William Ball, 1837.

–. "Correspondence and Other Papers Relating to the Hudson's Bay Company, the Exploration of the Territories ... and Other Affairs in Canada," dispatch nos. 19 and 33, 1858. In *Irish University Series of British Parliamentary Papers – Colonies: Canada, vol. 22*. Shannon: Irish University Press, 1969.

–. *Report of the Select Committee on New Zealand, together with the Minutes of the Evidence, Appendix, and Index, 1844.* In *Irish University Series of British Parliamentary Papers.* Shannon: Irish University Press, 1968.

Van Kirk, Sylvia, *"Many Tender Ties": Women in Fur-Trade Society, 1670-1870.* 2nd ed. Norman: University of Oklahoma Press, 1983.

–. "Tracing the Fortunes of Five Founding Families of Victoria." *BC Studies* 115/116 (Autumn/Winter 1997/98): 149-77.

Veracini, Lorenzo. "The Imagined Geographies of Settler Colonialism." In *Making Settler Colonial Space: Perspectives on Land, Race and Identity,* ed. Tracey Banivanua Mar and Penelope Edmonds. Basingstoke: Palgrave, forthcoming 2010.

Wakefield, Edward Gibbon. *A Letter from Sydney, the Principal Town of Australasia, Together with the Outline of a System of Colonization.* London: Joseph Cross, 1829.

Watson, Frederick, ed. *Historical Records of Australia.* W.G. Murray, Government Printer: Commonwealth of Australia, 1971.

Weidenhofer, Margaret, ed. *Garryowen's Melbourne: A Selection from the Chronicles of Early Melbourne, 1835 to 1852, by Garryowen.* Melbourne: Nelson, 1967.

Westgarth, William. *Personal Recollections of Early Melbourne and Victoria.* Melbourne: George Robertson and Co., 1888.

–. *A Report on the Condition, Capabilities, and Prospects of the Australian Aborigines.* Melbourne: William Clarke, 1846.

White, Jarrod. "Power/Knowledge and Public Space: Policing the 'Aboriginal Towns.'" *Australian and New Zealand Journal of Criminology* 30 (1997): 275-91.

White, Richard, and John M. Findley, eds. *Power and Place in the North American West.* Seattle: University of Washington Press, 1999.

Whiteman, Jeremy. *Reform, Revolution and French Global Policy, 1787-1791.* Farnham: Ashgate, 2003.

Wolfe, Patrick. "History and Imperialism: A Century of Theory, from Marx to Postcolonialism." *American Historical Review* 102, 2 (1997): 388-420.

–. "Land, Labour, and Difference: Elementary Structures of Race." *American Historical Review* 106, 3 (2001): 866-905.

–. "Nation and MiscegeNation: Discursive Continuity in the Post-Mabo Era." *Social Analysis* 36 (October 1994): 93-152.

–. "On Being Woken Up: The Dreamtime in Anthropology and in Australian Settler Culture." *Comparative Studies in Society and History* 33, 2 (1991): 197-224.

–. "Race and Racialisation: Some Thoughts." *Postcolonial Studies* 5, 1 (2002): 51-63.

–. *Settler Colonialism and the Transformation of Anthropology: The Politics and Poetics of an Ethnographic Event.* London: Cassell, 1999.

Wolski, Nathan. "All's Not Quiet on the Western Front: Rethinking Resistance and Frontiers in Aboriginal Historiography." In *Colonial Frontiers: Indigenous-European Encounters in Settler Societies,* ed. Lynette Russell, 216-36. Manchester: Manchester University Press, 2001.

Wright, Gwendolyn. "Tradition in the Service of Modernity: Architecture and Urbanism in French Colonial Policy, 1900-1930." In *Tensions of Empire: Colonial Cultures in a Bourgeois World,* ed. Frederick Cooper and Ann Laura Stoler, 322-45. Berkeley: University of California Press, 1997.

Wright, Nancy E. "Comparative Study of the Status of Women in Canada and Australia." *Australian Canadian Studies* 22, 1 (2004): 1-7.

Zaffaroni, Irene G.M. "The Great Chain of Being: Racism and Imperialism in Colonial Victoria, 1858-1871." Master's Thesis, Department of History, University of Victoria, 1987.

Index

Note: Page numbers followed by (f) indicate drawings, maps, or photographs. Terminology in the text is extremely precise. In the index, the same terminology is used as in the text, with appropriate cross-references. For more on the author's use of terminology, see page 19.

Loxton, John, 150
Lutz, John: on Europeans, 96; on First
  Nations economies, 31-33; on imperial
  vision, 104; on "Indian" as category,
  104; on labour, 226; on Lekwammen
  pre-contact population, 95; on smallpox, 27, 251n23; on trade, 111
Lydon, Jane, 172, 177

MacArthur, Gordon, 127
MacFie, Matthew, 227-28, 243
MacKenna, Suzanne, 54
Macneil, Rod, 59
Macquarie (Governor), 82, 87
*"Many Tender Ties": Women in Fur-Trade
  Society, 1670-1870*, 106-7
Maori, 40, 42, 102, 118-19. *See also* race
maps: of Adelaide, 65-66; of colony loca-
  tions, 21(f); cultural linguistic groups
  of Greater Port Phillip, 71(f); cultural-
  linguistic groups of Northwest Coast,
  92(f); of Melbourne, 83(f), 141(f); of
  Victoria, 190(f). *See also* art
mariculture, 42, 91, 93. *See also* agriculture
  (Indigenous)
Markus, Andrew, 153
martial law, 82. *See also* enforcement (of
  colonization)
Martineau, John, 66
Marx, Karl, 57-58, 136-37
Marxism, 32, 54, 57-58, 253n52
Mawani, Renisa: and liminal space, 201-2;
  on prostitution, 221, 223; on Victoria,
  200
May, Andrew, 146
Mayne, R.C., 186
McBride, Richard, 232
McCarty, John, 254n76, 275n8
McCleay, Alexander, 86
McClintock, Anne, 58
McCrae, Farquhar, 127, 131
McCrae, Georgiana, 131, 271n86
McDonald, Peter, 254n76, 275n8
McGuire, John, 151
McLoughlin, John, 94
McNeill, William Henry, 107
McNiven, Ian, 73, 260n13
Meek, R.L., 58, 258n36

Melbourne: Aboriginal camps, 122-23, 140,
  141(f), 142-48; and Aboriginal lands, 73;
  Aboriginal movement, 82; Aboriginal
  place names, 235; Adeney on, 46-47;
  colonialist period survivals, 84, 263n70;
  Dilke on, 179-80; early status of, 22-23;
  establishment of, 81-82; expectations
  of, 113; as illegal settlement, 79, 82;
  incorporation of, 133-34, 271n93; intercolonial exhibition, 170-79, 278n64;
  land sales in, 84-85, 125; layout of grid,
  83-84; as London, 157-58, 182; map of,
  83(f), 141(f); map of location, 21(f);
  Melbourne As It Is and Ought to Be,
  56-57, 61-62, 135; *Melbourne in 1846: A
  View from Collingwood*, 48, 49(f); original name of, 73, 260n16; population
  (1838), 113-14, 122, 269n37; population
  (1840), 154; population (1851), 36-37,
  254n76, 275n8; population (1903), 87,
  235; protests (modern period), 236-37;
  statue of Bunjil, 235, 235(f); from 1839-
  50, 113-52; from 1850-60, 153-83. *See also*
  Port Phillip
Melbourne Punch, 159, 160(f), 161, 167,
  167(f). *See also* newspapers
merchants, 125-26, 199, 210, 223
Meredith, Louisa, 117-18, 121
Merri Creek, 132-33
methodology (of author), 5-19, 239
metropolitan cities, 68
military power (display of), 31, 98, 129-30.
  See also enforcement (of colonization)
Mill, John Stuart, 67, 259n71
missions. *See* reserves (Australia)
Mitchell, Jessie, 125
Mitchell, Thomas, 73-74
mixed-race relationships: and burial records, 108-11; children of, 218, 284n46,
  284n49; in church marriage records,
  110; and class, 147, 165; and colonization,
  44-45; and fur trade, 32, 105-7, 182; and
  gold rush, 163-70; mixed-race colonial
  subjects, 147; and sealing and whaling
  industry, 262n50; and segregation, 225;
  views on, 218-19. *See also* race; whiteness; women
Monro, David, 113

Printed and bound in Canada by Friesens

Set in Minion and Helvetica Condensed by Artegraphica Design Co. Ltd.

Copy editor: Lesley Erickson

Proofreader: Valerie Warmington

Indexer: Natalie Boon